Office Organization and Method

To J.R.M.S.

Office Organization and Method

A manual of administrative management

Geoffrey Mills
FCIS, MBIM, F.Inst.AM

Oliver Standingford
OBE, FCIS, FBIM, F.Inst.AM

Pitman

PITMAN PUBLISHING LIMITED
39 Parker Street, London WC2B 5PB

Associated Companies
Copp Clark Pitman, Toronto
Fearon Pitman Publishers Inc, San Francisco
Pitman Publishing New Zealand Ltd, Wellington
Pitman Publishing Pty Ltd, Melbourne

© Geoffrey Mills and Oliver Standingford 1963, 1968, 1972, 1978

Sixth Edition published in Great Britain in 1978
Reprinted 1979

British Library Cataloguing in Publication Data
Mills, G and Standingford, O

Text set in 11/12 pt Photon Times, printed and bound
in Great Britain at The Pitman Press, Bath

ISBN 0 273 01121 9

Contents

Preface to sixth edition — vii

1 Introductory — 1

Part 1 General office services

2 Communication services — 13
3 Telecommunications — 38
4 Filing and indexing — 57
5 Reprography — 83

Part 2 Data processing

6 Fundamentals of data processing — 105
7 Computer components and programs — 111
8 Computers and their use — 136
9 Miscellaneous equipment — 159

Part 3 Financial and accounting services

10 Sales invoicing — 169
11 Sales accounting — 174
12 Purchases — 184
13 Cash control — 191
14 Wages — 199
15 Stock control — 212
16 Production records — 223
17 Management information — 237
18 Insurance — 247

Part 4 Environment

19 Furniture and layout — 263
20 Physical conditions — 276

Part 5 Personnel

21 Staffing — 287
22 Rewards — 306
23 Training — 320

Part 6 Planning and control

24   Methods   341
25   Day-to-day controls   363
26   Audit   374
27   Reports   382
28   Committee procedure   388

     Bibliography   394

     Index   397

Preface to the sixth edition

This book was written to provide a compact work of reference for company secretaries, accountants, cost accountants and administrative managers generally, and a textbook for students.

In surveying the entire subject of office work and the management of clerical staff, it is neither possible nor desirable to deal with matters in great detail. Emphasis is therefore laid upon purposes and principles which are then illustrated by some of the more common methods and practices. Machines and other equipment representative of the range available are described and illustrated. In relation to personnel and management practices, the field of policy is surveyed and examples provided of the more important techniques currently employed.

In preparing and revising this book, the authors have been fortunate in having the help and advice of others who have readily made available their knowledge and experience. In this connection, they wish particularly to acknowledge the work of the Institute of Administrative Management (formerly the Institute of Office Management) under whose aegis this volume was first published.

In addition to up-dating the text and illustrations generally, the authors have made some major changes in this sixth edition. The impact of new technology since the last edition was prepared has been of particular effect in two main areas: communications and data processing. In communications, electronic equipment has been applied to introduce a new concept of 'word processing' and to extend telecommunications which are now the subject of a separate chapter. In data processing, the advent of a new generation of equipment, cheaper in real terms and with substantially increased capacity, has widened the field of economic computer application. Whole classes of office machines have become obsolescent and it can be fairly stated that the office has entered a new era. The whole approach to study has, therefore, to change so that electronic data processing is regarded as the normal, with other methods as alternatives mainly for use in smaller offices. The whole of Part 2 (Data Processing Equipment) has therefore been re-arranged and largely re-written, and a greater emphasis given to computerized methods in describing systems and in dealing with the planning of procedures.

In recent years, there has been a spate of new legislation relating to health and safety in offices, and the relationships between employer and employee. The scope of legal requirements is now such that it must be regarded as a separate subject. It is still, of course, necessary for the administrative manager to be aware of the areas in which the law applies, so that he may seek professional advice when necessary. To this end, the principal Acts have been summarized in essence in the appropriate chapters.

The authors are deeply conscious of the responsibility which they bear towards the many teaching and examining institutions which have adopted or recommended this volume as a textbook. In revising its contents, due regard has been paid to the related syllabuses of professional bodies and those for Higher National Certificates and Diplomas.

Again the authors are grateful for the willing co-operation of manufacturers and others who have provided information concerning equipment and have permitted the reproduction of photographs and diagrams.

LONDON AND LIVERPOOL
1978

1 Introductory 17/2/81

Anyone commencing to study administrative management, from whatever point of view, ought firstly to be convinced that the subject is worthwhile—that the office provides an essential service. When costs are high, the burden of clerical work is often criticized. In industry and commerce, management wonder whether the organization might run as well, if not better, with fewer clerks and less paper. In matters of government, the taxpayers are not slow to react unfavourably to growing numbers of civil servants and local government officers.

In broad terms, there can be little doubt that the office can make an important contribution to economic and social life. Without paper-work, any complex industrial society would rapidly come to a standstill. Furthermore, it is to be observed that the wealthier nations of the world are those with the higher proportions of manpower engaged in 'white-collar' jobs. The efficient organization must provide its management with efficient information, planning, control and financial services.

It is obvious, however, that there must be a limit to expenditure on administrative services. If everyone were engaged in office work, there would be nothing to eat—except paper. The correct balance must be struck between the resources devoted to directly productive activities and those devoted to administration. This is as true for a nation as it is for an industrial or commercial undertaking.

In each individual organization, the manager or managers responsible for providing the office services must take positive steps to ensure as far as possible:

(a) that each service is necessary because it contributes to the overall effectiveness of the organization, and

(b) that, in providing that service, the best possible use is made of manpower, machines, equipment and other resources.

If there is any office task which does not result in more efficient production, distribution, service or finance, then it is truly unproductive and should no longer be carried out. If a task does contribute to the overall effectiveness of the organization, it must be done in the most efficient way.

1

THE PURPOSE OF THE OFFICE

The purpose of the office has been defined as the providing of a service of communication and record. This broad definition can be amplified and the functions of the office analysed under five headings as follows:

1. Receiving information   Examples of the form in which information is normally received are letters, telephone calls, orders, invoices, and reports on the various activities of the business.

In addition to receiving such information as may come in to the business, the office has the duty of obtaining any further information which the management may require.

2. Recording information   The object of keeping records is to enable information to be made readily available to the management when required. Some records are required to be kept by law but, other than these, records should be kept only to meet the needs of management in planning and controlling the business. Such records may show the details of negotiations, transactions, operations etc. (for example, correspondence, orders, invoices), or be summaries of detail (for example, financial and management accounts, stock records, sales analyses).

3. Arranging information   The information accumulated by the office is seldom in the form in which it is to be given out; data are collected from different sources, calculations have to be made. The office is responsible for supplying information in the form which best serves management, a function of the highest importance and one which must be carried out by properly trained staff. Examples of arranging information are preparing invoices, costings, accounts, statistical statements, financial statements, and reports generally.

4. Giving information   As the management may require, the office gives out information from its records. Some of the information given out is of a routine nature, some of a special nature, and it may be given verbally or in writing. Examples are orders, estimates, invoices, progress reports, financial statements, and instructions issued on behalf of management.

5. Safeguarding assets   The duties of the office would not be fully performed if they were restricted to the mere receiving, recording, arranging, and giving out of information. There is in addition a responsibility to observe intelligently the affairs of the business as shown in the records and to warn the management of anything untoward which may take place. In keeping stock records, any deficiencies must be reported; in keeping the accounts, any bad or doubtful debts must be reported before all hope of recovery is past; vital records such as major contracts must be properly protected; cash must be held in safety and banked. The office must look to the meaning of records and draw prompt attention to anything on which management should act.

These five broad functions must be performed in any organization. In a small one-man business, a separate office service may not be necessary. The proprietor can receive and give information himself, and many of his records may largely be contained in his memory. In the larger and more complex business, however, the managing director cannot deal personally with all inward and outward communications, he cannot remember or record all the facts relating to the business, nor can he exercise a detailed supervision over the handling of cash and other assets. The office is there to fulfil these functions on his behalf; the office is the servant of management.

THE CLERICAL CONTRIBUTION TO PRODUCTIVITY

In present-day industry and commerce there is a high degree of specialization. It often requires hundreds of different firms to complete the production and distribution of a single article. And within each firm there is again a more highly specialized division of duties. Hand-in-hand with specialization comes the need for the proper co-ordination of individuals, departments, and firms so that they may work as a balanced team. This co-ordination is the task of management, and the decisions that management makes should be based upon a proper knowledge of the facts. The provision of the facts on which the decisions of management are made is one of the most important functions of the office, and a very real and essential contribution to productivity.

The office can only make this vital contribution if there is both efficient office management and proper use of the office service by general management and by departmental managers (i.e. the production manager, the marketing manager, the chief designer etc.).

BUSINESS ORGANIZATION

In a small business, the manager, who may also be the owner, is in direct control. He sees for himself what is happening and takes immediate decisions as to what must be done.

As the business grows, there comes a point when one man can no longer exercise personal control; departments are formed so that the task of management is shared. The manager, by now known as the general manager or managing director, is still in control, but his control is indirect. Responsibility for the work of departments has been delegated, together with the authority to make decisions and take action. An organization has been created. It is usually found convenient to express an organization in chart form. A simple organization, such as might be established during the early growth of a business, can be illustrated thus:

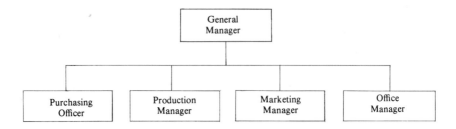

The lines connecting the general manager with the departmental managers can be regarded as lines of delegation and accountability; they also indicate the lines along which information flows.

As the business grows still larger and more departments are created, there comes a point when there are too many managers directly responsible to the general manager. The number of direct subordinates is termed the 'span of control'; this must be such that the manager in charge has time to meet them and deal with their problems. If he is too busy, the business will suffer. What the span of control should be is dependent on the facts of the case. When growth causes the span to exceed what is efficient, an additional level of management is introduced, for example:

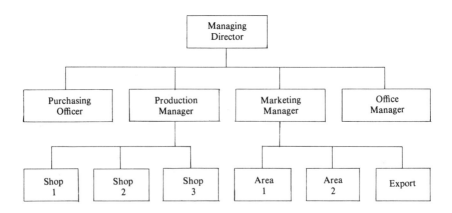

This pattern of organizational development can be continued as the business grows. In the chart shown above, there is a managing director and two levels of subordinate managers; in the very large business, there will be more.

OFFICE SERVICES IN RELATION TO THE ORGANIZATION

In any organization, 'the office' may mean different things to different people. To the salesman, it may mean the marketing manager and his supporting office staff; to a branch manager, it may mean head office; to the factory operative, it may mean the foreman's office. Often one hears that 'the office says we have to do it', as though the office had authority to give orders. In considering the office in relation to the organization, it is necessary to separate completely the concepts of *management* which decides and exercises authority, and *the office* which is a servant acting on behalf of management.

To those studying administration, or already responsible for the provision of office services, the office must be seen in wide terms; as anywhere where clerical work is done. The simple organization charts shown above, although they express the truth in broad terms, do not give the whole truth. They suggest that the administrative functions are in the hands of the office manager, whilst his colleagues are solely concerned with purchasing, production and marketing. In fact, all are involved in one way or another in the operation of clerical systems. The office manager undoubtedly has the principal responsibility, but he cannot fulfil this without the help of other managers, supervisors and, indeed, operative staff.

The main office relies on other departments for most of the data it processes. The facts of what happens in the course of business can only be reliably recorded by those present when incidents occur. The purchasing officer provides copies of the orders he places; the storeman records the goods he receives; the factory operative records time spent and goods produced; the salesman writes out a customer's order; the van driver obtains the receipt for goods delivered., etc., etc. The responsibility for the complete collection and accurate recording of these facts rests with the managers of the various departments where activity takes place.

Often, production, sales and other departments need immediate information which involves clerical work, if only to summarize the events of the day. In a factory, the supervisors may have to observe the rate of production from hour to hour. The marketing manager may need summaries of orders and despatches so as to assess the effects of these on available stocks. It is, therefore, not unusual for there to be small departmental offices in addition to the main office. Where an organization is highly computerized, these small offices may assume great importance: equipped with terminals, they can feed data directly into a central computer where stored information is held in a data-bank, available for all purposes. They can also extract information from the computer without calling on the services of the main office.

Whether clerical work is done manually or by computer, there must be co-ordination of systems and services. Each department cannot be left to devise its own methods and operate independently. The data used departmentally are the same data that are needed for the central accounting and recording processes. In the interests of efficiency, office work, wherever it is done, must be seen as part of one whole administrative process.

The provision of office services is a specialist function, having its own skills and its own body of knowledge. It cannot be expected that managers trained in disciplines such as engineering, chemistry or marketing shall also be expert in record-keeping, data processing or communications. In any organization there should be one authority—the office or administrative manager, by whatever title he may be known—responsible for the provision of central services, for the principal systems and for the machines and equipment wherever used.

If an effective office service is to be provided for management there must be full co-operation between the office manager and the managers of other functions. The records maintained should present a picture in words and figures of the activities of the business. It should be possible from the records to trace every transaction, every movement of goods, and every expense that has been incurred, and if these records are to be of proper value they must be kept in a form which truly reflects the business. For example, records of revenue and expenditure should be so maintained that it is possible to show them in relation to the delegation of responsibility within the organization. The financial effect of any decision taken by an individual manager should be capable of being made known without undue special work. It is clearly not possible for the office manager to provide records which give a proper picture of the business unless he is taken fully into the confidence of the general manager and functional managers. He must be kept fully informed of plans as they are made, and alterations as they are put into effect. His task is then to ensure that the work of the offices is so directed that the facts will be available when they are wanted.

The office manager, by constant consultation with other managers, must be in a position to know what information is likely to be necessary so that adequate records and adequate records only may be kept. There is, in some offices, a tendency to keep records 'just in case they are wanted', or to perpetuate records which have long since ceased to be of importance. This can only lead to excessive cost. There must be agreed routine statements which will be produced to meet the normal requirements of management, and there must be an understanding as to the type of special information which may from time to time be required and the degree of urgency with which it must be produced.

CENTRALIZATION OF OFFICE CONTROL

It has been argued above that, in the interests of efficiency, all office work should be co-ordinated by one office manager, even though some parts of it may be done in departmental offices not under his control. In some organizations, the principal office manager is given full responsibility for all offices, including those attached to operative departments. He is required to organize, equip, staff and manage these offices, providing such services as the departmental or functional manager may reasonably demand. Taking the simplest example of organization given above, the situation may be illustrated thus, the dotted lines indicating responsibility for providing service.

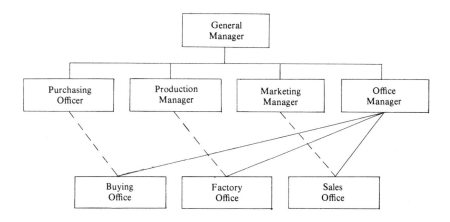

Again, it is emphasized that the office is not an end in itself but a service. If the service is best given by decentralization of offices then they should be decentralized, but this does not mean that those offices must be managed independently. A specialist office manager can control a group of small offices in just the same way as a sales manager can control groups of salesmen operating away from head office over a wide area.

OFFICE MANAGEMENT

The Institute of Administrative Management has defined office management as:

> that branch of management which is concerned with the services of obtaining, recording and analysing information, of planning, and of communicating, by means of which the management of a business safeguards its assets, promotes its affairs, and achieves its objectives.

Whilst this makes clear the office manager's purposes, it does not discuss the scope of his job in practice. In providing these various services, the office manager is responsible for the efficiency and effectiveness of his subordinates. The office staff must be efficient; each clerk should produce a reasonable day's work every day, in terms of both quantity and quality. But that alone is not enough. The work must be cost-effective, making a real contribution to the running of the business.

An earlier definition makes a broad analysis of the office manager's job as follows:

> Office management is the art of guiding the *personnel* of the office in the use of *means* appropriate to its *environment* in order to achieve its specified *purpose.*

The four principal elements which emerge are amplified below.

Purpose   Without an awareness of true purpose, the office manager cannot make correct decisions or ensure the effectiveness of work done.

Environment   This does not refer to the physical environment within the office. It is concerned with external factors: the business which the office serves, the industry or other activity within which the business lies, the customs and laws of the community within which it operates. These environmental factors are always changing and the office must react to change with them.

Means   The office manager must make the best use of premises, methods, computers and other equipment or techniques. New means are always being developed and should be applied whenever they will result in greater efficiency or effectiveness.

Personnel   The clerks who put the means to use are the most important of the four elements; they are also often the most difficult to understand. It is they who make office management an art as well as a science. No matter what machines are employed, management remains basically the leadership of people—and the ultimate goal remains the serving of humanity.

TERMINOLOGY OF OFFICE ADMINISTRATION

Every technique has its terminology in which words have special meanings, and the subject of this book is no exception. Those who study office work must learn to use the correct terms so that they may be understood by others—including examiners. In most offices there is a local slang and this must be discarded; familiar to a few colleagues, it will only serve to confuse others. Care must be taken not to use trade names as though they were technical terms in general use, e.g. 'Roneo' or 'Gestetner' when meaning any stencil duplicator.

'Office' should be interpreted as meaning any place in which clerical work is done, even though called by some other name, e.g. Accounts Dept, Computer Room or Town Hall. The term 'clerk' is used to refer to office workers generally, and may often include typists, machine operators, computer programmers etc. 'Office manager' or 'administrative manager' means the person in charge of all the office functions of an undertaking or some major part of them. It should be noted that, because the office or administrative manager often performs a technical or professional function also, he may have a job title which refers to this, e.g. Financial Director, Company Secretary, Accountant, Administrator, Local Government Executive etc.

A NOTE FOR STUDENTS

The chapters which follow are arranged in six parts, and in a sequence which experience has shown will facilitate study. Although this is a book for practising and student managers, the chapters dealing with management practices appear towards the end. This is because, before coming to the study of these, it is necessary to reach a comprehensive understanding of the services which offices provide and of the methods and equipment used. If the study of how to manage is to have meaning, it must be against the background of purposes and how those purposes are achieved.

Parts 1, 2 and 3 are concerned with the office services and the methods and equipment used in providing them. Efficient study should start with familiar things. For this reason, Part 1 deals with the general office services of communication, filing and reprography. In an electronic age, it is then necessary to master the principles and practices of data processing, explained in Part 2. Against this background, the various systems which provide the accounting and financial services are described in Part 3. These first three parts establish the purpose which the office serves and the ways in which the necessary work is carried out.

Parts 4, 5 and 6 deal with the various aspects of managing an office staff. Part 4 examines questions relating to environment; the physical conditions in which people work. At this point, it might be said that the plot is laid and the stage set. Part 5 turns away from the inanimate systems, equipment, furniture, etc., to consider the people who work in offices. Management has a duty to organize, recruit, train, promote, motivate, pay and generally care for those who serve under its direction, and this part deals with personnel policy and practices. Finally, Part 6 describes the techniques by which a manager plans and controls the office in action and maintains contact with those to whom the office services are given.

Part 1
General office services

Whatever may be the main technical purpose served by any particular office, there are a number of general duties with which it will almost certainly be concerned. These are:

Communication services
Telecommunications
Filing and indexing
Reprography

In one way or other these general services affect every department of the business. If efficiently carried out, they can make a considerable contribution towards the efficiency of management; if ill-planned or executed, they can render ineffective the best efforts of others in the organization. A well-conducted general office relieves the executive of the delays and irritations which can arise from poor typing, difficulty in finding files, and delay in getting in touch with people. It enables management decisions to be put into effect quickly.

These services which the office gives are of the most general interest, and are the most readily understood. It is appropriate, therefore, that the student of office administration should begin with them.

The methods and equipment described are not, however, related to secretarial services only. They are of equal importance in the financial and accounting services. To take but one example, if a data-processing department is to be truly efficient it must be supported by quick and reliable communications and the systematic filing of related documents.

2   Communication services

Communication is one of the fundamental functions of the office and a process essential to all forms of business. It is the process of conveying information from one person to another through the post, by telephone, teleprinter, messenger service, or by other means. The term communication should be interpreted widely and not taken as including only such obvious things as letters and telephone calls to and from persons outside the business; it includes also the transmission of memoranda, reports, instructions, invoices, orders, estimates, drawings, and even samples.

The majority of business communications are received or originated by the office in the course of its work. The office manager has, therefore, the responsibility of maintaining a communication service as part of the office organization. In most businesses he has the further duty of maintaining services such as the telephone switchboard and postal section for the convenience of all departments.

This chapter is concerned with general matters relating to communication and with secretarial, postal and messenger services. Telecommunications are dealt with separately in Chapter 3.

COMMUNICATION

There are certain basic principles of communication which should be understood and applied in all situations.

1. Communication is between the mind of one person and the mind of another   Legally, companies (which are legal 'persons') can write to other companies, but in practice companies can neither read nor write. Communication can only be between people. The most effective communication is between interested persons, face to face, when speech is supplemented by gesture and facial expression. It can then be seen immediately whether what has been said has been understood, and further explanation can be given should this be necessary. Communication is always more difficult between strangers. Some organizations take positive steps to establish personal relationships between members of their staffs and those of their suppliers, customers and other regular contacts; formal correspondence between people who do not know each other can be time-consuming and expensive. A telephone conversation between two directly interested people who quickly understand one another is effective and cheap. If a written record is necessary, a single letter can confirm what was agreed. The same principle should be applied in inter-departmental communications. The formal memorandum from the chief engineer to the chief accountant may at some stage be necessary, but the true effectiveness of the communication may rest in an understanding reached between George in the Engineers Stores and Henry in the Stock Records Section of the Accounts Department.

It is worthwhile to think in terms of people.

2. People can only understand one thing by relating it to something else already understood   It is in the nature of people that they can only comprehend by relating new ideas to existing knowledge. This is the basis of education; it is also the basis of effective communication. Whether speaking or writing, it is necessary to have some appreciation of what the person addressed already knows. When a lawyer writes to another lawyer, he can use legal language and know that he will be understood; when he writes to a lay client, he may have to choose other words. Similarly in business, the use of technical terms or departmental jargon must be limited to those who already understand them.

3. The communicator has a duty to make himself understood   It is useless to blame the recipient of a communication if he does not understand it. The reason for lack of understanding is that the speaker or writer has not chosen his words correctly, or has not given sufficient explanation.

4. The person who does not understand has a duty to ask for an explanation   If communications received are not understood, it is useless merely to blame the other party—or to guess what is meant.

SELECTING THE MEANS

In any office the majority of communications are of a routine nature and capable of being classified according to the purposes which they serve. The office manager should consider each class and lay down instructions as to the means to be used. It should not be left to the junior clerk to decide whether a letter shall be sent by registered post instead of ordinary mail, nor should it be left to the invoice clerk to decide whether forms shall be sent by first or second class mail.

In arriving at a decision as to the means of communication to be used in any circumstances, there are seven major factors to be considered:

(a) *Speed*   How urgent is the communication?

(b) *Accuracy*   Will the information be received accurately? If figures are spoken over the telephone they are liable to be misheard.

(c) *Safety*   What is the risk of losing the communication in transit? If an important legal document is to be sent through the post, it may be prudent to send it by registered mail.

(d) *Secrecy*   Does it matter if unauthorized persons become aware of the information communicated?

(e) *Record*   It is necessary that the communication should be in writing for purpose of record?

(f) *Impression*   Is the communication in such a form as to produce the desired reaction from the person receiving it? In some instances a form letter is adequate, but in others this might give offence or result in the communication being put into the waste-bin unread.

(g) *Cost*   All elements of cost must be taken into account. The greater proportion of cost usually lies in the stages of preparation rather than in transmission. For example, the cost of labour and material expended in preparing and posting a letter will far exceed that of the postage.

Not one of these seven factors can be said to be of greater importance than the others and all must be given proper weight according to the circumstances. The table below indicates the relative facilities offered by some of the more commonly used methods.

	Registered Mail	1st Class Mail	2nd Class Mail	Teleprinter (Telex)	Telephone
Speed	Fair	Fair	Poor	V. Good	V. Good
Accuracy	V. Good	V. Good	V. Good	Good	Fair
Safety	V. Good	Good	Good	V. Good	V. Good
Secrecy	V. Good	V. Good	Good	Fair	Fair
Record	V. Good	V. Good	V. Good	Good	Nil
Impression	V. Good	V. Good	Good	V. Good	Good

It will be seen that cost has been omitted from the table. In any particular situation, cost must be considered in relation to the service required. If the cheapest means is selected first, the question to be answered is 'are the additional facilities offered by alternatives worth the additional expenditure?'

ORAL v WRITTEN COMMUNICATION

The most common form of oral communication is, of course, direct conversation between two persons. Often the quickest and best way of ensuring co-operation is to talk the matter over with the people concerned. Too often, written memoranda pass between departments over a period, when a short discussion between the appropriate officials could settle the matter at once.

When several people are involved, a meeting may be the best means of communicating. All the benefits of direct conversation are obtained with the added advantage that all present are able to share in what is said; it is possible to reach a common understanding. It is sometimes said that meetings are a waste of time and this can be true if they are ill-prepared and allowed to deviate from a definite purpose. The strict formality of a legally-constituted company meeting is not, of course, necessary, but some formality can ensure that business is completed without delay and conclusions minuted, if necessary (see Chapter 28).

Great as may be the benefits of oral communication, whether face to face or by telephone, there are many occasions when writing is necessary or convenient. Most business transactions are the subject of written communications and without them there might be chaos. Wherever there is the possibility of legal dispute, a written record signed by the other party might be vital evidence. Many matters are so complex that no one could comprehend or remember the detail without a document to which to refer.

Oral and written communications both have their uses. The written method, being usually the more expensive, should only be used when there is good reason for so doing.

WRITTEN COMMUNICATION

Most written communications are typewritten and the machines available are described below. Typewriting, as compared with handwriting, is faster and the result is easier to read.

Handwriting is not, however, to be regarded as obsolete. Forms are entered and inter-departmental memoranda written as operations incidental to the main jobs of clerks who are not trained typists. If they are clearly written, they are ready for immediate despatch; if a typist is involved, there is extra work and delay. Where forms, letters or memoranda are drafted by hand for a typist to copy the question must be asked 'Why could not the original draft have been used and the typing process eliminated?'

Another question which might be asked is 'Why should not a clerk do his own typing?' It has become traditional to assume that simple typing is a skill that can only be exercised by specialist typists. In some organizations, and in some European countries, typing is regarded as a basic office operation which everyone engaged in clerical work should be able to perform. A clerk with a light-weight typewriter on a side-table could, with training, do his own typing as the need arose.

TYPEWRITERS

The typewriter is the most commonly used and best known of office machines and as such requires no general description. The standard model is designed for use in typing correspondence and reports on quarto, foolscap or A4 size paper and is satisfactory for most general office work. This basic standard machine can be modified in a number of different ways in order to meet special requirements.

Type   Most machines are fitted with a single type, usually Roman, but a variety of other styles is available (Fig. 1). There are also typewriters which

ADVOCATE: abcdefghi   ABCDEFGHIJ   1234567890

BOOKFACE ACADEMIC: abcedfghi   ABCDEFGHIJ   1234567890

MANIFOLD: ABCEDFGHIJ   ABCDEFGHI   1234567890

ORATOR: ABCEDFGHIJ   ABCDEFGHIJ   1234567890

PICA: abcdefghij   ABCDEFGHIJ   1234567890

DIPLOMAT: abcdefghij   ABCEDFGHIJ   1234567890

SCRIPT: abcdefghijk   ABCDEFGHIJK   1234567890

ARTISAN: abcdefghijk   ABCDEFGHIJK   1234567890

COURIER 12 METRIC: abcdefghij   ABCDEFGHIJ   1234567890

Fig. 1   Specimens of typewriter type (*Courtesy of IBM United Kingdom Ltd.*)

permit several styles of type to be used. Instead of the type being carried on bars, it is carried on a separate *printball* as on the machine illustrated in Fig. 2. The printball bearing the type required can be dropped into position in the machine. As a key is depressed the ball is turned until the required character is in position, when the printing action takes place.

Different sizes of type require different horizontal spacing. Ten letters to the inch (Pica) and twelve letters to the inch (Elite) are the most common; other examples are given in Fig. 1. Most machines are restricted to one horizontal spacing but some printball machines can work at either ten or twelve letters to the inch. Printball units can also be provided for universal, technical, chemical and mathematical symbols.

Fig. 2   Printball electric typewriter *(Courtesy of British Olivetti Ltd.)*

Line spacing   The standard spacing of lines is six to the inch, variable by the operation of a lever to three lines to the inch (double spacing) and two lines to the inch (treble spacing). Machines are also available which provide for half-line spacing or for four lines to the inch. Double spacing is commonly used in typing drafts, when room must be left between the lines for any corrections which may be necessary. Where office forms are duplicated from typewritten masters (Chapter 5), adequate space must be left for any entries which will subsequently be made by hand. Double spacing is the usual allowance for this purpose, but four lines to the inch is often sufficient.

Carriage sizes   The platen (roller) on a standard machine is usually between ten and eleven inches wide, a size well suited to take letter paper, envelopes, labels, and the majority of office forms. Where, however, large sheets of paper have to be used, as for legal documents, balance sheets, or involved statistical reports, a wider carriage is necessary. Carriages are obtainable in a variety of standard sizes, but for exceptional widths it may be necessary to modify the typewriter to carry the additional weight. On some typewriters, the carriage moves in relation to the type position; on others, a type-head moves along the length of the carriage.

Tabulating mechanism   Every office typewriter is fitted with some device to enable the typist to stop the carriage or type-head at predetermined positions, as an aid to setting out work accurately and quickly. In its simplest form, the tabulator consists of a rack at the back of the carriage on which small forked 'stops' can be fitted at any required point. When tabulating to insert figures in the columns of a form, for example, the typist has only to depress a key to cause the carriage or type-head to move and stop at the next column. Some machines are fitted with a more elaborate device, permitting the stops to be set from the keyboard simply by moving the carriage to the required position and depressing a key or lever. A further refinement is the provision of a series of tabulation keys which permit the carriage to be stopped at any one of a number of positions within a column. If, for example, the figure 10 has to be inserted, a key is depressed which will cause the carriage to stop two spaces from the right-hand side of the column. Other keys cause the carriage to stop at the correct position for typing 100's, 1000's and so on.

Ribbon   The typewriter imprint is normally made by type striking the paper through an ink-impregnated ribbon or coated plastic film. Ribbons may be of one or two colours, e.g. black and red, the colour being selected by means of a lever on the machine. Black and white ribbons are available, the white portion being used to conceal errors by over-typing, after which the correct characters are superimposed. Alternatively, some machines carry a separate white ribbon which can be brought into action when required.

There are also film ribbons which give high-quality impression by transferring a portion of the film to the paper. On some typewriters, there is a device which removes the film from the paper when an error has been made.

Portable typewriters

These machines, whether manual or electric, are of lighter construction than the standard typewriters. They are useful for casual office use and when travelling.

Comparison of manual with electric typewriters

In an electric typewriter, which should be regarded as the normal, both type and carriage movements are power actuated and only a slight depression of the keys is necessary. As compared with the manual machine, it offers the following advantages:

   (*a*) type impression is perfectly even;
   (*b*) more carbon copies obtainable;
   (*c*) typists can maintain a higher daily output.

Typewriters with variable type

There are typewriters which permit the use of a wide variety of styles and sizes of type. Instead of the type being carried on bars, it is on a block or printball which is dropped into position on the machine. As a key is depressed the block is turned until the required character is in position, when the printing action takes place. Type blocks can easily be interchanged without removing the paper from the platen, thus permitting a variety of type styles to be used on one sheet of paper as required. These machines are of particular value in preparing company and management accounts and for laying out involved statistical reports, when the range of type styles can be used to distinguish one set of figures from another, and to give whatever emphasis may be required.

Continuous stationery

When long runs of routine forms, such as invoices, are being filled in by a typewriter, a considerable proportion of the typist's time is occupied in interleaving carbon paper and inserting forms in the machine. These preparatory operations can be greatly reduced by the use of continuous stationery. An attachment is fitted to the typewriter carriage to take a quantity of forms printed on a long strip of paper which is usually folded in a zig-zag formation. Successive forms are thus fed into the machine with no more effort than is needed to turn the platen. The backs of the original and all but the last of the copies can be coated with carbon, or a device fitted which enables sheets of carbon paper or ribbons to be used again and again, by drawing them down into the next set of forms after each typing operation is completed. Use can also be made of chemically impregnated paper which produces copies without requiring carbon paper or backing.

WORD PROCESSING

Automatic typewriters of various kinds have been available for many decades. The term 'word processing' has been introduced to describe automatic typing processes which make use of electronic and magnetic equipment similar to that employed in data processing (see Chapter 7).

To review systems of word processing it is helpful to examine in turn three basic processes

(a) the initial recording of the text;
(b) the recall of the text from the magnetic record, and
(c) the final typing of the document required for use.

Initial recording

Whatever is entered on the keyboard can be made into both a visible record and a magnetic record.

Visible records   All word processing machines produce a typewritten record but some also have a separate display screen (Fig. 5) or a display panel built into the machine on which illuminated characters appear. Where a screen or panel is available the operator can delay the production of the typewritten record until a visual check has been made.

Magnetic records   There are three types of magnetic record: a magnetic card (see page 122) which can hold up to 12 000 characters but which often, for convenience, is used to hold the contents of one page, a magnetic tape cassette (see page 115) which can hold up to 125 000 characters, and a diskette (see page 118) which can hold up to 250 000 characters.

All word processing machines have an electronic store or memory (see page 125) and for this reason they are sometimes called *memory* typewriters. The store has two purposes: to hold a program of operating instructions (see page 132) and to hold part or all of the text.

The program relates to the entry of the text and ensures that when the text is recalled from the magnetic record and typed automatically, the machine follows the original operator's instructions as to line length, paragraphing, column headings, tabulations etc.

Fig. 3   Word Processor *(Courtesy of A. B. Dick Company of Great Britain Ltd.)*

The extent to which text is held in the store depends upon the system. Where there is a screen or panel, the store must be able to hold at least that part of the text being so displayed. Figure 3 illustrates a machine, that operates with magnetic cards for external storage, which has an internal electronic store for 8000 characters. Some systems are able to hold large quantities of text in a central computer. In this kind of system, which uses what is called *shared logic*, the computer is served by several connected keyboards. Each keyboard may have typing capacity or the computer may be linked to a fast printer.

Recall

An important feature of word processing is the ease with which it is possible to recall parts of the text from a magnetic record so as to make amendments, to add information or to retrieve information. For such purposes it is necessary to be able to transfer into the electronic store a particular page, paragraph, line, word or item of information. There are various ways of doing this of which the following are examples.

With a magnetic card or a cassette every paragraph can be given a code number which appears on all drafts but which is omitted from the final document. The program automatically associates the number with the exact location in the magnetic record of the corresponding text. When it is required to make an alteration the operator places the appropriate card or cassette in the reader on the machine and

(*a*) enters through the keyboard the reference number of the paragraph to be brought into the store,

(*b*) counts and enters the number of lines and the number of words along the relevant line to the point at which a change is to be made, and

(*c*) enters instructions to delete from, or add to, the text.

Working automatically under the operating instructions in the store, the system makes the changes and adjusts the spacing in the rest of the paragraph to allow for the change.

When recalling and editing text with the aid of a display screen, the entry of the paragraph number brings the whole paragraph on to the screen, or as much of it for which there is capacity on the screen. The text can then be *scrolled* back and forth until the line to be altered is at the top of the screen. A dot of light is moved along the line until the point is reached where the change is to be made. As soon as the entry has been made a key is depressed and the revised and respaced paragraph appears immediately on the screen.

With a system using a diskette it is possible to locate a point in the text by merely entering into a part of the store a phrase from the text of sufficient length to identify it; if the phrase is used more than once it will locate each use in turn. One system which uses a diskette has a display panel in which the phrase is displayed for checking and, when that phrase is located in the text, it can also be scrolled back and forth in the panel to display the text on either side.

Producing results

Since the final document is produced automatically the printing speed is important. The conventional type basket is never used and the printball, working at a speed of 15 characters a second had largely been replaced by the daisy wheel printer (Fig. 4) which works at 52 characters a second. It has 80 flexible spokes each with a different character or sign on one face at the end of the spoke. It is rotated back and forth at high speed to bring each

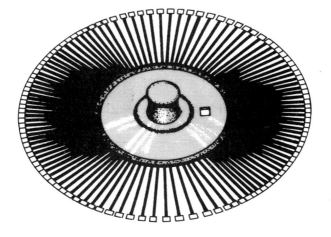

Fig. 4 Daisy Wheel (*Courtesy of Facit-Addo Ltd.*)

Fig. 5 Word processor with display screen and ink jet printer (*Courtesy of IBM United Kingdom Ltd.*)

required letter into place whereupon the spoke head is struck with a hammer. Like the printball the daisy wheel is interchangeable with different styles of type.

An even faster device is the ink jet printer. This is a separate free standing printer (Fig. 5) and the process is to squirt a stream of magnetized ink particles on to the paper; magnetic deflection ensures that these particles hit the paper in the shape of the required characters. The speed of printing is 90 characters a second. In a large installation this item may be justified because it enables the typewriters to be used only for composing and editing and does not leave an operator idle whilst the machine automatically types the final work.

Applications

Wherever typists are engaged in work that involves extensive repetition, word processing is likely to offer advantages. Many kinds of typing incur a great deal of repetition.

The preparation of technical reports, specifications, legal documents, manuals, minutes and a variety of long reports often causes extensive textual amendments. A draft is typed and returned to the author for checking and amendment; this may require the re-typing of whole pages if not an entire report. The cycle may be repeated several times and involve many different people whose views have to be taken into account before the finished document is released. Moreover, every time a report is retyped there is the possibility of a new error being made.

Much routine correspondence is highly repetitive particularly in matters such as a direct mail sales promotion, requests for quotations, and debt collection, where there is an attempt to 'personalize' what are in fact form letters. With word processing systems it is possible to merge form letters from one magnetic record with addresses and variable information either from another magnetic record or from a part of the memory where the information will have been entered in advance through the keyboard.

Word processing also has advantages to offer in the maintenance of, and data retrieval from, directories, lists, client and prospect files, inventories, staff records and a variety of other lengthy records that are subject to constant change and also where selection may involve the application of criteria.

Punched hole records

An earlier form of automatic typewriter is controlled by punched paper tape or edge punched cards (see page 124). On these machines at the same time as a proof page is typed, a paper tape or card is punched. Tape and cards can be fed into the reader to control the type, spacing and carriage movements and the recording can include instructions to stop at required points so that names and addresses and non-standard text can be inserted through the keyboard in the ordinary way.

DICTATION

There is an art in dictation which every manager should cultivate; it consists, broadly, in being sure in advance what ideas are to be expressed and in being able to put those ideas into good English. Too many writers of business letters still rely on hackneyed phrases—the so-called 'business English'. It is only too easy to memorize and use such expressions as:

'Reference yours of the 15th inst. . . .'
'Yours of the 15th inst. to hand . . .'
'Your esteemed instructions received'
'We would advise you . . .'

and to finish by assuring the addressee of 'our best attention at all times'. The effect of these well-worn and often curiously ungrammatical sentences can scarcely convey to the recipient the writer's desire to give real thought and personal attention to his affairs. Constant practice and self-criticism are necessary in order to be able fluently to dictate letters which are pleasing to read and which reflect the true personality of the writer.

Dictating machines

Dictating machines (Fig. 6) provide a means whereby correspondence, reports, instructions etc. can be recorded as speech and later transcribed by an audio-typist. Records may be *inscribed*, as where grooves are cut in a

Fig. 6   Dictating machines (*Courtesy of Philips Electrical Ltd.*)

plastic belt or disc, or *magnetic* on tape, disc, or belt. Inscribed records are permanent and cannot be corrected during dictation. They can, however, be stored with little danger of deterioration or accidental erasure. Some inscribed records can be shaved to remove the grooved surface and then re-used, the number of times depending on the thickness of the material. Magnetic records can be erased and corrected during dictation. They can also be erased and re-used, possibly hundreds of times.

In addition to machines for desk use, there are portable models, some being small enough to be carried in the pocket.

There is advantage in standardizing the type of record used in an organization for both desk and portable machines. If, for example, all recording is done on standard magnetic-tape cassettes, it can be transcribed in any department.

Dictating   Whatever the type of machine, facilities are provided whereby the dictator can start and stop the record instantly. By stopping the record when making even a brief pause in dictation, the whole surface can be used. The running times of records vary and may be classified as short duration (about 10 minutes), medium duration (10–20 minutes) and long duration (more than 20 minutes). If, in the course of recording, the dictator wishes to hear the record, this can be played back immediately. Magnetic records can be erased and corrected; inscribed records cannot be erased and corrections are usually indicated to the typist on a paper slip showing which parts are to be ignored and which substituted.

Whilst dictating machines can be operated after very little practice, executives are well-advised to listen critically to their own recordings and take pains to enunciate their words carefully. Carelessness in dictation leads to errors in transcription or, at the best, the wasting of time by the typist in listening to the record a second or third time in endeavouring to pick out an indistinct word or phrase. Typists who transcribe from dictating machines should be encouraged to express their difficulties, and to offer criticism of the dictation.

Transcribing   The audio-typist hears the record through earphones, stopping and starting the machine by hand or pedal controls.

The typist starts the record, listens, and types. Whilst some may require to stop the record before typing, experienced typists working from good records are able to listen and type simultaneously. Provision is made on the machine for the typist to be able to listen to any selected portion of the record without going back to the beginning.

Other applications   With special attachments, dictating machines can be connected so as to record telephone messages and conversations. By using a suitable microphone, they can also be used to record speeches and the proceedings of meetings.

If adequately packed, records can be sent through the post without risk of damage. Salesmen can, for example, dictate their reports and orders on portable machines and send the records for transcription at Head Office. Reports may, in fact, be heard and never transcribed. If a report is to be preserved for a time the record itself can be filed. With the aid of portable machines, inventories of stock, etc. can be dictated whilst moving from place to place.

These are but a few examples of the many ways in which speech recording can be used to save time and paper-work.

Stenographic machines

These are machines (Fig. 7) which enable an operator to take dictation, recording it in type (Fig. 8). Each line on the paper tape represents a syllable printed by the simultaneous depression of the appropriate combination of keys on the machine. The machine is easily portable and skilled operators can attain very high speeds. The operator does not usually transcribe from the tapes which he has prepared; they are passed to copy typists who can be quickly trained to read and type from them.

Stenographic machines are particularly suited for the reporting of meetings, as the tape can be passed to typists from time to time during the course of the meeting, the typing proceeding almost simultaneously.

Comparison of shorthand with dictating machine

The shorthand systems in common use are of two main types:

(a) those which can be written at high speeds, but only after extensive training and practice;

(b) those, often based on the normal alphabet, which are more easily learnt but cannot be written so quickly.

The ability to write at high speed is important in verbatim reporting, but the slower systems are often found to be adequate for general purposes.

The practice of dictating business correspondence, etc. to a shorthand writer is giving way to the use of dictating machines which offer the following principal advantages:

(a) the typist need not be present during dictation;

(b) dictation can be recorded item by item as matters arise;

(c) dictation can be recorded away from the office;

(d) recordings may be sent by post for transcription;

(e) transcription by an audio-typist from a good recording can be faster than transcription from shorthand notes.

Because of (a) and (e) above, the output of an audio-typist may be as much as double that of a shorthand-typist.

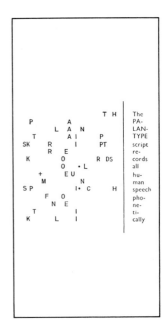

			T H	The
P		A		PA-
	L	A N		LAN-
T		A I	P	TYPE
SK	R	I	PT	script
	R	E		re-
K		O	R DS	cords
		O • L		all
	+	E U		hu-
	M		N		man
S P		I• C	H	speech
	F	O		pho-
	N	E		ne-
T		I		ti-
K		L I		cally

Fig. 7   Stenographic machine   **Fig. 8**   Stenographic machine script

(Courtesy of the Palantype Organization Ltd.)

SECRETARIAL DUTIES

It is not to be expected that private secretaries will understand as much about the business in hand as an executive, but they should have some understanding of the significance of the correspondence, reports, and instructions which pass through their hands. They should be able to fulfil some or all of the following duties:

(*a*) receive visitors and, if necessary, turn them politely away;

(*b*) receive and give messages verbally or by telephone, with understanding of their significance;

(*c*) compose routine replies to letters and memoranda;

(*d*) punctuate and correct grammar in transcribing dictation;

(*e*) maintain a filing system;

(*f*) keep an engagement diary, and see that engagements are fulfilled or other suitable action taken;

(*g*) operate a reminder system to ensure that necessary work is done at the due time;

(*h*) arrange business journeys, make reservations, obtain tickets, and prepare itineraries;

(*i*) arrange meetings by making contact with a number of executives or their secretaries to find mutually convenient dates.

Personal assistants

In some businesses, senior private secretaries are trained to act as personal assistants, relieving the executive of work which otherwise he would have to do personally. In this capacity, they should also be able to do the following:

(*a*) gather and collate information from within the business and from outside;

(*b*) draft reports, memoranda etc. for the executive;

(*c*) draft proposals for the executive to amend or approve;

(*d*) act as secretary to management meetings, drafting agenda, minutes etc.

CENTRALIZED TYPING SERVICES (TYPING POOLS)

Where each executive has his own typist, there is inevitably wasted time because the flow of typing work is not steady. On some days, the typist may be hard-pressed; on others, she may have little or nothing to do, perhaps because the executive is away from his office. In any case, it is rare for an executive to generate enough work to keep one typist fully occupied, even if her work is supplemented by other secretarial duties. This problem may be overcome by providing a typing or secretarial service to a number of executives or departments from a central department or 'pool'. The advantages to be gained are as follows:

(*a*) the total number of typists is reduced, sometimes by as much as half;

(*b*) expert supervision becomes possible;

(*c*) typists can be trained to do a wider variety of work;

(*d*) difficulties arising from absence are reduced;

(*e*) working conditions can be suited to the needs of typists;

(*f*) work can be allocated according to individual ability and experience;

(*g*) a wider range of machines and equipment can be made available because they can be shared.

On the other hand, there are disadvantages, for example:

(*a*) continuity of understanding is lost, because the work of one executive is not always dealt with by the same typist;

(*b*) the executive does not have the assistance of a private secretary immediately available.

The success or otherwise of the system depends to some extent on the complexity of the work. It has been found that the typing pool is a very efficient way of dealing with routine correspondence. It does not, however, provide a satisfactory substitute for the private secretarial service, which is generally retained for the higher executives.

Although a centralized typing service may provide shorthand writers, dic-

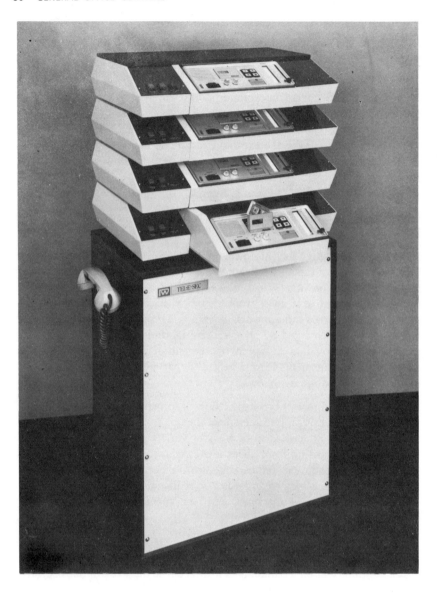

Fig. 9   Dictating exchange (*Courtesy of the Peter Williams Group*)

tating machines are more commonly used. The executive may dictate to a machine in his own office and send the record to be transcribed by the pool. Alternatively, the dictating machines may be installed centrally in the pool, being connected to the executives' offices by special circuits or through a private automatic telephone system (see Chapter 3). In the latter case, remote control permits the dictator to start and stop the machine and to play back his recording. The number of machines required is, of course, reduced. Two remote systems can be adopted:

(a) *Tandem*, in which each typist has two machines, so that one is available for recording whilst the other is being used for transcription.

(b) *Bank or exchange*, as illustrated in Fig. 9, in which executives are connected to one of a number of dictating machines, from which the records are removed when full and passed to the typists for transcription.

In either case, connection with a machine may be automatic or controlled by a supervisor.

Computer-assisted typing pools

Where the nature and volume of work warrants it, the conventional typewriter can be replaced by a keyboard and visual-display screen connected with a computer. The typists firstly key in instructions as to margin, tabulation positions etc., which are confirmed on the screen. The text is then typed in the ordinary way but without regard to line length which is automatically adjusted by the computer program. When a new paragraph is to be started or work is to be tabulated, it is sufficient to depress a control key. When a page is complete, the computer commences a new one without specific instructions.

What has been typed can be seen immediately on the screen. Corrections can easily be made by back-spacing to the required position and deleting or typing in. The computer automatically adjusts the position of the unaltered text to show the corrected version on the screen. When one task is complete, it is stored by the computer and the typist is immediately free to proceed with the next. Up to this stage there is nothing on paper.

An independent operator feeds paper (or continuous stationery) into a number of automatic typewriters which, under control of the computer, type accurately and at high speed. The computer checks the length of words and determines when to start a new line or a new page. If required, the first typing on paper can be treated as a draft for correction, whilst the computer file retains its recording. When the corrected draft is sent back to the pool, a typist recalls the recorded text to the screen and makes the required alterations. The final version is then produced on an automatic typewriter in the same way as was the draft.

The computer file record can be retained for as long as may be necessary and recalled on the display screen or typed out again. The system is of particular value where long documents are drafted and amended or must be updated, because repeated typing of the whole is avoided. Examples are contracts which may be altered in the course of negotiation, and specifications and price lists which may have to be up-dated in detail.

POSTAL AND MESSENGER SERVICES

Written communications may take the form of individually written letters, memoranda or reports, or may be formalized as in the case of orders, invoices or stereotyped letters. They may be conveyed in a variety of ways inside and outside the organization.

In organizing the communication services, economy of operation is not the only factor to be considered. It is both common courtesy and good business to have full regard for the convenience of other parties. For example, it should be seen that outgoing mail is properly addressed and bears the addressee's reference or department in a conspicuous position. A letter sent to a large business concern has not reached its final destination when delivered by the postman. It will need to be sorted out from numbers of other letters before it reaches the official for whom it is intended. The efficient operation of communications relies on full co-operation between departments, between businesses and between the public and the Post Office.

Postal services

The majority of written messages are sent through the post. There are a number of services available which are described in the *Post Office Guide*, and the office manager should be fully aware of their comparative merits and costs.

The rate of postage varies according to the type of package, and according to the speed of delivery or other special service provided, such as express delivery, registration, recorded delivery, and collection of cash on delivery (COD).

The Business Reply Paid service provides a means whereby postage on a reply can conveniently be paid by the addressee. Specially printed envelopes can be provided, for example, to a customer for his use in sending in orders. Postage stamps are not used, but an account of the number of letters delivered is kept by the Post Office and the addressee charged periodically.

Where a large volume of mail is handled by an office, special arrangements can be made with the Post Office for collection and/or delivery.

There is a preferential postal system for delivering packets overnight, known as Datapost (see page 150).

Private delivery services

Security companies and others undertake the collection and carriage of packages and will guarantee delivery by an agreed time. Such services are often used for the carrying of data and results to and from a computer.

Postal section

Where any considerable volume of mail is received and dispatched it is usual to set up a separate section of the office to deal with it. The arrival of the mail in the morning and the dispatch of mail in the late afternoon gives rise to peak loads of work in the postal section and it is common practice to supplement the staff during these busy times with personnel from other parts of the office. Whilst those handling the mail may to a large extent be juniors, it is advisable to include a number of trusted senior staff, particularly if postal remittances are being received.

In order that a proper control of incoming letters can be maintained, it is usual for the postal section to register the post as it is received. Each letter is stamped with the date of receipt and a serial reference number and marked to indicate the department to which it is sent in the first instance. Each letter is entered in a register, in which may also be recorded, in due course, the date on which the reply is sent.

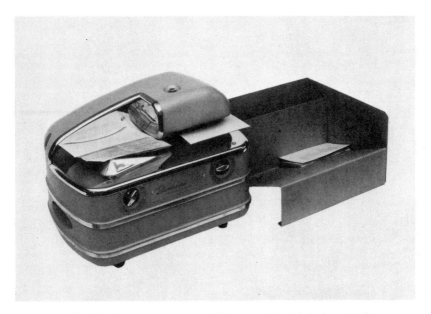

Fig. 10   Letter-opening machine (*Courtesy of Block & Anderson Ltd.*)

Much of the work of the postal section is manual, for example, opening letters, sorting, folding and stamping. Where the volume of mail handled is large, the provision of mechanical and other devices, such as the following, is often justified:

(*a*) *Letter opening machines* operate by cutting a very narrow strip from one edge of the envelope. The guillotine type, used in smaller offices, has a straight blade. The rotary type (Fig. 10) has a circular blade and can open envelopes at the rate of hundreds a minute.

Fig. 11 Franking machine (*Courtesy of Pitney-Bowes Ltd.*)

Fig. 12 Collating/inserting/mailing machine (*Courtesy of Pitney-Bowes Ltd.*)

(b) *Envelope sealing machines* dampen and stick down the flaps of envelopes. For some types of package, adhesive tape provides a rapid means of sealing.

(c) *Franking machines* (Fig. 11) print a form of postage stamp on an envelope or adhesive strip for affixing to a package. Payment of postage is made to the Post Office in advance, when a meter is set to show the amount paid. As stamps are printed, this amount is automatically reduced by their value until it reaches zero, when the machine locks. Machine-franked mail must be handed in at a post office.

(d) *Paper folding machines* fold sheets of paper to sizes convenient for placing into envelopes at the rate of up to 20 000 an hour.

(e) *Mailing machines* (Fig. 12) collate several sheets, fold, envelope and seal automatically at speeds of up to 7500 envelopes an hour.

Sorting devices These fall into three broad types:

(a) *Sorting benches*, which are merely flat surfaces, sometimes marked out into areas on which papers can be sorted according to a limited classification. This method should be used only where the number of different classifications is such that a clerk can sort to them without undue arm or body movement.

(b) *Pigeon holes and vertical racks*, which are particularly suited for the sorting of bulky packets.

(c) *Flap sorters*, which permit papers to be sorted under a large number of classifications in a restricted working area. Simple forms of flap sorter can easily be made in the office, consisting of a series of strips of light manila card, glued to a more substantial cardboard base. They can be used on a clerk's desk when required and removed and stored when not in use. They are readily portable so that the sorted papers can be carried from one part of the office to another in the sorter itself. Fig. 13 shows simple flap sorters in use, the clerk having available within easy reach some 150 compartments.

Sorting devices, similar in principle but more elaborate in construction, can be purchased. These may be mounted on runners so that a clerk, by drawing them past his chair, can gain quick access to any one of many hundreds of compartments without body movement.

Messenger service

In all but the smallest businesses, it is a wasteful practice for each department to deliver its own messages to other departments. Unless a message is particularly urgent, a centrally controlled messenger service should collect and deliver. In establishing such a service, the following principles should be applied:

(a) messengers should be based on a central point, often the postal section, from which collection and delivery rounds are made throughout the day;

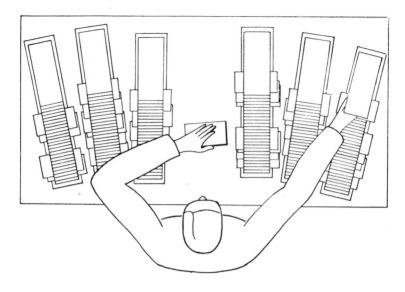

Fig. 13   Desk sorting with flap sorters

(*b*) each department should have recognized collection and delivery points at which the messengers will call. These points should be equipped with trays or other containers for the inward and outward messages;

(*c*) messages collected should not be taken back to the central point if they are for delivery to a department visited later in that round. To aid the messenger, he should be provided with a portable sorting device (which may be no more than a concertina file as shown in Fig. 14) into which messages can be sorted as they are collected;

(*d*) rounds should be planned so that departments with the most outgoing messages are visited first, thus allowing the maximum of direct delivery;

(*e*) collection, particularly in the late afternoon, should be so arranged that outgoing mail can be picked up and taken to the postal section in time for posting.

Simple verbal messages can be conveyed by a messenger, but care should be taken only to use this method when assured that the message will be accurately delivered. Messages should be short and, if possible, capable of being understood by the messenger rather than merely committed to memory.

Conveyors

Where there is a large volume of written messages to be conveyed within a business the problem can often be effectively solved by introducing conveyor systems. The type of conveyor to be employed will depend upon the

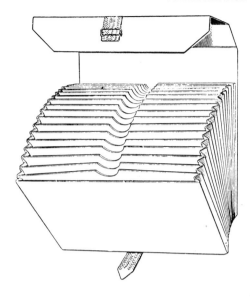

Fig. 14 Concertina file

particular circumstances as to distance, weight of papers, books, files, etc., to be conveyed and their volume. Common types of conveyors are:

(*a*) *Pneumatic tubes* through which cartridges containing the messages are propelled by means of compressed air.

(*b*) *Gravity chutes* down which papers can be dropped, if necessary in some special container in order to provide protection and weight.

(*c*) *Small lifts* similar to service lifts.

(*d*) *Moving bands or railways* similar in principle to those used in factories.

3 Telecommunications

With the advance in technology, telecommunications have become quicker, more reliable and cheaper by comparison with other methods of communication. This chapter is concerned with telecommunication services other than those relating to computers, which are dealt with in Chapter 8.

Telecommunications embrace communications over telephone and telegraph circuits and by radio. They may convey speech, handwritten material, facsimile drawings, pictures, etc., or television images. Systems may be *internal*, i.e. between points in the same building or group of buildings, or *external*, i.e. linking through Post Office connections with more distant points in the same or another country.

POST OFFICE TELEPHONES

The Post Office telephone service is so widely used as to require no general description, and the purpose of this section is to outline briefly the equipment and services which are of particular importance in business.

The smallest telephone installation is a line connecting directly from a public exchange to the subscriber's instrument. A telephone which is connected directly to the public exchange is known as a 'main' instrument. There are various types of instrument, including some suited to special situations such as exposure to the weather. Those in most common use (Fig. 15) are:

Tablephone and *Trimphone* for standing on a desk-top;
Wallphone for attachment to a wall;
Loudspeaking telephone leaving the hands free when speaking.

Arrangements can also be made for a *pendant* telephone to be fixed out of sight in the knee-hole of a desk.

Instruments may be fitted with a rotary dial or with a digital keyboard (*keypad*).

Extensions The basic main instrument can be added to by connecting extension instruments. There are a number of extension circuits to suit

Tablephone (dial)

Tablephone (keypad)

Wallphone

Trimphone

Loudspeaking telephone

Fig. 15   Post Office telephone instruments (*Courtesy of the Post Office*)

varying requirements and the more important of these are illustrated in diagrammatic form in Figs 16 and 17. Of these, plans 1A and 107 are in the most common use.

Plan 1A consists of additional instruments allowing the one line to be used from two or more places. Plan 107 offers the additional facility of inter-communication between the main and extension instruments. The main instrument is provided with switches to give the following facilities:

(*a*) *Speak to exchange*, when the main instrument is connected to the public exchange for the making or receiving of external calls.

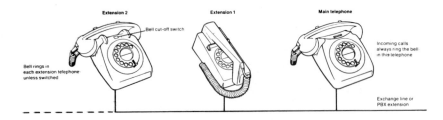

(*a*) Plan 1A. Main set and one to five internal extensions in parallel

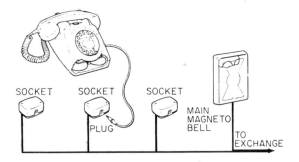

(*b*) Plan 4. One exchange line or private branch exchange extension with jacks in parallel and portable telephones

Fig. 16 Post Office telephone extension circuits (*Courtesy of the Post Office*)

(*b*) *Speak to extension, exchange held*, when conversation can take place between the two instruments whilst an outside caller is held on, though unable to overhear.

(*c*) *Extension to exchange*, when the extension instrument is connected to the exchange for conversation with the outside caller. (In a variation of Plan 107 the main instrument is unable to overhear the conversation between the extension instrument and the caller.)

(*d*) *Release*, when the main and extension instruments can be used for internal conversations without the circuit being connected to the public exchange.

This type of extension is particularly useful where a manager wishes to have telephone calls taken in the first place by his private secretary and passed over to him only if they require his personal attention. It also provides a ready means of communication between his office and that of his private secretary.

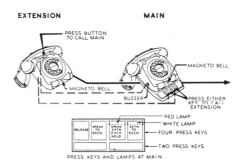

(*a*) Plan 107. Main set and one internal or external extension with inter-communication

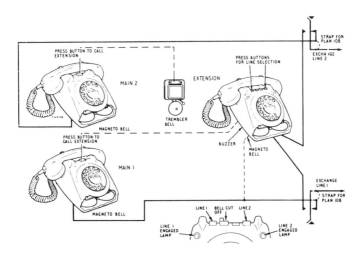

(*b*) Plan 108. Two exchange lines and one internal extension in parallel

Fig. 17 Post Office telephone extension circuits (*Courtesy of the Post Office*)

Where a single line with one or a few extensions is not enough, some form of private exchange system is necessary; one or more lines from the public exchange, the 'exchange lines', terminating at a special switching instrument or a private branch exchange (PBX). These devices enable any exchange line to be connected with any one of a number of extensions, of which there might be hundreds. They also provide for one extension to be connected with another for internal communication.

Keymaster system The Post Office Keymaster telephone system (Fig. 18) offers excellent facilities for the small office. It provides for up to ten press-button intercommunicating extensions and up to two lines from the public telephone exchange. Incoming calls are normally received at the main station which can transfer them to the extension required. Each instrument is provided with a number of press buttons by means of which any other extension on the installation can be called. A connection is thus made without intervention of the operator. It is also possible for any extension to obtain direct connection with the public exchange by pressing a button. More than two extensions can also be connected together permitting a number of persons to confer by telephone.

Fig. 18 Post Office Keymaster system (*Courtesy of the Post Office*)
Capacity 2 exchange lines and 10 extensions

Private manual branch exchange (PMBX) Manual switchboards are of two main types: for the smaller installations up to five exchange lines and twenty-five extensions, they are key-operated (Fig. 19), and for larger in-

Fig. 19   Post Office cordless (key-operated) switchboard (*Courtesy of the Post Office*)

stallations there are various cord-operated switchboards (Fig. 20). The PMBX is worked by an operator who may be full-time or combine this task with other duties. The operator is able to connect any one of the extensions to any one of the exchange lines for the purpose of receiving incoming calls or making outgoing calls, and to connect any two extensions together to permit inter-departmental telephone conversations.

Extensions from a switchboard can in turn be fitted with certain of the 'plan' extensions previously described.

Private automatic branch exchange (PABX)   The private automatic branch exchange combines manual operation with the facilities of an automatic, dial-operated exchange. There are two main types of PABX: for the smaller installations of up to five exchange lines and twenty extensions, the manual operation is through a telephone instrument equipped with a dial and press-button switches (Fig. 21). For the larger installations, there is a manual switchboard which may be cord-operated (Fig. 20) or cordless (press-button) (Fig. 22).

The various classes of call are dealt with as follows:

(*a*) external calls coming in are received by the operator and connected to the appropriate extension;

(*b*) each extension instrument is able to make connection with any other extension through the automatic exchange without the intervention of the operator;

(*c*) outgoing external calls can be made from extensions by dialling '9' followed by the required number; alternatively, by dialling '0', the service of the operator can be obtained.

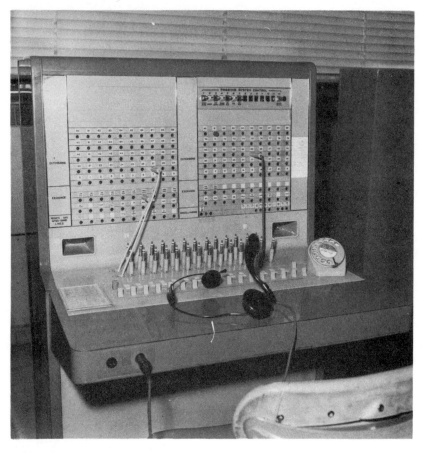

Fig. 20   Post Office cord-operated switchboard (PMBX4) (*Courtesy of the Post Office*)
This unit can be combined in suites of up to four units giving a total capacity of forty exchange lines and 200 extensions

As compared with the manual exchange (PMBX), the PABX reduces the workload by relieving the operator of the tasks of handling internal calls and possibly some outgoing calls. In addition to permitting simpler operation, the system has means whereby:

(*a*) an incoming call may be held for a busy extension and automatically connected as soon as the line is free;

(*b*) one extension can transfer an incoming call to another without involving the operator;

(*c*) an extension can hold an incoming call whilst speaking to another extension without being overheard.

Fig. 21   Post Office private automatic branch exchange (PABX6) (*Courtesy of the Post Office*)
This instrument controls up to five exchange lines and twenty extensions

Additional equipment   The Post Office provides a range of accessories which can be fitted where necessary. The following are common examples:

(*a*) *Bells* of various sizes for use where the standard bell would not ring loudly enough to be heard.

(*b*) *Lamp signals* which augment the normal bell.

(*c*) *Head-sets*, a combination of receiver and microphone supported on a wire headband. Though normally provided for switchboard operators, this apparatus can also be installed for order clerks, inquiry clerks, and others who use the telephone and require to have both hands free.

(*d*) *Coin boxes*, including a portable version, used to collect charges from members of the public or staff making private telephone calls.

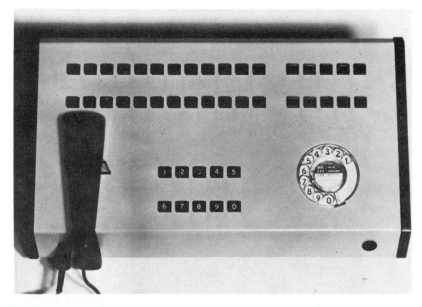

Fig. 22 Post Office automatic branch exchange (PABX1) (*Courtesy of the Post Office*)
This unit provides for up to twenty exchange lines and 100 extensions

(*e*) *Callmakers* (Fig. 23) which can be used for the automatic dialling of frequently-used telephone numbers. *Key callmaker* stores up to thirty-two numbers, each of which can be dialled on pressing the appropriate button. *Card callmaker* dials when a pre-punched card is inserted. *Tape callmaker* stores up to 400 numbers on magnetic tape. A knurled wheel is turned until the name of the subscriber to be called appears in an aperture, when on pressing a button the number is dialled.

(*f*) *Key and lamp units* (Fig. 24), which enable incoming calls from a number of lines to be taken at any one of a number of answering positions, as might be required in an office receiving orders by telephone.

(*g*) *Meters* to enable the cost of calls to be assessed.

In addition, there are devices, such as automatic alarms, which can be purchased from manufacturers. Before making use of them it is advisable to ascertain from the Post Office that they are officially approved.

Private circuits   Where there is need for frequent or prolonged contact between two points, e.g. head office and a branch, a permanent private telephone circuit can be rented from the Post Office. Rental having been paid, there are no call charges.

Tape callmaker
Stores up to 400 numbers on magnetic tape

Card callmaker
Numbers stored on plastic punched cards

Key callmaker
Up to thirty-two numbers stored

Fig. 23   Post Office callmakers (*Courtesy of the Post Office*)

Special circuits   The Post Office will, when it is technically possible, supply and install special telephone circuits to suit the subscriber's particular needs. The local Telephone Manager should be consulted whenever the normal equipment does not provide the service required.

Fig. 24   Post Office key and lamp unit (*Courtesy of the Post Office*)
Provides for selective connection with any one of twenty exchange lines, extensions or private circuits

Telephone answering sets   These devices (Fig. 25) will automatically answer an unattended telephone, and may:

(*a*) transmit a recorded message to the caller;
(*b*) invite the caller to record a message;
(*c*) be used as a remote dictating machine;
(*d*) automatically repeat any messages recorded by callers, when required to do so by a secret code word spoken over the telephone by an authorized person.

Radiotelephony   Radio forms a useful means of communication between a central station and mobile units such as cars, vans, or people equipped with portable apparatus.

In certain areas there is a Post Office radio service linking vehicles with the public telephone system.

Confravision   This a Post Office service whereby individuals or small groups of people in studios in different cities can be linked by both sound and monochrome (black and white) television. Business conferences can be held in this way without the necessity of travel. There are close-up facilities for showing documents, drawings etc.

Fig. 25   Telephone answering set (*Courtesy of Ansafone Ltd.*)

PBX Operation   The efficient telephone exchange must be adequately equipped and adequately staffed. Post Office travelling supervisors are available to visit subscribers and advise on the problems of the private branch exchange, and the office manager should make use of their services whenever the need arises.

Telephone operators should be carefully selected bearing in mind that their voices will, in many cases, be the first contact with the organization which those outside it will have. If they speak clearly and are both courteous and helpful, the goodwill of the business will benefit. Few things can be more annoying to a caller than to be answered by a junior who started work the previous day and knows nothing of the organization or the people in it.

The operators should be provided with an index enabling them to determine quickly the extension to which a caller should be connected. An index in terms of names and departments alone is not always adequate, since the caller may not know the name or department of the person to whom he needs to speak. An index by subjects may also be necessary. In a large private branch exchange a separate inquiry desk should be provided, manned by a senior operator who can help callers in difficulty. Where there is a public address system or a signalling system for locating executives, it should be controlled from the telephone exchange.

Push button (*Courtesy of the Reliance Telephone Co. Ltd.*)

Automatic (digital buttons) (*Courtesy of Centrum Electronics Ltd.*)

Fig. 26   Internal telephone systems

PRIVATE INTERNAL TELEPHONES

Although the Post Office switchboards provide a means of making internal telephone calls, it is often found necessary to provide a supplementary private system. These are available from the Post Office or from a number of firms which offer systems for purchase or for hire. When the apparatus is hired it is normal for the contract to cover maintenance, but where the equipment is purchased a separate arrangement has to be made.

Small systems with up to, say, twenty stations are often of the direct-connection type (Fig. 26) with cables connecting each instrument with every other instrument, or with a selection suited to the user's needs. Calls are made by pressing buttons or keys which serve to make the connection and actuate the bell, buzzer or other signal at the distant station. The alternative, necessary for large installations, is a system using a Private Automatic Exchange (PAX) to which all stations are connected. Calls are then made by means of a dial or digital buttons.

In either system, there may be one or more master stations, normally provided for senior executives. These can be equipped to give additional facilities, including some or all of the following:

Executive key calling   Buttons or keys marked with the names of persons or departments will, when pressed, automatically call the required station.

Loudspeaking instruments   Where a loudspeaker is used, feedback from this to the microphone must be prevented. According to the particular system, the microphone may be controlled during a conversation by depressing an on–off button or key, or there may be automatic voice switching to ensure that only the microphone or loudspeaker is live at any time.

Privacy   Arrangements can be provided to ensure that no other station can listen-in on a master-station conversation.

Group calling   A number of stations can be called simultaneously.

Conference facilities   The linking of several stations so that all can speak and hear over a common circuit.

Paging   Connection is made with a public address system.

Executive priority   An ability for a master station to break in on a conversation between other stations.

Caller identification   Indication of which station is calling by means of a lamp or other signal.

TELEGRAPHS AND CABLES

The *Post Office Guide* contains full details of the various home and overseas telegraph services which are available. Messages may be sent in plain language or in code or in combinations of the two, subject to the regulations imposed by various countries from time to time. A number of recognized codes are published and the use of these results in considerable economies.

Telegrams and cables may be dispatched and received through the Telex service (see under Teleprinters below).

TELEPRINTERS

The teleprinter (Fig. 27) is to the written word what the telephone is to the

Fig. 27   Post Office Telex Service teleprinter (15) with reperforating and tape-transmitting attachments (*Courtesy of the Post Office*)

spoken word. It is a machine on which messages can be typed, the text being reproduced at a distance on a similar machine. The sending and receiving machines are connected by telegraph cable or radio. Although technically the maximum speed is 70 words a minute, a competent operator will normally transmit at 35–40 words a minute.

Teleprinters may be hired from the Post Office under the Telex Service. These machines may be connected, by dialling, with any other Telex subscriber's machine, including those in many countries overseas. A call fee is charged for each connection according to the time occupied. In addition, the apparatus can be used for the receipt and transmission of telegrams and cables. On some machines, the message to be transmitted can be coded on perforated paper tape and then transmitted automatically at 70 words a minute. Incoming messages can also be received in the form of perforated tape for subsequent decoding into printed form. Automatic transmission can save time and money where there are any number of long-distance and overseas connections.

A teleprinter connected with the Telex network may be left switched on but unattended throughout the day and night. Incoming messages are received and printed automatically, a service of particular importance for international communication between different time zones. If desired, messages can be 'scrambled' so as to remain secret until unscrambled by an authorized person.

Teleprinters can also be purchased and installed internally for the purpose of communication between departments. They are particularly useful where it is necessary to transmit information quickly and accurately in circumstances where the use of verbal messages by telephone might lead to misunderstanding and error.

FACSIMILE TELEGRAPHS

By facsimile telegraph (or graphic communication), written matter, drawings, pictures etc. can be transmitted over public or private telephone lines or by radio. The material to be transmitted is fed, on A4 or A5 size paper, into the sending machine and passes round a drum (see Fig. 28). A similar drum on the receiving machine carries photographic paper. The sender makes contact with the distant station by telephone in the first instance. A button is then pressed at the sending point to start the drums on both sending and receiving machines revolving at the same speed. As the drum at the sending point revolves, the paper is scanned by a light beam, and as the beam falls on light or dark areas, signals are transmitted to the receiving point. Here the signals are re-converted into light which falls on the photographic paper, thus producing the facsimile copy.

Arrangements can be made for material to be broadcast simultaneously to a number of receiving stations.

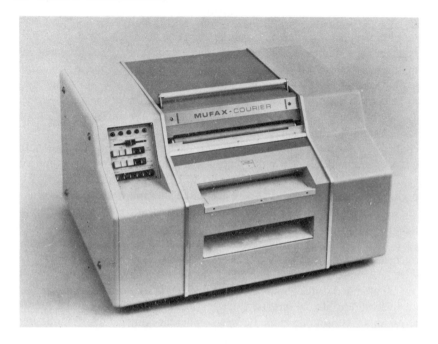

Fig. 28   Facsimile telegraph (*Courtesy of Muirhead Ltd.*)

TELENOTE

This is a system (see Fig. 29) for the transmission of hand-drawn or written material over telephone circuits, whether private, national or international. The sender draws or writes, using a ball-pen connected by a flexible wire to the transmitter. Simultaneously, the same outlines are traced on paper by a receiver at the other end of the telephone circuit. Transmission can take place at the same time as a telephone conversation, permitting verbal messages to be supplemented by drawn illustrations, formulae and other information which cannot readily be expressed in words.

Equipment for sending and receiving can be as separate units, or incorporated in one instrument, a transceiver.

OTHER COMMUNICATION SYSTEMS

Public address systems   Loudspeaker systems are now widely used in factories, shops and offices as a means of giving instruction or of locating individuals who may be away from their offices. When used in offices, they have the disadvantage that, in order to attract the attention of one person, it is necessary to distract all of the clerks from their work.

Fig. 29 Telenote (*Courtesy of Standard Telephones and Cables Ltd.*)

Staff location The simple system of signalling by bell or buzzer in order to summon messengers or clerks is too well known to require comment. There are also signalling systems designed to trace executives and others who move about a large building or area in the course of their duties. These signals may be by sounds, by combinations of coloured lights, or by radio. If the signals are by radio, each person likely to be called carries a small receiver which emits signals under control of a central transmitter. The pocket receiver may also provide one- or two-way speech facilities for passing messages.

Closed-circuit television   This is a means of communication which has widely differing uses. A system consists of a video-camera, a linking circuit and a television screen; a sound link can also be provided if required. It may have associated with the system a video/sound recorder which will store signals passing through the circuit, enabling them to be 'played back' on a television monitor screen later. Essentially, closed-circuit television is a means of seeing at a distance, normally over private circuits.

In offices, warehouses, shops etc. closed-circuit television is used as an aid to security, enabling guards to observe many critical areas from a central room. It is also used to convey information, e.g. financial and stock-exchange news, and as a means of displaying documents held in a central filing department on a screen in any one of a number of distant offices.

4 Filing and indexing

Filing is the process of so arranging and storing original records, or copies of them, that they can be readily located when required. Indexing is the process required to enable records to be located. In this chapter the two processes are discussed separately.

FILING SYSTEMS

The maintenance of an efficient filing system is one of the perennial problems of the office, and its solution demands a proper understanding of principles. There is no one ideal system, and no one ideal type of equipment which will meet the requirements of every record in every office. The office manager must in each case analyse the problem and decide upon the solution which he considers most proper. An efficient filing system is one in which:

(*a*) the records required at any time can be produced without unreasonable delay;

(*b*) the records are adequately protected during the period over which they are retained for reference;

(*c*) the cost of installing and maintaining the system is reasonable having regard to the service which is required.

The first step in planning the filing system should be to schedule all the different types of documents and records to be stored. The responsible management should be consulted about each type and decisions obtained as to:

(*a*) *Storage period*   How long is it necessary, for legal or administrative reasons, to retain the records?

(*b*) *Protection*   What degree of importance is attached to the records? Are other copies available or, if necessary, could they be reconstructed from another source? What are the conditions necessary to give adequate protection against dust, dampness, theft and fire?

(*c*) *Acceptable delay in location*   What delay in producing the record can be regarded, in normal circumstances, as reasonable? It is not sufficient to assume that every record must be produced on demand; for example, businesses often keep records in a bank strongroom, despite the delay before they can be consulted.

(*d*) *Person normally using*   Who uses the records? Who in the ordinary way will need to refer to them? Who will need to refer to them in special circumstances, and how frequently will these circumstances arise?

(*e*) *Mode of description*   How will the record be asked for? The answer to this question is a fundamental requirement, because it will determine the system of classification to be adopted. Records can be thought of in different ways: the sales manager may think in terms of the customer's name, the factory manager in terms of product ordered, the progress clerk by job number. When the person usually requiring to see the record needs it, how will he think of it, and how will he ask for it?

The completed schedule showing, in relation to each type of record, the requirements under the five headings given above, is a document of the greatest importance. On the basis of this information, the office manager can plan how to classify, where to store, what type of equipment to use, and when to destroy old records.

CLASSIFICATION

In deciding the headings under which documents are classified, the object is to be able to select any one paper from among all the papers stored in the office. The method is to divide and subdivide the papers into groups, so that the final selection is from a limited number only.

In the schedule of documents suggested above, broad types will have been established: orders, invoices, correspondence, etc. All those papers falling within one such major classification should have certain characteristics in common, namely the five factors already given:

(a) storage period;
(b) protection;
(c) acceptable delay in location;
(d) person normally using;
(e) mode of description.

If, for example, papers requiring different storage periods are kept together, they must either all be retained for the maximum period, or they must be sorted periodically to extract those due for destruction. The first method entails unnecessary storage equipment, and the second, unnecessary labour. Also, if documents requiring varying degrees of protection are kept together, they must all be protected to the degree necessary for the most important among them. This, again, entails unnecessary expense for equipment. Carried to the ridiculous extreme, it would mean all records being kept in fire-proof, burglar-proof safes.

Each broad classification must in turn be subdivided in the most convenient manner. For example, correspondence is commonly classified according to the names of correspondents. A folder is opened for each person or firm with which the business has dealings, and letters arranged within the folder in date order. To find a particular letter, reference is made firstly to the broad type 'correspondence', then to the group in the person's folder, and finally to the date position within the folder. This follows a logical sequence proceeding from large groupings to smaller, until the individual document is found.

The method adopted for classifying within each broad type should depend upon how the person using the file thinks of the individual documents. If a letter is required for reference, it is often thought of in terms of the name of the correspondent—'the letter from Smith'. But, it may be that the letter is thought of as being about a certain subject—'the letter about the office cleaning contract'. How people think of documents determines how they ask for them, and this, in turn, should determine the reference headings in the files.

Having determined how each major group should be subdivided, it must be decided in what order the individual documents or folders shall be arranged in the files so as to facilitate their location. For this purpose, they can be classified by five main methods—Alphabetical, Geographical, Subject, Numerical, Chronological, or some combination of them.

Alphabetical classification

Alphabetical classification, of which the telephone directory is an example, is so commonly used as to require no explanation. It is particularly suitable where the headings of classification can be adequately expressed in one main word, as where the classification is according to names of people, or of products. It is a simple method, having a number of advantages:

(*a*) clerks can understand it without long training;

(*b*) it is elastic, i.e. new headings can be introduced at any point without disturbing the classification;

(*c*) it is self-indexing, i.e. no separate index is required.

On the other hand, it is not always the fastest system, and difficulties may arise through the mis-spelling of names. Where large numbers of files are arranged alphabetically, it is necessary to lay down strict rules, of which the following are examples:

(*a*) file under the initial and subsequent letters of the surname and the first (and, if necessary, subsequent) Christian name initials;

(*b*) file together variants of the prefix MAC, treating, for example, McDonald and Macdonald as MacDonald;

(*c*) file together under SAINT, names with the prefix St or Saint;

(*d*) file under O, in alphabetical sequence, names commencing with O', such as O'Brien;

(*e*) disregard ranks and titles (Captain, Sir, Lord etc.);

(*f*) file hyphenated names under the first name. For example, Chapman-Hunt should be filed under CHA, but R. Chapman Hunt, under HUNT;

(*g*) file business names under the first main word, or letter if no words are included in the name, for example:

A. L. L. Co Ltd
Aagar, T.
Allan, Dr B.
Allan & Co.
Allan, Mrs D.

The telephone directory is a convenient guide when there is any doubt as to the rules to be followed.

Geographical classification

In this system, the location or address is used as the identifying heading. In the extreme, the arrangement would be by country, then by county, town, street, and number. It is, however, often convenient to use the geographical system for the major groupings only and then introduce an alphabetical or other system, for example:

Home sales correspondence. By sales territory and thereafter alphabetically by name of customer.

Export sales correspondence. By country and thereafter alphabetically by name of customer.

Branch correspondence. By town and street, and thereafter by subject.

The geographical system has inherent disadvantages. A correspondent's address must be known in order to find his file and because of this a separate alphabetical index of names may have to be kept. Also, clerks must be trained to recognize the names of towns and know the counties or other territories in which they are situated.

Subject classification

Whilst some records lend themselves to simple alphabetical or geographical classifications, many others do not and must be filed according to subjects. This means that all documents relating to a subject are brought together in one file, even though they may have come from many different sources, and may include letters to and from many different people. Filing by subject is comparatively slow, because it requires that whoever files the documents shall have an understanding of their contents, and shall know in what connection they are likely to be required. Subject filing cannot be handled by a junior clerk according to a simple set of rules. Often the executive himself must undertake the task of deciding the file into which each document shall go.

Great care should be exercised in selecting the titles for files. Each title should be kept as short as possible, should be descriptive of the contents of the file, and should not be ambiguous. The title should be in ordinary everyday language, and the subject should be described in the same way as it is spoken of in normal business conversation.

In subject filing, the principles of classification and sub-classification can often be carried a stage further with advantage. The field which the records have to cover can be divided in the first place according to main subject headings, which can in turn be subdivided and so on. The following is a simple example showing main headings and sub-headings:

PREMISES	STAFF	EQUIPMENT
Rent	Applications	Purchases
Rates	Salary scales	Maintenance
Heating	Holidays	
Maintenance	Training	
	Statistics	

Numerical classification

This is, where applicable, the simplest method of classifying. Each record or group of records is given a number and filed in numerical order. There are fundamentally three methods of numbering, suited to differing situations.

Natural numbers   These are numbers which are used naturally by people in their everyday language. A common example is the registration number of a motor vehicle. If drivers, mechanics, loaders and everyone else concerned with a vehicle calls it CGT 249 or more likely 249, this number provides a suitable file heading. In many businesses, numbers attached to drawings, specifications, factory operations, or catalogue items are also commonly used and understood as part of the local language.

Random numbers   These are numbers allocated to records or groups of records in sequence as they are produced or as they are added to the filing system. If the last customer's file opened was 1264, the next will be 1265, no matter what the customer's name or business connection. It may be convenient always to add new files at the end of the shelf, but the random number offers no other advantages. Normally, a separate index must be maintained and time spent in referring to this. There are, however, circumstances in which another existing record may serve as the index. If, for example, copy sales invoices are filed in serial-number order, the sales ledger can be the means of discovering the invoice numbers relating to a particular customer.

Number languages   Numbers can be constructed so that they have meaning and, after a comparatively short period of training, can be quickly translated. This approach is generally used in computer coding systems, where numbers are used to identify data which must be sorted into logical sequence, summarized and analysed. The significant factors in any subject are identified and arranged in order of importance. For instance, the significant factors relating to a customer might be:

(*a*) the geographical area in which he is situated (1 digit);

(*b*) the salesman who calls on him (1 digit);

(*c*) the nature of his business, e.g. wholesaler, multiple retailer, independent retailer, consumer etc. (1 digit);

(*d*) the branch of industry or commerce in which he is engaged (1 digit);

(*e*) a unique number distinguishing him from others having the same characteristics as identified by (*a*)–(*d*).

The code number, say 324509, could be built up to mean a customer in Scotland, called on by salesman James Robertson, and in the wholesale grocery trade. He is number 9 in the list of such customers. If the first four digits of the number were random, clerks could not understand their meaning without turning to an index or memorizing up to 9999 separate cases. If, however, each digit in each position has a meaning, any number can be translated with the knowledge of up to $4 \times 10 = 40$ digits. Only the last two digits, which are serial and have no meaning, must be interpreted with the aid of an index.

Where computer coding systems of this type are in use, it may be found useful to adopt the same system when filing related documents.

Numerical classification, by whatever system, makes for ease in sorting papers prior to filing, although care must be taken to avoid errors arising from the mental transposition of figures.

Chronological classification

In this system, records are identified and arranged according to date and sometimes even according to the time of day. It is often employed in filing invoices and other vouchers associated with accounts, particularly when these constitute a journal. In correspondence filing, letters may be filed in order of the date of writing as shown on them. Except in the smallest of businesses, this system cannot be used in isolation. It is, however, commonly adopted in arranging papers within folders which are in turn arranged in some other order. Sales correspondence, for example, may be kept in folders, one for each customer. The folders are arranged in alphabetical order of customers' names; the letters within each folder are arranged according to date.

FILING EQUIPMENT

Equipment, however well designed, will not by itself make for efficient filing. A muddled system will still be a muddled system whether it is kept in a cabinet or in a cardboard box. This does not mean that equipment is unimportant, but that it should be considered only in relation to the purposes which it serves:

1. Protection of documents against:

   (*a*) loss through careless handling;
   (*b*) loss or damage by fire or water;
   (*c*) deterioration through dust or dampness.

2. Prevention of theft or unauthorized reference.
3. Reduction of physical effort on the part of filing clerks in inserting, locating and extracting documents.

In selecting the equipment necessary for the storage of a particular class of document, all of these purposes should be taken into account. Protection against dust and dampness is of more importance if the records are to be kept for a long time than if they are to be destroyed after a few months. The need for special protection of documents against loss by fire will vary according to their importance and also according to the nature of the premises in which they are stored. The risk of fire in a wooden building, or in an office attached to a warehouse containing highly inflammable goods, is obviously greater than in a steel and concrete office building. Some documents may need to be kept secret, and for these it is worth while spending money on providing substantially constructed containers fitted with locks. The provision of elaborate mechanical aids to inserting, locating and extracting files from the cabinets or other containers will be of far greater importance if very frequent reference is made to them than if reference is made only at long intervals.

The task of the office manager in selecting equipment is to determine what are the purposes to be served and the relative importance of each, and to match these against the facilities which the various designs afford.

Small containers

If the number of documents to be filed is small, there is a variety of simple filing equipment available. Certain of these simple devices are sometimes referred to as 'old-fashioned', but, if the principles set out in the preceding paragraphs are applied, they may often be found to be both economical and effective.

Lever arch files consist of heavy-gauge cardboard covers, in which papers are retained by means of stout arch-shaped wire loops which pass through holes punched in the margin. The wire loop is opened by means of a lever to permit documents to be inserted into or removed from any position in the file.

Box files are flat cardboard, metal or plastic boxes, usually provided with a spring clip or other retaining device.

Concertina files (see Fig. 14) provide a series of light cardboard pockets, usually sufficient to permit simple alphabetical classification. They are readily portable.

Wallets made of light card, sometimes with cloth inserts to give flexibility, are commonly used for the protection of legal and other bulky documents.

Guardbooks are books, the leaves of which are of stout, usually brown, paper. Documents are pasted to the leaves as in a scrap-book. Guardbooks are mainly for storing small papers of varying sizes such as press cuttings.

Loose-leaf binders   Records which are uniform and required in portable book form can often be most conveniently filed in loose-leaf binders. Unlike the bound book, new leaves can be inserted in any order and each leaf can be removed or replaced at will. Loose-leaf binders are commonly used for hand-posted and some machine-posted ledgers, for personnel records, sales statistics, instruction manuals and many other types of record. Because the leaves can readily be removed and re-arranged, these binders are particularly valuable for records which are required to be self-indexing.

Although there are numerous types of binder manufactured (Fig. 30), they can be broadly classified under three heads as follows:

(a) *Ring binders,* which are fitted with metal rings, cut and hinged to enable them to be broken open for the insertion or removal of papers. Any number of rings may be arranged along the fastener, and holes are punched in the papers at corresponding positions.

(b) *Post binders,* which retain the leaves by means of posts passing through the covers and through holes punched in the leaves. These binders, in their simplest form, do not permit of such easy insertion or removal of leaves as the other types. Developments of the fundamental type, however, employ two sets of posts, enabling rapid alterations to be made.

(c) *Thong binders,* in which sheets are retained by pressure between the binding edges of the front and back covers. The leaves are slotted to enable them to be slipped on to stout canvas thongs passing between the two covers. Means are provided for the thongs to be tightened, drawing the two covers together so that they press on the binding margins of the leaves. As soon as the thongs are slackened, sheets can readily be inserted or removed.

Ring binder

Post binder

Thong binder

Fig. 30 Types of loose-leaf binding (*Courtesy of Twinlock UK Ltd.*)

Folders   Where papers are of varying sizes, as in general correspondence, it is usually convenient to keep them in folders, clearly marked to assist location.

Many different types of folders are available and manufacturers have exercised considerable ingenuity in designing them to meet varying requirements. Folders and their 'fittings' may be classified into broad types as follows:

(a) *Simple folders*   The simple folder consists of a sheet of heavy or light-gauge manila cardboard or of paper, folded so as to form a cover. The fold is usually a little off-centre so that the back of the folder projects about half an inch beyond the front, providing a visible strip on which the reference heading is written.

Fig. 31   Cabinet suspension files (*Courtesy of The Shannon Ltd.*)

Simple folders are also used for the temporary storage and protection of papers in use. In this situation, transparent plastic folders have the advantage of permitting the contents to be seen and identified without labelling.

(*b*) *Suspension folders*   When manila folders are stacked on edge, it is possible that one may slip down beneath the rest and become lost. Even if the folder is not altogether lost to view, it may become difficult to read the reference heading. The suspension folder is designed to overcome these difficulties. For vertical filing (see page 69), it is fitted with attachments which enable it to be suspended from rails along the sides of a drawer (Fig. 31). For lateral filing (see page 69) the folder is fitted with hooks by which it is suspended from a rail running the length of a shelf or rack (Fig. 32).

(*c*) *Pockets*   Vertical or lateral filing equipment can be fitted with a series of canvas or cardboard pockets suspended from rods. When plain folders are placed in the pockets, the effect is similar to that obtained with the suspension folder.

(*d*) *Labelling*   Folders should bear descriptive titles in a manner suited to the type of equipment in use. They may be written along the spine, along the edge or on a tab which projects so as to be readily visible (see Fig. 31).

Fasteners   Whilst documents are often filed loose in folders, it is generally considered prudent to have some means of retaining them. If a clerk should accidentally drop a folder of loose papers, they will probably become scattered and some may be lost. At the best, time must be spent in reassembling them in the correct order. Also, if individual papers can be readily removed from a file, the tendency is for them to be extracted and mislaid. Among the many methods for fastening documents in folders are the following:

(*a*) *Paper fasteners*   Holes are punched in both the folder and the papers and a two-pronged brass paper fastener passed through. If one fastener only is used, there is a danger that papers may be torn out by careless handling.

(*b*) *Tagged cords*   Short lengths of cord, fitted with metal tags, are passed through holes punched in the folder and the papers. As with the paper fastener, if only one cord is used, there is a danger of papers becoming torn out and lost.

(*c*) *Spring-backed folders*   A spring is built into the folded edge of the cover and grips the papers.

(*d*) *Flexible strip or prong fasteners*   A device is attached to the folder, consisting essentially of two metal or plastic strips or prongs projecting from the back cover. Papers are punched with two holes in the left-hand margin

Fig. 32 Lateral filing

(Courtesy of Sperry Rand Ltd.)

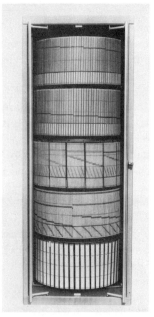

Fig. 33 Revolving filing *(Courtesy of ADM Business Systems Ltd.)*

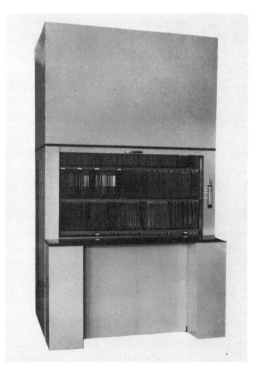

Fig. 34 Automatic filing *(Courtesy of The Shannon Ltd.)*

and the strips or prongs passed through the holes and secured in various ways. This method gives the advantage of two-hole fixing, ensuring that papers do not become disarranged or fall away from the protecting cover.

(e) *Elastic cord fasteners*   Elastic cords with tagged ends are attached to the folder, passed through holes punched in the papers to be filed, and secured by some form of clip. If the cords are secured whilst stretched, they exert pressure on the binding edges of the papers. This form of fastening is often used when filing bulky computer print-outs, the cords being passed through the sprocket holes in the paper.

(f) *Ring fasteners*   These employ the mechanism already described earlier in this chapter in the section dealing with Loose-leaf Binders.

Storage equipment

Before considering in detail the various types of storage equipment, three terms must be defined:

(a) *Horizontal filing*   The papers, folders or other containers are piled *one on top of another* on shelves or in shallow drawers.

(b) *Vertical filing*   The papers etc. are stacked on edge *one behind another* usually in drawers or box-type containers. Compared with horizontal filing, this method offers the advantage that any item may be withdrawn or replaced without disturbing the remainder.

(c) *Lateral filing*   This method is strictly 'vertical' in that the papers etc. are again stacked on edge. The term lateral is used to mean that they are arranged *side by side*, usually on shelves or racks.

Desk filing   Both executives and clerks may need to keep close at hand papers relating to matters with which they are actively engaged. In these circumstances, some sort of desk filing system may reasonably be employed, although it should never be used as an alternative to the main system. Many desks are provided with a deep drawer which can be fitted with rails to take suspension files, and these will be found a useful means of retaining, in an orderly fashion, papers for immediate use. A 'work organizer' similar in design to the flap sorter (see Fig. 13 on page 36) can also be used. A well-planned desk filing system has considerable advantages. It ensures that no papers are retained except in connection with a specific current job, and it enables papers to be cleared quickly into the permanent files as soon as they are no longer of immediate use.

Shelving   Box files and other small containers are usually kept on steel or wooden shelves or in cupboards. Equipment for this purpose can be made up from standard units and altered from time to time as necessary. The units consist of uprights and cross-pieces which can be assembled to form a framework to carry shelves. Sheets can be attached to the top, back and sides of the framework to enclose the shelving and, when required, door units can be added to form cupboards. Alterations can easily be made in the office.

Drawer filing   For general use in offices, vertical filing cabinets are fitted with two standard sizes of drawer: the quarto size, to take folders containing papers up to quarto (10 in. × 8 in.), and the foolscap size to take folders containing papers up to foolscap (13 in. × 8 in.) or International size A4. The number of drawers in a cabinet varies, usually from one to five; the most common is the four-drawer size which is the maximum height for convenient use. Drawers are usually mounted on ball-bearing runners for ease of operation, and are easily removed for cleaning, maintenance or the transfer of filing to other containers. Cabinets containing shallow drawers are available for the horizontal filing of duplicator masters, photographs, plans etc. which might become damaged if stacked vertically.

Documents of uniform size sometimes lend themselves to filing in drawers without first being in folders. Examples are copy invoices which can be filed in serial number order with guide cards inserted after, say, every hundred forms so as to provide support and to facilitate location.

Lateral filing   Suspended by hooks, folders may be stored laterally in cupboards or racks, appearing end on as shown in Fig. 32. Lateral files have the advantage of requiring less floor space than drawer cabinets of the same capacity.

Revolving filing   Folders may be stored in circular containers mounted horizontally (see Fig. 33) or vertically. The floor space required is less than that for drawer cabinets of the same capacity and movement by filing clerks may be reduced.

Automatic filing   Lateral filing containers are arranged on a revolving mechanism which can bring any one of them to the clerk's working position. The clerk can select the container required by means of a control panel. Automatic filing units may be fitted with up to about 16 containers, each having a capacity of about 5 ft 6 in. (1·68 m) shelf length (see Fig. 34).

Fire-resisting equipment   Documents of particular importance are sometimes stored in steel cabinets or cupboards lined with some fire-resisting material. Whilst not completely fire-proof, these offer greater protection than the ordinary steel equipment. Where protection against fire is of particular importance, the office manager should consider the erection of a fire-proof room inside which records can be filed in ordinary standard equipment.

Micro-filing   Original records can be photographed on microfilm or micro-fiche (see Chapter 5) with a saving of up to 98 per cent of storage space. After the photographs have been developed and checked for clarity, the originals are usually destroyed.

The Civil Evidence Act, 1968, permits microfilmed records to be produced in evidence subject to certain conditions, which include the establishing of authenticity at the time of photographing. On each roll of film, two certificates should be photographed with the documents. At the commencement of the roll, a *Certificate of Intent* identifies the nature of the documents to be photographed and declares the intention to destroy the originals after the film has been inspected and found satisfactory. At the end of the roll, a *Certificate of Authenticity* declares that the images contained in the film are true and correct. Both certificates should be dated and signed by the camera operator and by a senior official of the organization.

Computer-originated micro-records   Information held in computer files need not be printed out on paper but may be output in the form of page images on microfilm or micro-fiche. To aid location, the computer can be programmed to prepare an index to the contents of a reel of film or a fiche and this will appear as one of the images. For example, a micro-fiche size A6 (105 mm × 148 mm) can contain 208 pages of information or 207 pages plus an index. As an alternative to bulky files of computer print-out, the micro-record images enlarged on a projector screen can provide a more convenient means of reference as well as being more compact.

OPERATING THE FILING SYSTEM

If the filing system is to be operated so that documents are not mislaid but are available for use when required, strict rules should be laid down and steps taken to see that they are followed.

The responsibility for deciding the heading under which any document should be filed must be clearly defined. It is seldom satisfactory that this is left to a junior clerk. In some cases it may be a task capable of being undertaken by a senior filing clerk or by a private secretary, but in many businesses a rule is made, particularly where subject filing is adopted, that the decision as to the heading under which any document is filed shall be taken at executive level. The executive who is concerned with the matter to which the document relates understands its significance and may be expected to know the heading under which he will think of it when he wishes to refer to it again. Many managers, therefore, set aside each day the few minutes necessary to mark up the day's filing with file numbers, subsequently handing it over to a clerk to be put into the folders.

The senior filing clerk should be responsible for operating a system of control over the folders which are withdrawn from the files. When a folder is taken from the file for reference, a note should be made of the person into whose custody it has passed. If the folder is not returned to the file within a reasonable time, inquiries should be instituted to see that it is not mislaid or being held unnecessarily. It should be made a rule that only in the most unusual circumstances should an individual document be extracted from a folder once it has been inserted. Anyone wishing to refer to an individual document should have a photocopy of it, or the entire folder.

In order to ensure that every letter eventually finds its way into a file, arrangements are sometimes made whereby the letter register is used as a control to ensure that correspondence is filed, and not retained in the drawer of some executive's desk, where it may become forgotten and be as good as lost.

The rules outlined above may appear, at first glance, to be over-exacting. The amount of time spent in keeping a close control over records and files is, however, small compared with the time which can easily be expended in tracing misfiled or mislaid papers under a system less strictly controlled.

Long-term storage

The current files in the office should contain only those papers which are likely to be wanted in the ordinary course of business. Bulky files containing unwanted papers make it the more difficult to control items of immediate use. When the need for quick reference has diminished, filing should be transferred to long-term storage, usually in a separate room, until it is due for destruction.

If the methods of classification have been correctly selected, it should not ordinarily be necessary to examine and select individual papers for transfer or destruction. Ideally, whole batches or folders should be moved according to age.

Destruction of filing   Filing which is no longer of any value should be destroyed without undue delay. If the records are confidential, the papers can be rendered illegible by passing them through a shredding machine or they can be destroyed by burning. Otherwise, the paper can be sold as waste.

Except where there are legal requirements to be fulfilled, there are no generally adopted periods for keeping records. Investigations have shown that policies vary widely. It is therefore necessary for each business to draw up its own regulations for the retention and destruction of filing, according to its particular needs.

CENTRALIZED FILING

There are degrees of centralization and 'centralized filing' may mean:

(a) all files kept in one place;

(b) all files of general interest kept centrally, while those of purely departmental interest are kept by departments;

(c) all, or most, files held by departments but controlled and staffed from one central point.

There is no overriding virtue which makes any one of these systems the more appropriate in all circumstances. The principles stated at the beginning of this chapter should be the basis on which any judgment is founded. Files should be located in such a position that they can be readily available *where* and *when* wanted. If a central filing department results in files being made available more quickly and more easily, then it should be established, but each case must be fully considered on its merits.

Physical centralization possesses the following advantages:

(a) no duplication in that only one copy of any document need be retained;

(b) specially trained filing staff employed;

(c) uniformity of system throughout the organization;

(d) economy of equipment and space;

(e) tighter control over the records.

On the other hand, in a large office there may be considerable disadvantages:

(a) delay in bringing records to those who need them;

(b) inconvenience to some departments through the necessary enforcement of the same rules for all.

Generally, it will not be found convenient to carry the centralization of filing to an extreme. Documents which must regularly be referred to by a number of departments lend themselves to storage at one central point, but it is more efficient to keep papers which concern one executive only as close to his office as possible.

COMPUTER FILING

Computers, which are described in Part 2, are capable of storing large quantities of information retrievable in printed form or on a display screen. The information may appear in graphical form (drawings or graphs) as well as in alphabetical and numerical characters. The recovery time will vary according to whether or not the computer file is available on line, but the delay in bringing a display to the screen might be only a matter of seconds.

It is possible to index automatically every significant word in texts stored in a computer file and this is sometimes done in technical information files. On feeding in, for example, the word 'ships', the screen would show how many documents contain that word. If that number is too large for detailed examination, the search can be narrowed by adding 'cargo', then 'container' and so on until a reasonable number appears. The pages containing the required combination 'container cargo ships' are then called for and appear in detail on the screen with the key words highlighted by greater brilliance to draw attention to them.

The use of a computer as a means of filing and retrieving text is expensive if all the information stored must be specially copied in order to place it on record. For this reason, such systems are likely to be restricted to technical reference libraries etc.

Where the original material is typed on word-processing machines and a magnetic recording is made in any case, the wider application of computer filing may be economically justified.

INDEXING

The purpose of an index is to facilitate the location of records. The index may be kept apart from the records to which it refers, or the records themselves may be so arranged as to be 'self-indexing'. The index of this book is a separate index; it is apart from the text but serves to assist the reader to locate those pages on which various matters are mentioned. The Telephone Directory, on the other hand, is self-indexing; the subject-matter is arranged in alphabetical order of subscribers and reference to the name leads directly to the telephone number. Where a separate index is employed, two steps are necessary to reach the record: firstly, the index must be consulted and, secondly, the record located. Where, on the other hand, a record is self-indexing, one reference only is necessary. Wherever possible, therefore, folders, ledger cards, and other unit records should be arranged so as to be self-indexing.

Indexing equipment

Vertical card index   This consists of a number of cards, each concerned with one item of the index. The reference heading is written along the top edge of a card, and the remainder of the space is devoted to indicating where the corresponding record is to be found. If the card index is to be used as a self-indexing record, then the remainder of the card is used to contain the record itself. Cards are arranged vertically in a drawer or tray, leaving sufficient room to enable the cards to be parted for the reference headings on the top edges to be read. To facilitate the location of an individual card, tabbed guide cards may be inserted at intervals (Fig. 35).

Fig. 35 Vertical card index (*Courtesy of the Art Metal Construction Co.*)

Automatic card index Trays of cards are suspended from a revolving mechanism under push-button control, by means of which a clerk can obtain quick access to more than 100 000 cards (Fig. 36).

Fig. 36 Automatic card index (*Courtesy of Sperry Rand Ltd.*)

Strip index (Fig. 37)   This consists of a frame into which strips of stout paper or card can be fitted in any required order and subsequently withdrawn and rearranged as changes become necessary. Each strip is devoted to one item of usually not more than two or three lines. Frames can be made up in various forms to suit different purposes: they can be fixed to the wall, made up in book form or, where a large number are necessary, arranged on a rotary stand which is easily turned to give reference to any desired portion of the index.

Fig. 37   Strip index (*Courtesy of the Art Metal Construction Co.*)

Visible card index   This is an index which offers the ready visibility of the strip index and also the additional record space provided by the vertical card index. It consists of a series of cards, arranged so as to overlap, leaving a strip of each card exposed. This exposed edge is used for the reference heading, the remainder of the card being readily available for record purposes (Fig. 38A). The trays in which these cards are kept are fitted with

Fig. 38A   Visible card index *(Courtesy of Roneo Vickers Ltd.)*

devices which enable the cards to be held in position, and yet permit individual cards to be written upon, withdrawn, replaced, or rearranged as may be necessary. The trays of cards are usually kept in a cabinet but, as in the case of the strip index, frames can be arranged in book form when they make an easily portable record (Fig. 38B).

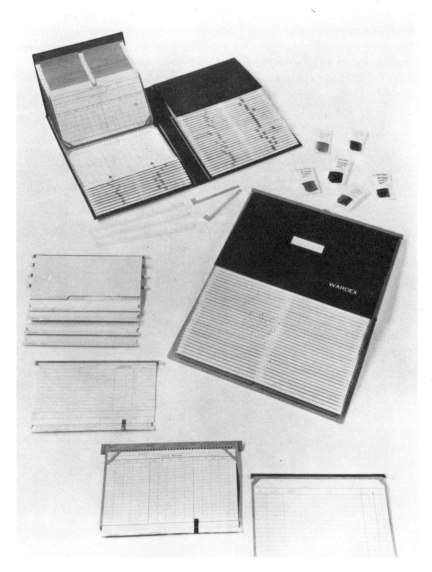

Fig. 38B   Visible card indexes (*Courtesy of Roneo Vickers Ltd.*)

Visible books   Overlapping visible index records can also be kept in book form. A visible book (Fig. 39) consists of a loose-leaf binder in which paper pages are arranged in a similar formation to the cards in the visible card index.

Wheel index   This is a form of vertical card index in which the cards are arranged about the circumference of a wheel which may be portable (Fig.

Fig. 39 Visible book (*Courtesy of Kalamazoo Ltd.*)

Fig. 40 Wheel index (portable) (*Courtesy of C. W. Cave & Co. Ltd.*)

40) or set in a cabinet or desk (Fig. 41). Some thousands of cards can be attached to one wheel and as many as six wheels set up within reach of one clerk seated at his desk. The capacity is further increased when wheels of greater diameter are arranged horizontally.

Fig. 41   Wheel index (*Courtesy of Art Metal Construction Co.*)

Staggered card index   This is an arrangement of the vertical card index which has been developed to give easier reference to the headings. Cards are arranged in groups, and overlapped so that the reference headings on the corners of a whole group can be seen at once. This system of indexing is sometimes applied to ledger cards to facilitate the extraction of accounts for posting (Fig. 42).

Slotted cards   Slotting is a device by which cards can be selected or sorted (Fig. 43). The cards are punched with holes along one or more edges, each hole representing a classification or a figure in a code number. Written information is recorded by hand or typewriting in the centre of the card. The information in terms of which it is required to select or sort can be recorded around the edge of the card by cutting the appropriate holes into slots. Once they have been prepared, the cards may be filed in trays in any order. To select the cards for a particular classification, a batch of several hundred cards is removed from the tray and a long needle is passed through the holes

Fig. 42   Staggered cards (*Courtesy of the Copeland Chatterson Co. Ltd.*)

representing the class required. When the needle is lifted, the cards which have been slotted at these holes fall out and so separate themselves from the remainder.

Alternatively, the punched holes may be in the central area of the card and elongated when a code position is significant. The cards are then held in a frame from which those selected protrude for reference but do not fall free from the pack.

This method can be applied to a variety of tasks including sales analysis, costing, and staff records. For example, staff record cards can be slotted so as to permit sorting and selection according to age, sex, grade, trade, department, and other groupings. If the employee code number is among the items punched, the record of any individual can be selected.

Signals

The location of particular folders, record cards, ledger folios etc. can sometimes be made the easier by attaching signals. These may be in the form of metal clips, plastic tabs or adhesive material. The significance of a signal is shown by its shape, colour or position along the edge of the folder, card or sheet. Some types also provide space for the writing of descriptive matter. Signals are sometimes used to provide a quicker and easier identification of the normal main classification. Their principal advantages lie, however, in supplementing this: they may be used to indicate a second or subsidiary classification. Sales correspondence folders, for example, might be arranged alphabetically by names but have signals showing sales areas.

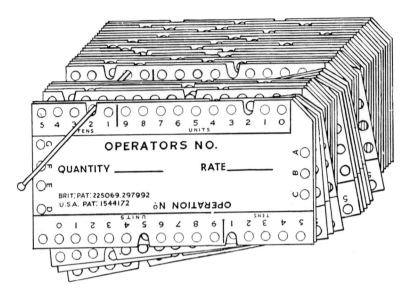

Fig. 43   Slotted cards (*Courtesy of The Copeland Chatterson Co. Ltd.*)

Alternatively, the signals may be used to indicate some temporary significance, as when they are attached to accounts to show when credit is stopped.

Where records are kept in the form of a visible index, metal clips or adhesive signals are often used along the visible edges of the cards or sheets. Examples of this application may be seen in Fig. 39 (see p. 79).

5 Reprography

It frequently happens that more than one copy of a document is required. The simplest method is to create the copies at the same time as the original. This is usually done by using carbon paper, carbon backing or chemically impregnated NCR (No Carbon Required) paper, any one of which will provide a small number of legible copies. When copies are required in greater numbers, or cannot be made in the first instance, duplicating or copying processes are employed.

The term *duplicating* is used when substantial numbers of copies are made from a prepared master copy, and the term *copying* when one or a few copies are taken direct from an original. With the development of new machines and processes, the distinction between the two terms tends to become blurred. Some machines will as easily make a few copies or many hundreds direct from an original and may be called *duplicator–copiers*.

In this chapter, consideration will be given firstly to the duplicators and addressing machines which require the preparation of some kind of master copy, and then to the photocopying and other processes which operate direct from an original document.

DUPLICATING

Duplicators serve to produce circulars, price lists, reports, office forms etc., when either cost or urgency makes printing unsuitable. There is a wide range of equipment from the simple tray of hectographic jelly to the small printing press. No one process is best for all circumstances and when selecting a machine the following questions should be considered:

(a) *How many copies are required?* Different processes produce different numbers of copies from the one master copy. Provided that the normal needs are met, unusually large quantities can be run off by preparing two or more masters.

(b) *What type and quality of paper is to be used?* Some processes require particular types of paper, and these should be considered in relation to the purposes for which copies are made. If office forms are duplicated, the paper must usually be suitable for typewriting, or for handwriting in ink or pencil.

(c) *Are colours, or combinations of colours, to be reproduced?*   Where catalogues, charts, drawings or plans are to be duplicated, colours may be of importance.

(d) *Are pre-printed forms to be overprinted?*   It is often economical to have quantities of a limited number of basic forms printed for use in the office, and to overprint the detailed headings for various jobs. This over-printing process requires a duplicator with reasonably accurate *registration*, i.e. the impression on every copy must come in the same place in relation to the edges of the paper.

(e) *Is the machine required for intensive or for casual use?*   If the volume of duplication is such that the machine will be in use throughout the day, sturdy construction, power drive, automatic feed and other labour-saving refinements are of more importance than if the machine is for casual use.

The duplicating processes outlined below are not the only methods, but represent those more commonly used in offices.

Spirit hectographic duplicators

Spirit duplicators (Fig. 44) will reproduce typewriting, handwriting or drawing in a variety of colours.

(a) *Preparation of the master copy*   A master copy is prepared on a sheet of art paper (shiny surfaced) by means of hectographic carbon paper. The carbon paper is placed with the coated surface upwards, and the art paper placed on it, with the art surface down. The matter to be reproduced is then written by typewriter, pencil or a ballpen on the exposed side of the art paper, causing a carbon impression in reverse to be obtained on the art surface. Master copies can also be made from originals by the heat-transfer copying process.

If a standard ruling, heading or other matter is required on large numbers of master copies, the carbon can be applied by a typeset printing process.

(b) *Colours*   This is the only type of machine which will reproduce in several colours in one run. Combinations of colours are possible on a single master copy by the simple process of writing or typing over different coloured carbon papers in turn.

(c) *The duplicating process*   The master copy is fixed round a roller on the duplicator. Paper fed into the machine is first dampened with spirit and then pressed against the master copy. The spirit dissolves a small proportion of the carbon impression, thus taking a copy on the paper.

Fig. 44 Spirit hectographic duplicator (*Courtesy of Block & Anderson Ltd.*)

(*d*) *Number of copies* According to the quality of paper and carbon paper used, 100 to 250 copies can be taken. The master can be removed from the machine and stored, permitting a number of short runs to be taken. Alterations to the master are possible between uses.

(*e*) *Applications* Because of the low cost of preparing masters, the process is particularly suited when relatively few copies are wanted, say from ten upwards. By suitable layout of the master, it is possible to print the same information, or different portions of it, on forms of varying sizes, e.g. invoices, delivery notes and works orders. There are special types of duplicator which enable selected lines from a list to be printed individually. With special stationery interleaved with hectographic carbon paper, masters can be prepared as computer output.

Stencil duplicators

Stencil duplicators (Fig. 45) will reproduce typewriting, handwriting or drawing.

(*a*) *Preparation of the master copy* Stencils are used, consisting of a layer of material with a coating that is impervious to ink. The stencil is cut, either on a typewriter (with the ribbon out of action) or by writing or drawing with a special pen. Masters can also be prepared by the heat-transfer copying process or on an electronic stencil cutter (see Fig. 46).

Fig. 45　Stencil duplicator (*Courtesy of Gestetner Ltd.*)

Fig. 46　Electronic stencil cutter (*Courtesy of Roneo Vickers Ltd.*)

(*b*) *Colours*   If two or more colours are required on the finished copy, separate stencils must be cut, and a separate duplicating run made for each colour.

(*c*) *The duplicating process*   Ink is pressed through the cuts in the stencil on to the paper which is held in close contact. Rotary machines (Fig. 45), which may be hand- or power-operated, are usually employed when the process is regularly used. There is also a flat-bed model, which is the cheapest type of stencil duplicator and is adequate where the volume of work to be done is small.

(*d*) *Number of copies*   Up to 4000 copies can be obtained and stencils can be stored and re-used if carefully handled and protected.

(*e*) *Applications*   Stencil duplicators are often limited to producing copies on fairly thick absorbent paper. Whilst suitable for reports, specifications, price lists etc., this paper may not serve for catalogues or office forms. There are, however, some machines which make use of non-absorbent paper and do not therefore have these limitations.

Offset-litho duplicators

Offset-litho duplicators (Fig. 47) will reproduce typewriting, handwriting, drawing or photographs.

(*a*) *Preparation of the master copy*   Masters are prepared on thin metal sheets or specially surfaced paper. They can be typewritten with the aid of a special ribbon, handwritten, or drawn by using a special ink or ballpen, or produced by the diffusion transfer, gelatine transfer or electrostatic copying processes.

(*b*) *Colours*   A separate master and a separate duplicating run is required for each colour.

(*c*) *The duplicating process*   The master copy, after treatment with a chemical wash, is fixed round a drum where it is brought into contact with water and an oil-based ink, separately or as an emulsion. The process relies on the fact that oil and water will not mix. The blank portions of the master become wet and do not, therefore, pick up any printing ink; the greasy impression made by typed or handwritten matter, on the other hand, rejects water and takes the ink. Unlike the hectographic master, the impression on the master is not in reverse, and must therefore be reversed before contact with the paper. A second roller, the printing roller or 'blanket', is therefore interposed between the master drum and the paper. The ink on the master is picked up in reverse by the blanket and transferred in turn to the paper on which the impression appears the right way round.

Fig. 47   Offset-litho duplicator (*Courtesy of Addressograph-Multigraph Ltd.*)

(*d*) *Number of copies*   Up to 50 000 copies can be obtained from a metal master, and up to 100, 500 or 2000 copies from various types of paper master. The metal masters can be stored and revised.

(*e*) *Applications*   All ordinary types of paper or light card can be used, and the copies are of a high quality. The process is well suited to the production of office forms, particularly those with complex rulings.

Typeset duplicators

These machines are, in fact, small printing presses employing letterpress type. The process of setting type is slow and calls for some skill but long runs of high quality work are possible.

Addressing machines

Whereas the duplicator provides a number of copies at one run, it is sometimes necessary to take a few copies, perhaps even one copy only, but to do this repeatedly at intervals. Examples of this are the addressing of envelopes to regular correspondents, or the preparation of labels for sending goods to regular customers.

Fig. 48   Addressing plate (*Courtesy of Addressograph-Multigraph Ltd.*)

Addressing machines print from media which differ according to the method of production and the number of impressions which can be obtained from them.

Metal or plastic plates are embossed on a special machine so as to provide a raised representation of what is to be printed. When required, an impression is struck on to paper or card through an inked ribbon. For the smaller office in which an embossing machine may not be justifiable, manufacturers will prepare plates for a small fee. Metal plates can be altered by flattening the raised type and re-embossing, and may be used and re-used indefinitely.

Metal foil plates can be produced on an ordinary typewriter by typing on the foil against a rubber backing.

Stencils can be prepared on an ordinary typewriter and mounted in a protective card frame. They are not as sturdy as metal or plastic plates and will not give as many impressions before having to be replaced.

Hectographic masters are prepared in the same way as those for the spirit hectographic duplicator (see page 84). As impressions are taken, the carbon is worn away, the life of a master being thus limited.

Whilst addressing equipment was originally designed for preparing envelopes and labels, it has since been developed and adapted and is suitable for a wide variety of office tasks. It is used, for example, for addressing invoices, preparing account cards, clock cards, payrolls, pay envelopes, dividend sheets and warrants, to mention but a few of the common applications.

In that which follows, the operations of equipment using metal or plastic plates are described. Equivalent facilities are obtainable from those using stencils or hectographic masters.

Masking plates can be fitted to the machines so that part only of the matter on a plate need be printed. This enables the one master to be used for a variety of purposes; for example, an employee's plate might be used to print clock card, payroll, pay envelope, deduction and other staff records by successively masking out all but the matter appropriate to each job.

Fig. 49   Electrically-operated addressing machine (*Courtesy of Addressograph-Multigraph Ltd.*)

The plates are usually stored in drawers or racks in alphabetical or some other convenient order, in much the same way as the cards in a simple index.

When used for addressing circulars or for payroll preparation, it is usual for all or most of the plates in a series to be active. The addressing machine (Fig. 49) used on this type of work has a hopper into which the plates can be stacked, and from which they are fed automatically to the printing position. These machines can include the following devices:

(*a*) a repeat-print control, which determines the number of prints from each plate;

(*b*) a skip control, which passes unwanted plates without printing;

(*c*) an automatic plate selector, operated by tabs fixed to the plates, which enables only a predetermined selection of plates to be printed;

(*d*) a listing attachment for printing in list form from a number of plates.

When used for addressing invoices or labels, individual plates may have to be selected. For this purpose it is usual to employ a simpler type of ad-

Fig. 50   Hand-operated addressing machine (*Courtesy of Addressograph-Multigraph Ltd.*)

dressing machine (Fig. 50), into which the plates are fed individually by hand.

THE OFFICE PRINT ROOM

The offset-litho duplicator (see pages 87 to 88) has the capacity for producing a wide range of output from departmental reports to catalogues and display material illustrated in colour. It can reproduce on various weights and classes of paper from bank, through art papers to light card. From being an office duplicator for casual use, it can become the central machine of an office print-room for which the following ancillary equipment is available.

Composing   The standard typewriter is suitable for typing offset masters for duplicating reports, price lists etc. Where a wider variety of work is undertaken, it may be necessary to use a range of type sizes and styles to give emphasis to headings or matters of particular importance and to improve general appearance.

In the smaller office, the use of ingenuity and a variety of sources of material can produce an original of 'professional' appearance from which a master can be made photographically. An office form, for example, can be prepared by a combination of hand ruling, typing and characters taken from sheets of 'press-on' type such as are obtainable from stationers. The distinctive style of a company name, trade marks, trade association crests etc. can be added by cutting them from existing stationery and pasting them into position.

Where the volume and nature of work justifies the cost, use can be made of a typewriter with variable type (see page 19). By exchanging the type blocks or printballs, a variety of styles and sizes of type can be introduced in the one typing process. This can, if required, be supplemented by the occasional use of press-on type and by pasting in material from other sources.

The large print room may need an electronic composer (Fig. 51). This is a typewriter with variable type having an associated electronic memory. The keyboard is used firstly to insert layout instructions and then to type and, if necessary, correct the text. When a page is complete and correct, the final version is typed automatically at high speed, set out in accordance with the layout instructions.

Fig. 51   Electronic composer (*Courtesy of IBM Ltd.*)

Platemaking   Paper and metal litho plates can be made by several of the office photocopying processes (see pages 93 to 97), or special equipment can be installed including facilities for reducing or increasing the size of the image.

Guillotining   Paper can be cut to size or trimmed with a guillotine. The smaller types will cut only a few sheets at a time, but the heavier power-driven models can slice through a pile of paper up to 150 mm high. All guillotines of whatever size must be treated as dangerous and all necessary safety precautions observed.

Numbering On some offset-litho machines, serial numbering can be carried out at the same time as duplicating. For short runs, a hand-numbering stamp is normally used.

Perforating As with numbering, this may be done on the duplicator or as a separate hand operation.

Punching Where holes are required for filing, small quantities can be punched with a heavy-duty office punch; for large quantities, a *drill* may be necessary. Special punches must be used for some binding processes, for example comb binding.

Collating Small numbers of sheets can be collated into sets by hand on a desk top. Where large numbers of sheets must be collated for binding and the task arises frequently, a collating device should be used. Collators vary according to the number of sheets that can be assembled and according to speed of operation. The simpler devices consist of an arrangement of compartments from which sheets are plucked by hand. Power-driven collators are available of varying capacities; up to fifty different sheets can be assembled at the rate of 2000 sets an hour.

Binding For some purposes, standard loose-leaf ring binders may be suitable. For more permanent binding, there are the plastic comb and other methods which require special equipment. A simple method of binding reports etc. is to place a sheet of manila card at front and back of the pages and staple all together. Adhesive tape can be used to join the covers along the spine and conceal the staples.

Padding Forms can be padded by holding the batch of sheets firmly in a press whilst applying an adhesive to the top or left-hand edges of the papers. When dry, the adhesive will hold the pad together, but allow each copy in turn to be torn away.

PHOTOCOPYING

There are several processes whereby an original document can be quickly reproduced photographically. The copies may be made on plain paper, on specially sensitized paper, on transparencies, or on duplicating masters (see pages 84–88). Subject to the limitations of certain of the processes which are described below, a photocopy is complete and accurate, and may even be clearer than the original from which it is made.

In all cases, photocopying is more expensive than the taking of carbon copies when the original is made, and should not be regarded as an alternative to this simple method.

The cost of photocopying, allowing for depreciation and maintenance of

Fig. 52   Rotary thermographic copier (*Courtesy of Ozalid (UK) Ltd.*)

equipment (or hire charge) and the consumption of paper and other necessary materials, varies according to the process. So also do the quality and durability of copies, the ability to make duplicator masters, transparencies and double-sided copies. There is therefore no one best process for all purposes, although the electrostatic methods usually offer the widest range of output for general office use.

Photocopying machines differ in mode of operation. Some are *rotary* (Fig. 52), the original and copy paper being fed together round a drum. Others are *flat-bed* (Fig. 53), in which case the original, which might be a page in a bound book, is placed on a glass plate and held in position whilst the photographic exposure takes place. Another distinction is as to whether the copy paper is fed in *sheets* individually or automatically from a stack, or from a *roll* from which varying lengths are cut to match the size of the original. Some machines have both roll and sheet feed, the latter being used for unusual sized copies, or when duplicator masters or transparencies are required.

Photocopiers, sometimes described as duplicator-copiers, may be equipped with a dial to be set according to the number of copies to be taken of one original. This quantity is then produced automatically without further intervention by the operator. The process is so quick and easy that clerks may acquire the habit of taking copies unnecessarily. In some offices, the use of photocopiers is strictly controlled by a responsible official from whom

Fig. 53 Electrostatic copier (*Courtesy of Rank-Xerox Ltd.*)

permission must be obtained before any copies are taken. Machines are usually fitted with meters which record the number of copies made. By recording the meter reading after each use, it is possible to apportion cost to departments or jobs. One type of photocopier has plug-in meters on which each department can record its own usage.

In addition to making copies of documents, photocopiers have many possible system applications. For example, several forms serving different purposes might be produced from one original:

(*a*) by masking unwanted items when copying;

(*b*) by overlaying the original with transparencies bearing headings and rulings so as to produce a composite copy.

Computer print-out on plain paper can be converted into various forms in this way. Where the volume of work justifies it, rolls of copy paper may be pre-printed with a form outline.

The essential features of the different processes are described below. In selecting a process for a particular purpose, the following factors should be considered:

(*a*) *Originals to be copied:* bound book; double-sided paper; single-sided paper; translucent paper; transparency.

(*b*) *Copies required:* on special paper; on ordinary paper or card; on pre-printed forms; on duplicator masters (stencil, spirit hectograph or offset-litho); on transparencies.

(*c*) *Processing:* single stage or two-stage; wet chemicals, semi-dry or dry.

(*d*) *Speed:* copies per minute produced; delay before copies usable.

(*e*) *Size of originals* to be copied.

(*f*) *Restrictions* (some processes are limited as to colours or writing materials copied).

(*g*) *Cost:* capital outlay; maintenance; copy papers; toner, developer and other supplies.

Reflex   A negative copy (white on black) is produced on photographic paper. After wet processing and drying, this is used in turn to produce one or more positive copies (black on white) by further exposure and developing.

Diffusion transfer   The original is exposed with a special negative paper. This negative is immediately placed in contact with a positive paper and the two passed together through a chemical solution. After allowing 10–15 seconds for action to take place, the two copies are parted and the positive image appears. The negative can be used several times before it becomes exhausted.

Gelatine transfer   After wet developing, a negative copy is squeezed in contact with a plain sheet of paper to which the image is physically transferred.

Direct positive (auto-positive)   This process uses a photographic paper which produces positive (black on white) copies from single-sided originals in a single stage. If a double-sided original is used, the initial copy will be positive but reversed. This can be corrected by using this reversed copy as an original in a second exposure and processing. Copies may be sufficiently translucent to enable them to be used as originals for making dyeline prints.

Dual spectrum   This is a dry-contact process which will produce positive copies in a single stage. Originals may be single or double-sided and may be written in any colour.

Dyeline (diazo)   This process requires a transparent or translucent original which may be on film or on paper of suitable texture. Copies are produced on chemically impregnated paper which is comparatively cheap. After exposure to ultra-violet light, the copy is developed by either a wet or a dry process. The image is liable to fade if exposed to strong light and the process is therefore used mainly for system purposes where the copies are not of permanent value.

Heat transfer (thermography)   For the heat transfer process, the document to be copied must be drawn, written or printed in a mineral-based ink or pencil. The original is put through the machine with a sensitized paper and subjected to heat from an infra-red lamp. The infra-red rays are reflected from the plain areas of the original but absorbed by the mineral-based writing, where the heat generated causes the copy paper to turn black. The operation is quick and no chemical processing is necessary. The blank areas of the copy, however, remain sensitive to heat and will blacken if exposed to direct sunlight or, for example, to an electric radiator.

Electrostatic processes   Xerography is a process of electrical photography which uses ordinary papers and which requires no chemical treatment. The original document is placed in the machine, where its image is projected through a lens system on to a selenium drum which has previously been given a positive electrical charge. The properties of selenium are such that where light falls, the electrical charge is lost but where it is shaded, the charge remains. The image of the original is, therefore, transferred to the surface of the drum as an invisible pattern of positive electrical charges. Negatively charged resinous ink powder toner is cascaded or wiped over the drum and, because opposite charges attract, adheres only to this pattern. The powder is then automatically transferred to the surface of a plain sheet of paper, to which it is firmly bonded by exposure to heat. The machine illustrated in Fig. 53 automatically turns copies over so that a second image can be made on the other side.

There are other electrostatic processes which differ in that they require special copy papers or make use of liquids.

MICROPHOTOGRAPHY

Microphotography is the process whereby letters, forms and other documents are photographed to a much reduced size. If the original papers are then destroyed or used for other purposes, the microphotographs provide a compact record which can easily be transported from place to place.

Microfilming

Documents are photographed in the office as positive or negative images as shown in Fig. 54 on:

(*a*) *Roll microfilm:* 16 mm, 35 mm or 70 mm film held on spools or in magazines, or

(*b*) *Micro-fiche:* A sheet of film on which appears a group of related items (alternatively, a jacket in which frames cut from roll films are inserted), or

(*c*) *Aperture cards:* Plain or punched cards in which one or a few frames of film are mounted, as in slides.

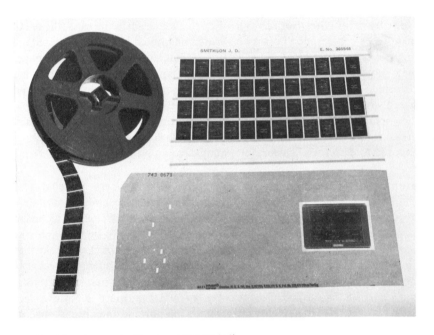

Fig. 54   Microphotography (*Courtesy of Kodak Ltd.*)

There are two basic types of microfilmer for office use:

(*a*) flat-bed equipment in which papers to be copied are placed individually on a platform beneath the camera. This enables large or non-flexible originals to be microfilmed;

(*b*) rotary equipment (as in Fig. 55), often with automatic feed, which enables up to 600 cheque-sized documents or quarto sheets to be microfilmed per minute. At the same time, index numbers or code markings can be applied to the film to aid subsequent retrieval.

Various size reduction ratios are employed. The machine in Fig. 55, for example, can be set to operate at any of four ratios: 24:1, 32:1, 40:1 or 50:1. With the lowest ratio, one image occupies the whole width of the film,

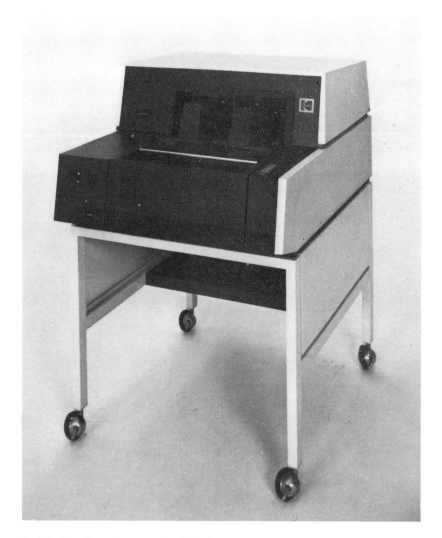

Fig. 55   Microfilmer (*Courtesy of Kodak Ltd.*)

and a 100 ft reel will contain about 3200 quarto or A4 pages. With the higher ratios, there can be two images in the width. These can be the two sides of a document filmed at the same time, or the two halves of the film can be exposed separately to double the storage capacity.

Another form of automatic feed enables continuous stationery such as computer print-out to be microfilmed at 166 ft a minute. Computer output can also be converted to readable microfilm without ever being printed on paper. A combination of cathode-ray tube and camera records the output directly on to film from a magnetic tape at the rate of 90 000 characters per second, equivalent to 300–500 pages of print-out a minute (see page 130).

Processing

Films may be developed in an automatic processor in the office or sent out to a service bureau.

Storage

The reduction in size permits a saving of up to 98 per cent of the storage space which would have been occupied by the original papers. A microfilm spool containing as many as 12 000 A4 documents can be stored in a cardboard carton or 'magazine' measuring 4 in. × 4 in. × 1 in. Films may be cut

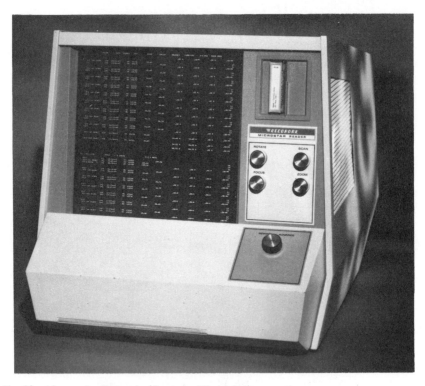

Fig. 56   16 mm microfilm reader (*Courtesy of Kodak Ltd.*)

and each frame mounted separately in an aperture card or in suitable groups on a backing sheet or in a transparent jacket (see Fig. 54). Any of these latter methods permits records to be filed by subject title and the records updated with addition over a period of time.

Retrieval (viewing and printing)

Microfilmed records are read by projecting to about original document size on a screen (Fig. 56). Some readers can also produce prints on paper; others can provide copies as offset-litho masters or as transparencies for use in the dyeline process or for projection.

Where coded markings have been added to the microfilm during the camera operation, automatic retrieval equipment may permit the rapid location of an image, no matter where it lies, along the length of the film.

Certification of microfilm records

If microfilm records are likely to be used in legal evidence, it is necessary to conform with the requirements of the Civil Evidence Act, 1968 (see page 71).

MANIFOLD REGISTERS

Where a small number of copies of a frequently used form are to be prepared in manuscript, the repeated operation of arranging carbon paper between the various copies can be avoided by the use of continuous stationery in a manifold register (Fig. 57A). The register consists of a box in

Fig. 57A Manifold register (*Courtesy of Lamson Paragon Ltd.*)

which strips of forms are stored in rolls or in fanfold (Fig. 57B). By the turn of a handle, the forms are automatically fed to the top surface of the box, where they become interleaved with carbon paper and are ready for writing. Use can also be made of chemically impregnated paper which produces copies without the need for carbon paper. When a form has been filled in, the handle is turned, causing the form to be ejected and the next blank copies to come into position. If desired, one or more carbon copies can be made to return to the box to be

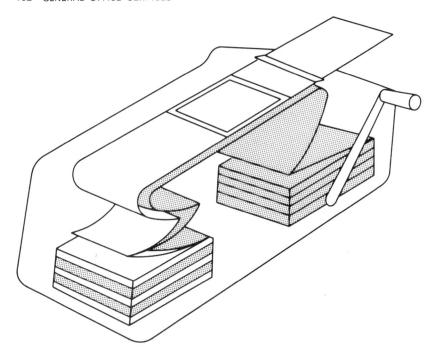

Fig. 57B   Manifold register (*Courtesy of Lamson Paragon Ltd.*)

retained there until required. The box can be fitted with a lock, so as to prevent access to, and possibly fraudulent alteration of, the carbon copies. In addition to the type illustrated, smaller portable registers are available.

Part 2
Data processing

Before considering the accounting services it is appropriate to describe the kinds of data-processing equipment available. Data processing is the basis of all the accounting services dealt with in Part 3, namely sales and purchase accounting, calculating and recording wages, cash control, stock control, production records, financial records and other forms of management information. The equipment is explained in four chapters:

Fundamentals of data processing
Computer components and programs
Computers and their use
Miscellaneous equipment

6 Fundamentals of data processing

The term 'data processing' embraces many and various office systems employed in business, governmental and other organizations. It is as much data processing to record and issue driving licences or to keep hospital-patient records as it is to keep the financial and management accounts of a business. The subject itself is therefore broadly based.

The electronic and other equipment used in data processing varies widely from the simplest visible-record computer to the largest, mainframe computer with its satellite terminals. All computers are general-purpose machines, able to be used for any system; subject, of course, to limitations imposed by the size of the machine.

It is necessary, before going into detail, to establish the fundamentals in simple terms and to define the meanings of some of the words which will be used in later chapters.

DATA-PROCESSING FUNCTIONS

The purpose of data processing is to take original information (*data*) and from it produce other information in useful form (*results*). In the course of converting data into results, there may be many—hundreds and perhaps thousands—of operations which a computer carries out automatically under the control of a *program* of *instructions*.

Although the program may be complex, there is a limited number of basic functions which must be performed:

(1) To take in the program and data (*input*).
(2) To *store* the program and data and hold these available for reference.
(3) To carry out *arithmetical and logical processes* on stored data.
(4) To *store* the intermediate and final results of processing.
(5) To *print* or otherwise give out stored data or the results of processing.

There is a *control* unit which causes the various functions to be performed in the sequence dictated by the program.

DATA-PROCESSING SYSTEMS

All data-processing systems are designed to produce one or usually several results, employing various sorts of data collected from different sources.

The fundamental processes can be seen by examining a relatively simple example: the preparation of a sales invoice for goods normally sold to a regular customer. The end-product, or one of them, is a form as illustrated in Fig. 95. The data which must be taken in and stored ready for use are:

the date of dispatch of the goods;
the name and address of the customer;
the description of the goods and the price;
the quantity of goods;
the trade discount percentage to be allowed;
the rate of Value Added Tax (VAT) to be applied.

From the data, it is possible to calculate:

quantity × price   = gross value
value × discount % = discount
net value   = gross value minus discount
VAT   = net value × VAT %
invoice total   = net value plus VAT

Given the data and the results of calculation, the process can be completed by printing entries in the pre-determined spaces on the form.

It should be noted that all the processing could be done by hand and brain, with or without the aid of simple machines such as calculator and typewriter, just as well as by computer. The advantages which the computer offers are speed, accuracy and automatic control by means of the program.

In a basic hand system each item of data would have to be found and entered separately on each invoice. One of the objects of data-processing systems is that data, once stored, should be recovered and used automatically as many times as are necessary. To this end, a store is divided into *files* for different purposes and a file and each item of its contents can be located by an *address*.

Data can be broadly classified as *fixed* or *variable*. The fixed data can be extracted from the store and used again and again. The variable data applies to one particular case. In the example, the fixed data are:

(1) The date which, once stored, can be printed on every invoice until changed.

(2) The name and address of a regular customer which can be stored and recovered automatically if identified by a code number.

(3) The description and price of goods which can be stored and recovered automatically if identified by a code number.

(4) The trade discount percentage which can be stored in association with the customer's name and address.

(5) The rate of VAT which can be stored in association with the description and price of the goods.

Most of the data required for processing can therefore be held in two files: a customer file and a goods file. To produce an invoice it is only necessary to add the quantity of goods dispatched.

In practice, the variable data necessary to produce the invoice would be:

Customer code: 1234
Goods code: 4567
Quantity: 12

Under instruction from the program, a computer could then proceed to extract the fixed data from its files, carry out the necessary calculations and print the invoice.

THE BASIC FUNCTIONS

From consideration of the example given, it will be seen that the following functions must have been carried out:

INPUT:	Program taken in
	Fixed data taken in
	Variable data taken in
STORE:	Program of instructions stored
	Fixed data stored
	Variable data stored
	Results of calculations stored
	Information to be printed,
	assembled and stored
ARITHMETICAL	
UNIT:	Calculations carried out
OUTPUT:	Results taken from store and printed
CONTROL:	Operations carried out in the sequence
	required by the program

BASIC COMPONENTS OF A COMPUTER

The basic components of a computer perform the functions listed above. The diagram at Fig. 58 shows their relationships, the solid lines indicating the notional flow of data and results from one to another, and the broken lines representing the control exercised.

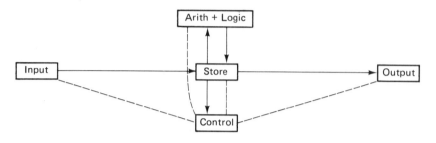

Fig. 58   Computer data flow

All input goes into some designated part of the store which must be able to hold in various files:

Program
Fixed data
Variable data
Intermediate results
Final results awaiting output.

All data to be used in calculation or logical processes is taken from store to the arithmetical/logical unit and the results taken back into store. All output is taken from store.

The store, the arithmetical/logical unit and the control unit together are known as the *central processor*. This is the heart of the computer to which may be connected the various means of input and output according to the needs of the user.

As will be seen in later chapters, the family of computers ranges from the small *visible-record computer* in which data are directly entered by an operator using a keyboard, to the large *mainframe computer* which operates for long periods at very high speed without human intervention.

The simple diagram in Fig. 58 will remain valid as representing the basic pattern. The differences will lie in the wide variety of devices of different sorts, speeds and capacities which fulfil the functions.

THE BINARY SYSTEM

In describing the functions and basic components of an electronic computer, reference has been made to data and results moving from component to component without mention of how these are represented. The computer is essentially a machine that deals in numbers; even the letters of the alphabet and symbols become converted into numbers during input and reconverted during output. The significance of each item of data is identified by a code number and the address or position in the store in which data is held also has its number.

Instead of working in the decimal system, electronic computers make use of the binary system which has only two digits, 0 and 1. Following are a few decimal numbers and their binary equivalents:

1 = 1	5 = 101	9 = 1001
2 = 10	6 = 110	10 = 1010
3 = 11	7 = 111	11 = 1011
4 = 100	8 = 1000	12 = 1100

In the decimal system, once 9 has been reached, higher numbers are indicated by making use of other positions which indicate tens, hundreds, thousands etc. The difference with the binary system is that since there are only two signs it is necessary to use further positions for any number above 1. Thus, in the decimal system one move to the left raises the power by ten (10, 100, 1000 etc.), whereas in the binary system a move to the left raises the power by two (10 = 2, 100 = 4, 1000 = 8 etc.). It follows that 11 = 3 or 2 + 1, 101 = 5 or 4 + 1, 10111 = 23 or 16 + 4 + 2 + 1. Using this system it is possible to carry out all the ordinary arithmetical functions of addition, subtraction, multiplication and division.

The advantage of the binary system, so far as electronic computers are concerned, is that numbers can be recognized by the presence or absence of electrical pulses. A pulse at a point in time indicates 1; the absence of a pulse indicates 0. Thus 10111 (or 23) can be expressed as

Pulse	No pulse	Pulse	Pulse	Pulse
1	0	1	1	1

This method of expressing numbers may at first sight appear laborious, but it is the key to the computer's speed. Pulses in an ordinary computer are only of one millionth of a second duration (micro-second) and in some computers one-thousandth of one-millionth of a second (nano-second).

In order to store data it is, of course, necessary to 'freeze' these minute pulses in some way. The most common method is to convert the electrical energy into magnetism on tapes, discs, drums etc. The binary pattern thus becomes one of magnetism (1) or no magnetism (0) in a particular physical position. When it is required to recover what has been stored, the magnetism is used to generate new electrical pulses. Other methods involve the punching of patterns of holes in paper tapes or cards, which can be stored away from the computer and used as input at a later time.

THE BENEFITS OF DATA PROCESSING

Data processing, and in particular electronic data processing, has the advantage of reducing the need for human effort. In general, data processing involves:

(*a*) recording original data;

(*b*) processing data including copying, calculating, comparing, sorting, storing and indexing;

(*c*) communicating data that is understandable, accurate and relevant.

The greater part of all routine administrative work is attributable to these processes and it is sensible that as much as possible shall be performed automatically by equipment of some kind. Compared with manual methods, data-processing equipment offers many advantages: greater legibility, greater accuracy, greater speed, the facility for automatic control and the simultaneous processing of more than one record.

Even more significant is the avoidance of recording that which has already been recorded. An overwhelming proportion of all routine administrative work involves the repetition and use of information that has been recorded previously; only a small proportion relates to new facts. For example:

(*a*) on a sales invoice the only new facts are the actual quantities ordered, whereas the customer's name, address, prices, descriptions and date will in most cases have been recorded previously;

(*b*) when calculating wages and salaries the new facts are, at most, hours and overtime worked, any bonus or commission earned and, occasionally, days absent sick or a non-recurring deduction; all else will be on record including employee's name, code number, base rate, fixed deductions, information for calculating income tax, loan balances and any other cumulative information required;

(*c*) when an entry is made to any form of account, nothing is new since the debit or credit amount, the date, any description, reference and any data required for up-dating the balance and for control will already have been recorded.

These three examples are sufficient to establish the potentiality of the benefits that can be obtained if human clerical effort can be confined, so far as is possible, to recording that which is entirely new. This potential can be realized because, as has been seen, electronic equipment has the advantage that it can read information that has been precoded for its use and store it in a variety of ways for subsequent access and re-use.

The computers by which electronic data processing is carried out are *systems* or *configurations* of interconnected electronic components. These components and the programs of instructions by means of which the components are put to work are the subject of the next chapter.

7 Computer components and programs

Every computer consists of a system of interconnected components. These may be built into a single item of equipment or be arranged as a group of free-standing units. In some cases, components may be remote from the main system and connected to it as necessary by cable or through the public telephone network.

The variables of main interest to the computer user lie in the fields of input, storage and output and these will be described in some detail. The arithmetical/logical and control functions carried out by the central processor are predetermined for a particular computer and are not ordinarily a matter of choice.

INPUT

There are two fundamentally different methods of feeding data into a computer. The first is *direct entry* where data are transmitted directly into the computer store; this is called *on-line*. The second method is to produce an intermediate record *off-line*, later to be fed into the computer when required.

On-line entry can be performed by the use of a keyboard or by means of a document reader. The keyboard method is used in the smaller *visible record computers* and also in the larger *mainframe computers* provided they have the facility for receiving input whilst at the same time doing other work. A document reader, which also would only be used with a computer able to receive input whilst doing other work, automatically reads characters or bar marks.

Off-line records take the form of magnetic records or punched-hole records that can be fed into the computer automatically. They can be produced by keyboard, by document reader or by a computer as a form of output after processing has taken place.

On a mainframe computer there is an *operator console* which has a keyboard which the operator uses for systems control; it is not normally used as a means of data or program input. There is usually a separate *engineer's console* which is used by the computer engineers for the location and rectification of faults in the equipment.

On-line entry

Most on-line input is by the use of keyboards in the ways described in this section. Document readers, which operate either on line or off line, are dealt with in the next section.

Visible record computer keyboards   Part if not all of the data to be fed into the smaller visible-record computer (VRC) is directly entered by the operator. There are usually two keyboards, one similar to that of a typewriter and the other a digital keyboard with a series of function keys relating to the execution of programs (Fig. 59). In some machines the typewriter keyboard is not connected with the store and it is used only to write directly on to a form, a visible record, which is being produced. Numbers entered through the digital keyboard are translated into their binary equivalents and passed into store for processing.

Fig. 59   Typical VRC Keyboard (*Courtesy of British Olivetti Ltd.*)

Direct data entry (DDE)   Where a computer is equipped to carry out more than one program at a time, it is possible to feed in data from a number of different DDE stations, local or remote, without interrupting whatever other work may be in progress. Many DDE stations consist of a keyboard and display screen similar to a television screen (Fig. 60); others have only a keyboard. The keyboard may include a separate digital keyboard. The operator can feed directly into store both alphabetical and

Fig. 60 Direct data entry station (*Courtesy of IBM United Kingdom Ltd.*)

numerical data. What is typed appears on the display screen so that it can be verified and edited before being released to the computer.

If necessary, data already in the store can be called for and seen on the screen before being added to or adjusted. Some stations employ an illuminated marker, known as a *cursor*, to aid this process. By means of function keys, the cursor is moved vertically and horizontally until stopped at the point where it indicates the first character of information to be changed. The new data is then entered through the keyboard and replaces the old.

Where it is required to select an item displayed on the screen in order to cause some predetermined action to take place, this can be done by means of a *light wand*. This is a pointer attached to the equipment by a flexible cable. When the required item is touched a signal is generated which is intelligible according to the controlling program. For instance, the screen might show a list or index of records available in the store. By touching the one required, all the detail of that record becomes displayed.

With the necessary programs, the computer can be caused to show on the screen the items of data it requires as an instruction to the operator, and draw attention to any deficiencies or apparent errors in data submitted. Messages such as 'out of stock' or 'no credit to be allowed' can also be displayed.

Direct-data entry can save labour and also speed up the input process and consequently the availability of resulting information.

Off-line entry

The most widely used forms of input are magnetic; punched-hole records occupy more space and are slower to feed into a computer.

Magnetic tape   This is coated plastic tape on which data can be recorded at a density of up to 1600 binary digits (*bits*) to the inch by magnetized spots. A tape is usually 2400 feet long and can hold up to 46 million bits which can be read or written at speeds of up to 300 000 bits a second. Magnetic tape is held on exchangeable reels and operated in tape-drive cabinets (Fig. 61). It has to be handled with great care and kept free of dust; it is available in sealed units which have automatic threading.

Fig. 61   Magnetic tape drive (*Courtesy of IBM United Kingdom Ltd.*)

Although magnetic tape is a convenient form of input because of the speed at which it can be fed into a computer it is not a convenient medium for the initial entry of data by an operator because an encoding machine with keyboard and tape drive is an expensive machine. Most of the tape used is written under the control of a computer after data processing has taken place. New data are usually transcribed by an item of equipment called a converter from data that has first been written on to magnetic disks (see below).

Also available are processing units which can be used to merge and verify the data on several tapes, to rearrange it and to write the result on a further tape.

Short lengths of tape are available in cassettes. These can be used to hold data recorded at remote stations or that recorded as a by-product of some other process. Cassettes may also be used to hold programs for feeding into a computer.

Key-to-disk   This is a system in which a number of stations, not unlike DDE stations, are linked to a special small computer, the main purpose of which is to assemble data. The computer has a store, a part of which consists of a series of magnetic disks. Each disk carries a number of circular tracks on which magnetic recordings are made. When in use, disks are spun at high speed whilst adjacent 'heads' record and retrieve information as required.

The means of entering data is called a *key-station* (Fig. 62) which has a keyboard and a display screen. Key-stations may be local or remote from the computer and linked by a telecommunications network (see page 148).

Programs to control the entry of data are held in the disk store of the computer. An operator has only to enter the type of transaction and the system selects the appropriate program and, on the display screen, specifies the format for the operator. If necessary, data can be entered in a form convenient to the operator and then automatically rearranged to a form convenient for input to the main computer.

A program can apply data checks (see page 152) with alternative ways of dealing with errors. In one method, if an item fails a test the keyboard will lock and the operator can either cancel and re-enter or *flag* the media for later correction. Another method is to have a subsequent and separate data-checking run and to use a printer to prepare a list of rejected data.

Verified data is stored temporarily in the disk store until it is transferred to magnetic tape for subsequent off-line input to the main computer.

The system can include a line printer (see page 129) to print output that might otherwise take up the more expensive time of the main computer.

Diskettes   These, also called floppy disks, are single disks held in sealed covers 20 cm square. A diskette can hold 250 000 *bytes* (see page 126) which is equivalent to two operator days' work.

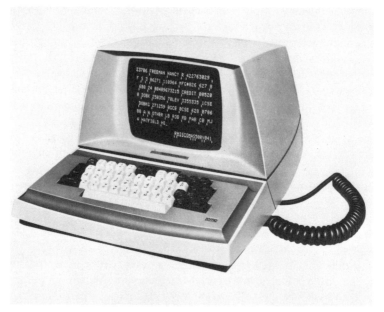

Fig. 62   Key-to-disk key-station (*Courtesy of Computer Machinery Company Ltd.*)

Data can be entered on what, in this system, is called a data entry station (Fig. 63). The station has a display screen for error recognition and since, as with every form of disk, each entry has an address, it is possible to locate a record for verification or up-dating.

Diskettes can be held over for the entry later of data of the same class, they can be passed to other departments for the entry of additional related information, and they can be sent through the mail; a diskette and cover weighs less than 60 grammes.

A data entry station at a remote point can pass data from a batch of diskettes to a main computer via a telecommunications network. Alternatively, data on diskettes can be transferred on to magnetic tape by means of a data converter which will take twenty disks at a time, apply data checks and pass the verified data at high speed by telecommunication to a main computer.

On a visible record computer, data can be fed direct from diskette to a disk store. Diskettes can also be employed to actuate a printer.

Special-purpose terminals   These are available for a variety of purposes, particularly in the retail trade as in the example illustrated in Fig. 64, and can perform many functions.

Fig. 63   Diskette data station and converter (*Courtesy of IBM United Kingdom Ltd.*)

With the aid of a light wand, a product number can be taken in from a bar-coded merchandise tag on which the bars represent 0 or 1 in binary notation. Alternatively, a coded tag can be fed into an aperture or a number can be entered through the keyboard.

Charges, discounts and VAT can be calculated and invoices, sales dockets or other forms can be printed. Where cash is handled, if the amount tendered is keyed in, the correct change can be displayed or a warning given if the amount tendered is insufficient.

For the purpose of credit sanction a warning can be given when a total purchase exceeds a given limit. Alternatively, if the terminal is on line to a computer, credit can be authorized or withheld when a customer number is read in from a card or keyed in.

Data for stock control, sales accounting, statistics and management reports can be retrieved in several ways. The data could have been:

(*a*) written on magnetic tape in a cassette for later transfer to a central computer;

(*b*) recorded through a direct link with a local item of equipment called a data collecter;

(*c*) held on magnetic tape until each terminal is *polled* (called up) after hours by a central computer acting through a telecommunications network.

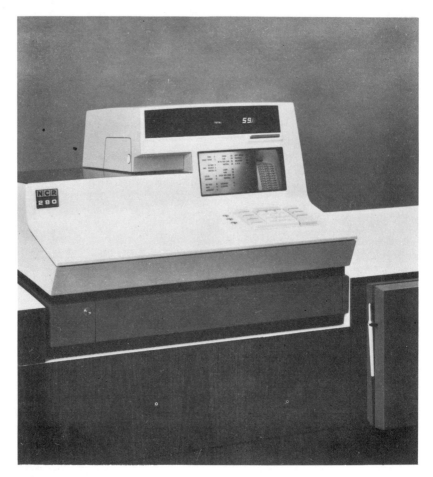

Fig. 64   Retail terminal (*Courtesy of NCR Ltd.*)

Portable data-capture unit (fig. 65)   This portable device is designed for use with such procedures as stock control and order entry. It measures 35 cm × 10 cm × 18 cm, weighs 3 kg and is carried by a shoulder strap. Power is provided by a rechargeable battery.

Fixed data, such as product numbers, can be read by light wand from bar-marked labels. Check digits can be used and if an item is unacceptable, an audible warning is given and no further data can be taken in until the error condition has been cleared. Other data are entered through the keyboard with each item being shown on the display panel for visual check.

The record is on a magnetic-tape cassette and can be recalled, item by item, on the display panel. The cassette, which has a capacity of 21 000 sixteen-digit places, can be fed direct to a computer or, alternatively, to a converter for transfer to a computer by a telecommunications network.

Fig. 65   Portable data-capture unit (*Courtesy of Plessey Telecommunications Ltd.*)

Document readers   Computer input can be prepared automatically by machines which read printed characters, bar marks or even handwritten characters. These characters must be in a special form which can be read by humans and also recognized by a machine. The data, having been read, is translated into binary notation. Document readers can be used on line, in which case data are fed into the store, or off line, in which case the data are recorded on magnetic tape.

(1) *Optical bar-mark readers*   This is the most simple form of optical reader. Forms are designed to enable numerals to be indicated by drawing bar marks in closely defined spaces. A customer or employee code number or other items of permanent data can also be entered in bar marks by the use of an embossed addressing plate (see page 89).

(2) *Optical character recognition (OCR)*   These are readers which can read characters printed in special founts or even handwritten numerals, provided these are written according to particular rules to avoid irregularities which might be quite acceptable to the human eye but not to the machine. So-called 'document readers' can read a few lines in a fixed position whilst the more expensive 'page readers' can read, under electronic control, from anywhere on the page.

(3) *Magnetic-ink character recognition (MICR)*   These are document readers which read characters printed in magnetic ink and in special founts. The process has been widely used by the banks for identifying cheques.

(*4*) *Models* The range of document readers available is wide. Some read bar marks, handwritten numerals and several different printed founts. Some carry out checks (see page 152) or, if a doubtful figure is read, will call for intervention by an operator. This intervention can take various forms and the following are two examples:

(*a*) where the data are being recorded on magnetic tape the reader causes signals to be recorded so that in a subsequent print from the tape, called a data-vetting run, symbols show where the queried data occurs thus enabling new data to be input separately to make good the deficiency,

(*b*) where data is being read directly into the computer store the reader stops and a message appears on the screen of a DDE station so that the operator can enter corrected data through the keyboard of the station.

The first of these methods allows faster recording but the information cannot be used until the data-vetting run has been completed. The second slows the initial recording but once it is completed the data are ready for use. Figure 66 illustrates an optical character reader which reads several founts, as well as handwritten numbers, from a variety of sizes of document; there is one model which works on line and another that works off line on to tape.

Fig. 66 Optical character reader (*Courtesy of IBM United Kingdom Ltd.*)

Magnetic stripe cards   These may be used in systems where accounts or other records are posted on a visible-record computer. Each ledger card bears a stripe or stripes of magnetizable material on which information as printed on the card can be recorded by the computer as it leaves the machine. On the card shown in Fig. 67 the magnetic stripe is the black

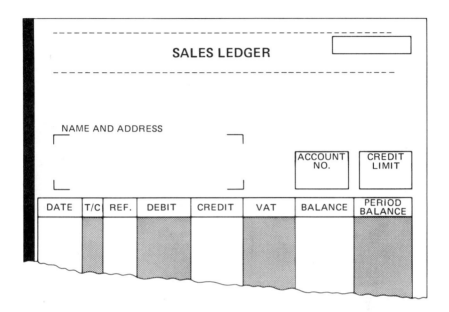

Fig. 67   Magnetic stripe card (*Courtesy of Philips Data Systems Ltd.*)

column on the left. When the card is next fed into the computer, the magnetically-recorded data are recovered and taken into store for use. The capacity of the stripes varies and may be sufficient to carry, say, a customer's name and address to be automatically printed on an invoice form. In a simple ledger-posting system, the stripe might carry the account code, an indicator of the position of the last posting made, and the balance brought forward. The following processes are then automatic:

(*a*) *Alignment.* When the card is fed into the forms handler (see page 137) it is stopped in the correct position for printing.

(*b*) *Account number check.* When the account number shown on the posting medium is set up on the keyboard this is compared with the number already magnetically recorded on the card and, if it is not the same, the machine locks.

(*c*) *Balance.* The balance to date is recorded magnetically as well as printed so that when the card is next fed in, the old balance is picked up and used with the new posting to calculate the new balance to date.

Automatic readers (Fig. 68) are available to read a batch of cards without the attention of the operator, to list and summarize the data recorded or to select overdue accounts.

Fig. 68   Automatic stripe-card reader (*Courtesy of NCR Ltd.*)

Magnetic edge stripe cards (Fig. 69)   These measure about 19 × 8 cm and a stripe can hold up to 250 bytes (see page 126). It is used as a unit record with the cards being held in a fixed sequence. On some computers, as one batch is fed in and read into the store, and after any calculation has been made, another up-dated batch is produced for input on the next occasion.

Magnetic cards (Fig. 70)   These are plastic cards which measure about 19 × 7 cm on which data are recorded magnetically. When prepared on a computer terminal under the control of a program they can hold over 12 000 characters.

Fig. 69 Magnetic edge stripe card (*Courtesy of British Olivetti Ltd.*)

Fig. 70 Magnetic card (used to record a computer word-processing program) (*Courtesy of Dataplex Ltd.*)

Punched cards   These are cards (Fig. 71*a*) on which information in numbers and words is recorded by punching holes in columns. Each column has punching positions corresponding to the digits '0' to '9' together with two additional positions; each column can be used to designate any digit or letter. A card can be used to hold a discrete item of information such as the details of an item bought or sold. Punched cards can be:

(*a*) punched and verified by manually-operated equipment;

(*b*) read into a computer by a card reader which translates the data into binary code;

(*c*) sorted into a convenient sequence for computer input by means of a sorting machine;

(*d*) punched automatically by equipment connected to a computer and under the control of a program;

(*e*) interpreted by the card punch, the equivalent of the punching being printed in clear language along the edge of the card.

The standard card has eighty columns but there are others of greater capacity. Punched cards provide unit records which can be used more than once if the same data are to be fed in repeatedly. When punched automatically under the control of the computer, they can serve as a form of external data storage, being used as input at some later time.

Punched paper tape (Fig. 71*b*)   Paper tape about 2·5 cm wide is punched with a pattern of holes, those in each row across the tape representing in binary code a number, letter, symbol or control instruction. Where a hole is punched, this represents the binary digit 1, and where a position is left unpunched, this represents 0. There are ten rows of holes to 2·5 cm of tape. The number of punching positions across the tape varies from five to eight, the latter, known as eight-track tape, being the most popular.

Paper tapes can be punched on special manually-operated punches or as computer output for subsequent re-processing. They can also be produced as a by-product from a variety of machines of original entry including typewriters and printing calculators. Where paper tape is used to hold a program or data for repeated use it may be held in a cassette.

Paper tape is less expensive, occupies less space and input speed is faster than for punched cards. However, it is necessary for the data to be punched in the sequence in which it will be used unless there is sufficient storage capacity available in the computer to hold it all.

Edge-punched cards (Fig. 71*c*)   Data are recorded along one edge of a card in the same way as in punched paper tape. As compared with paper tape, they provide unit records which can be manually selected, sorted and assembled as required. They can be *interpreted* automatically so that the card bears the equivalent of the punching in clear language.

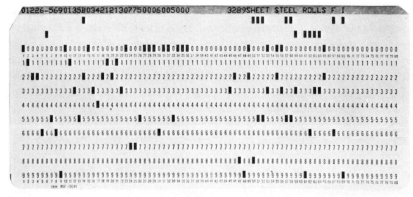

(a) Punched card

(b) Punched paper tape

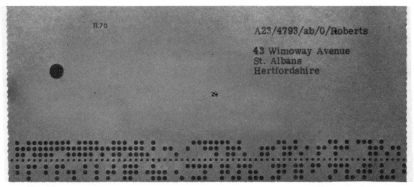

(c) Edge-punched card

Fig. 71   Punched-hole records

STORAGE

The store holds the program of instructions and the data until they are required for use, and may be visualized as a number of locations each of which can be identified by an *address*. Stores are of two types: immediate-access stores and backing stores which are of slower access.

Immediate-access stores

There are many forms of electronic storage for immediate access and this function is subject to frequent innovation so as to provide greater numbers of locations in less space at less cost. One way to visualize a store is as a complex network of microscopic 'printed' circuits. Because there are no moving parts, data can be manipulated in the store at almost the speed of light.

The way in which a store is organized to hold data and the capacity of each location varies. One system adopts the *byte* as the smallest addressable part of the store. A byte consists of eight binary digits and can hold + or − 127. For larger numbers of up to + or − 32 767, two adjoining bytes are used together. Four adjoining bytes will hold a number of up to + or − 2 147 000 000. Alternatively, a byte can be used to store an alphabetic character or a decimal digit.

The number of locations in an immediate-access store varies greatly. Because the basis of the numbers is the binary system, the quantity is usually a product of the power of two; thus a store will have 64 rather than 60 locations; 1024 rather than 1000 and 1 048 576 rather than 1 000 000. Stores are usually built in units of 1024, this unit being called a *K*. 1000K is called a *megabyte*.

On most computers the basic immediate-access store is incorporated in the central processor (see page 132), but it is also possible to add further units of immediate-access storage in multiples of, say, 2K bytes on small computers whilst on the largest computers each additional unit may have a capacity of a megabyte.

Read only storage   Some small computers employ a limited form of storage to hold only programs. Whilst instructions can be read from this kind of store, data cannot be entered and altered. This is known as ROM (Read Only Memory).

Backing stores

Because of its comparatively high cost, immediate-access storage is necessarily limited in size. Other and slower forms of storage are therefore used to hold the data until they are fed into the immediate-access store for use when required. This is called backing storage and may be one of the following types:

(a) Magnetic tape   The magnetic tapes described on page 114 provide a store of the serial type. In a *serial store*, it is necessary to search from beginning to end, or as far as may be necessary, in order to find one required item of data. This is to be contrasted with a *random-access store* from which a single item can be selected quickly through some system of indexing.

In a large computer installation, sixteen magnetic-tape drives can be on line, thus providing a capacity of some 700 million bits capable of being read at a speed of 300 000 characters a second. The program would provide for the automatic transfer of data from the appropriate tape reel as and when they are required in the immediate-access store. In addition, any number of reels can be held off line for manual transfer to the tape drives when needed.

Serial stores are most effective when most of the items are active so that data processing is carried out in a fixed sequence. A typical case is payroll,

Fig. 72 Disk pack (*Courtesy of IBM United Kingdom Ltd.*)

where all the brought-forward data would be held on magnetic tape in the employee code-number order. Current data, such as hours worked, would be fed through the input channels in the same sequence.

(b) Removable magnetic disks   Magnetic disks (see page 115), when not wanted on line can be removed in their disk packs (Fig. 72) from the disk drives and held elsewhere, and provide extremely large on-line random-access storage combined with virtually unlimited storage off line. A disk pack can store 200 million bytes and a large computer can employ on line sufficient disk drives to give access to several thousand million bytes. Data are transferred at speeds of 800 000 bytes a second whilst being indexed automatically by the computer program or operating system (see page 133). An item can be located in an average of about 1/30 of a second.

(c) Non-removable disks   Disks that remain sealed in their drives provide even faster access and, whilst storage capacity cannot be unlimited, it can be sufficient for many normal requirements. Fig. 73 illustrates a disk drive that has a capacity of over 500 million bytes, a transfer rate of over a million bytes a second and an average access time of 1/40 of a second. This unit also has an optional feature which enables 1·1 million bytes in the disk area to be covered by a fixed read-write head to give an average access time of 1/200 of a second.

Fig. 73   Non-removable disk drive (*Courtesy of IBM United Kingdom Ltd.*)

(d) **Magnetic drums**   These are similar in operation principle to the magnetic disk, except that the tracks lie around the circumference of a cylinder. They are fast in access but limited in storage capacity as well as being expensive. With the reduction in access time for non-removable disks and the enlargement of immediate-access stores they have been superseded.

(e) **Unit records and paper tape**   Diskettes, magnetic cards of various kinds, punched cards and paper tape are all forms of backing storage. They are comparatively slow in action and are commonly employed with the smaller computers.

Hierarchy   It will be seen that having regard to speed of access, there is a hierarchy of backing storage:

(i) First are the non-removable disks which provide very fast random access. There is an upper limit on the volume of data which can be stored, albeit counted in hundreds of millions of characters.

(ii) Next are the exchangeable disks, for random access, and magnetic tapes, for serial access. These are slower and less expensive but unlimited in capacity.

(iii) Then there are the diskettes and magnetic cards where the volume of data on the unit is low compared with normal disks but high in comparison with other unit records.

(iv) Finally there are magnetic stripe cards, punched cards and paper tape where access is relatively slow, serial and limited at any time to the next card in the pack or item on the tape.

OUTPUT

A computer has a number of channels designed to feed various kinds of output device according to the purpose for which the information is intended.

Printed output   Visible-record computers have built into the main, and sometimes only, unit, a printer using a print-ball, print-wheel, dot matrix or other device, which prints one character at a time and is called a *serial printer*. Associated paper-handling equipment holds forms which may be inserted individually, as well as continuous stationery. Whilst part of the entries made on the forms may be generated by the computer, some part may be entered directly from the keyboard by the operator.

Most large computers are linked to free-standing *line printers* (Fig. 74) which print one line at a time, some at speeds of more than 2000 lines a

Fig. 74   Line printer (*Courtesy of IBM United Kingdom Ltd.*)

minute. Where narrow forms are used several can be produced simultaneously side by side. More than one printer may be on line in a large installation whilst additional printers or special typewriters may be off line and actuated by magnetic tape produced by the computer.

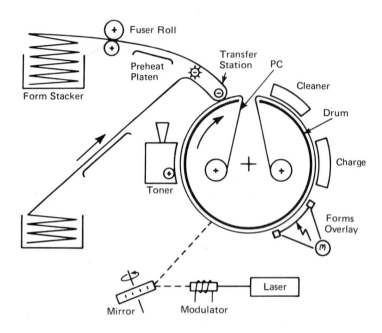

Fig. 75   Diagram of laser-beam printer (*Courtesy of IBM United Kingdom Ltd.*)

An even faster printer, a diagram of which is given in Fig. 75, produces more than 160 forms a minute. The forms can be eleven inches long and, with eight lines to the inch spacing, giving the equivalent of 13 000 lines a minute. A form layout, with computer-output entries, is printed on to blank paper by the use of a photo-conductive drum exposed to a computer-controlled laser beam and a negative of the form layout.

Microfilm   Where results are for reference, possibly over a long period, and only a small percentage of the information is likely to be required, equipment (Fig. 76) is available which will translate magnetic-tape output into microfilm in an indexed or self-indexing sequence. The microfilm records are in plain language so that when a query arises the appropriate reel of film is placed in a viewer similar to one of those employed with ordinary microfilm records (see Fig. 56). This form of record is particularly valuable where the reference records need to be held at scattered and distant branches.

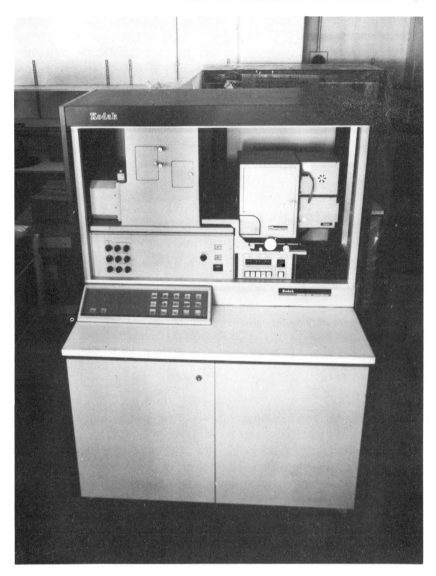

Fig. 76 Computer-output microfilmer (*Courtesy of Kodak Ltd.*)

Visual display units (VDU) The direct data entry station illustrated in Fig. 60 on page 113 is also a means of output when it may be called a visual display unit. By setting up codes on the keyboard, information contained in the immediate-access store of the computer can be seen on the screen in whatever pre-determined arrangement is convenient.

This device can be used by clerks or by management needing to refer quickly to a limited amount of stored information. A buyer, for example, might wish to know from the stock-control file the level of stock of a commodity, what is currently on order and when delivery is expected.

With suitable programs (see operating systems on page 133), data can be displayed from more than one file; many VDUs may have access at the same time and, if some of these are at distant places, telecommunications equipment (see page 148) must be employed.

Magnetic and punched output   A significant part of the output of a computer may be produced only for use on a subsequent occasion by the same or by another computer, in which case it may be written on magnetic tape, disks or cards, or punched into cards or paper tape.

CENTRAL PROCESSOR

The central processor contains the arithmetical logical unit which performs the productive work of a computer. It consists of a series of electronic circuits which carry out the logical functions in a program as well as all the calculations. It contains the control unit which controls the other parts of the computer, i.e. the input, the output and the store according to the program of instructions. In most computers, the main immediate-access store is contained in the central processor and, as a separate free-standing item of equipment, this is sometimes called the *mainframe*.

PROGRAMMING

The processor controls the components but the element which directs the processor so that the components do useful work is the program. Thus the components become a computer capable of performing a variety of data-processing functions including the ability to solve business problems through the application of mathematical and logical or decision-making techniques. Throughout each job the physical nature of the computer remains unchanged. The ability of the computer to turn from one kind of job to any one of a wide range of entirely different jobs resides in the power of the programs that can be employed.

Program instructions relate to such actions as reading in data submitted through an automatic input device, placing it in designated locations in the store, making calculations, manipulating data in the store and outputting results in the form required.

A computer reacts only to data and instructions which are expressed in binary notation. It is the practice first to plan and write the program steps in an alpha-numeric code and for this *program* or *source* language to be converted into binary *machine* language by some automatic process. Once converted into machine language, programs can be fed to the computer in many ways, including by magnetic tape in a cassette, magnetic stripe cards, punched paper tape or cards or by plugging in a circuit.

Source languages

Certain languages have been developed for general use, such as COBOL (common business oriented language) which is suitable for business operations, and FORTRAN (formula translator) a more mathematical language. Other languages have been developed by manufacturers for use on particular computers.

High-level languages With the larger computers, source languages known as *high-level languages* are employed. With some such languages, apart from normal mathematical symbols and a few standard code words, the programmer is free to adopt whatever short words he chooses, provided these are used consistently. Translation from source language to machine is then made by a *compiler* program which not only translates each source instruction into a string of orders in machine language, but also allots portions of the store for specific purposes and keeps account of the location addresses so established.

Low-level languages On the smaller computers it may be necessary to use a mnemonic code to detail all the instructions that the computer will carry out, including the specification of the particular location in which an item is to be stored. This is called a *low-level language* and subsequently it is translated order by order, by means of an *assembler* program.

Software

Software is the term used to describe the programs supplied by the manufacturers in contrast to the *hardware* of the computer and associated items of equipment. The term software is also used to refer to any program whether bought from the manufacturer, a software supplier, or written by the user's programmers.

In addition to the compiler and assembler programs referred to above, many other kinds of program can be supplied by manufacturers.

Packaged programs These are suppliers' programs designed for complete applications for any user and may deal with stock control, journey planning, critical path analysis etc. Other programs deal with particular operations common to many routines, such as sorting.

Executive routines These are programs held permanently in the store to control parts of the computer operation such as the transfer and verification of data from an input device to the central processor, or from the central processor to an output device.

Operating systems These are programs supplied by the manufacturer to enable the operators to obtain maximum performance by the computer particularly where several programs are carried out at the same time. Some computers operate with such complexity that there is no practical distinction between the part performed by the circuitry of the hardware and that performed by the manufacturer's operating systems. Some of the more simple examples include:

(*a*) to overlap high-speed calculating or other processing with the relatively slow operations of reading input or printing results;

(*b*) to turn from one program to another so as to make best use of the capability of the computer whilst following predetermined priorities;

(*c*) to enable a computer to be interrogated for information in the store with a minimum of delay to other jobs being processed at the same time;

(*d*) to determine where in the backing store a required batch of information is held, to transfer it to the immediate-access store at the proper time and to protect every batch of data from misuse by any other program except that to which it relates.

Programs and the user

The quality and the appropriateness of the programs is crucial to the effective use of computers. Users of the larger and more sophisticated installations have a team of experienced programmers to meet the precise needs of the employing organization. For the smallest visible-record computers, programs are almost certainly produced by the manufacturer. In between these two extremes there is room for a choice between:

(*a*) using standard programs and operating systems available from the manufacturer or from suppliers of software; and

(*b*) having special programs and operating systems prepared by a software supplier or by programmers in the employ of the user.

Programs written to a user's requirements are likely to be more economical of computer time and of storage space and to provide a closer fit with existing procedures. They are, however, very much more expensive: the cost of exclusive programs may be between a half and the whole of the capital cost of the computer and its associated equipment.

Standard programs are far less expensive and they will have been tested and proved, an aspect which can be a costly phase in the installation of a new program. It may be wise, therefore, for the user to agree to alter the layout of some forms or even to change some business procedures so as to be able to use standard programs. Most manufacturers have a range of packages to meet normal data-processing functions. In addition, packages are available from software suppliers, computer service bureaux, some consultants and the National Computing Centre, which can in particular provide programs suitable for small businesses. These sources also offer:

(*a*) integrated suites of programs to enable all the data processing of a business to be performed by computer;

(*b*) sets of programs to meet the specialized requirements of a particular industry or section of commerce;

(*c*) programs in modular form to go towards meeting a user's particular needs.

So many are the standard packages available that several agencies produce and up-date lists of programs on the market.

Programs capable of carrying out all but the most simple routines are extremely long and so require extensive storage space in the computer. The user may be inhibited in particular applications by lack of space in the store. Moreover, in all but the largest computers the space available for the user programs and data may be more limited than would at first appear:

(*a*) In the smallest visible-record computers most of the store may be a *read only memory* (see page 126) to hold the programs whilst the true storage available for the results of calculations may be limited to a few locations described as registers.

(*b*) In other small to medium-sized computers, part of the store, whether read only or otherwise, may be occupied with permanent programs without which the computer cannot function. These programs carry out logical functions which would be performed by hardware circuitry in a larger computer or carry out executive and logical functions. Such programs may occupy more than half the so-called store and so place limits on how the computer can be employed.

It follows that when considering the use of a computer, or comparing one with another, regard must be had not only to the components but to the size of the store available for user programs and data and to the cost of the programs that will put it to work.

8 Computers and their use

In the preceding chapter the various alternative components of computers have been described under the headings of input, storage and output. The broad concept of the computer as illustrated by the diagram in Fig. 58 can now be expanded and developed. It will be seen how computers of varying capabilities are made up from the components, and how they are put to use.

The classification of computers is difficult because the data-processing ability of a central processor can be varied greatly according to the nature, speed and capacity of the other components associated with it. Indeed, a user starting with a small computer may be able by successive modifications to build up his installation until it is able to handle many times the volume of work and carry out systems of much greater complexity. Manufacturers often use a numerical code to indicate a family of computers within which there are many variations, but are unable to draw hard boundaries between one class and another. It is nonetheless helpful to recognize three main categories:

(*a*) at the start of the range the visible record computer;

(*b*) at the advanced end the mainframe computer; and

(*c*) an intermediate category which, although generally recognizable, has no clear demarcations at the boundaries with the other two.

Visible record computers A typical visible record computer (see Figs 81 to 83) consists of a main unit, approximately of desk size, incorporating the following parts:

Processor and immediate-access store This holds the program, carries out its logical functions and calculations, controls the operation of the other parts of the system and holds at least some of the data as well as the results pending output.

Keyboard This usually has:

(*a*) An alpha-numeric keyboard for the entry of descriptive information on the form being entered. On some machines this data, or part of it, may also be held in the store for later transfer to some other form of output.

(*b*) Ten number keys for the entry of numerical data to be processed. This may be associated with a buffer store which enables the operator to enter and confirm data while the unit is performing some other function such as printing.

(*c*) Various control keys relating to the handling of forms and the operation of the program.

Forms handler   This consists of a platen with guides for controlling forms and cards of various sizes, tally rolls, continuous stationery, journal sheets and any other documents on which entries are to be made. There may also be some form of automatic line feed.

Printer   A print-wheel, print-ball, dot-matrix device or some other form of serial printer.

Program reader   This is a device to read and place in the store the programs which will have been pre-recorded, typically on a magnetic tape held in a cassette.

Other devices   In addition, there may be other devices or components such as:

(*a*) a display screen, either built-in or free-standing, by which to pass instructions from the program to the operator;

(*b*) a magnetic stripe-card reader, usually built-in;

(*c*) free-standing card and paper tape punches and readers;

(*d*) free-standing magnetic tape and disk drives;

(*e*) free-standing line printers;

(*f*) a channel, built-in, which enables the computer to be linked to a central mainframe computer through a telecommunications network.

Characteristically, a visible record computer produces traditional *hard copy* records on paper and card and requires an operator to enter through the keyboard some part of the data for each transaction. Some visible record computers, however, have the ability to hold some brought-forward data on magnetic or punched cards. Moreover, provided the computer has a sufficiently large store to enable it to operate with a complex program, as well as, say, a disk store and a line printer, batch processing may be possible which requires only minimal intervention by an operator. In circumstances such as these the visible record computer overlaps the intermediate range.

A diagram showing the functions and possible components of a visible record computer is given in Fig. 77.

Mainframe computers   The term mainframe is synonymous with central processor, which in the case of the most advanced category of computer is a separate free-standing item of equipment in a plain cabinet without visible or

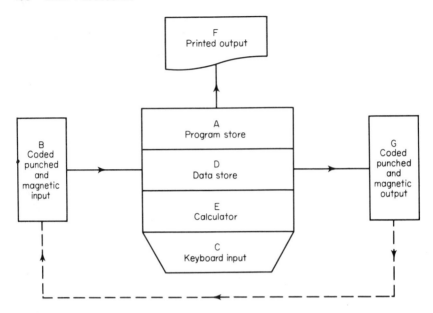

Fig. 77   Visible record computer diagram

moving parts. The total assembly of components controlled by the central processor, called a configuration, typically consists of the following parts:

Central processor and immediate-access store as already mentioned.

An *operator console* consisting of a typewriter keyboard and display screen. This is used by the operator to pass messages to and take messages from the processor, including instructing it to take in and act upon a program.

An *engineer console* with rows of small lamps by which to establish the status of parts of the system. This is used by computer engineers in the location of faults.

An extensive variety of input and output devices such as:

(*a*) document readers and line printers;
(*b*) magnetic disk and tape drives;
(*c*) punched-card and paper-tape readers and punches;
(*d*) telecommunications control gear.

To the outside observer the general impression of a mainframe installation (Fig. 88) is one of much unidentifiable equipment, ample space, few people, and an air of antiseptic cleanliness; in short, mainframe installations offer little to indicate what work is being done. A diagram showing the functions and possible components of a mainframe computer is given in Fig. 78.

Intermediate computers   These are commonly known as mini-computers or small business systems. Not only are these terms also used by

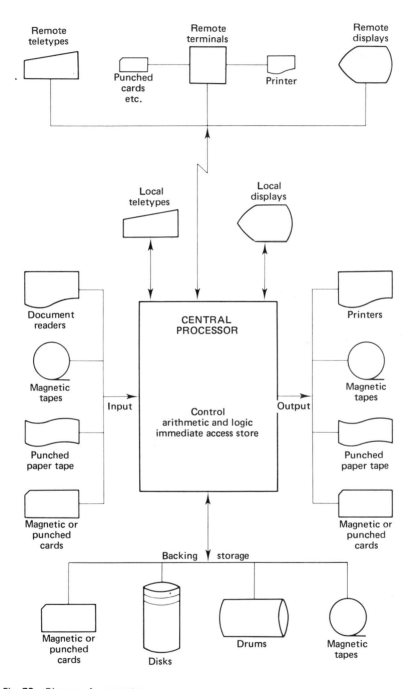

Fig. 78 Diagram of a computer

some manufacturers to describe visible record computers but the terms are unsatisfactory in themselves:

(*a*) a mini-computer has no recognizable relationship to the other categories as to size or capacity;

(*b*) neither the systems nor the businesses they serve are necessarily small.

The distinguishing characteristics of the intermediate computers are that the central processor may not be free-standing and separate and it may not require to be housed in a dust-free and temperature-controlled environment. Otherwise they are similar in configuration to a mainframe computer.

Examples of computers   Having drawn attention to these somewhat amorphous categories, it is now appropriate to give some examples of the wide and constantly changing range of computers available. These examples, whilst they are typical, are not comprehensive and the intending

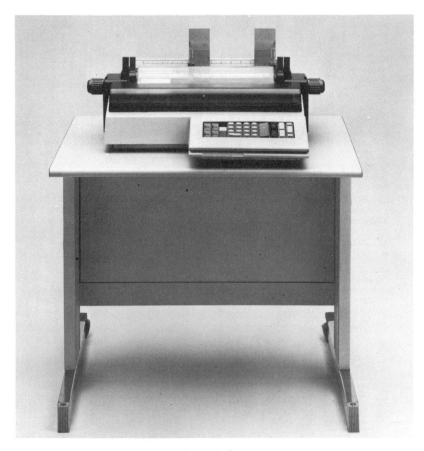

Fig. 79   Olivetti A4 (*Courtesy of British Olivetti Ltd.*)

buyer, as well as the student, would be advised to visit showrooms, exhibitions and actual installations.

Olivetti A4 (Fig. 79)   This is an electronic accounting machine without an alphabetical keyboard. It is designed for payroll, ledger posting and other accounting work for which eleven 16-digit registers are provided. The maximum program capacity is 223 bytes, programs being fed in from cassettes which contain a drum with a 93-byte capacity.

Output is printed at 16 digits a second by a moving print-head. Additional output devices are available to write magnetic tape or paper tape.

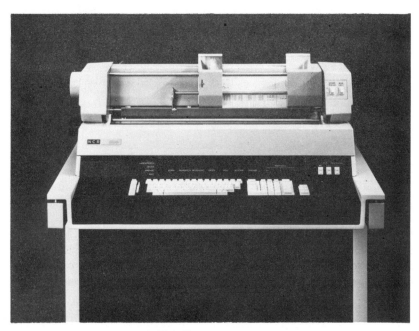

Fig. 80   NCR 299 *(Courtesy of NCR Ltd.)*

NCR 299 (Fig. 80)   This also is an electronic accounting machine with a store that has 50, 70 or 100 registers each of 17 digits. Input is normally by the numeric keyboard and output is by a print-ball serial printer with 88 characters printing at 15 digits a second. The program is compiled by the entry of vertical bar marks in columns on a large sheet of light card the width of the platen, which is read line by line into the program store by an optical reader.

Additional input and output devices which can be provided include a continuous-forms feeder, magnetic stripe card reader, punched cards, edge-punched cards, paper tape and magnetic tape cassettes. The tape cassette can also be used as a faster way of feeding in a program.

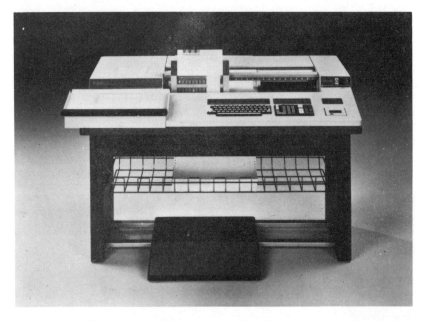

Fig. 81   Philips 300 (*Courtesy of Philips Data Systems Ltd.*)

Philips 300 (Fig. 81)   This visible record computer has an immediate-access store of 4K, 6K or 8K bytes for the application program, data tables and analysis. Standard operational routines are held in additional storage. Input is through the keyboard and output by the built-in matrix printer. A model is available which can handle magnetic stripe cards. There are also facilities for the use of diskettes or magnetic-tape cassettes. The unit can be connected direct to a modem (see page 149) for data transmission to a central computer.

Olivetti A5 (Fig. 82)   The immediate-access store on this visible record computer can be $\frac{1}{2}$K, 1K, 2K bytes and, in addition, there is read-only storage of from 8K to 12K bytes. Built-in is a read/write unit for magnetic edge-striped cards which provide backing storage in sequential form; each card holds 250 bytes and can be used to store data or programs. At the same time that a set of brought-forward cards is fed in to the unit, an up-dated carry-forward set is automatically produced. Additional backing storage is provided by a magnetic-tape cassette drive, each cassette having a storage capacity of 250 000 bytes. Up to five tape-cassette drives can be attached.

Other input is through the keyboard and output from the associated serial printer. For input to another computer, paper tape can be punched and there is a control unit for data transmission by telephone line.

Fig. 82   Olivetti A5 *(Courtesy of British Olivetti Ltd.)*

NCR 499 (Fig. 83)   This visible record computer has a basic immediate-access store of 16K bytes, which can be expanded to a maximum of 32K bytes in increments of 4K bytes. Programs are written in a high-level language and are fed in from a magnetic-tape cassette. The basic model has two cassette stations built in. Input is through the keyboard, from a magnetic-tape cassette with a capacity of about 250 000 bytes, or from punched cards or paper tape. Magnetic stripe cards can be used and an automatic magnetic stripe-card reader can be linked. Output is from the built-in bi-directional matrix printer at either 75 or 130 characters a second.

Additional input and output devices include a choice of two line printers working at either 200 or 300 lines a minute, two additional cassette stations, two continuous-forms feeders and a disk unit of nearly 10 million bytes for

Fig. 83   NCR 499 (*Courtesy of NCR Ltd.*)

random access. This unit is also capable of being linked as an intelligent terminal (see page 148) to a central computer.

Olivetti A7 (Fig. 84)   In this system, the basic immediate-access store of 8K bytes can be expanded to 12K or 16K bytes. In addition, there is a hierarchy of backing stores available:

(*a*) Magnetic edge-striped cards and magnetic-tape cassettes as in the case of the Olivetti A5, described above.

(*b*) Fixed-head disks which provide random access to 40K, 80K, 120K or 180K bytes with an average access time of 800 nano-seconds (a nano-second is a thousand-millionth of a second).

(*c*) Cartridge disk packs consisting of a fixed-head disk and a removable disk. With four disk drives under the control of the processor, there is access to 40 million bytes.

In addition to the built-in serial printer, a second serial printer can be employed as well as line printers from a range operating at between 300 and 1200 lines a minute. Magnetic stripe cards, punched cards and paper tape can be used and there is a unit for data transmission by telephone line. The basic equipment can be employed as a visible record computer or the expanded system can be used for batch production under program control. Two independent programs can run simultaneously.

Fig. 84   Olivetti A7 (*Courtesy of British Olivetti Ltd.*)

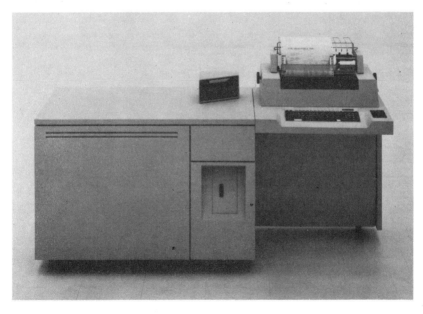

Fig. 85   IBM System 32 (*Courtesy of IBM United Kingdom Ltd.*)

IBM System 32 (Fig. 85)   In this range, the processor has immediate-access storage of 16K, 24K or 32K, backed by from 3 to 13 million bytes of disk storage. Diskettes, each holding about 250 000 bytes, are used for recording data at remote locations for transfer by mail or through a telecommunications network, for holding data off line for transfer to the on-line disks when required and for feeding in programs.

Output can be from a serial printer or from a line printer, the latter being available with speeds of 50, 100 or 155 lines a minute. There is also a display screen.

A unit with a serial printer can be used as a typical visible record computer and the store is large enough to carry a program capable of writing on the display screen step-by-step instructions to the operator. Alternatively, if fitted with a line printer it can perform batch production under the control of a program.

BCL Molecular 18 (Fig. 86)   This equipment has a processor with immediate-access storage of 24K bytes, backed by a disk drive which provides 10 million characters of storage. Input to the system is either through the keyboard or the visual display units and output is from the free-standing line printer which takes information direct from the keyboard or the visual display units as well as the storage.

Fig. 86   BCL Molecular 18 *(Courtesy of Business Computers (Systems) Ltd.)*

Computers in this range have direct-access storage of from 8K to 64K bytes and disk storage of from 5 to 200 000 million characters with facilities for up to thirty-two input and output devices such as keyboards, visual-display units and line printers.

ICL 2903 (Fig. 87)   This system has a processor with immediate-access

Fig. 87   ICL 2903 (*Courtesy of International Computers Ltd.*)

storage ranging from 16K to 48K 24-bit words or the equivalent of from 48K to 144K bytes. The backing storage includes a disk store of 60 million bytes with an average access time of 5·2 milliseconds, or up to 200 million bytes with an average access time of 38·3 milliseconds and magnetic-tape systems with alternative transfer rates of 20 000 or 80 000 characters a second. Other input devices include up to eight keyboards with video monitors for direct data entry, and punched card and tape readers.

Output devices include line printers operating at speeds of from 150 to 1500 lines a minute, up to sixteen visual-display units, card and tape punches, a graph plotter and a coupler for data transmission by a telecommunications network.

IBM 370/168 (Fig. 88)   This system has, in the processor, immediate-access storage of up to 8 megabytes whilst an operating system enables designated parts of the backing storage to be called into the main store automatically, increasing it to 16 megabytes.

Associated disk storage can provide 200 megabytes on each drive with an average access time of 25 milliseconds. The magnetic tape sub-system has a transfer rate of up to 320 kilobytes a second.

There is available a variety of keyboard input stations for local or remote

Fig. 88   IBM 370/168 (*Courtesy of IBM United Kingdom Ltd.*)

data entry and interrogation. Punched cards can be read at speeds of up to 1200 a minute.

Line printers available for output have speeds of 1100 lines a minute, 2000 lines a minute with forty-eight characters, 2500 lines a minute with thirty-six characters, or the equivalent of 13 000 lines a minute by the photo-conductive drum illustrated in Fig. 75 on page 130.

TELECOMMUNICATIONS

The use of a telephone line to connect a remote terminal to a central computer has led to a number of important developments such as:

(*a*) a single high-powered computer serving an entire national or multi-national company;

(*b*) a service bureau serving clients spread over a wide area;

(*c*) computerized airline reservation and other specialized systems.

In consequence, telephone lines are used to transmit data across countries and continents whilst space satellites are used to transmit data across oceans.

All terminals have the capacity to initiate the transmission of data to a central computer and to print or display data received from it. Many, the so called 'intelligent' terminals, also have the capacity for some data processing. Some merely apply checks to data; others are capable of extensive data processing. Where there is a computer terminal, the opportunity exists to decide what processing is appropriate to the central, more powerful installation, with the high cost for computer time and transmission, and what is appropriate to the comparatively low-cost terminal.

Despite the option to use local computers, the volume of data transmission to central computers is increasing. It has been estimated that by 1985 the number of terminals, with a substantial proportion of them intelligent, will approach $1\frac{1}{2}$ million in Europe alone; a few years later, 100 000 million words, say the equivalent of a million novels, will be transmitted in Europe every day.

Data can be transmitted by public telephone lines or by leased telephone lines. Leased lines have the advantage of being more reliable and less subject to data corruption; moreover, they are cheaper with sufficient volume, say of the order of six or more hours a day. However, the use of either kind of line requires the employment of sophisticated equipment, some of which is described below.

Modem   For data to be transmitted by telephone line it has to be converted to a form compatible with equipment designed for the transmission of speech; this process is called *modulation*. At the receiving end, the reverse process is needed and is called *demodulation*. Both processes are performed by an item of equipment called a *modem*, the name being a contraction of the words modulator and demodulator.

Post Office telephone lines may not be used to relay data to and from a computer other than by employing the Post Office Datel Services which provide the required modems. The speed of transmission depends upon the type and, consequently, the cost of the modems employed. Normal speeds range from 110 bits (binary digits) a second to 2400 bits a second. Faster speeds may be achieved by means of modems supplied by the manufacturers but permission to use these must first be obtained from the Post Office.

Multiplexer or concentrator   The cost of using telephone lines to send large volumes of data over long distances is appreciable. The multiplexer reduces the cost because it enables data to be transmitted at high speeds, say 9600 bits a second. It can also combine outputs from a number of terminals. For example, the equipment can be used in the following way:

(*a*) A network of local terminals, each with a low-speed modem, employs public lines to pass data to a multiplexer.

(*b*) The multiplexer, with a high-speed modem, is linked by a leased telephone line to another distant high-speed modem and multiplexer which passes the data to a central computer.

Similarly, output from the computer can be distributed to a number of terminals by the same network.

Multiplexers provided by various manufacturers may only be used on a leased, rather than a public, telephone line. The Post Office Datel Service also provides a multiplexer service.

Communication controller   This monitors in turn a series of terminals to discover which have data ready to be taken into the computer and ensures the proper channelling of data transferred in different modes depending upon the terminals, modems and multiplexers employed for transmission.

Front-end processor   This performs functions similar to those of the communication controller and, in addition, applies data checks and performs other functions that would otherwise take up extensive and valuable processing facilities in the main computer.

DATAPOST

Although designed for a wide range of documents, samples and other material, this service can be used to send data to and from computers. It operates overnight from door to door in Britain and has to be at regular intervals from once a week to, say, several times a day. It is subject to contract, the minimum period for which is three months.

The service is also available for overseas destinations, for example:

(*a*) Collections in London before 5 p.m. reach many cities in Belgium, France and the Netherlands on the following morning; collections from elsewhere in Britain reach these cities on the following afternoon.

(*b*) A package collected in London before 2 p.m. reaches New York by 9 a.m., local time, on the following morning and by 10 a.m. for many other American cities.

(*c*) A package collected in London before 5 p.m. reaches Sao Paulo on the second morning or reaches Hong Kong and Tokio after 48 hours.

Two-way services are available for some countries.

A protective packing, the Envopak, can be provided and for this a sealing device is available. There is also the 'Datapost D' service for irregular deliveries provided the packages are taken to any of 150 designated post offices throughout Britain.

ASPECTS OF COMPUTER USAGE

It is crucial to the effective use of computers to obtain, with the minimum of human effort, accurate data in a form that is intelligible to the machine.

It is of prime importance to reduce the extent of human effort. The level of clerical salaries has risen steeply as has the cost of supporting a staff, including accommodation, national insurance and a growing range of benefits arising out of the increase in expectations by the population in general. At the same time, the cost of equipment has not only risen less steeply but has in some cases fallen dramatically; indeed, with the impact of miniaturization in electronic equipment, the balance is likely to move more sharply in favour of automatic procedures in place of manual and mental procedures. Computer users, therefore, employ an ever-widening variety of techniques to reduce human effort and to increase accuracy.

Data capture   Most data originate in a form acceptable to humans (*man legible*) and must be translated into a form acceptable to the computer (*machine legible*). If the cost of data capture is to be kept within reasonable limits, the initial entry into a machine-legible form must involve the minimum of human effort; this can be done by the use of sophisticated equipment, by systems ingenuity, or by a combination of both. Examples follow:

(*a*) The key-to-disk system (page 115) simplifies the task of an operator making the initial machine-legible entry by prompting the operator on a display screen and by enabling the entry to be made in a form convenient to the operator.

(*b*) The diskette (page 116) is a flexible machine-legible record which can be made close to the point at which a transaction occurs because it is produced on a device sufficiently simple to enable it to be provided to a number of out-stations.

(*c*) Special-purpose terminals (page 117) and portable data-capture units (page 118) can eliminate or greatly reduce the human effort required to produce an initial machine record.

(*d*) A direct data entry station provided with a display screen and a cursor (page 112) has labour-saving potential. When used for recording branch orders, for example, the operator enters only the branch number and there can appear on the screen the branch identification and the relevant list of goods; by the use of the cursor, the operator has only to enter the quantity ordered against each item to put the order into the system.

(*e*) If a document, such as an order form for example, is printed under the control of a computer it can:

(i) be selective and print only those products which a particular customer is likely to order;

(ii) print code marks to identify the customer and the products when the completed form is read by the document reader for input.

By the use of automatic equipment, once the initial machine-legible records have been produced, the data can be rearranged to suit the computer operation, transmitted over distance and fed into the computer, all at very high speeds.

Instructions to operators   The prompting of an operator, mentioned under key-to-disk, has wide applications to simplify training and to draw attention to errors in entering data. This requires, in addition to a display screen or panel, a store of sufficient size to hold what is likely to be a long program.

Check digits   The speed at which a computer can calculate makes it possible to verify numbers whenever they are transcribed, whether manually or automatically, by the use of 'check digits'. Circumstances in which an automatic verification process is vital include where:

(a) data are carried on public telephone lines;
(b) an operator enters numbers through a keyboard;
(c) paper tape or a card is punched or a magnetic recording is made automatically.

Check digits are most frequently applied to permanent reference numbers, such as customer numbers and account numbers, but they can also be employed for variable data.

The use of check digits requires the application of a calculation formula to each number before it is finally recorded. This calculation can either be carried out by the computer or else the punch, encoder or receiving station can contain an electronic calculator for this purpose.

In order to detect an error in the transposition, as well as in the transcribing of numbers, a formula can take the following form:

(a) each digit in the number is multiplied by a fixed multiplier, according to its position, and a total is produced;
(b) the total is divided by a fixed number (the modulus) and the remainder is deducted from the modulus to produce the check digit.

An example follows:

Original number: 7953
Weights from left to right: 5, 4, 3, 2
Modulus: 10
Calculations: $7 \times 5 = 35$
$\qquad\qquad\quad 9 \times 4 = 36$
$\qquad\qquad\quad 5 \times 3 = 15$
$\qquad\qquad\quad 3 \times 2 = 6$
$\qquad\qquad\quad$ Total $= 92$

$92 \div 10 = 9 + 2$ remainder
$10 - 2 = 8$

Number with check digit: 79538

When a reference number is first created, the computer, the encoder or a check-digit generator makes the calculation and adds the check digit at the end (right) of the number. Thereafter, whenever the number is read by a unit which has the means of verifying check digits, the calculation is repeated and if the result does not correspond with the check digit the entry is rejected.

A more simple form of check digit is the 'parity bit' used on paper or magnetic tape recordings. In this case one track of the tape has 1 or 0 recorded so that the line of binary digits, known as 'bits', adds up to, say, an odd number. The prime purpose of the parity bit is to reduce errors caused by a fault in the equipment.

Data storage A significant part of the output of a computer may be produced only for use on a subsequent occasion by the computer. This data may be produced for another kind of job; data for sales statistics might be produced as the by-product of invoicing and stock control. Alternatively, data to be carried forward may be produced for use in the same job on a subsequent occasion as in the case of the daily keeping of accounts, or the weekly preparation of a payroll.

In some computer systems, data to be carried forward may be written on magnetic tape or cards, removable disks, or punched cards and tape; this is the backing-store concept. In advanced computer systems, employing extensive fixed-disk storage with the capacity for holding a vast amount of data on line, the concept of a data bank emerges. All the carry-forward data is permanently on line and is constantly being up-dated; input is then confined to new current data.

Mode of use Most work on visible record computers, as has been pointed out, is performed item by item with the concurrent intervention of an operator. More advanced computers carry out the much faster batch production described below. But advanced computers are also capable of operating in the interactive mode or on the data-bank principle and it is appropriate to compare the three methods.

Batch In this kind of application the computer is set to carry out one function at a time, say invoicing or payroll. The input for each batch tends to be built up outside the computer and the computer files of brought-forward data may be held on line or assembled by an operator. This is often the most economical way in which to use a computer.

Interactive In this kind of application the computer deals with one transaction at a time and performs all the relevant functions relating to that one item. It ensures that all parts of the system are always up-to-date so that the system can be responsive to management needs. It is appropriate, indeed essential, to applications concerned with planning and control such as, for example, production control. With the availability of computers with increased memory capacity and with greater understanding by management of how a computer system can function as a management tool, it can be expected that increasing use will be made of the interactive mode.

Data bank   The concept of a data bank emerged as large disk stores became available and it was possible to hold large quantities of information on line. Notionally and practically, every fact about a business can be input and held in store, to be recovered when required in a fraction of a second. Computer programs are then of two kinds: those which put data into store and those which recover data, possibly from several different files, and process it to provide required information. The restrictions of self-contained systems are removed and management reports can contain any facts no matter what the source or the file in which they are stored.

INSTALLING A COMPUTER

Surveys of computer installations over a wide range of companies have shown that not all have a history of success. Many have failed to recover the cost of equipment, planning, programming and retraining. Not only have they failed to take the opportunity to improve the control of operations but they have failed even to improve routine data processing. Nonetheless, for all but the smallest concerns there is no viable alternative to electronic data processing and it is not a question of whether or not to adopt computerization but of what equipment to install and how to prepare to make proper use of it.

Often the trouble arises from managerial attitudes. Some managers regard the computer merely as a superior machine for carrying out traditional data processing cheaper and faster; some regard computerization as a mysterious function to be left in the hands of the experts.

If it is to be effective, a computer installation should be seen as the opportunity for:

(*a*) improved control of operations, improved product innovation, improved customer service and improved decision making based on new information systems and on simulation models;

(*b*) the data processing of the business to be planned as an integrated whole to give faster data processing, improved accuracy and increased but selective information.

For most companies, these aims will only be achieved over a period of years and then only provided there is:

(*a*) high-quality business management;

(*b*) competent computer staff;

(*c*) appropriate training of both line management and computer staff;

(*d*) integration of line management and computer staff when planning computer applications;

(*e*) openness of mind among managers when considering adapting business practices to the potentialities.

The kinds of actions that have to be taken to bring this about will depend upon the size of the company.

In a large company, if there is to be a feasibility study (see page 360), a new computer installed, or the existing installation put to better use, it is desirable that there shall be formed a multi-disciplinary team to conduct the project. This might include a board member, an accountant or financial manager, a functional manager to represent the users, and the senior computer and systems managers. It is helpful if, before the team starts work on the project, some time can be spent on team building.

Some large companies even arrange for such a group to meet in a hotel for a day or two to take part in a special seminar. This is to give each member the opportunity to express the concerns, as well as hopes, that exist whenever changes are foreshadowed and particularly when members of different disciplines work together for the first time. It can also be helpful to have present someone from outside the team, perhaps the personnel manager, to act as a catalyst.

Appropriate training is of paramount importance, not merely of the project team but of all the line managers and computer managers, planners and programmers who are to be concerned with the use of the computer:

(*a*) The computer staff need not only to be skilled in their computer techniques, they also need to be trained in business management and given an understanding of such aspects as accounting, costing, forecasting, business planning and operations management.

(*b*) Line managers, on the other hand, have to be brought to understand computer techniques, not so that they can apply them but so that they learn something of the problems of the specialist and are able to contribute to the discussion and solution of computer problems.

Finally, the management development policy of the company should provide career paths to allow interchange between computer managers and those of other functions.

For the smaller business, the directing team will necessarily be smaller. Indeed, it may consist only of the managing executive but, ideally, he should be supported by reliable lieutenants. There may not need to be a computer specialist since the business will not be large enough to sustain one and will, no doubt, rely on standard programs supplied by the manufacturer or by a software supplier. The prime requirement is an open attitude of mind rather than extensive training which, in any case, would not be practicable for the head of a small business. Ideally, he and his lieutenants should attend a short computer appreciation course related to the smaller business.

The tasks then to be performed are:

(*a*) select a limited number of suitable suppliers;

(*b*) examine a range of data-processing equipment suited to the needs of the business;

(*c*) examine the standard programs available for the particular business; some software suppliers specialize in particular computers and others in particular industries;

(*d*) make judgements on the support services offered by each supplier;

(*e*) try to get the experience of other small concerns which use the equipment and programs.

The process of examining estimates of costs and savings is an exacting one because of its significance to the future of the business. Consideration should be given to obtaining the advice of a consultant with experience of computer operations in small firms. Alternatively, and less expensive, may be to obtain advice from staff in a nearby polytechnic or technical college which has a school of data processing; staff members are usually well informed and are glad to extend their contacts with operating businesses.

Off-setting factors

In order to obtain the advantages offered it is necessary to change attitudes as well as to be aware of additional cost liabilities.

Forethought   There is a need for precise planning and rigid operational discipline. A clerk's working methods can be changed immediately by verbal instruction, but the computer requires a program which may take weeks or even months to prepare. A clerk could interpret information received by a variety of means, but the computer demands data in an exact form.

Because of the need for precise planning and programming, computer systems are comparatively inflexible. Unless the program and computer facilities provide for interrogation of the data held in the backing storage, it may be more difficult to produce random information at short notice. This has always presented a difficulty in any office; in an office where the computer takes the work in one operation from the original data to the finished results this difficulty is accentuated. In designing any procedure, therefore, due weight must be given to possible demands for special information and plans made for dealing with them.

Planning and programming cost   It is advisable to develop an open attitude to the use of standard programs even though this may involve changes in practices, procedures and forms layout. The preparation of special programs is time-consuming and expensive. To make the necessary plans and to write the associated programs may be measured in man-months or even man-years. Moreover, it is difficult to foresee all the problems which will arise and experience shows that the costs of planning are often greatly underestimated. It is all the more important, therefore, to relate these costs to the expected usage of a program.

One approach to this aspect is to apply some such formula as the following:

$$\frac{\text{Cost of program}}{\text{Number of usages}} = \text{Cost per usage}$$

The cost of the program is the cost of:

(a) the time spent by the systems analysts and programmers, being salaries, incidentals and overheads; and

(b) the computer time spent in testing and proving the program.

The elements of cost discussed on pages 353–4 are all pertinent: staff, machines and equipment maintenance, stationery and sundries, premises and installation costs.

HUMAN ASPECTS OF COMPUTER USAGE

It is to be expected that any major technological innovation will have its effects upon the human way of life. Whilst there are wider social aspects, business has its own problems arising from the effects upon individuals and on the organizational structure.

Managers at all levels have to understand what the computer can do for them—and also what it cannot do. They must accept its inflexibilities and learn to determine their requirements well in advance. They must appreciate how to interpret the information provided to them and how to make correct decisions based on it. Attitudes and working methods must be adapted to enable the computer to take its proper place as an opportunity rather than a master or an enemy.

Those below management levels have also to adapt themselves. For example, a number of branches might be provided with terminals linked with a central computer. Those working in the branches would transmit data and in return receive balances, totals, and other calculated results. If they are unable to accept these as correct and work to them without seeing the supporting details, the scheme will fail.

The solution to these human problems lies generally along three main paths:

(a) Guiding the period of transition. As soon as there is an intention to change to computer methods, all levels of the staff who will be affected by the change, or who may think they will be affected, must be kept informed of the plans and of the company's intentions as to job opportunities, retraining and, if need be, redundancy. It is rarely too early to inform the staff even although the plans may still be tentative. Moreover, managers, supervisors and all other levels must continue to be informed at intervals. As plans develop, opportunities should be created to demonstrate plans and equipment.

(b) Integration and training. Throughout the development period, training should take place at all levels and in all functions to bring about understanding and collaboration (see page 155).

(c) Attention to output. Particular regard must be given to producing the output to be used by people in a form that is acceptable to them. Experience shows that whilst planners and programmers can be relied upon to take care to ensure accurate input and processing they, and those who will use the output, often fail to give adequate attention to the form of the output until there are complaints about having to handle cumbersome and incomprehensible tabulations.

9 Miscellaneous equipment

For routine systems in the medium or large-sized organization, the tendency is for data processing to be carried out by means of the computers and electronic accounting machines described in Chapter 8.

In the smaller offices, data-processing equipment may consist of adding machines, calculators, mechanical book-keeping machines and the manifold posting board. These may also be found in the larger offices for casual use or for system use where the volume of data is such that the more complex equipment is uneconomic.

These smaller, cheaper means of data processing are the tools whereby clerks can achieve greater productivity. As compared with the equivalent unaided manual and mental processes, mechanical and electronic devices offer many advantages including:

(*a*) *higher working speeds*, which can be maintained over longer periods without the effects of fatigue being felt;

(*b*) *greater accuracy* because mental fatigue is avoided;

(*c*) *less skill and concentration* demanded.

With the increasing use of electronics, the cost of equipment has become less significant than its ability to increase a clerk's productivity. In such a situation, every clerk should be given the best tools available, recognizing that they may well prove economic even though used only part of the time. It must also be recognized that it may be beneficial to scrap and replace obsolescent machines, even though they are not worn out.

ADDING–LISTING MACHINES

The mechanical adding–listing machine has a long history and was the foundation of the whole family of devices including mechanical cash registers, accounting machines and punched-card tabulators. With the advent of electronics, mechanical adding and subtracting has become obsolescent but simple machines are still produced.

They add, subtract and provide a printed record on a tally roll or on a form. Most have the standard ten-digit keyboard, and amounts set up on this are transferred to the adding register and printed by the operation of a function (+ or −) key. By means of a *total* lever or key, the total may be cleared from the register and printed. On some models a sub-total to date may be printed, leaving the amount in the register for further items to be accumulated.

Some machines have a full keyboard with a column of keys numbered 1 to 9 for each digital position. When used intensively, the full keyboard may be faster in operation because all keys representing a number of several digits can be depressed at the same time. It is, of course, necessary for the operator to be trained and practised in this method.

Adding–listing machines equipped with paper-tape punches or optical character-printing heads can be used for recording data for subsequent computer input whilst accumulating an immediately available control total.

ELECTRONIC CALCULATORS

The electronic calculator is cheap and easily operated by anyone having a knowledge of the basic rules of arithmetic. Little training in its use is necessary; dexterity and regular practice in operation are relatively unimportant. It is, therefore, a machine which can usefully be provided for any clerk whose duties include casual calculation.

Electronic calculators are available in great variety as to capacity, number of accumulating registers (or memories) and automatic features. The more expensive calculator is not necessarily the best for a particular job. Before selecting one, it is advisable to define carefully the work that is to be done in terms of the size of numbers to be processed, the nature of the calculations and the extent of repetition of similar calculations.

Every model has a ten-digital keyboard with keys for automatic and instant multiplication, division, addition and subtraction. Among the variable aspects are:

(a) the keyboard arrangement and the extent of provision for percentages, constants, square roots, decimal points, reciprocals and other mathematical needs;

(b) the size, clarity and convenience of display panels for factors and results;

(c) the number of registers (or memories) and the means by which data are entered to and recalled or removed from a register;

(d) the number of digits that can be held in the registers;

(e) the power source and, where not on mains, the method of recharging batteries;

(f) the extent to which, and the means by which, a program of operating instructions can be held so that, upon the entry of the variable factors, a long and complicated series of calculations can be carried out without the delays that would be incurred by further operator intervention.

Figs 89 and 90 illustrate examples of electronic calculators.

(a) Desk display

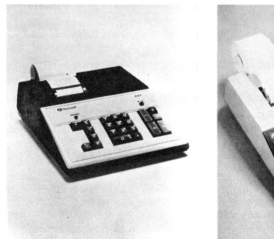

(b) Desk printer   (c) Programmable printer

Fig. 89   Commercial electronic calculators (*Courtesy of Rockwell International Ltd.*)

Electronic programmable calculators

Some calculators have, in addition to built-in sub-routines, the facility to be programmed to enable more complicated routines to be carried out automatically. Figure 90c illustrates a calculator that can be fed by

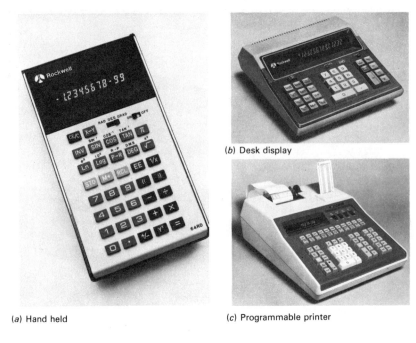

(b) Desk display

(a) Hand held   (c) Programmable printer

Fig. 90   Scientific electronic calculators (*Courtesy of Rockwell International Ltd.*)

magnetic card with scientific programs of up to 1000 steps; it can have up to eighty data registers.

Electronic printing calculators

Electronic printing calculators provide printed records of both factors and results. All the facilities provided on the electronic calculators described above are available except that the printed tally roll replaces, or is provided in addition to, the display panel (Figs 89b, 89c and 90c).

MECHANICAL CALCULATORS

The speed and convenience of electronic calculators has rendered most earlier machines and devices obsolescent. As some will still be found in use, the following is a brief outline of their nature.

Key-driven calculators   On this type of machine the result is read from dials; it is sometimes described as a non-listing adding machine. These machines have a full keyboard with a column of keys numbered 1 to 9 for each digital position.

As the keys are depressed, the digits they represent are added in total dials so that no function key is required in its operation other than to clear totals from the dials at the end of an adding run. Machines may be provided with two sets of dials to provide batch totals and grand totals.

Although a key-driven calculator can be used for addition, subtraction, division and multiplication, by comparison with an electronic calculator it is only effective for adding. Indeed, in the hands of a trained operator it enables adding to be performed more rapidly than by any other form of equipment. Other than for adding, the operation of these machines is not automatic: subtraction, division and multiplication require extensive training, regular practice and some mental work on the part of the operator. Subtraction is performed by complementary addition; multiplication is carried out by a form of repetitive addition; whilst division involves various methods of repetitive complementary subtraction. All three can be carried out far more rapidly by the electronic calculator.

Rotary calculators   These machines were designed for multiplication and division rather than addition and subtraction. Essentially, they consist of the following parts:

(a) a setting register to hold a factor for repeated addition or subtraction in the product register;

(b) a product register which can be moved in relation to the amount in the setting register to raise or lower its power;

(c) a rotary mechanism to enable an amount in the setting register to be added in the product register by a clockwise rotation and subtracted by an anti-clockwise rotation;

(d) a revolution counter to show the number of times an amount has been added or subtracted;

(e) dials from which the results are read.

Compared with the electronic calculator, the operation is laborious and very slow.

READY RECKONERS

These are of particular value where the same calculations are made repeatedly. Provided that the factors and result can be located quickly as a single reference, the process may well be faster than machine calculation. In invoicing, for example, the price record might be extended as a ready reckoner, giving the values of various normal quantities. Pricing and valuation can then be done as one operation.

MECHANICAL BOOK-KEEPING MACHINES

Mechanical book-keeping machines have been largely replaced by their electronic equivalents but are still used in some offices, particularly those of small organizations. For the purpose of a general description, it is convenient to deal with three aspects: keyboards, carriages and calculating facilities.

Keyboards   Most book-keeping machines have the standard ten keyboard, but some have a full keyboard with the keys numbered from 1 to 9 arranged in columns. In addition, there are usually a few *limited description keys* which, when depressed, cause abbreviations to be printed, for example INV for invoice, GDS for goods, CSH for cash, DIS for discount. These are satisfactory for posting ledger accounts, stock records and preparing wages records, where figures are of prime importance.

The keyboard can also include a standard typewriter keyboard to replace or supplement the limited description keys. With the facility for typing full descriptions, the applications of the posting machines may be extended to include, for example, invoicing.

Most machines have an automatic date-printing device which can be set up at the beginning of the day and remain unchanged throughout. Alternatively, a set of date keys enables the date to be changed for each item, if necessary.

The reference number may be entered on a special non-adding section on the keyboard. If this is not available, reference numbers can be entered from the ordinary keyboard with the use of a non-add key, which causes figures to be printed but not added. Some machines can be set up by control bars (see below, Calculating facilities) so that the sequence in which numbers are entered determines whether or not they are added.

Carriages   Most machines have a controlled carriage which moves automatically from one position to the next, and finally restores itself to the starting position. The carriage can include special attachments to ensure correct registration of forms of different sizes, so that by means of carbon paper, entries made on the top form are repeated on the forms underneath.

Some machines have carriages into which a number of forms can be inserted side by side. Once the keyboard has been operated, the printing processes are repeated in different positions so that all the forms bear original impressions and no carbon paper is used.

Calculating facilities   The calculating mechanism is built into the body of the machine and consists of two or more adding mechanisms to enable balances to be calculated and postings to be totalled. Machines can, however, have twenty or more registers for calculating and analysis purposes. Balances are printed either upon the depression of a single key, or automatically when the carriage moves to the appropriate position.

On most machines it is possible to carry out a variety of jobs by means of interchangeable control bars or other devices to activate carriage movements and use of the registers.

By-product output   Some models can be linked to paper tape punches (see page 124) so as to produce input for a computer used for a subsequent and related function. For example, whilst invoices are being prepared, *by-product* output can provide data for stock control, sales analysis and sales accounting. For this purpose, transactions, items and customers are designated by code number as well as, or instead of, by name.

POSTING BOARDS

Data processing generally, if not always, leads to the preparation of more than one type of record. One of the inherent benefits of the computer is that it is able to take in data once, store them and then process them to produce as many different results as may be necessary. This benefit, to a lesser degree, is provided by the book-keeping machine in that one keyboard entry may produce a journal or proof sheet, ledger folios and statements or remittance advices.

The small office may not have enough work to justify even the simplest book-keeping machine. It can, however, obtain some of its advantages by using a manifold posting board on which to make hand entries, and an adding machine to arrive at the necessary balances and totals.

The posting board (see Fig. 93 on page 177 and Fig. 96 on page 203) consists of a base board to which papers or cards can be held in various positions by pegs passing through punched holes, or by some form of clip. In the process of posting a sales ledger, for example, a journal/proof sheet is attached to the board and covered with a sheet of carbon paper. The customer's ledger card on which the first posting is to be made is selected and attached to the board so that the next vacant line on it corresponds with the next vacant line on the proof sheet. The statement form for the customer, with carbon paper behind it, is then similarly lined up and attached over the ledger card. A single entry made by hand with a ball-pen will appear on all three forms. If the old and new balances are written in, the journal/proof sheet can be totalled at the end of the posting run and used as a check on accuracy similar to that provided by a book-keeping machine. The same board can be used for a variety of systems, for example:

(*a*) in preparing a payroll and simultaneously producing the tax-record card and payslip for the employee;

(*b*) in keeping material stock records and simultaneously producing job, batch or process cost records;

(*c*) in writing cheques and simultaneously posting the cash book.

The ingenious design of forms and the entry of key code numbers can enable accuracy to be checked and controlled with little effort.

The system is sometimes called 'three-in-one' but this is misleading. The number of forms entered at the same time may be less or more than three, the only limiting factor being the number of satisfactory carbon copies obtainable with an acceptable grade of paper or card.

The manufacturers of posting boards usually supply standard forms for common systems such as accounting, payroll and stock control. For the smaller office, such systems may be found both satisfactory and economical.

Part 3
Financial and accounting services

The purpose of this part is to deal in broad outline with one of the prime functions of the office: the financial and accounting services. The main headings are:

Sales invoicing
Sales accounting
Purchases
Cash control
Wages
Stock control
Production records
Management information
Insurance

The principal intention is to establish purposes and, whilst in each chapter reference is made to some common methods and common forms used in relation to each subject, this is only to give some indication of the kind of problems which arise in fulfilling these purposes.

In studying basic systems, it is best firstly to consider each separately and in terms of operations such as might be carried out manually or with the aid of simple machines and devices. When the more advanced machines described in Part 2 are employed, these same operations have to be performed, but advantage may be taken of a computer's ability to integrate systems which are similar in nature, or which make use of the same original data.

10 Sales invoicing

Clerical services in regard to sales range from the initial handling of customers' orders, through the many operations relating to their execution and the collection of payment, to the provision of information required to stimulate future orders. This chapter is concerned with the preparation of the invoice and the other clerical work necessary to get the customer's order executed. The subsequent accounting processes are dealt with in Chapter 11 (Sales accounting).

THE PURPOSE

Whilst the prime purpose of an invoice is to inform the customer of his indebtedness, the operation of making out the invoice is often the key to the provision of important information for many other sections of the business. The following list gives the principal departments interested and the purposes served:

(a) *The factory* may want advice of goods to be produced.

(b) *The warehouse* may want advice of goods to be drawn from stock.

(c) *The dispatch and transport departments* may want details of goods to be packed and shipped, and may require acknowledgement of receipt from the customer.

(d) *The customer*, in addition to notification of his indebtedness, may require advice of shipment or delivery.

(e) *The accounts office* will want to know the amount to be charged and collected from the customer.

(f) *The sales or marketing department* may want analyses of sales and records of business with individual customers for use in planning and control.

THE MEANS

If the various requirements noted above are to be met economically and effectively, careful thought must be given to the means to be adopted. The operation of invoicing should be combined with the provision of as much as is practicable of the information required in the execution and delivery of orders. Merely to make numerous copies of the order or invoice and provide them to all concerned is not sufficient. Such a method is apt to cause excessive cost through wasted clerical effort since, whilst modern equipment makes it easy and cheap to take additional copies, the mere existence of these copies involves increased handling costs and may lead to duplicate records being kept in different parts of the organization. The better practice is to arrange for the invoicing section to provide other departments with the required information in whatever form is best suited to their purposes and to discourage the origination of records elsewhere.

In the following pages some of the more common practices in relation to invoicing are considered.

Forms

The principal forms used are the order, the delivery note and the invoice.

Order   Many businesses encourage the use of their own order forms, particularly when orders are taken personally by salesmen. The order form may be nothing more than a headed sheet providing a blank space for details. Alternatively, it may be pre-printed with the range of goods available and may contain elaborate conditions relating to warranties, delivery, discounts and payment. Many orders are, of course, received on the customer's own order form or by letter.

Delivery note   Goods sent to a customer are normally accompanied by a delivery note (which may be a copy of the invoice) stating what goods are being delivered. This need only state quantity and description, without either price or value. Sometimes the customer is asked to sign a copy of the note as an acknowledgement of receipt of the goods.

Invoice   This is a notification to the customer of his indebtedness. It should be a clear and concise statement of the goods or services charged, together with the price, value, any additional charges for transport and other services and any taxes chargeable.

Method

The method will be determined by the particular needs of the business and, since no two cases are exactly alike, it would not be appropriate to describe any one particular system. It is best, therefore, to consider the fundamental needs and some of the ways in which these are met.

Acceptance of orders   When an order is received, the following tasks have usually to be carried out:

(a) *General scrutiny* to ensure that the order is complete and intelligible and that descriptions, code numbers etc. are correct.

(*b*) *Terms and conditions*, including those printed on the customer's order form, are checked to see that they are acceptable.

(*c*) *Availability* of goods is checked, or if they are not stocked, the possibility of obtaining or manufacturing them.

(*d*) *Credit* to be allowed to the customer is checked, unless cash has been received with the order.

It is sometimes the practice to pass orders to the sales department for general scrutiny and acceptance of terms and conditions, to the warehouse for availability check, and then to the sales ledger section for credit sanction. The movement and delay which this procedure involves can be avoided if the tasks are carried out by one clerk at one time. The order acceptance clerk is provided with lists of the goods *not* available and of the customers *not* to be given credit. His function is then to extract and refer to the appropriate department only those orders for goods or customers appearing on his 'stop lists'; other orders can go forward for action.

In some mechanized systems, the stopping of orders which cannot be executed in the normal way is achieved by withdrawing punched cards or addressing plates from files so that they cannot be used, or by inserting coded instructions in computer data files. Such automatic stops reduce the possibility of human error.

Invoice preparation   The procedure can vary greatly from simple manual methods to the highly automatic operations of a computer. It can also be broken down into stages so that different clerks using different machines or devices contribute to the ultimate invoice. In any case, the basic document is the order form and it is common practice to use this to assemble the information which is eventually to appear on the invoice. The processes, which may or may not be carried out separately, are as follows:

(*a*) *Prices and terms*   Prices, trade discounts, tax rates (if any), delivery charges etc. are checked if they have been entered by the customer or, if not already entered, inserted and checked.

(*b*) *Calculation*   The quantity of each item is multiplied by its price and the amount entered. The amounts are then totalled. Trade discount and tax calculations may be made on each item or on the invoice total according to custom, which varies from trade to trade. All calculations, including the final net total, should be checked.

Calculation may be by machine, but where prices are fixed and the range of quantities ordered is limited, specially prepared ready reckoners may save time by permitting the pricing clerk to enter the price and value together.

(c) *Writing the invoice* (*and associated documents*)   Normally, as an invoice is written, additional copies are taken to serve as, for example:

(i) *delivery note*, on which prices and values may be omitted or obliterated;
(ii) *sales ledger posting copy* for use in posting the customer's account and retained for audit and record purposes;
(iii) *stock record posting copy*;
(iv) *sales record copy* to be filed in the sales department.

The method used in writing the invoice will depend to some extent on the number of copies required. Care should be taken not to produce more copies than are strictly necessary. It may be found, for example, that the sales department could file the copy used for stock record posting after that task has been done. Possible methods are as follows:

(a) *By handwriting*   Where the volume of invoices is small and the details to be written are brief, manual methods may be the most economical. Normally, however, not more than three legible copies can be obtained. Sets of forms may be made up as manifold books or as continuous stationery for use in a manifold register (see page 101).

(b) *By typewriting*   The typewriting of invoices is commonplace and permits more legible copies to be produced. In addition to improved neatness and legibility as compared with handwriting, typewriting is likely to be quicker when long descriptions are necessary. Some electric typewriters can be equipped with punched paper-tape output so that contents of the invoice may subsequently be fed into a computer as data for accounting, stock control and sales analysis purposes.

(c) *By addressing machine*   Addressing plates or stencils are prepared for each item normally sold and for each quantity normally ordered. Quantity, description, price and value are recorded and the invoice is prepared by selecting the appropriate plates and printing from them on to the invoice form. This method may be advantageous where the number of items sold and the range of quantities ordered is restricted.

(d) *By other simple methods*   Where more copies are required than can conveniently be produced by hand- or machine-written methods, duplicating or photocopying processes may be employed.

(e) *By computer*   The simplest visible record computer is sometimes called an invoicing computer. Consisting of a typewriter connected with an electronic calculator with limited storage capacity, it is particularly suited to invoicing as a task in isolation. The operator can type the details of customer and of goods or services supplied and, using the separate digital keyboard, put in quantities, prices, discount rates etc. The calculation, addition and subtraction processes are then automatic, and control totals can also be accumulated. By adding a suitable punched or magnetic-recording output, selected information can be extracted to be used as input data for further computer processing. Using more sophisticated visible-record computers, some fixed data may be retrieved from storage and typed automatically in response to codes entered through the keyboard, e.g. customer's name and address, descriptions and prices.

As a further development, the visible-record computer can be adapted to combine the writing of the invoice with the posting of the customer's personal account or the up-dating of a warehouse stock record.

When using a mainframe computer, the fixed data will normally all be stored and the current data reduced to the minimal identifying codes and quantities. The computer will then produce the invoices and, from the same data, up-date the sales ledger and stock control records, prepare sales analyses, commission records etc. Invoicing is then but one of a series of related operations. If the sales ledger and stock records are on line when the invoicing is done, the processes may include credit control, checks on availability of stock and the preparation of warehouse assembly and loading lists.

Addressing the invoice   In the simpler systems the writing of the customer's name and address on the invoice is often done as a separate operation by addressing machine. It is, of course, only economical to do this where the same customers are invoiced regularly so that plates or stencils can be used repeatedly. Where this method is adopted, it is usual to take advantage of it to address labels, head ledger cards and statements, prepare lists of customers etc.

Export invoicing   It is regrettable, but true, that whenever goods are sold across international boundaries the number of documents to be produced increases substantially. In collaboration with business men, the UK Government has approved and published a system for producing complete sets of export documents from a duplicator master copy and it may be found convenient to adopt this.

Layout of invoice forms   The invoice is a form which must serve the needs of the customer as well as of the seller. It is, therefore, courteous to conform as far as possible with general commercial practice as well as the principles of good form design.

11 Sales accounting

Following the consideration of sales invoicing and related operations, this chapter is concerned with sales accounting, including charging and collecting payment, sales statistics and information for reference.

THE PURPOSE

Stated briefly, the principal purposes of the sales accounting records are:

(*a*) to ensure that all the goods invoiced are charged accurately to the right customer;

(*b*) to ensure that payment is collected in accordance with the terms agreed;

(*c*) to provide information concerning debtors and sales.

THE MEANS

The keeping of customers' ledger accounts, whilst not the only means of achieving the objects mentioned above, is the commonly adopted practice.

When the number of credit customers is large, it is usual for their accounts to be kept separately from the purchase book and other accounts of the business. Since they relate to customers, it is important that sales ledger accounting shall be carried out expeditiously and accurately. Particular attention has therefore been paid to creating efficient sales ledger methods. Much of what is said here, however, applies equally to other types of ledger. Computer or other mechanized accounting is widely used for sales ledger purposes and a brief account of its principles is given here.

Forms

Owing to the impact of mechanization, the forms used originally, and as described in simple book-keeping theory, have altered in appearance considerably.

Sales journal A principle of book-keeping is that sales are first entered into a journal or daybook, which serves as a diary of sales transactions. From the journal, the amounts are posted to the debit of the individual

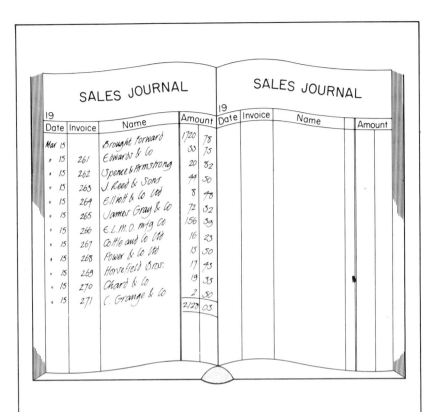

Fig. 91 Sales journal compared with invoices and tally roll

(a) Hand-posted sales ledger account

Anderson and Co Ltd

April 1	To Balance	B/d	24	18	April 9	By Cash	354	23	58
„ 4	„ Goods	87	3	18	„ „	„ Discount	82		60
„ 18	„ „	106	12	14	May 1	„ Balance	c/d	15	32
		£	39	50			£	39	50
May 1	To Balance	B/d	15	32	May 6	By Cash	376	14	93
„ 3	„ Goods	123	7	34	„ „	„ Discount	85		39
„ 14	„ „	146	22	23	„ 22	„ Returns	162	2	23
„ 20	„ „	158	26	37	June 1	„ Balance	c/d	53	71
		£	71	26			£	71	26
June 1	To Balance	B/d	53	71	June 2	By Returns	178	4	63
„ „	„ Goods	172	24	63	„ 24	„ Cash	394	47	86
„ 2	„ „	177	18	68	„ „	„ Discount	91	1	22
„ 24	„ „	192	37	27					

(a) Hand-posted sales ledger account

Name ANDERSON & CO LTD. Acct. No. 1443.

Address 77 ARCHWAY ROAD Sheet No. 6.
HIGHGATE. N.

Terms: 2½%

Date		Particulars	Debit	Credit	Balance	Previous balance
1 APR					24.18 T	
4 APR	GDS	667. SLOUGH.	3.18		27.36 T	24.18
9 APR	CSH	1,022.		23.58		27.36
9 APR	DIS			.60	3.18 T	3.18
18 APR	GDS	714. SLOUGH.	12.14		15.32 T	3.18
3 MAY	GDS	787. PERIVALE.	7.34		22.66 T	15.32
6 MAY	CSH	1,665.		14.93		22.66
6 MAY	DIS			.39	7.34 T	22.66
14 MAY	GDS	854. NOTTINGHAM.	22.23		29.57 T	7.34
20 MAY	GDS	965. SOUTHEND.	26.37		55.94 T	29.57
22 MAY	RET	94.		2.23	53.71 T	55.94
1 JUN	GDS	1,214. LEIGH.	24.63		78.34 T	53.71
2 JUN	GDS	1,296. PERIVALE.	18.68		97.02 T	78.34
2 JUN	RET	425.		4.63	92.39 T	97.02
24 JUN	CSH	2,141.		47.86		92.39
24 JUN	DIS			1.22	43.31 T	92.39
24 JUN	GDS	1,474. SLOUGH.	37.27		80.58 T	43.31

(b) Machine-posted sales ledger account

Fig. 92 Comparison of hand- and machine-posted ledgers

Fig. 93   Manifold posting board for ledger (*Courtesy of Lamson Paragon Ltd.*)

customer's personal account. The totals of all the sales entered in the journal are credited to the sales account of the business, thus completing the double entry.

In mechanized methods, it may still be wise to have a 'journal' of some kind, providing a control total with which the machine total can be reconciled. This journal may be no more than an adding-machine tally roll of invoice totals, sometimes known as a pre-list, supported by a batch of invoice copies (Fig. 91). If the adding machine is fitted with a paper tape or other coded output, the preparation of the journal or pre-list may also provide the means of feeding data into the computer.

Where an accounting machine or visible-record computer is used, the journal may be the proof sheet bearing copies of the entries made on the ledger folios. Where a mainframe computer is used, with direct data entry, a printed journal may be produced, listing a day's entries. This provides a means of routine checking and auditing.

Ledger   The form of the ledger has also changed. Ledgers, whether posted by hand, by accounting machine or by visible-record computer, usually consist of loose-leaf sheets or cards, one for each account. Instead of having a debit and a credit side, there is a columnar arrangement permitting the balance to be shown after each entry (Fig. 92*b*).

Statement   Customers who settle their accounts periodically are normally sent a statement showing the amount outstanding on the due date (often the end of the calendar month). Cash discounts are deducted from the statement rather than from the invoice. If a ledger is posted by hand with the use of a manifold posting board (see Fig. 93), the statement is produced simultaneously, whereas in a computer application statements are likely to be produced as a separate print-out. In any system which produces a form of ledger folio, the statement may be a photocopy of this.

Method

Sales ledgers may be kept by a variety of methods ranging from simple hand posting to the use of computers. In the paragraphs which follow, the basic operations common to all systems are described and it is then shown how these are performed by the principal manual and mechanized methods.

Basic entries and operations   The typical entries to be made in sales ledgers and their sources are as follows:

(*a*) goods or services sold to customers—from copy sales-invoice totals;
(*b*) goods returned by customers—from copy credit-note totals;
(*c*) payments received from customers—from cash-book entries;
(*d*) corrections and adjustments—from journal entries.

(*1*) *Journalizing*   The first operation is to journalize each type of entry separately, either by hand in the traditional manner or by machine listing. The journal totals serve as a check on subsequent operations and can be posted to control accounts.

(*2*) *Ledger posting*   The second operation is to post each separate entry to the appropriate customer's account in the debit or credit area as necessary. Each entry should show the date of the transaction, sufficient coded or written information to identify the transaction and link it with its source, and the amount.

(*3*) *Balancing*   The third operation is that of balancing and proving the accounts. The opening balance of each account (normally debit) is adjusted by adding to it the debit entries and subtracting the credit entries to arrive at a new closing balance. The same procedure is followed in the control account which has been posted in batch total from the journals. If all the entries have been made correctly, the balance of the control account will equal the sum of all the balances on the individual customers' accounts.

An arithmetical 'proof' of this kind is not, however, complete. It is possible that one error may have offset the effect of another or that, whilst the correct amount was posted, it was posted to the wrong account. Complete accuracy can rarely, if ever, be guaranteed. The objective should be to make the best possible use of visual and automatic checks to cover the essential elements in the system (see pages 363 and 364).

(4) *Statement*   The final operation is the preparation of a copy of the customer's account, known as a statement of account, which is sent to the customer, usually monthly. Although many regard this form primarily as a reminder that payment is due, it is part of the proving system. If an entry has been made in the wrong account, it is likely that one at least of the two customers involved will challenge the balance shown.

Manual methods   For the small business or professional partnership, the traditional hand-posted journal and ledger may be adequate. Speed and accuracy can, however, be improved in the simplest system by pre-listing and balancing with the aid of an adding–listing machine.

A more highly developed manual method is that which uses a *manifold posting board* (Fig. 93). This is a metal or plastic board which provides a hard writing surface and has down one side, pegs or other devices for holding forms firmly in position. A proof sheet, which may also serve as the journal, is placed on the board and held. To make a posting, the ledger folio is selected and fixed over the proof sheet so that the next vacant line on the folio is directly over the next vacant line on the proof sheet. Similarly, the statement form may also be aligned over these two. The rulings on all three forms coincide. The entry is made on the statement and carbon copied on to the ledger and proof sheet below. To facilitate daily proofs of accuracy, the new balance on an account is calculated and entered when postings are made, as is the case with mechanized accounting.

At the end of each batch of postings, the proof sheet showing carbon copies of all the entries and balances is totalled. If the opening balances on active accounts have also been entered on the proof sheet, the following checks on accuracy can be made immediately, without waiting for the monthly closing of accounts.

(*a*) the totals of entries made can be compared with the totals of pre-lists of posting media;

(*b*) the total of opening balances on active accounts, adjusted by the totals of entries made, can be compared with the total of closing balances;

(*c*) if need be, the individual entries can be checked conveniently from the proof sheet instead of from the individual ledger folios.

The manifold posting board affords some of the advantages of machine accounting in that several forms are entered simultaneously and a proof sheet is provided for daily checks. Because new balances are calculated at each posting and statements are built up as exact replicas of the ledger folios, the monthly tasks of closing accounts and issuing statements are completed more quickly.

Accounting-machine methods The accounting or ledger-posting machine was described in Chapter 9. After pre-listing the posting media to obtain control totals, the operator posts to each active account folio in turn by:

(*a*) picking up and entering on the keyboard the balance shown on the account;

(*b*) feeding into the machine the ledger card and statement form and aligning these with the proof sheet;

(*c*) reading from the posting medium and setting up on the keyboard the date, reference number, description code (or detail), and the amount as debit or credit.

The machine will then print the entry to appear on the proof sheet, ledger folio and statement, and automatically calculate and print the new balance. Registers are also available for the machine to accumulate and, at the end of the posting run, print out the control totals of postings and balances.

Visible record computer methods Whilst larger computers may be used for sales accounting as part of a wider scheme, the smaller of the visible-record computers are more likely to be used for ledger posting as a separate task. The visible-record computer is described and illustrated in Chapter 8. The forms used may be similar in design to those used with an accounting machine. The operation may be wholly through a keyboard or might be made partially automatic. Opening balances may be picked up from magnetic stripes on the ledger cards; data relating to the postings may be fed in by punched or magnetic records.

Mainframe computer methods The larger mainframe computer is not suited to up-dating individual account cards as entries are made, even though it is technically possible on some machines to have a special terminal for this purpose. Most systems store data and balances and print out whatever information is required on continuous stationery. Methods vary and the following is by way of example. Three disk files might be maintained:

(1) Fixed data for each account, with the current balance and possibly the balances at the end of each month for as long as two years previously; control totals.

(2) Detail of all entries made in the current financial year.

(3) Open entries, i.e. all entries not yet cleared by payment or adjustment.

From these it is possible, with the use of suitable programs, to print out the following as required:

(1) Trial balance or list of all current balances with supporting detail.

(2) Full accounts over any period of time for examination and audit.

(3) Statements of account.

(4) Details of overdue accounts.

(5) Analyses of debtors or of trade.

If required, there could be a monthly print of accounts in the traditional form.

Where the computer is able to have the sales accounting files always on line, direct data entry methods may be used by the sales office staff. With the aid of visual display units, it may also be possible for sales and accounts staff to make direct enquiries of the computer as to balances outstanding, credit ratings etc.

Allocation of duties   Whereas a book-keeper posting by hand may carry out a wide range of duties, mechanized procedures must be designed to keep the machines fully employed. The machine operator should be provided with batches of work which can be posted quickly and without interrruption.

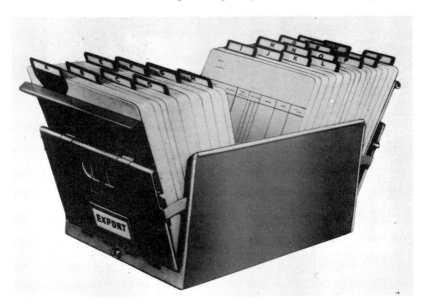

Fig. 94   Ledger-card posting tray (*Courtesy of the Copeland-Chatterson Co. Ltd.*)

One time-consuming operation is the selection of the cards on which entries are to be made from the tray in which the ledger is housed. Whilst indexing systems may be used to aid location (see Fig. 94), the operator may be relieved of this task altogether in one of two ways:

(*a*) a junior clerk can extract the cards and interleave them with the posting media so that they are ready for use, or

(*b*) a junior clerk can 'stuff' the posting media in the tray in front of the cards to which they refer.

The operator can also be relieved of the tasks of proving accuracy. Each batch of work, when completed, can be passed with its proof sheets to a senior clerk responsible for checking and balancing.

In judging the effectiveness of methods the total cost, including that of these ancillary operations, must be taken into account.

Integration of systems   Where the larger computer is used, it is unlikely that the sales accounting will be an isolated operation. Some data are likely to be drawn from the stored results of other systems, e.g. invoice totals from the invoicing system, cash receipts from the cash-control system. Other less frequent entries may be made by the normal input process.

It is of the essence of computer usage that data should be entered once only and thereafter drawn on by as many programs as necessary to give the results required. These results will, of course, be no more accurate than the data. Indeed, one error in data input could produce errors in many outputs. Whereas in a manual-accounting system, proofs of accuracy might await the end of a month when the books are closed, in a computer system the weight of endeavour must be placed on ensuring that each item of data is correct before processing is undertaken.

Where a computer is used, overdue accounts can be automatically identified and listed. Sometimes the computer is programmed automatically to write letters calling for payment, but such impersonal communications are not always as effective as a more personal approach.

Each batch of data must be controlled by a senior clerk to ensure that it is entered in the computer files and entered correctly. Usually, data are entered in the simplest form, an amount being identified by codes relating to nominal account, departmental account and personal account. The computer can be programmed to produce a journal for each batch of data, printing in clear language the significance of the codes it has been given. This can then be visually checked against the original data source. It is much quicker and more reliable to check words which have meaning than to check code numbers.

Collecting payment   Whilst there are variations from one trade to another, it is usual to expect customers to pay their accounts monthly after having had a reasonable opportunity to check the statements of account sent to them. The majority are likely to do this but there will always be some who do not settle by the due date.

The sales ledger must be examined regularly to discover those customers who are taking extended credit. This is usually the duty of a senior clerk who will write letters in an approved form calling for payment. In extreme cases, legal pressure may be necessary but this should only be applied as a last resort and after consultation with sales management.

Sales information

Sales analysis   Where an analysis of sales turnover is required by area, salesman, type of customer etc., the information can often be produced as part of the accounting procedure. Invoices might be sorted according to area etc., before pre-listing, so that the control totals provide a suitable analysis of the day's sales. The sales ledger might be divided into groups of customers according to area or type so that statistics can be extracted from the individual accounts and the control accounts.

Where a computer is used, sales data will ordinarily be stored and analyses printed at required intervals. To facilitate this, customer codes and commodity codes should be designed as logical patterns in which digital positions have significance, e.g. the first two digits of a customer's code might identify area and salesman, the third the type of customer (wholesaler, retailer etc.) and the remainder the approximate position in an alphabetical sequence of names.

Coding in a logical number language may also be useful when sorting documents for analysis by clerks using simple machine aids.

Quantity analysis   Statistics in quantity cannot usually be extracted as a by-product of the accounting processes. Simple information may be obtainable from warehouse stock records but if complex analyses are required these may have to be obtained by hand abstracting or by computer.

Customer records   It is sometimes necessary to review in detail the business done with individual customers. Where a computer is used and data are stored, there is no difficulty in producing the required information. In smaller businesses, the sales ledger expanded to record more detail of transactions may suffice. If reviews of all customers are not required regularly it may be more economical to extract information only when necessary. If, for example, copy invoices are filed in folders, one for each customer, the business done with any one can be examined or analysed quite simply.

12 Purchases

Purchasing procedures vary considerably according to the authority delegated to departmental managers. At the one extreme, the office may merely be required to receive purchase invoices already certified as correct by a departmental manager, post these to the accounts and make payment at the due time. At the other extreme, the office may have to play a much larger part in checking the invoice and otherwise seeking to prevent or disclose fraudulent practices.

Whatever the general policy of the business, there are likely to be differences in the treatment of various kinds of purchases. There may be one procedure for dealing with raw materials received into a factory store, another for capital purchases. Charges for machine maintenance, electric power, telephone service, rent or local rates may require different procedures again. All goods and services received are regarded as 'purchases', the one exception being the services of employees which are treated as 'wages' (see Chapter 14).

In this present chapter, it is assumed that the office is to play a major part in the procedures, and that the principal functions are apportioned as follows.

Purchasing Purchasing officers (or buyers) are responsible for entering into contracts for the supply of goods or services. They negotiate with suppliers on all relative matters, including quantity, quality, price, discounts, delivery charges, packaging, delivery date, and so on. The terms of purchase are notified to the office.

Receiving The department receiving the goods or services is responsible for checking these and notifying the office of the details.

Accounting and payment The office is responsible for ensuring that the business pays only for what it has received and in accordance with the terms of purchase.

THE PURPOSE

The office has four main duties in relation to purchases:

1. To ensure as far as possible that value has been received.
2. To record indebtedness and payments made.
3. To record expenditure under suitable nominal account headings.
4. To keep management accounts by department, cost centre, etc.

THE MEANS

Forms

The principal commerical forms are the buyer's order, the receiving department's 'goods received' record, the supplier's invoice, the supplier's statement, the purchase journal and the ledger.

The order   The terms of the contract are usually set out on a simple order form (Fig. 95(*a*)). This should bear:

(*a*) name and address of supplier;
(*b*) date of placing the order;
(*c*) place and date for delivery;
(*d*) precise details of goods ordered, including description, quantity and quality;
(*e*) the price including, as appropriate, discount and such additional costs as carriage, packaging, VAT and, in the case of foreign goods, customs duty;
(*f*) any other special terms;
(*g*) signature of the buyer.

In addition, the order form may be pre-printed with any terms and conditions imposed by the business in accordance with its policy, by custom of the trade, or by statutory regulations applying to the type of goods involved. Copies of the order serve to provide the office and other interested departments with information concerning the contract.

Where the terms of a purchase are complex or cover a long period, a more formal contract may be entered into, but again a copy of the relevant parts should be provided for office use.

Goods-received record   Any form used for recording the details of goods received should include:

(*a*) the name of the supplier;
(*b*) the date of receipt;
(*c*) the description and quantity of the goods;
(*d*) the condition of the goods.

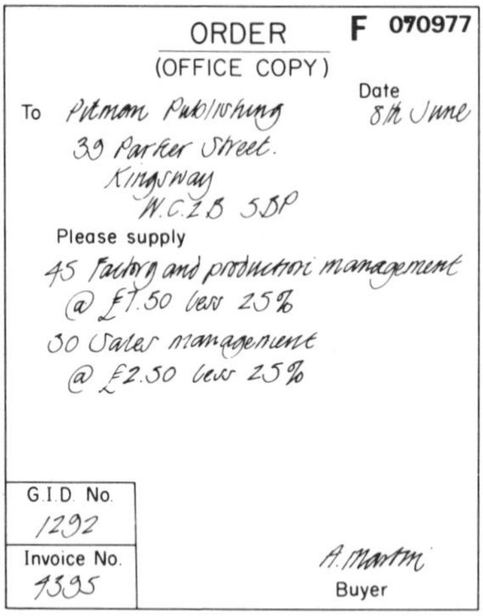

ORDER F 070977

(OFFICE COPY)

To Pitman Publishing
39 Parker Street.
Kingsway
W.C.2B 5BP

Date 8th June

Please supply

45 Factory and production management
@ £7.50 less 25%
30 Sales management
@ £2.50 less 25%

G.I.D. No. 1292

Invoice No. 4395

A. Martin
Buyer

(*a*) copy order

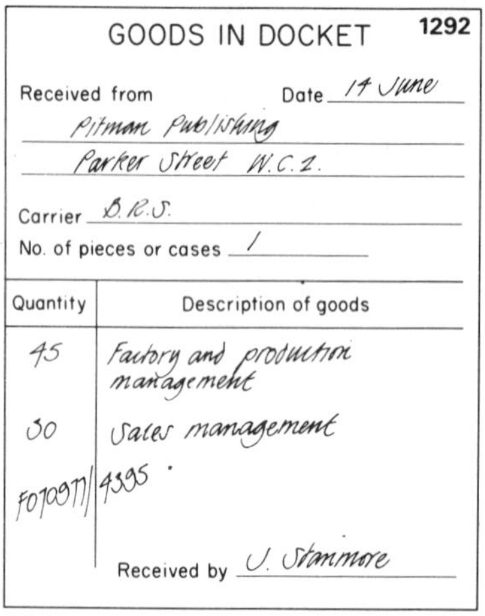

GOODS IN DOCKET 1292

Received from Pitman Publishing
Parker Street W.C.2.

Date 14 June

Carrier B.R.S.

No. of pieces or cases 1

Quantity	Description of goods
45	Factory and production management
30	Sales management
F070977	4395

Received by J. Stanmore

(*b*) goods in docket

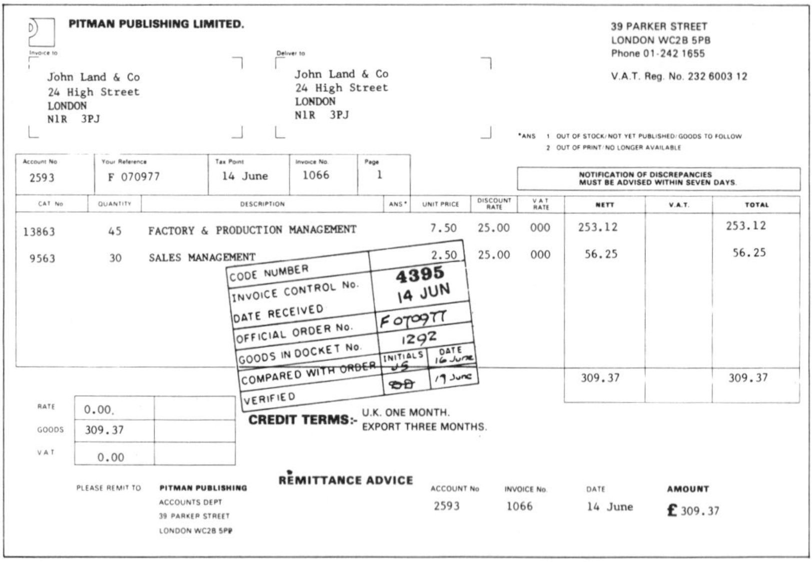

PITMAN PUBLISHING LIMITED.

39 PARKER STREET
LONDON WC2B 5PB
Phone 01-242 1655

V.A.T. Reg. No. 232 6003 12

Invoice to
John Land & Co
24 High Street
LONDON
N1R 3PJ

Deliver to
John Land & Co
24 High Street
LONDON
N1R 3PJ

*ANS 1 OUT OF STOCK/NOT YET PUBLISHED/GOODS TO FOLLOW
2 OUT OF PRINT/NO LONGER AVAILABLE

Account No	Your Reference	Tax Point	Invoice No.	Page
2593	F 070977	14 June	1066	1

NOTIFICATION OF DISCREPANCIES MUST BE ADVISED WITHIN SEVEN DAYS.

CAT No	QUANTITY	DESCRIPTION	ANS*	UNIT PRICE	DISCOUNT RATE	V.A.T RATE	NETT	V.A.T.	TOTAL
13863	45	FACTORY & PRODUCTION MANAGEMENT		7.50	25.00	000	253.12		253.12
9563	30	SALES MANAGEMENT		2.50	25.00	000	56.25		56.25
							309.37		309.37

CODE NUMBER	4395		
INVOICE CONTROL No.			
DATE RECEIVED	14 JUN		
OFFICIAL ORDER No.	F070977		
GOODS IN DOCKET No.	1292		
		INITIALS	DATE
COMPARED WITH ORDER		JS	16 June
VERIFIED		BB	19 June

RATE	0.00.	
GOODS	309.37	
VAT	0.00	

CREDIT TERMS:- U.K. ONE MONTH.
EXPORT THREE MONTHS.

PLEASE REMIT TO PITMAN PUBLISHING
ACCOUNTS DEPT
39 PARKER STREET
LONDON WC2B 5PB

REMITTANCE ADVICE

ACCOUNT No	INVOICE No.	DATE	AMOUNT
2593	1066	14 June	£ 309.37

(*c*) purchase invoice

Fig. 95

For convenience in matching with supplier's invoices a separate form may be employed for each consignment (Fig. 95(*b*)). This is called a goods in docket or goods-received note. Alternatively, where deliveries are accompanied by a supplier's delivery note, this itself may be used, certified by the official who checks the receipt of the goods.

Supplier's invoice   This is the notification from the supplier giving details of the goods and the charges relating to them (Fig. 95(c)).

Supplier's statement   This is the notification from the supplier of the amount outstanding on a specific date, usually when payment is due.

Purchase journal   This is similar to the sales journal and the principles set out on page 174 apply.

Ledger   This is similar to the sales ledger and again the principles set out on page 177 apply.

Method

The operations necessary in authorizing purchase invoices for payment are mainly manual and mental, although simple machines such as calculators may be of assistance. The accounting processes too may be less highly mechanized than in the case of the sales ledger because the number of postings made is often much smaller.

In fulfilling the purposes defined above, the methods adopted must ensure reasonable accuracy and safeguard the business against loss through fraud. It should not, however, be assumed that absolute accuracy and safety must be achieved at any cost. In recent years, some businesses have decided to accept invoices without detailed check and this development is discussed separately below. In the first place, consideration will be given to the situation in which complete checking is required.

Receiving the goods   The office needs a reliable record of goods received. It has, therefore, the duty to draw attention to any lack of facilities in other departments which make it difficult to prepare accurate goods-received notes. The mere copying of the supplier's delivery note by a clerk is not enough unless it has previously been carefully checked against the actual goods. Ideally, the check should be 'blind'; the checker should discover and record what has been received without knowing exactly what to expect to find. Proper equipment for counting, weighing, measuring etc. and for testing quality should be available.

Checking the invoice   The sequence of tasks to be carried out in the office is as follows:

(a) *Control of forms*   Copy orders and goods-received notes should be controlled by serial number to ensure that none is missing.

(b) *Check authorization*   On receipt, copy orders and goods-received notes should be scrutinized to see that they are complete and bear the signatures of authorized persons. They are then filed under suppliers' names to await the arrival of the invoices.

(*c*) *Receive invoices*   Serial reference numbers should be marked on the invoices as they are received.

(*d*) *Check goods or services* charged on the invoice against both order (or contract) and goods-received note as to quantity, quality and description.

(*e*) *Check prices, discounts and charges* for tax, delivery, containers etc. against the order (or contract).

(*f*) *Check arithmetic.*

(*g*) *Certify*   If the invoice is correct in all particulars, it should be clearly certified as in order for payment and bear the initials of the clerk responsible.

(*h*) *Cancel and cross-reference documents*   It is important to prevent the possibility of accepting a second invoice for the same transaction. The copy order and goods-received note should be endorsed as cleared, and all documents cross-referenced as an aid to audit and tracing.

In large offices, some operations such as the sorting and matching of forms may be done by junior staff, but the authorization of payment is a responsible task requiring a clerk of proved ability and relatively high grade. As a further precaution against possible fraud, a second, more senior clerk or internal auditor should at least scrutinize all invoices accepted and carry out random checks of detail.

When inaccuracies are discovered, it is usual to inform the supplier of corrections made. It should, however, be noted that letters and adjustments cost money—possibly more than the amount of the error. Clerks are often given discretion within defined limits to allow incorrect invoices to be paid as rendered.

Checking invoices for services   Where invoices are for services, as distinct from tangible goods, the checking procedure may, of necessity, be different, although the same basic principles are applied. If the office is to certify the invoice, it requires evidence that a contract was entered into and carried out.

In some cases, however, charges for services may not be capable of assessment before the work is completed. In others, payment may have to be made in advance, for example, insurance premiums and telephone rentals. If the office is unable to certify on clear evidence, the invoice must be passed to a responsible manager for authorization and possibly also to higher management for confirmation. When invoices are dealt with in this way, it is prudent for the office to keep a register of them and check to ensure that duplicates are not accepted.

Acceptance of invoices without complete check The principles applied above assume that every precaution must be taken to ensure that purchases are paid for exactly. Complete checking is, however, costly and the amount spent may exceed the value gained.

In some businesses, purchase invoices are classified according to the probability of error or fraud and varying degrees of check imposed. The following are examples of pertinent considerations:

(a) provided that the quantities and prices are correct, there is unlikely to be an arithmetical error in an invoice prepared by a computer;

(b) invoices from local authorities, public services and nationalized industries are unlikely to be deliberately fraudulent;

(c) invoices for small amounts cannot contain large errors.

Experienced senior clerks can often scrutinize invoices and see at a glance that the amount is 'about right' without checking each calculation and addition.

It is neither possible nor desirable to attempt to state rules as to when checks should or should not be applied. When checks are forgone, a risk is taken. This should be a calculated risk having regard to all the circumstances, and should be approved by top management.

Accounting Simple book-keeping theory requires that details of invoices should first be entered into a purchases journal. Each amount is then posted to the credit of the supplier's account and to the debit of a nominal account. Usually the nominal account to which each invoice is to be charged is noted on the invoice at the time when it is authorized for payment.

Many small businesses continue to use an analysed purchases journal. This is provided with a number of columns, each allotted to a different nominal account, so that instead of items having to be posted separately to the nominal accounts concerned, only the totals of the columns need be posted.

If there is any considerable volume of transactions, the journal is generally replaced by a simple machine list of invoice totals. For this purpose, the invoices are sorted into batches according to nominal accounts before listing, so that the batch totals on the list give the amount to be posted to each nominal account. In addition to the requirements of financial accounting, it may be necessary to charge purchases and expenses to departmental accounts, or to specific processes or jobs for cost-accounting purposes. If only departmental accounts are kept these can usually be treated as a subdivision of the nominal accounts and so will be dealt with when the nominal accounts are posted. If, however, it is necessary to dissect purchase invoices to specific processes or jobs, this may have to be dealt with as a separate operation. This is not always necessary, as bulk supplies of materials may be charged to a store from which issues for individual processes or jobs are in turn charged out (see Chapters 15 and 16).

Invoices are next sorted under names of suppliers, after which they are posted to the credit of suppliers' personal accounts. Until they are paid the invoices are usually held in separate files for unpaid invoices (see below).

Methods of keeping both nominal and personal accounts are similar in principle to those described for sales ledgers.

Making payment   There are alternative practices with regard to payment for purchases. Some businesses wait until the supplier's statement is received and pay only those items agreed on that statement. Others ignore suppliers' statements and pay on a fixed day each month all the invoices authorized for payment in the preceding month, regardless of whether or not a statement has been received. In this latter case, it is customary to make out a payment statement or remittance advice, which is a list of the dates and amounts of the invoices covered by the payment. A further variation is prompt payment, when invoices are paid as soon as possible after receipt, in order to obtain a cash discount.

When the supplier's statement is received, or the business's own payment statement is originated, it should be verified before payment by checking with the items posted to the supplier's account or with the corresponding original invoices. In the latter case it is customary to keep unpaid invoices separate from paid invoices. If a supplier's statement does not agree, it is customary to amend it without reference to the supplier.

When agreed, the statement is endorsed as an authority for the cashier to draw a cheque or originate a bank transfer to pay the supplier, and the invoices or the corresponding entries in the ledger are marked to indicate that they have been paid.

To reduce the possibility of fraud, it is a good practice to place into different hands the two separate responsibilities:

(a) checking the statement against the invoice or against the ledger, and
(b) drawing the cheque or originating a bank transfer.

Methods of making payment and the relative cash entries in the ledger are dealt with in the next chapter.

Using a computer   Computers provide an opportunity to remove from the task of authorizing the payment of purchase invoices much of the mental and manual work associated with it. If details of orders placed, of goods received, and of suppliers' invoices can be fed into the computer, the process of matching these sets of information and of authorizing payment can become completely automatic. Such a computer application lends itself more readily to those transactions which deal with standard or branded goods. As always, the computer should enable clerks to deal only with queries where human skills are required. Moreover, the computer application should be part of a suite of programs which also cover purchase ledgers, stock control and cost accounting.

13   Cash control

The responsibility of the office for looking after cash is, of course, well established and it is obviously necessary for the most stringent controls to be exercised, whether cash is held in the bank or in common currency. Within the office it is customary to segregate duties in this connection from all others. Normally the control of cash is the responsibility of a cashier or, in a large office, of a section under a chief cashier.

THE PURPOSE

The cashier is responsible for receiving, paying and safeguarding all moneys. Normally he is also responsible for recording these transactions in the cash book, but he does not take any part in keeping other accounts.

THE MEANS

Cash may be handled by cashiers at cash desks, by salesmen in retail shops, by travelling salesmen, by clerks handling inward mail and, or course, by the cashier's office. The differing demands of each determine the particular forms and methods to be used.

Forms

Numerous forms are used in the control of cash and often the titles given to these vary from one business to another. For the purpose of this chapter only the most common are given.

Cash book   In principle, the cash book is merely an elaborated ledger account, with the additional distinction that it also serves the purpose of a day book or journal of cash transactions. As with other accounts, the impact of modern methods has somewhat altered the original form. It is quite common, for example, for the receipts side of the cash book to be separated from the payments side.

The cash book may include separate columns for cash in hand and cash at bank or, alternatively, separate cash books may be kept for these two accounts. In addition, the cash book usually includes a column for recording discounts.

Cheques   The cheque forms provided by the banks and by which payments are made generally conform to a standard pattern. Payments may also be made by transfer through banks or National Giro.

Receipts   When payments are made by cheque, receipts are not usually required. If payment is in cash, it is normal to issue a receipt in distinctive form and to warn that this official form alone will be recognized. Receipts may be made out by machine in conjunction with other forms.

Bank paying-in slip   The banks provide their own paying-in forms covering payments into the bank. Arrangements may, however, be made with the bank to use a form especially designed to meet the needs of the business.

Cash-receipts list or book   Cash received should be recorded immediately it is received. The receipts list can be in book form, on carefully controlled loose sheets, or produced by a cash register. The making of an immediate record, even when it may not be convenient to make a complete cash-book entry, provides a safeguard against loss or misappropriation.

Method

This section is primarily concerned with the principles of control and the manner in which responsibility for handling cash is spread among several persons to reduce the possibility of fraud. The actual details of any particular system, that is, of the way in which these principles are applied, are of less significance. In each case these will depend upon the circumstances, the amount of money handled, and the extent to which opportunities for misappropriation exist. Only the more common types of transaction are mentioned.

Cash received by mail   It is not uncommon for the mail to be opened by relatively junior staff. Because any closed envelope may include some form of money (cheques, money orders, postal orders, bank notes, or even coin), the mail is, however, usually opened under the supervision of a senior and trusted employee.

Any cash received should be recorded at once on a cash-receipts list, which need show no more than the name of the sender and the amount. If the receipts are in loose-leaf form, they should be numbered and controlled.

Identifying documents received with the cash should be marked with the list folio and attached to the list together with the cash. If the only accompanying and identifying documents have to be released immediately for some other purpose, as in the case where cash accompanies an order which must be released at once for execution, further details need to be entered on the receipts list.

Uncrossed cheques, money orders, or postal orders should be immediately crossed with the name of the bank and account. As soon as possible, receipts lists and cash are passed to the cashier.

Cash received direct Circumstances vary but, where appropriate, arrangements should be made for the cash to be accompanied by some form of bill, paying-in slip, or other advice showing to what the money relates. Alternatively, every item should be entered at once on to a cash-receipts list. Cash registers are widely used for this purpose, particularly where cash is received from members of the public. Most cash registers provide a printed and totalled list of the amounts received. Dissection totals for different classes of receipts can also be provided.

Issuing receipt forms This is generally the responsibility of the cashier, and limitations should be imposed as to who have authority to sign receipts.

Payments Normally, the cashier is responsible for making all payments with the exception of petty-cash payments (see below), but he should always act upon the authority of some other official. The cashier draws cheques and may sign them but, if so, he should sign jointly with a director or some other person independent of the cashier's office. Certified authorities for the payment (for example, invoices authorized for payment) should be available when the cheques are signed. Wherever it can be assumed that the payee has a banking account, the cheque should be crossed and marked 'Account payee only'.

Cash book The cash book is kept by the cashier or carefully controlled by him if machine posted elsewhere for convenience. It should be entered without delay, preferably on the day on which receipts or payments are made or notified.

Because of its central position in the accounting system and because of the need to prevent or disclose fraud, the cash book should be designed so that every entry can be readily traced. It should also facilitate reconciliation with:

(*a*) the initial records of cash received or paid out, for example the list of remittances received by post;

(*b*) the amounts posted to contra accounts;

(*c*) the bank statement.

Manifolding methods, whether by posting board or machine, help in achieving these ends and reducing work. Using suitably designed forms, the following might be produced simultaneously:

(*a*) *Receipts cash book:* cash-book folio, bank paying-in list, ledger-posting slips and receipts (if required);

(*b*) *Payments cash book:* cash-book folio, ledger-posting slips, and cheques or bank-transfer list.

Where a computer is used for ledger-posting, the posting slips might be replaced by a punched paper-tape or other coded output from the typewriter or other machine used in writing the cash book.

Banking   It is good practice to pay cash into the bank daily. Cheques should be endorsed by the cashier, and he should compare the cheques so endorsed with the corresponding entries on the receipts list to ensure that all are paid into the bank account. If large sums are collected after the bank has closed, and there are no adequate facilities for safe-keeping on the premises, use should be made of the banker's night safe or of security services (see pages 196 and 255).

Standing orders   Where pre-determined payments must be made at regular intervals, for example rents and subscriptions, a standing order may be given to the bank to make payment at the due time. Care must be taken to note these liabilities so that management is not misled as to the cash resources available.

Direct debit   Banks operate a system whereby, authority having been received, debits to their customers' accounts will be accepted and payment made. This means that a supplier may be free to obtain immediate payment in respect of goods or services as soon as the invoice is rendered, without the delays which are normally experienced whilst clerical operations take place. This system may be convenient when regular payments of variable amounts are expected. Many businesses, however, prefer to control their bank balance and decide what shall be paid and when it shall be paid.

Balancing the cash book   Where any considerable sum of money is handled, it is usual for the cash books to be balanced daily. An idependent clerk should check the entries in the cash book with the relative authorities including the receipts list, paying-in slips, receipt counterfoils, cheque counterfoils, vouchers and any other related documents. Any balance in hand should be checked with the corresponding money and documents.

The bank statement should be reconciled with the bank cash book at frequent intervals. This should be done by an independent authority and, if possible, the cashier should not have access to the bank statement.

Receipts by travelling salesmen   Where salesmen collect money from customers, they should bank the takings daily and send a certified copy of the paying-in slip to the cashier, together with a collection list or other documents identifying the sums collected. The cashier is then responsible for entering these amounts in the cash book.

Cheque-writing machines   Apart from machines for the simultaneous writing of cheques and cash book, there are machines for writing and protecting cheques. These provide some form of indelible impression by penetrating below the surface of the paper when entering the amount. In addition to writing the amount in words and figures, these machines may also be used to enter a limiting clause such as 'account payee only', or 'not over £10'. Machines for printing signatures and endorsements on cheques are also available; a business making use of a machine for cheque signing may have to indemnify its bank against possible loss by reason thereof.

Petty cash If the business is a large one or sections of it are separated by distance, it is usual for small cash floats to be held at convenient points. The amount of the float should in each case be restricted to actual needs and it is usually sufficient if it is approximately one and a half times an average week's disbursement. Petty-cash vouchers should only be signed by authorized persons and the float should be reimbursed weekly. Cash balances should be checked periodically by the cashier or his representative.

Stamps, tickets etc. Stocks of postage and insurance stamps and other vouchers of monetary value, such as canteen tickets and trading stamps, are usually controlled in a manner similar to that for petty cash.

Payment of wages The cashier is usually responsible for the making up of wage packets and for their distribution to the employees. The responsibility for the preparation of the payroll must, however, be placed elsewhere, and under no circumstances should clerks who calculate the payroll either make up the packets or distribute them.

Clerks making up wage packets should work in pairs, one making up the cash and the other checking it into the packets. The packets for each wages sheet, or group of wages sheets (see Chapter 14, Wages), should be made up as a separate batch. The exact amount of cash required for the batch should be given to the pair of clerks, and if the last packet exactly exhausts this sum, it may be taken that, subject only to compensating error, the packets have been made up correctly. The checker should be responsible for sealing the packets and for their safe custody until they are handed back to the cashier or to the pay clerk. Pay clerks should be frequently interchanged so that no one clerk continually pays out to employees in any one section of the business. Strict control should be exercised over wage packets which are not handed out at the normal time. Equivalent precautions should be taken when wages are paid by cheque or bank transfer.

Some security organizations provide a service whereby they will:

(a) draw cash from the bank and deliver it to where the pay packets are to be made up;

(b) hold the pay packets in safe custody for the time between making up and paying out;

(c) draw cash from the bank, make up the packets and deliver them to the point of payment.

Branches   Close controls should be instituted where a distant branch handles large sums of money. In general, the procedures mentioned above should be adopted. Daily banking should be enforced and occasionally an auditor should visit the branch to check the receipt counterfoils and other documents with the cash book and with the payments into the bank.

As a safeguard, an arrangement may be made for two bank accounts to be kept for each branch: a No. 1 Account for receipts and a No. 2 Account for payments. All payments from the bank are made from the No. 2 Account which is reimbursed up to an agreed limit each week from the No. 1 Account. The amount of the limit should be determined in advance according to requirements, and no more than this amount would be paid out in any one week without reference to head office.

Control of forms   As far as possible all forms such as cheques, receipts and anything else which might be used in the misappropriation of cash, should be numbered and stocks should be carefully controlled and kept under lock.

Computer-accounting systems   In computer-accounting systems, the cash account is likely to be posted at the same time as the contra entries are made in other accounts. If it is possible by direct data entry to make cash postings on the day of receipt or payment and receive an immediate confirmatory journal list, the computer cash account alone may be adequate. If, however, there is delay because of account-coding processes or because the accounting program is not always available on line, a separate cash-book system should be maintained, even if by hand. The principle of accounting for cash daily as it is received and paid out should not be discarded, nor should the principle of making the cashier completely responsible for sums passing through his hands.

Security

Where substantial sums of cash must be held in the office or carried in transit to and from the bank, adequate protection against theft must be provided. More important still, there must be protection for staff who might suffer assault during an attempted robbery.

Ancient fortresses illustrate the principles of security. Those who attacked had first to break through a series of outer defences, during which time the alarm was given, summoning help. If the outer barriers failed, the attackers eventually reached the inner 'keep': a strong point which could withstand an extended seige, allowing still more time for help to arrive. For an office, the first line of defence may be the site gate, the second the door of the office building and the third the door of the cashier's department. The inner 'keep' is usually the strong-room and/or safe.

The objective is to prevent any breach of the lines of defence and, if any should fail, to raise the alarm for help before the attacker has time to reach and effectively attack the inner areas. The combination of delay and alarm is essential. Delay alone is ineffective if the thief has time to break in, steal and depart before assistance arrives.

Secure areas   A secure area must be such that entry is denied to unauthorized persons. Those who try to break in by force must be resisted by strong doors and locks, barred windows etc. Those who try to enter during working hours must be identified before doors are opened to them:

(*a*) by a member of the staff able to recognize them face to face or through closed-circuit television;

(*b*) by the production of a pass bearing a personal photograph; or

(*c*) by the use of a pass card which will release a lock.

Alarms   The simplest form of alarm is a loud bell which is set off by a push-button or foot-operated switch. To be effective, such an alarm must be audible over a wide area and staff must be instructed how to act when it is heard.

Other forms of alarm are remote, so that an attacker is not immediately aware that help has been summoned. These may send a signal to a security guard on the premises or directly by telephone line to the police station or the offices of a security company.

Automatic systems can be installed to cover the hours when there are no staff on duty. If thieves attempt to break in, an audible or remote alarm is activated by the opening of doors or windows, by breaking through walls, floors or ceilings, or by the detection of movement within the premises.

Safes   Safes may be free-standing, built into a wall or floor, or placed in a strong-room. They are available in a wide range of sizes and vary in the degree of protection afforded. In selecting a safe, regard must be had to the value of the contents and the difficulty which an intending thief would have in reaching it. A relatively inexpensive safe may provide adequate protection against the petty thief. A safe which is to deter and, if necessary, defeat a professional gang of thieves may have to be proof against attack by drilling, cutting and explosives.

There is a choice of key-operated locks and keyless combination locks. As an additional precaution, time controls may be fitted to ensure that a safe can be opened only during certain pre-determined hours of the day. The strict control of keys, or availability of combinations, is essential and it may be considered necessary to fit more than one lock so that two or more persons must be present before the safe can be opened.

Cash in transit   When money is being carried through the streets to and from the bank, an escort should be provided and the time and route varied. If large amounts are to be carried, it is usual for the transfer to be made by a security company using its specially-equipped vans and trained staff.

Planned protection   Improved technology provides improved protection; it also provides more formidable means of attack. Periodical reviews of security arrangements should be made, expert advice being obtainable from the police, insurers and security companies.

14 Wages

For a number of reasons the system of paying wages is of great importance. Its ramifications extend throughout the business and every employee is affected personally. Specialized knowledge is required to deal with the statutory provisions; protection from fraud is essential because large sums of money are involved; finally, the maintenance of a timetable is of the utmost importance: the wages must never be late.

THE PURPOSE

Wages systems are required to fulfil a great many purposes and among those more generally involved are the following:

(*a*) to calculate the wages earned by each employee, in accordance with the terms of employment. This may involve, besides the rate of pay and the time worked, the work produced, bonus, overtime, commission, expenses, allowances, holiday pay and sick pay;

(*b*) to conform with statutory requirements. These may be general legal requirements in the cases of income tax, National Insurance, redundancy payments etc., or varying from one industry to another;

(*c*) to deal with various kinds of deductions. These may include pensions contributions, savings, repayment of loans, hospital funds, club contributions and similar matters, according to the policy of the business;

(*d*) to have regard to the employees' requirements. These include payment at a recognized time, the provision of adequate and legally acceptable information as to how the amount paid is calculated, and conforming with trade union agreements;

(*e*) to provide the cashier with such information as he may require to enable him to pay the amounts due;

(*f*) to account in the books of the business for the sums paid out and to analyse them for departmental or cost accounts;

(*g*) to apply the sums deducted according to their purposes;

(*h*) to record the terms of employment of each individual, to note changes in rates of pay and status when authorized by the management, and to keep certain basic staff records so as to provide information from time to time for the management, for supplying references and for any other purpose.

THE MEANS

The number of different systems in operation is very large; almost every type of equipment can be used in one way or another, and in each industry and each business any general method requires modification to meet particular needs.

Forms

It is possible to select a few forms which are characteristic of the great number used.

Application form   This is usually the basis of the contract of employment although further details of contractual terms may appear in the statutory written particulars which can be prepared later.

Time and attendance records   To pay wages, the office requires evidence of continued attendance at work in accordance with the initial contract. Where wages are based upon an hourly rate or where overtime is paid, some form of daily time record is required (Fig. 98, page 206). Where wages or salaries are on a weekly or monthly basis, attendance sheets are usually sufficient (see Fig. 99, page 207).

Payroll (wages sheet)   The basic practice is for all the information relating to wages to be assembled on a weekly payroll with one line or section for each employee.

Earnings-record card   The Commissioners of Inland Revenue require that a record be kept for each employee showing wages paid and PAYE income-tax deductions made therefrom. This is also of value to the employer for reference purposes. The Commissioners provide a suitable card for this purpose. Alternatively, the employer may design his own form (see Fig. 97B) by arrangement with the local tax office provided it conforms to certain principles.

Pay slips   Because the make up of wages is generally somewhat complicated, most employees require a slip showing full details which may exceed any minimum legal requirements (see Fig. 97A).

Pay packets   Wages are usually paid in special envelopes with the employee's name, number and department visible.

Staff record   It is usual for a central staff record to be maintained for each employee giving details of service. It is convenient for this to be kept by the wages office since much of the information is required by it.

Method

Apart from the maintenance of staff records (see pages 210–11), the principal tasks are concerned with the preparation of the payroll, the employees' pay slips and earnings-record cards, and the various journals, analyses and reconciliations associated with the payment of wages. The pay slips and earnings-record cards contain information similar to that on the payroll and all three documents are frequently produced together by carbon or other manifolding method. The journal entries etc. are drawn from the various payroll totals. It is therefore convenient to consider firstly the preparation of the payroll in the knowledge that other routine records are likely to stem from this.

Payroll   The weekly payroll or wages sheet is fundamentally a list of the names of employees, one on each line, with columns for each of the several items making up the gross wages, and for the various deductions which together produce the net wages to be paid. The names should be arranged in alphabetical or code-number order under departments or sections. In a large business, there will be a separate sheet or series of sheets for each department.

The items entered on the payroll are of three kinds, and it is important to distinguish one from another:

(*a*) *Fixed data:* items which generally remain unchanged from week to week, e.g. employee's name, code number, basic rate of pay and deductions for national insurance, pension contribution etc.

(*b*) *Balances brought forward:* totals of gross pay and tax deducted to date, balances outstanding on loan accounts etc.

(*c*) *Current data:* the information relating to the week for which wages are to be calculated, e.g. normal hours, overtime hours, days absent sick, bonus, commission etc. and any non-recurring deductions.

All three types of information must be assembled on the payroll in order that the net pay for the week may be calculated. The sources will differ and so may the methods of entry, as follows:

(*a*) *Fixed data*   Because these items do not change frequently, it is customary to use some duplicating device to enter them on the payroll. One common method is to prepare addressing plates or stencils (see page 89), one for each employee. From these, the fixed data are printed on the payroll and pay slips. New plates can be added and unwanted ones removed each week as necessary. Alterations in detail, as when rates of pay change, can be made without difficulty. Where changes in personnel are few, the fixed data may be held on a duplicator master or photocopying transparency, from which payrolls can be copied as required.

(b) *Balances brought forward*   These items change weekly and it is often found convenient to record them all on the earnings-record card from which they can be picked up as the current data are entered.

(c) *Current data*   The principal source of current data is the clock card, time sheet or other attendance or work record. From this, the days or hours worked at basic rate, the overtime hours, pieces produced etc. are entered as the means of calculating the gross pay due. In some systems, the gross pay is calculated on the time or work record and the amount only transferred to the payroll. This is not usually the most economic method clerically but may be justified by the need to show the employee in detail how his gross wage is made up. In such cases, the clock card or other record is often returned to the employee for him to check and later surrender in return for his pay packet.

Other current data may include sick pay, holiday pay, bonus, commission etc. It may facilitate the preparation of the payroll if all payments authorized are assembled on the time or work record rather than being taken from different source documents (see Fig. 99).

Calculation of net pay   With all the requisite information entered, it remains to calculate the sum due to each employee:

(i) the amounts earned are cross-cast and the total entered in the column for gross wages;

(ii) the income tax payable is calculated (see page 208) and entered;

(iii) the amounts to be deducted (including tax) cross-cast and entered in the column for total deductions;

(iv) the total deductions are subtracted from the gross wages and the amount payable is entered.

Mechanized payroll preparation   If the number of employees is small, the work described above can be done by hand, but if the number is large, firms are justified in using machines or devices such as the following:

(a) *Manifold posting board*   The payroll sheet and a perforated copy which can be torn to provide individual pay slips are placed on the board (see Fig. 96). Each earnings record is in turn placed over the payroll and held with its line for the week over the payroll line for the employee. Entries are made on the earnings record and appear as carbon copies on the payroll and pay slip. An adding machine is used to make the calculations and to total and balance each sheet.

(b) *Accounting machine*   Accounting machines (see Chapter 9), whilst producing the necessary forms simultaneously, offer the advantage of automatically cross-adding and subtracting to give the employee's net pay. According to the number of vertical adding registers available, they will also

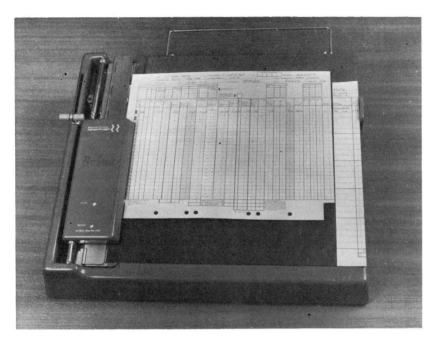

Fig. 96 Manifold posting board for payroll (*Courtesy of Lamson Paragon Ltd.*)

provide totals of some or all of the columns.

(c) *Computers* The more simple visible-record computers can be used in the same way as an accounting machine, but with the additional facility for calculating gross pay from the original data. Where magnetic stripe cards are used as earnings records, the balance brought forward can be picked up and the new balances calculated and recorded automatically. Dependent on the capacity of the stripe, items of fixed data can also be recorded, enabling more operations to be carried out without action by the operator.

Where a computer has disk storage, the whole of the fixed and brought-forward data can be available for automatic recovery and use. The operator has then only to insert the stationery, and enter the employee's code and current data. The computer, with varying degrees of operator or program control, can then calculate the gross pay and carry out all subsequent processes.

Where a mainframe computer is used, there will be no individual record cards inserted. The whole of the fixed and brought-forward data will be available on file on a disk or other form of storage. The current data are entered by direct data entry or other method of input. The program or programs then produce all the necessary forms, with accounting journals, reconciliations and analyses.

Because the amount of current data is small compared with the amount of fixed and brought-forward data, and because there is a standard routine which must be followed many times each week, the computer has from its earliest days proved to be an economical means of doing payroll work where there is a substantial number of employees (Figs. 97A and B).

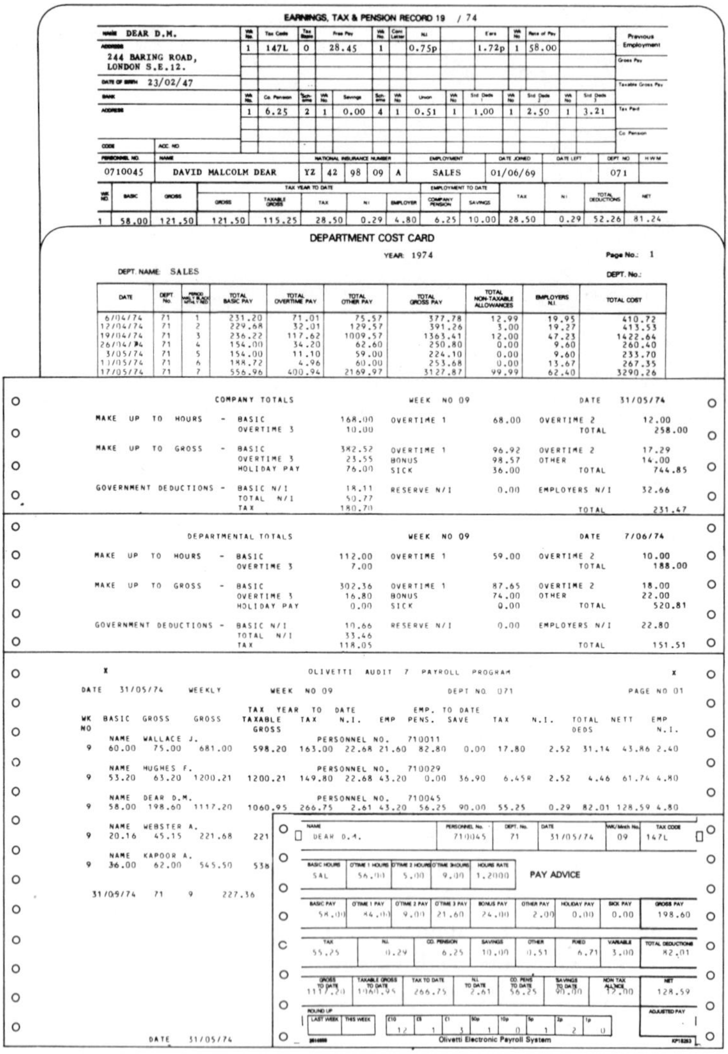
EARNINGS, TAX & PENSION RECORD 19 / 74

NAME DEAR D.M.
ADDRESS 244 BARING ROAD, LONDON S.E.12.
DATE OF BIRTH 23/02/47

Wk No.	Tax Code	Tax Basis	Free Pay	Wk No.	Cont Letter	NI		Ears	Wk No.	Rate of Pay
1	147L	0	28.45	1		0.75p		1.72p	1	58.00

Wk No.	Co. Pension	Scheme	Wk No.	Savings	Scheme	Wk No.	Union	Wk No.	Std Deds 1	Wk No.	Std Deds 2	Wk No.	Std Deds 3
1	6.25	2	1	0.00	4	1	0.51	1	1.00	1	2.50	1	3.21

Previous Employment: Gross Pay; Taxable Gross Pay; Tax Paid; Co. Pension

Personnel No.	Name	National Insurance Number					Employment	Date Joined	Date Left	Dept No	H W M
0710045	DAVID MALCOLM DEAR	YZ	42	98	09	A	SALES	01/06/69		071	

Wk No	Basic	Gross	Tax year to date: Gross	Taxable Gross	Tax	NI	Employer	Employment to date: Company Pension	Savings	Tax	NI	Total Deductions	Net
1	58.00	121.50	121.50	115.25	28.50	0.29	4.80	6.25	10.00	28.50	0.29	52.26	81.24

DEPARTMENT COST CARD
YEAR: 1974 Page No.: 1
DEPT. NAME: SALES DEPT. No.:

Date	Dept No.	Period	Total Basic Pay	Total Overtime Pay	Total Other Pay	Total Gross Pay	Total Non-Taxable Allowances	Employers N.I.	Total Cost
6/04/74	71	1	231.20	71.01	75.57	377.78	12.99	19.95	410.72
12/04/74	71	2	229.68	32.01	129.57	391.26	3.00	19.27	413.53
19/04/74	71	3	236.22	117.62	1009.57	1363.41	12.00	47.23	1422.64
26/04/74	71	4	154.00	34.20	62.60	250.80	0.00	9.60	260.40
3/05/74	71	5	154.00	11.10	59.00	224.10	0.00	9.60	233.70
10/05/74	71	6	188.72	4.96	60.00	253.68	0.00	13.67	267.35
17/05/74	71	7	556.96	400.94	2169.97	3127.87	99.99	62.40	3290.26

COMPANY TOTALS WEEK NO 09 DATE 31/05/74
MAKE UP TO HOURS - BASIC 168.00 OVERTIME 1 68.00 OVERTIME 2 12.00
OVERTIME 3 10.00 TOTAL 258.00
MAKE UP TO GROSS - BASIC 382.52 OVERTIME 1 96.92 OVERTIME 2 17.29
OVERTIME 3 23.55 BONUS 98.57 OTHER 14.00
HOLIDAY PAY 76.00 SICK 36.00 TOTAL 744.85
GOVERNMENT DEDUCTIONS - BASIC N/I 18.11 RESERVE N/I 0.00 EMPLOYERS N/I 32.66
TOTAL N/I 50.77
TAX 180.70 TOTAL 231.47

DEPARTMENTAL TOTALS WEEK NO 09 DATE 7/06/74
MAKE UP TO HOURS - BASIC 112.00 OVERTIME 1 59.00 OVERTIME 2 10.00
OVERTIME 3 7.00 TOTAL 188.00
MAKE UP TO GROSS - BASIC 302.36 OVERTIME 1 87.65 OVERTIME 2 18.00
OVERTIME 3 16.80 BONUS 74.00 OTHER 22.00
HOLIDAY PAY 0.00 SICK 0.00 TOTAL 520.81
GOVERNMENT DEDUCTIONS - BASIC N/I 10.66 RESERVE N/I 0.00 EMPLOYERS N/I 22.80
TOTAL N/I 33.46
TAX 118.05 TOTAL 151.51

X OLIVETTI AUDIT 7 PAYROLL PROGRAM X
DATE 31/05/74 WEEKLY WEEK NO 09 DEPT NO 071 PAGE NO 01

WK NO	BASIC	GROSS	GROSS	TAX YEAR TO DATE: TAXABLE GROSS	TAX	N.I.	EMP	EMP. TO DATE: PENS.	SAVE	TAX	N.I.	TOTAL DEDS	NETT	EMP N.I.
	NAME WALLACE J.				PERSONNEL NO. 710011									
9	60.00	75.00	681.00	598.20	163.00	22.68	21.60	82.80	0.00	17.80	2.52	31.14	43.86	2.40
	NAME HUGHES F.				PERSONNEL NO. 710029									
9	53.20	63.20	1200.21	1200.21	149.80	22.68	43.20	0.00	36.90	6.45R	2.52	4.46	61.74	4.80
	NAME DEAR D.M.				PERSONNEL NO. 710045									
9	58.00	198.60	1117.20	1060.95	266.75	2.61	43.20	56.25	90.00	55.25	0.29	82.01	128.59	4.80
	NAME WEBSTER A.													
9	20.16	45.15	221.68	221										
	NAME KAPOOR A.													
9	36.00	62.00	545.50	538										

31/05/74 71 9 227.36

DATE 31/05/74

PAY ADVICE

Name	Personnel No.	Dept. No.	Date	Wk/Mnth No.	Tax Code
DEAR D.M.	710045	71	31/05/74	09	147L

Basic Hours	O'time 1 Hours	O'time 2 Hours	O'time 3 Hours	Hours Rate
SAL	56.00	5.00	9.00	1.2000

Basic Pay	O'time 1 Pay	O'time 2 Pay	O'time 3 Pay	Bonus Pay	Other Pay	Holiday Pay	Sick Pay	Gross Pay
58.00	84.00	9.00	21.60	24.00	2.00	0.00	0.00	198.60

Tax	N.I.	Co. Pension	Savings	Other	Fixed	Variable	Total Deductions
55.25	0.29	6.25	10.00	0.51	6.71	3.00	82.01

Gross to date	Taxable Gross to date	Tax to date	N.I. to date	Co. Pens to date	Savings to date	Non Tax Allnce	Net
1117.20	1060.95	266.75	2.61	56.25	90.00	12.00	128.59

Round up: Last week | This week — £10 12, £5 1, £1 3, 50p 1, 10p 0, 5p 1, 2p 2, 1p 0 — Adjusted Pay

Olivetti Electronic Payroll System

Fig. 97A Wages records produced by visible record computer (company requirements) (*Courtesy of British Olivetti Ltd.*)

Recording time and work Although time and work records are primarily the responsibility of the operative departments, the office is also concerned. These records must be accurate, and it is necessary to ensure that they are made out under conditions which facilitate accuracy. They

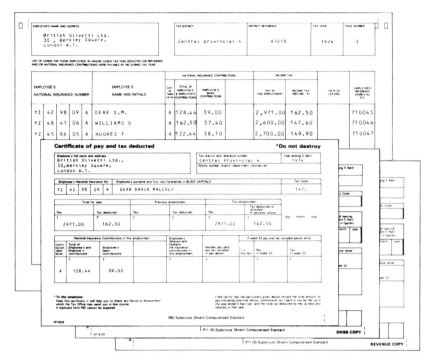

Fig. 97B   Wages records produced by visible record computer (Government requirements)
(*Courtesy of British Olivetti Ltd.*)

must also be convenient, not only to those who originate them, but also to the clerks who use them as the basis of other records.

For time records, clock cards used in conjunction with time-recording clocks are widely used (Fig. 98). These simplify the recording of stopping and starting times where large numbers of employees work at varying hours; it is advisable, however, for them to be used under supervision to avoid the possibility of employees making false recordings. The centralization of clocks, to save the expense of placing them in every department, has the disadvantage that time may be wasted between clocking in and starting work in the department; this will not be shown by the record.

Where flexible hours are worked (see page 311), special equipment may be installed whereby the employee uses a key to start and stop his own time-recording device (see Fig. 120 on page 313).

An alternative to the clock card is the simple attendance sheet maintained by a supervisor at the place of work (Fig. 99). Whilst this calls for some effort by the supervisor, it helps him to see that subordinates start work at the agreed time. It can be used as a simple record of daily attendance or it can be extended to become a complete statement of all the information required for the payment of wages, including time worked, bonus, sick pay, expenses, and so on.

DAY	IN	OUT	IN	OUT	Ordinary time	Over-time
NO						
Name						
Week ending ....19..........						

DAY	IN	OUT	IN	OUT	Ordinary time	Over-time
AM **S** PM						
AM **SUN** PM						
AM **M** PM						
AM **TU** PM						
AM **W** PM						
AM **TH.** PM						
AM **F** PM						
Ordinary time						
Overtime						
Total wages						
Deductions						
Amount paid		£				

Fig. 98   Clock card

Another form of record is the job time sheet (Fig. 100) filled in by the individual employee, or by a supervisor for a group of employees. In addition to showing time at work, it also records how the time has been spent. It can, therefore, also be used for costing purposes and for the calculation of bonus.

Some costing systems require, as a variation of the work sheet previously described, a job sheet which is a record of the time spent or the work done on a single job by one or more employees. As to which is appropriate (the sheet which records all the jobs done by a single employee, or the sheet

WEEKLY ATTENDANCE SHEET   Section_Sales Ledgers_   W/E_16 April_

| Name | Attendance | | | | | | Overtime | Holidays | Sick pay | Special payments | Bonus |
	Mon.	Tue.	Wed.	Thu.	Fri.	Days to pay	Hours to pay	Days to pay	Days to pay		
DOBBIE R. C.	✓	✓	✓	✓	✓	5					
DOBSON T.	✓	✓	✓	✓	✓	5					
DOLBY B. J. R.	✓	✓	✓	✓	✓	5					
DOLLOND A. F.	s	s	s	s	s	—			5		
DOMMETT L.	✓	✓	✓	A	✓	4					
DONALD C.	✓	✓	✓	✓	✓	5					
DORMER S. W.	✓	✓	✓	✓	✓	5	2½			5o	
DOWLING F. H.	✓	✓	✓	✓	✓	5					

Fig. 99   Weekly attendance sheet

JOB TIME SHEET

KEY NO....2169.......   NAME....*J. Watson* ....

DEPARTMENT........*Engineers*...   DATE....*6 April*......

| JOB AND DEPARTMENT | TIME | | | | Total Mins | |
	Start	Stop	Start	Stop		
Taking down Trunking—Stores	8.0	10.0			120	
Lining Chute—Boiler House	10.0	11.15	3.0	4.0	135	
Alterations to Roof Plates—Welding	11.15	12.30			75	
Fitting Conveyor Belt—Dispatch	1.30	3.0			90	
Running and Testing—Dispatch	4.0	5.0			60	

Fig. 100   Job time sheet

which records all the time spent by different employees on a single job) must depend upon the requirements of the situation, and neither can be said to be a superior method without reference to the circumstances.

Whatever form the record takes, it should be scrutinized and authorized by the supervisor, and passed to the wages office as soon as possible after the end of the working period.

Changes   New engagements, employees leaving, transfers from one department to another, changes in status, alterations in deductions, and similar matters have to be dealt with carefully and speedily. Authorities for changes are usually received separately and signed by a responsible official. In the case of engagements, the application form is received, whilst in the other cases, a memorandum or some kind of special form may be used.

It is advisable to avoid a multiplicity of forms, one for each of the many possible changes that can take place. One carefully designed form may be able to cover many situations and, where a computer is used, be a satisfactory medium for the recording or direct entry of data.

Income tax   An example is given below of the procedure for the calculation of tax deductible under the PAYE scheme. The 'year' mentioned is the 'income tax year' and not the calendar year. Weeks in the years are numbered and the example assumes that the current week is week 10.

Stage 1   Calculate taxable pay

	Gross pay for the year to week 9—brought forward	£450·00
PLUS	Gross pay for current week 10	50·00
EQUALS	Gross pay for the year to week 10	500·00
MINUS	Tax-free pay for the year to week 10 (taken from PAYE tables according to the employee's tax code)	142·50
EQUALS	Taxable pay for the year to week 10	£357·50

Stage 2   Calculate tax deductible

	Tax due on taxable pay for the year to week 10 (taken from PAYE tables)	£125·10
MINUS	Tax already deducted for the year to week 9— brought forward	112·50
EQUALS	Tax to be deducted in week 10	£ 12·60

Holiday pay and sick pay Special authorities from the appropriate management are usually required before payments are made to those absent for any reason. It is an advantage if the authority is entered on the attendance list or time record, so that the information is to hand when entering the payroll.

Pay slips Employees are normally provided with a form showing details of the make-up of their wages. This is often produced, whether manually or mechanically, at the same time as the wages sheet is made out. The entries on the wages sheet are then spaced sufficiently far apart to enable a copy of it to be torn into strips with one for each person.

In manual systems, another method is to use a photocopy of the clock card for this purpose. In this case, space is provided on the clock card for the complete calculation of wages including the entry of all additions and deductions. Some businesses require the clock card itself to be signed as a receipt and retained by the office.

Pay packets Where used, these are usually prepared in advance by the entry of employee's name, code number and department. Address plates, where available, can be used for this purpose. To enable the cashier to make up the amount it is usual to enter also the net wages due. For both secrecy and convenience in filling packets, this amount can be entered on the inside of the envelope under the flap. The envelope can also be used to provide the employee with full details of the make-up of the wages, but this has the disadvantage of lack of secrecy. (See also Chapter 13, Cash control.)

If suitably designed pay slips are produced, whether manually or mechanically, they may be folded to reveal the name and net pay and inserted with the cash in a transparent packet. This method avoids the need for any special preparation.

Packets are sometimes designed so that the corners only of notes protrude. These can then be counted by the recipient without opening the packet. Queries as to the correctness of the amount can then be settled without any suggestion that money might have been fraudulently extracted by the recipient beforehand.

Lying time Where wages are based on hours worked or bonus earned, it is almost impossible to arrange for wages to be paid on the last day of the week in which they are earned, because of the time that must be occupied by the clerical work involved. The usual practice, therefore, is to arrange for the pay day to be some days after the last day of the working week. The intervening period is known as lying time. For example, the week may run from Monday to Saturday with the wages paid on the following Friday.

New employees who for personal reasons cannot wait for payment may be given a loan to be repaid over a period.

Accounting   The payroll serves as a journal and should be designed so that the totals of its columns provide the various entries to be made in the financial accounts for wages, national insurance, income tax deducted, pension contributions, loan repayments etc. and, of course, for cash paid.

Where entries are required for departmental and cost accounts, the payroll should be arranged in an order which will facilitate the taking of subtotals under suitable headings.

Where a computer is used, the program can provide for separate but reconciled journals to be printed to serve various purposes.

Protection from fraud   Reference has already been made to the need to avoid any one person having immediate control over all the operations in connection with wages. The several parties among whom the responsibilities should be spread are:

(*a*) the manager of the employee's department, who directly or through one of his subordinates authorizes the terms of employment and the hours to be paid;

(*b*) the wages office supervisor, whose staff calculate the net amount to be paid in accordance with the authorities received from the management or accumulate and control authorized data to be fed into a computer;

(*c*) the cashier, who makes up the pay packets from the information provided by the wages staff;

(*d*) the pay clerk, who hands the packet to the employee.

Each of these should be a separate person. In addition, as a further check, copies of the wages sheet should from time to time be sent to the managers of the departments concerned for scrutiny.

In general, it should be noted that the wages office has no power to authorize either payment or deduction. Care must be taken to see that all documents which support the payroll are signed by a duly appointed official or, where necessary, by the employee.

APPLICATION FORMS AND CENTRAL STAFF RECORDS

Because of the various records required in the calculation and payment of wages, duplication is avoided if the wages section of the office is responsible for keeping the central record of all the employees. This record is built up from the application form and from notices of subsequent changes.

The application form

As already stated, this is commonly the basis of the contract of employment. It is sometimes convenient to design the form so that one copy shall serve as the written notice of terms of employment required by law.

This is not, however, the only purpose which the form may serve. It may require the candidate for employment to give certain personal information, which would include name, age, marital status, date of birth and health record. Other items may be included, but the form should only call for information for which there is a specific purpose.

In the case of successful applicants, the form shows the engagement rate, the capacity and department in which the employee is to start, and any other particular information relating to the terms of engagement.

The form may include certain reminders to the engaging officer on matters which have to be dealt with at the time of engagement, for example:

(*a*) obtaining the employee's income-tax certificate which he should have received from his previous employer;

(*b*) obtaining the employee's insurance card;

(*c*) arranging for the employee to undergo a medical examination if this is part of the terms of employment.

The form is completed by the signature of a manger or other authorized engagement officer.

Central staff records

The central staff record consists of a sheet or card for each employee. The records are usually filed in binders or card-index cabinets in alphabetical order. The record contains much of the information shown on the application form, to which is added, as they occur, changes in rate, capacity, status, department in which employed, and similar information. When an employee leaves, the date and possibly the reason for leaving are also entered, so that a complete record of employment is provided.

Since it is necessary to preserve the application form as the basis of the employment contract, the form may be designed to be used as the permanent staff record. If so, space should be provided for alterations to capacity, rate, and other information, and for information relating to leaving. The reverse side of the application form is commonly used as the record of the employee's service and the forms filed, with the reverse side facing upwards, in alphabetical order of employees' names.

In addition to the central record, additional and more detailed records may be kept by the department in which the individual is employed. If there is a personnel department, it is sometimes required that a third record should be held by the personnel officer or in his department. The value of a multiplicity of records is questionable. Not only has the initial cost to be considered, but every change which takes place must be recorded on all the various records, and the procedure necessary to see that none is missed can be expensive. As always, it is desirable to make one record serve many purposes; the possibility of the personnel department sharing either the central record or the departmental record should be considered.

15 Stock control

It is as important to control the goods in stock as it is to contról the cash. The value of the stock will probably exceed that of the cash and there are many ways in which losses can occur; goods may be stolen, they may be wasted and they may be the subject of fraud of one kind or another.

It is also important to ensure that only the right kinds of goods are held in stock and, further, that the right goods are available when they are wanted and where they are wanted. Money must not be tied up in unwanted stocks; men and machines must not fall idle because materials are not to hand; warehouse and showroom must not run out of the lines required by customers.

This chapter is concerned with the clerical records kept as an aid to the control of stocks. It should be remembered, however, that more important than the record is the physical control which is exercised; it is more important to prevent losses than to record them. Goods need to be held in a suitable store and under a responsible storekeeper who should see that they are kept in good condition. Particularly valuable stocks and those subject to pilferage should be kept in separate rooms or cages which can be locked. Stock should be issued only against requisitions signed by properly authorized persons.

THE PURPOSE

The purpose of stock records can be placed under the following headings:

(*a*) to account for the goods which have been purchased and, as far as practicable, to trace them through the business until they have been delivered and charged to the customers;

(*b*) to report on stock losses and wastage;

(*c*) to report on goods held, or on order, in relation to requirements for production and selling programmes;

(*d*) to report on inactive stocks;

(*e*) to provide information for the accurate pricing of goods, if required for departmental charging or costing purposes.

THE MEANS

Stock-control records are concerned with quantities of goods; they are records in kind rather than cash. Because they provide information of day-to-day use to management, they are usually best kept near the goods to which they refer. This does not, of course, mean that stock records are entirely divorced from the financial records. They must be reconciled periodically with the accounts of the business and any system should enable this to be done.

The methods described below assume that a thorough control is to be exercised over all items of stock. There are, however, circumstances in which less stringent control is adequate (see page 222).

Forms

Among the forms used the following are common to most stock-control methods:

Buyer's order   See page 185.

Goods-received record   See page 185.

Stores requisition and delivery note   To ensure the close control of stores, the storeman should only issue goods against a properly authorized requisition, and all issues should be accompanied by a delivery note. The requisition should state clearly:

(*a*) the quantity and description of the goods;

(*b*) the store which is to issue them and the department which is to receive them;

(*c*) the authority for issue.

The same information is also required on the delivery note with the addition of the date of issue and an acknowledgement of receipt. It is, therefore, often convenient to combine the two forms, thus saving clerical work and avoiding mistakes in copying. Provision is made for entering the quantity issued in case this should be different from the quantity requisitioned. It is sometimes possible to prepare the combined requisition and delivery note as a copy of a material schedule (see page 228).

Stock record   This, in its simplest form, is a record of one line of stock showing the quantities received and issued, and the balance in hand (Fig. 101). It can, in addition, show the value of each transaction and of the balance or it can be an elaborate record covering not merely the quantities in stock, but also ordering levels, goods on order, goods allocated, and other items of information which may interest the management.

Ref. No.	1155 /64/3		Bin:	75
Description:			Unit:	
152 mm Base Plates			each	

Date	Description	In	Out	Balance
July 1	Stock taking			4200
" 3	Assembly. 330		430	3770
" 4	Invoice 3692	1000		4770
" 5	Assembly 335		500	4270

Fig. 101   Stock record in kind

Method

Requirements vary; those of the factory, for example, may be very different from those of the warehouse. Moreover, controls can be exercised in cash, in kind, or in both cash and kind. It is, therefore, only possible to mention the more important components. How these are arranged into a particular method must depend upon the circumstances obtaining in each individual business.

Stock records in kind   A simple record (see Fig. 101) shows, in kind, the receipts, issues and stocks. Normally, the receipts are entered from goods-received notes (or suppliers' delivery notes), whilst the issues are entered from copies of the stores delivery notes. If required, the new balance is calculated as each entry is made.

If these records are to be fully effective, they must be kept up to date and be available near the goods, where full use is likely to be made of them. They should, however, be as simple as possible and the storeman should not be expected to deal with prices and values.

One form of elementary record is the bin card, kept with the goods to which it relates. Sometimes, however, it is more convenient to keep cards at some central place in the store, perhaps in the form of a visible index (see Figs 38A, 38B and 39).

Where the records of stock and stock movements are required for several purposes, a manifold posting board (see Fig. 93) might be used so that entries on the stock-record cards appear also on a proof sheet/journal and other forms. In addition to facilitating the checking of accuracy, these copies might also be used for charging materials to job or process-cost accounts.

In some circumstances, particularly where the number of stock items is small, a weekly stock sheet may be used. The sheet has a line for each item and on it shows the opening stock, receipts, issues and closing stock (Fig. 102). This method is particularly useful where a salesman or branch is required to account to head office for goods held and for related cash or credit sales.

Checking stocks   The stock record provides an inferred stock balance or 'book stock': the quantities that should be available if all receipts and issues have been accurately entered and all calculations correctly made. To complete the cycle of control, it is necessary to count the physical stock and compare it with the book stock. If there is a difference between the two, it should be reported immediately to the store manager and to the office so that the records in cash terms may be adjusted (see below). There are two principal methods of stocktaking:

(a) *Periodic stocktaking*   All stocks are counted at one time. Dependent upon the size of the store, stocktaking may take a few hours or several days. Where a factory closes for annual holidays, this may provide an opportunity since no receipts or issues take place. If movements cannot be halted, elaborate arrangements may be necessary to record these and adjust the physical counts so that all are correct as at one point of time.

(b) *Perpetual inventory*   The purpose of this method is to avoid the overtime and disorganization of work associated with periodic stocktaking. A number of items of stock are counted each day. Any differences with the book stocks are reported and the records are adjusted to agree with the physical stock found. The number of items checked each day must be such that the whole of the stock is taken over a selected period. Some items may be checked more frequently than others, particularly those likely to be pilfered or of special value.

When stocks are to be listed for valuation, the balances are taken from the stock records. Some balances may be incorrect but, if the frequency of stocktaking is appropriate to the risk of error, any discrepancy is likely to lie within acceptable limits.

Replenishing stocks   Where it is not possible or desirable to hold large reserve stocks, and particularly if goods are not readily replaceable, it is customary to use stock-control records for signalling the need to re-order. For each item of stock there is fixed a minimum stock level which is estimated as sufficient to cover the consumption during the period between placing an order and having a new consignment in the store available for

GENERAL STORES

WEEKLY STOCK CONTROL SHEET

W/E......8 May............

DESCRIPTION	Unit	Cost (Office Use) A	RECEIPTS							Opening Stock C	Total D (B+C)	ISSUES							Book Stock F (D−E)	Actual Stock G	Stock	
			Mon.	Tue.	Wed.	Thu.	Fri.	Sat.	Total B			Mon.	Tue.	Wed.	Thu.	Fri.	Sat.	Total E			Over H (G−F)	Short J (F−G)
Boxes—Plain—Z3152	m						50		50	209	259	5	10		10			15	244	231		13
,, —Printed—Z615	m						100		100	373	473					20		30	443	436		7
Cellophane 8″ × 11″	lb						10		10	27	37			4			6	10	27	28	1	
,, 10″ × 4″	lb									50	50				7			7	43	43		
Greaseproof 7″ × 10″	Rms				12				12	36	48					6		6	42	42		
,, 9″ × 3″	Rms				18				18	64	82					12		12	70	70		
Gummed Labels—ZL/152	m									117	117		15					15	102	106	4	
,, ,, —ZL/5	m									89	89				5			5	84	84		
Insert Labels—6189	m							20	20	39	59			10				10	49	48		1
,, ,, —3094	m									56	56		10					10	46	46		
Packing Cases																						

Fig. 102 Weekly stock-control sheet

issue. The minimum stock level is shown on the stock card, and when the actual stock approaches this figure, the buying department is informed. Sometimes maximum stock levels are also recorded to indicate the quantity which should be ordered.

The stock card may also be used to show details of outstanding orders. If so, a copy of each order placed by the buying department is provided for the records clerk, who enters on the cards the quantities ordered. When a delivery is received, the quantity on order is reduced accordingly, and transferred into the stock column.

Inactive stocks   At least once in each year, a report should be issued on any items of stock which have been inactive over a specific period. Unwanted stocks waste storage space and represent working capital unprofitably employed; it is among the duties of the office to draw attention to such matters.

Stock availability   It is sometimes necessary for the stock records to distinguish between allocated stocks, or stocks earmarked for specific jobs, and free stocks. In this case, the stock record has additional columns to show the quantity of free stock held.

Stock records in cash   As has already been pointed out, the office is usually responsible for exercising a control by value over the goods held in store. Where a record in kind is held by the store, the most simple control is by means of a bulk stores stock account.

Purchases taken into the store are charged to this account from the suppliers' invoices. Issues from the store are credited from the stores delivery notes valued at cost prices (see below, Valuation of goods) and debited, according to circumstances, to the receiving department, or to a cost account. At any time the balance on the stores cash account should equal the value at cost of the goods held in stock, as detailed in the record in kind held by the store. At intervals, the balance on the account is compared with a valuation of a stock inventory at the same date or, if the perpetual inventory method is adopted, with a valuation of the balances shown on the stock records in kind. At the same time any reported stock losses are taken into account. In summary form the balance may be shown as follows:

DR	Opening Stock	*CR*	Issues
DR	Receipts	*CR*	Reported Losses
		CR	Inventory Stock

Any difference remaining on the account reveals an unreported stock loss or a clerical error.

Because of the possible need to check detail, the cash accounts may be divided into control groups for the main classes of goods held in the store. If

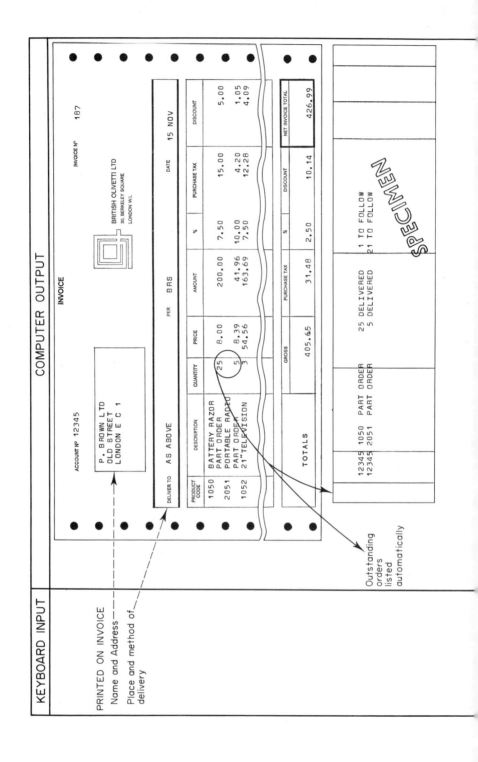

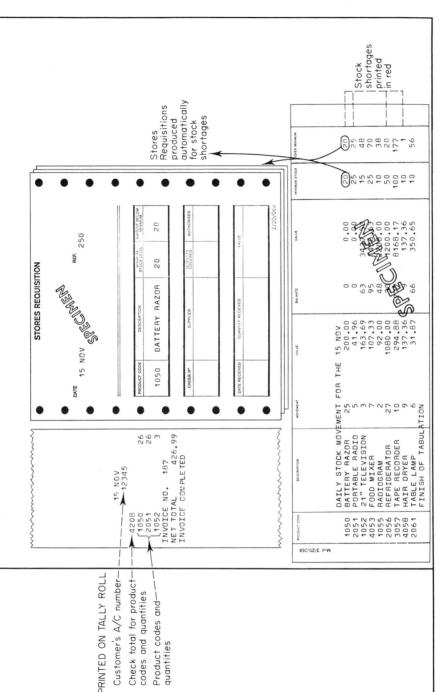

Fig. 103 Invoice and stock-control forms produced by visible record computer (*Courtesy of British Olivetti Ltd.*)

an error is made it is then only necessary to check the entries in the particular control group concerned.

An alternative method of control is to combine the accounts in cash and kind. In this case, the three columns for receipts, issues, and balance are duplicated so as to provide columns for quantities and for values. This method helps to reduce errors and certainly to simplify their location. It tends, however, to lead to duplication, unless the accounts can be kept at the store, where the records in kind are required.

Mechanized methods   Whilst stock records in kind are usually kept by hand, records in cash or in cash and kind together may be kept by machine, examples of which are as follows:

(a) *Accounting machines* (Chapter 9)   Because they are able to print records simultaneously, these machines can produce journals and stock records in cash or in cash and kind. They may also post at the same time to departmental or cost accounts.

The methods of proving accuracy usually adopted with posting machines can be applied to the cash entries and also to the entries in kind, provided these are expressed in whole units. All quantities, whether grams, kilograms or litres etc., may then be added by the machine to produce a total for balancing purposes, even though it is a meaningless conglomeration of units.

(b) *Visible record computers*   The ability of the visible record computer to multiply and divide as well as add and subtract facilitates the keeping of records in both kind and cash. The value of stock or of consignments received can be divided by the quantity to arrive at a unit price. Quantities issued or written off can be evaluated at unit prices for accounting and cost-accounting purposes. If magnetic stripe cards are used, the price can be recorded on the stripe and picked up automatically.

(c) *Computers* (Chapters 7 and 8)   The computer is able to undertake all the processes of stock control in kind and/or in cash. In addition, it can be programmed to calculate the quantities required for replenishing stocks and may even be used to produce purchase orders automatically as the need arises (see Fig. 103).

Data can be fed into the computer and information obtained from it at a remote terminal (see page 113) in the store or warehouse. In this way, the whole stock-control process can be centralized and the need for separate records in the store and in the office eliminated.

(d) *Punched or magnetic cards*   For high-value stocks, control is sometimes exercised through tokens in the form of punched or magnetic cards. As goods are taken into stock, the computer issues card tokens; as goods are issued, the tokens are surrendered and used as computer input to cause the stock records to be up-dated. Cards may also be issued by a computer as authority to issue goods from stock, later being returned as notification that the issue has taken place (see Chapter 15). These methods have the advantage of reducing the possibility of human error once the right card has been selected.

Valuation of goods   In any business, it is necessary to price and value goods for the purpose of stock valuation and costing. Where cost accounts are kept, the pricing of raw materials, indirect materials and finished products are major operations.

Sometimes the nature and high value of goods demands that articles be individually identified and priced. Where goods are handled in quantity, less exact methods are usually adequate and avoid excessive clerical work. The following are among the methods which may be used:

(a) *Lot method*   Each consignment of goods received is kept separately and given a 'lot number'. An average price per unit is calculated for each lot and is used thereafter for stock valuation and cost-accounting purposes. This method demands that each issue from stock must be identified by lot number and priced accordingly. It also infers that a separate stock record or sub-record is kept for each lot.

(b) *First in first out (fifo)*   Sometimes known as the *Exhaust Method*, this is not dissimilar in effect to the lot method. When each consignment is received a price is calculated and issues charged at this price until a quantity equal to that of the consignment has been issued. Subsequent issues are charged at the price of the next consignment and so on. It is assumed that stocks are used in strict rotation, although this may not, in fact, be so.

(c) *Last in first out (lifo)*   Issues from stock are priced at the price paid for the last consignment received. When prices are rising, this may ensure that costs are not under-estimated but it will obviously give rise to discrepancies in stock reconciliation. *Lifo* is not acceptable as the basis of stock valuation for tax-computation purposes.

(d) *Continuing average method*   In this case, a new average price is calculated each time a consignment is received. This is done by taking the value of the stock in hand at the old price, adding to it the value of the new consignment at the new price, and calculating a new average price to be effective from that date.

(e) *Standard price method*   In this case, estimated standard prices are used over a period for charging out issues, regardless of the actual cost of the various consignments. The standard price is, therefore, calculated on the expected cost of each item of goods. When a new consignment is received, the actual value is compared with the standard value. If there is a difference, this is transferred to a price-variance account, so that the charge to the relative control account can be made at the standard price. If significant differences occur and are maintained, it may be necessary to alter the standard price from time to time.

Valuation of work in progress   Unfinished products or jobs in stock have some value but it is difficult, if not impossible, to assess this exactly. The method of valuation is usually a matter of management policy, having regard to the peculiarities of the industry or trade. Where standard costs are employed, these are often used as the basis of calculation.

Degrees of stock control   The cost of stock control must not exceed its value to the business. In general, the strictest control should be reserved for goods of high value which are attractive to would-be pilferers and which are readily portable. A gold watch requires a more strict control than a 20-tonne section for a specially built bridge—even though the latter may be the more valuable.

Each class of goods should be considered on its merits. In retailing, the stock in a bulk warehouse might be controlled in kind whilst that displayed is controlled in cash and profit terms only. In factories, some items of general use and low value (e.g. nuts, bolts and washers) may be classed as 'free issue'. Operatives help themselves and the only control is over bulk reserves from which bins are replenished. In offices, stationery may be put in charge of a responsible supervisor who issues what is necessary and re-orders when stocks run low.

16 Production records

In any business function there is a direct connection between the practical working and the clerical operations. The office receives information from the buying, productive, sales, and other departments and, having processed it, gives information to the management generally. Whilst this function can in most cases be performed adequately by the general office, the clerical work concerning production control and its allied activities is often carried out in a local factory or cost office. This is done for two reasons: firstly, the work calls for some technical knowledge of the productive processes and, secondly, the information provided must be immediately available to the factory manager, foremen and others so that they may act upon it.

The factory office may be staffed largely by technicians and technical clerks of one sort and another: draughtsmen, estimators, ratefixers, cost clerks, progress chasers and the like. Although their work demands technical knowledge, it nevertheless contains a high proportion of essentially clerical processes. If full use is to be made of the technical skill, this clerical work must be made as simple and straightforward as possible. The use of modern methods and, where appropriate, machines can often yield even greater economies here than in the general office.

Whereas the functions of the general office in one business have much in common with those of any other business, this does not apply to the same degree in factory offices. Here the nature of the product and of the productive processes can cause wide variation in the detail of functions and methods. In engineering there will be differences according to whether there is flow production, batch production or jobbing. In textiles, chemicals, food production and, indeed, any industry there are peculiarities which call for special treatment. In spite of this wide variation, there are, however, basic principles which may be followed to advantage and the purposes to be achieved are fundamentally the same. In that which follows the examples given are from engineering and it is, of necessity, left to readers in other industries to apply the principles and methods enunciated to their own particular problems.

THE PURPOSE

The factory office serves management in a number of ways, all of which are interrelated in that they reflect the productive processes and their cost. These comprise:

(a) the detailed planning of production in terms of material requirement, labour and machine time;

(b) the estimating of cost for price quotation and cost control;

(c) the requisitioning of material to be available in due time;

(d) the scheduling of work so as to maintain an even load on the factory capacity, and fulfil delivery dates;

(e) the progressing of work through the factory in accordance with the production plan;

(f) the recording of material, man-hours and machine-hours used in various processes and jobs;

(g) the gathering of information necessary for calculating piece-work payments or other incentive bonuses;

(h) the provision of information concerning production performance and cost, so that the management and supervision may be aware of any deviation from the plans laid.

These objectives are all broadly concerned with setting the production plan, informing those who are to put it into operation, and taking steps to inform the factory and general management of the extent to which the plan has or has not been achieved. In carrying out the clerical work necessary to these ends, much will be done which is directly linked with the work of the general office and other departments. When material requirements are calculated, the buying department and stores are concerned. When records of time worked on operations are being made, the wages department may be concerned. When cost accounts are being compiled, they must be reconciled with the financial accounts. The factory office systems cannot therefore be considered in isolation if duplication of work is to be avoided. There should be full integration of clerical work no matter where it is done.

This does not mean that the needs of accountancy come first and that all other records are mere by-products of these; rather the reverse. The factory management needs information in a form which reflects the realities of production. They must be able to see readily the significance of the facts and comparisons set before them and be able to take immediate action accordingly. If these requirements are met, it is not usually difficult to produce from the same sources the figures needed for other purposes.

THE MEANS

The service given by the factory office is to all levels of management within the factory: the manager, the foreman and the chargehand. Each requires information upon which to judge performance and take action. It is not sufficient to provide the records needed at the higher levels only; to do so may result in unofficial clerical work being done within the factory, probably at greater cost than if it were done in the office.

Forms

The following forms are representative of those used in engineering factories. Where they are illustrated, the forms have been simplified in order to bring out their salient features and are not intended as the prototypes for any particular system. Their counterparts, under perhaps different names, are to be found in other industries since the pattern of information required is naturally similar.

Material schedule From an examination of drawings, specifications etc., a schedule is prepared showing what material is required for a job or product and whence it is to be obtained (Fig. 104). It is often convenient to have separate schedules for material to be drawn from stock and material which must be purchased specially. The schedules can serve four main purposes:

(*a*) a record against which to check the availability of material when loading work into the factory;

(*b*) a notification to the buying department of material to be purchased or to the stores of stock to be reserved;

(*c*) a record from which material can be requisitioned;

(*d*) a basis for costing the material requirements.

It is usual, therefore, to make copies of the schedule for eventual distribution to the buying department, stores, progress, and costing departments as may be necessary. As the dates by which the various items are required will depend upon the placing of the job in the production programme, some of the copies will not be released until the job has been entered on the production control chart (see below).

In suitable circumstances it may be possible to use a form one copy of which will in due course serve as a material requisition (see below and Fig. 105).

Operation schedule Again by reference to drawings, specifications etc., a list of the productive operations necessary is prepared (Fig. 104). This list may include detailed instructions as to method or, where such are not necessary, short descriptions such as 'turn' or 'mill' and a reference to the drawing. Against each operation is shown, among other things:

(*a*) type of operator necessary, e.g. turner, fitter;

(*b*) the machine to be used (if any);

(*c*) special tools required (other than those generally available);

(*d*) man-hours and/or machine-hours for the operation.

MATERIAL SCHEDULE

FOR DELIVERY TO:
JOB DESCRIPTION
DELIVERY DATE:

JOB No.
PAGE No.
No. OF PAGES
DATE

DRAWING No.	ITEM No.	DESCRIPTION	BIN No.	QTY.	REQ No.	STOCK AVAILABLE	DATE ISSUED	ITEMS TO BE PURCHASED				NOTES
								SUPPLIER	ORDER No.	EST'D. DEL. DATE	DATE RECEIVED	

LABOUR / MACHINE SCHEDULE

FOR DELIVERY TO:
JOB DESCRIPTION
DELIVERY DATE:

JOB No.
PAGE No.
No. OF PAGES
DATE

DRAWING No.	OPERATION	QTY.	MAT. SCHED. REF.	LAB. OR MACHINE TYPE	EST'D. TIME	STARTING DATE		COMPLETION DATE		TOOLS, ETC.
						EST'D.	ACTUAL	EST'D.	ACTUAL	

Fig. 104 Material and operation schedules

The operation schedule can serve four main purposes:

(*a*) a record from which the production control chart can be entered (see below);

(*b*) a notification to the factory foreman and chargehands of the work to be done;

(*c*) a record from which operation tickets and similar forms can be prepared by non-technical clerks;

(*d*) a basis for costing the labour and machine-time elements of the operation.

As in the case of the material schedule it is usual to make copies for distribution to the progress and costing departments. The copy to be used in progressing will not, of course, be released until the job has been included in the production programme and the date for completion entered. It is sometimes possible to design the schedule so that one copy is perforated and can be divided so as to provide operation tickets (see below).

Costing The material and operation schedules set out what the job requires in terms of quantity and time. The costing or cost estimate translates quantity and time into value. The content and layout of the costing form will depend upon the costing system in use.

It is often possible for the estimation of material and direct labour cost to be done on carbon copies of the material and labour schedules, thus avoiding copying and the possibility of error. In such cases, the cost-estimate form consists of a summary of totals brought forward from the schedules with the addition of allowances for indirect costs, scrap etc. In appropriate circumstances, the costing may be expanded by the addition of overhead and profit allowances to arrive finally at the selling price.

Material requisition From the material schedule, material requisitions are prepared as authorities for the factory to draw material from store (Fig. 105). After the material has been issued the requisition may also be valued and serve as the medium from which stock and cost accounts are posted.

Operation ticket From the operation schedule, individual tickets are prepared for each operation showing what work is to be done and the estimated time, standard time or piece rate, according to the output control methods employed. These tickets may be used by the foreman in the day-to-day loading of the factory and also serve as the record of time spent on operations.

Production control chart The production control chart sets out the production programme and shows when it is intended that each operation shall be done. From this it follows that it also shows, by reference to the available man-hours and machine-hours, the capacity remaining available at any time.

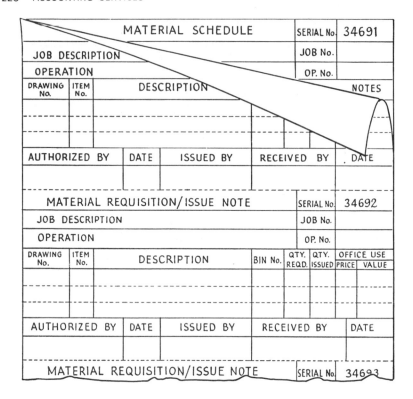

Fig. 105   Material requisition

This chart is a key document and is usually extended to show actual production as compared with the programme. If it is to be of full value to the factory management it must be kept up-to-date at all times, and the programme amended as circumstances demand. For this reason it is often kept on a specially designed board (such as that shown in Fig. 106) which permits alterations to be made readily as the need arises.

Job record   The production control chart gives an overall picture of the state of work in the factory and for this reason can contain little detail. It may, therefore, be necessary to have in addition a job record showing when each operation was completed and giving a comparison with the estimates of the actual material consumption and hours spent. Where the actual performance is significantly different from the estimate the reason should be noted.

Such records should be kept up-to-date so that any failure to work according to plan may be made known to the management without delay. When a job is finished the record should be filed for reference as it can be of great value in setting future estimates for similar work, or in revising standard costings where these are used.

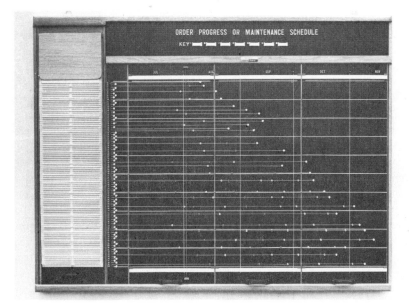

Fig. 106   Control board (*Courtesy of Movitex Signs Ltd.*)

Bonus record   Where incentive bonuses are paid, it is probably necessary to produce a record of each employee's performance on individual operations in addition to the record relating to the job as a whole.

Cost summary   The ultimate object of all production control is to contribute to the efficient working of the factory. In the long run, efficiency or inefficiency is measured in terms of cost, and the cost summary is therefore the ultimate guide as to the ability of the factory to make profits. On this form are accumulated the costs of material, labour and/or machine time expended and the total cost of a job calculated. The reasons underlying any failure to meet estimates should be noted on this form by reference to the job record.

Method

The method will, in detail, depend on the nature of the product and of the productive processes. It will depend also on the number of products being made, the number of different operations involved and the number of employees. Whether there be job, batch or continuous production, the purposes to be achieved and the principles to be applied are the same. Where, however, there is repetition in production, there can equally be repetition in the associated clerical work, and full advantage must be taken of this possibility in designing forms and procedures.

Whatever method is employed, it should not be planned or operated in isolation. Production planning and control are closely linked with other activities such as purchasing, stock control, the calculation of wages and bonus, with cost accounting and, eventually, with the financial accounts. If separate clerical systems are employed by the buying office, the stores, the wages office, the cost office and the production control department, there will inevitably be duplication of records and of work. There is even the possibility of apparently conflicting information being provided to the management from these various sources because of error, or differences of emphasis or interpretation. The ideal is that the work of all these departments should contribute to one general procedure agreed by all. Whatever information is required by any department should come only from the most reliable and most economic source.

Planning   The operation schedule is prepared by an estimator or other technically qualified person from drawings and/or specifications. As this process involves the decision as to the productive methods to be employed, it is often only possible after consultation with the production management. The operation schedule records in concise terms the operations and their sequence. It defines for each operation:

(*a*) the department in which the work is to be done;
(*b*) the grade and skill of the operator to be employed;
(*c*) the type of machine to be used (if any);
(*d*) the tools, jigs, fixtures etc. to be used;
(*e*) the man-hours and/or machine-hours estimated as necessary.

From the same drawings and specifications, material schedules are prepared showing the descriptions and quantities of material and components required and the operation at which each is first required. It is usually convenient to list separately the material which can be drawn from stock and that which must be purchased specially. In the latter case, some consultation with the buyer may be necessary in order to determine probable delivery dates. These can be of vital importance subsequently, since they may govern the entire production programme.

Except in the smaller organizations, it is usual to prepare a number of copies of the material and operation schedules. These schedules are key documents which are the basis of the subsequent stages of planning and control and may be required by several other departments.

Costing   There are widely varying policies as to the costing formula and as to the basis on which allowances are calculated. In general, a costing should be set out in such a way as to illustrate the sequence of productive processes and arrive at a realistic total estimate of cost.

Estimates of cost are vital to any business. They are the means whereby profitability is forecast, and the standards by which efficiency is judged. It is therefore important that they should be approved in detail by the management, and not treated as purely clerical products.

From the material schedule and operation schedule, an estimate is prepared, according to an appropriate formula, for example:

Material ex Stock	. . . .
Material to be Purchased	. . . .
Total Material Cost	. . . .
Direct Labour/Machine Hours	
at rate per hour	. . . .
Indirect Labour Allowance	. . . .
Total Material and Labour Cost	. . . .
Oncost Allowance	. . . .
Total Material, Labour and Oncost	. . . .
less Scrap Allowance	. . . .
Total Estimated Cost	

Factory loading   When work has been accepted it must be included in the production programme, taking its place according to:

(*a*) the existing load on types of labour and machine;

(*b*) the date by which material is expected to be available;

(*c*) the date by which work must be completed for delivery.

Whilst the factory office can and should make proposals in the light of all the facts at its disposal, the decision as to where new work should take its place in the overall plan must rest with the production management.

It is often found convenient to express the production programme as a chart which also shows the progress made. The best of plans are liable to go unfulfilled, and the production programme usually requires constant amendment. Suppliers may fail to keep to their delivery dates; estimated times may be exceeded or beaten; machines may break down; urgent work may have to be given priority. The production control chart must therefore be capable of being amended from hour to hour as conditions change or work is added or completed. For these reasons it is often found convenient to use a mechanical chart such as that illustrated in Fig. 106.

Job documents   When work is loaded into productive departments it is necessary to inform them of the material which must be drawn from store and the operations which are to be carried out. In a small factory it may suffice to issue copies of the material and operation schedules to the foreman, leaving him to organize the production from the information so provided. In the larger factory, however, there may be many departments and many foremen involved and the production management has the task of directing and co-ordinating their efforts. In these circumstances, it is usual to break down the main schedules and issue unit documents for each operation, i.e. material requisitions and operation tickets. By the issue and control of these the factory office can implement the decisions of management and provide information as to progress.

The nature of the information contained in the job documents will depend upon the nature of production. If production is repetitive and the operations familiar to all concerned, there need only be a short description of the operation. If, on the other hand, the factory is engaged in jobbing it may be necessary to supplement the unit document with drawings and a copy of the complete schedules so that each foreman may see his own responsibilities in relation to the job as a whole or some major part of it. Where unit documents are employed, it is often possible to have them serve more than one purpose. For example, the material requisition can:

(*a*) inform the foreman of the material on which his department must work;

(*b*) authorize the store to issue the material;

(*c*) act as an issue note and receipt to the store for the goods released by it;

(*d*) notify the progress department that material has passed into the factory;

(*e*) provide the cost office with the means of evaluating the material consumed;

(*f*) act as the medium through which stock records, and stock and cost accounts are posted.

The operation ticket can also serve a multiplicity of purposes; it can:

(*a*) inform the foreman as to the work to be done, the type of labour and/or machine to be employed, and the estimated time to be taken;

(*b*) aid the foreman in loading his department and assigning work to operators;

(*c*) provide a record of the actual time spent on the operation and a comparison of this with the estimate;

(*d*) notify the progress department of the completion of an operation and of the time taken;

(*e*) provide the cost office with the means of evaluating the time spent on an operation;

(*f*) provide the basis for bonus calculation;

(*g*) act as the medium for posting cost accounts and for reconciling labour expended with the payroll.

In view of these possibilities it is desirable to design the job documents so that they may serve the needs of all departments.

Progressing   In any factory which is undertaking a multiplicity of operations or producing many different articles, progress control is usually carried out by the factory office on behalf of the production management. Whilst the progress clerks or 'chasers' may spend much of their time on the factory floor, it is important that there should be proper records of the position as they find it. The material schedules, operation schedules, and the production control chart provide the programme. As work proceeds these same documents can be marked to indicate what has, in fact, been achieved, and may thus provide the management with the information required. If there is a considerable volume of such information, the management may prefer a daily or weekly report summarizing those points at which the programme has not been achieved, and those departments or machines which are underloaded or over-loaded.

Quality control   Among the items recorded is likely to be the quantity of production which is rejected on inspection as being below the required standards of quality. In addition to evaluating any losses arising from this, the office may be required to keep running records of the percentage of rejects from each operation and/or operator, so that management may be informed of any adverse trend.

Cost control   The nature of cost records and accounts should depend largely on the nature of the business. In principle, they should provide a reflection of what has occurred in the course of production. The value of cost information diminishes with the passing of time, and it is important that it should be available to the management quickly. If costs have risen above an economic level, corrective action must be taken as early as possible. The procedure must therefore provide for documents such as material requisitions and operation tickets to reach the cost office promptly.

The clerical processes usually necessary are as follows:

(*a*) receipt and control of job documents to ascertain that none have been mislaid in the factory or stores;

(*b*) pricing of material issues as shown on the material issue notes (which may be the requisitions serving a dual purpose);

(*c*) valuation of material issue notes;

(*d*) pricing of labour and/or machine-hours expended as shown on operation tickets, time sheets, clock cards or punched cards according to the system in use;

(*e*) valuation of operation tickets etc.;

(*f*) summarizing of the values of material issued and labour or machine-hours expended for control and accounting purposes;

(*g*) analysis of material and labour costs according to operation, job or process, as may be required for cost accounts and statistics.

Rarely is this work done as part of a cost-control procedure in isolation. Every cost-accounting system has in its very nature close links with the stock accounts, wages and bonus calculation and its results must be reconciled with the financial accounts. There is much to be gained therefore by integration of system. The pricing of material issues may well be combined with the posting of stock records since, if the prices are shown on these records, the need for a separate catalogue is avoided. The valuation of material issues is as necessary to the keeping of stock accounts as to cost accounts. The records of time spent may serve as the basis for wage and bonus calculation as well as for cost control.

Mechanized methods The range of operations associated with the office services to production is such that many of the machines and devices described in earlier chapters may be applied in one way or another. It is convenient initially to consider some of the common situtations in which mechanization may assist, such as the following:

(a) *Preparation of job documents* It is often necessary to prepare several copies of schedules and also unit documents authorizing the issue of materials and the carrying out of individual operations. Where the same processes are carried out repeatedly, identical sets of documents may have to be produced again and again. Duplicating and copying processes can be used so that one carefully-checked master schedule may be the means whereby working copies are made as required. Material requisitions and operation tickets can be made by cutting up a suitably designed copy or by masking unwanted matter when photocopying.

There are specially designed *spirit hectographic duplicators* which enable impressions of single lines of a schedule to be taken on small forms and tickets. *Addressing plates or stencils* can also be used to prepare lists and also single-item documents.

(b) *Data collection* Production control and cost-accounting systems usually involve the collection of numerous items of data from stores and from the factory floor. As the stores and factory staffs are non-clerical, the amount of recording should be kept to a minimum. Wherever possible, the job documents which act as instructions should serve also as the records of what actually occurs. Thus, if an instruction is carried out exactly, it may only be necessary to endorse the material or operation ticket to that effect, adding the date, operator's name etc. If the instruction is not carried out exactly, the actual quantities, times etc. must, of course, be inserted. These principles can be applied whether the methods are manual or mechanized.

(c) *Pricing and calculation* Where material, man-hours, production etc. must be priced at standard rates, the rates can often be incorporated in the master documents so that they appear with the quantities. If quantities are also standardized, the value can be shown, thus avoiding repeated calculation.

(d) *Accounting*   The items to be summarized as part of a production control or cost-accounting system must often be recorded for other purposes too. The possibility of producing more than one record at the same time by means of *an accounting machine* (see Chapter 9) or *manifold posting board* (see Fig. 96, page 203) should thus be considered. For example, records of material issued to jobs or processes might be made as carbon copies of the entries on stores stock records; records of finished production might be similarly made as copies of warehouse stock records. When summarizing the time spent on jobs, carbon copies of the entries could be made on operators' time sheets or bonus records.

(e) *Data processing*   The more advanced machines are able to combine many or all of the processes necessary in planning production, preparing job documents and producing cost accounts and other types of management information.

The *visible-record computer* (see Chapter 8) has facilities for:

(*a*) automatic pricing from stored lists of material prices, labour rates etc.;

(*b*) automatic calculation for the evaluation of costs;

(*c*) automatic calculation of standard cost variances;

(*d*) accumulation of control totals;

(*e*) simultaneous entering of a number of related forms;

(*f*) provision of punched or magnetic output for further processing.

The *mainframe computer* (see Chapter 8) is able to undertake a complete cycle of work embracing both planning and control. Given the production required and data as to material stocks, machine/operator capacity available and optimum quantities, it can be programmed to calculate the production plan which will make the best use of resources. In addition to the master plan, it can print out the necessary schedules and job documents. On receiving data relating to what has actually occurred in the factory, it can then compare this with the plan and print out reports showing deviations. In some systems, the job documents are produced in the form of punched cards which, after the minimum of additional punching, are fed back into the computer for further processing. In addition, the computer can produce magnetic cards or printed forms which can be read again by optical means.

Given material prices, labour rates etc., the computer can also prepare cost accounts with detailed explanations of any variances from standard performance.

Complete production planning and control systems should be co-ordinated with the raw material, work in progress, and finished-goods stock control and, in some respects, with the payroll system. The object is that data common to two or more systems shall be recorded once only and that the results shall be fully reconciled.

The computer's ability to discriminate makes it possible to print out the full details of those variances from standard performance which are large enough to require the attention of management, whilst suppressing those which are insignificant.

Where the computer is able to have data files always on line, direct data entry methods may be used by the production office staff. With the aid of visual display units, it may also be possible to make direct enquiries of the computer as to the availability of stock or work in progress, and obtain other information dependent on the nature of the production processes and the control system employed.

17 Management information

The term 'management information' should be interpreted widely as including financial accounts, divisional and departmental accounts and cost accounts, as well as statistical statements of one sort and another. In the preceding chapters of this Part, it has been shown how information in quantity or value, in detail or in total, may be extracted as part of a routine procedure. It has been convenient, and realistic, to consider separately the processes relating to sales, purchases, wages, stock control etc. In business generally, clerical work is done according to such separate systems. But eventually, all must be seen as parts of one pattern of records, illustrating the affairs of the business in varying degrees of detail and in total.

Management requires information for two main purposes: planning and control. When laying plans for the future, decisions must be based on estimates, and these are usually calculated with reference to the records of past experience. When controlling the business in operation, management requires to know what has happened in the immediate past in order to correct any undesirable trends. Management includes all levels from the foreman or supervisor to the chief executive. It is just as important that a foreman should have information illustrating the affairs of his section, as that the board of directors should know the total profit or loss resulting from the business as a whole. Indeed, if every supervisor could ensure that his section was operating according to plan, top management might have little cause for concern about the overall result.

Office systems generally start with the collection of factual information in terms of quantity and/or value. They then summarize this to provide totals and balances which will eventually be brought together to give the final profit and loss account and balance sheet, or other financial statement. During these processes of collection and collation, management information can be extracted to suit the needs at various levels of responsibility. The foreman can be expected to require information in terms of quantity: numbers produced, man-hours worked, weights of material consumed etc. The departmental or functional manager may require totals in quantity, together with accounts in money value to correspond with these. Top management will require some totals in quantity, with complete accounts in value. For the greatest benefit to be gained, the figures provided at any level must be capable of being related directly with those provided at levels above or below.

Factual information is only meaningful when compared with some concept of what is satisfactory or unsatisfactory. The most commonly adopted comparison is with the corresponding period of time in a previous year, but there are other types of comparison which will be mentioned in this chapter. In the more advanced management information systems, comparison is with a pre-determined target of achievement: a budget or standard.

It is not to be assumed that the more advanced techniques, some of which require mathematical rather than accounting methods, should be adopted in all situations. The smaller business may be well served by simple reports, whilst the large and complex business might find these completely inadequate. The office manager or accountant is not always told what information to produce. He must try to understand the business and the needs of management so as to be able to suggest useful new forms of accounting or statistical statement.

The development of the computer and other advanced machines has made it possible to provide a better management information service. It has also drawn wider attention to the need to integrate accounting and statistical systems. The records of a business, by whatever names they may be described, are parts of one whole system. Whether a computer is employed, or simple hand methods, the possibility of integration should be pursued.

FINANCIAL ACCOUNTS

All procedures which are directly or indirectly concerned with accounting, whether in quantity or value, should be regarded as parts of one accounting system. Eventually, the detailed facts about purchases, sales, stocks, production, cash, wages etc. become summarized as totals and balances on accounts. At this point, the administrative function with which this book is concerned has fulfilled its task. It is now for the accountant to construct the trading account, profit and loss account and balance sheet, or other form of final accounting statement.

The routine systems should provide the figures needed by the accountant without his having to go back to the original sources. For example, a total of directors' expenses is of little help if this has later to be analysed to separate the amounts incurred by individual directors. In such a situation, it is better that an account be kept for each individual in the first place and totalled in a control account.

The financial accounts must, in some respects, conform with legal requirements. It should, however, be borne in mind that accounts were primarily intended to provide information for management. To separate the financial accounting procedures from those producing management information is to duplicate work. The objective should be to so arrange the methods that all the information required for any purpose can stem from one sequence of operations.

DIVISIONAL OR DEPARTMENTAL ACCOUNTS

In the small trading concern, the traditional trading account, profit and loss account, and balance sheet may provide all the management information necessary. As businesses grow in size and complexity, however, these basic accounts are not enough. They still show the overall profitability and liquidity, but they do not provide many answers to the questions which the accounts themselves may pose. The need to answer questions has led to the subdivision of accounts, so as to narrow to some extent the areas of further investigation. The breaking down may be:

(a) by divisions, where a business is engaged in more than one major activity; or

(b) by departments, according to the responsibilities of the various managers and supervisors.

Such accounts are generally termed departmental accounts because they show how the various parts of the business have contributed to the total of revenue, expenditure, investment etc. Inevitably, some items in the accounts remain the sole responsibility of top management and require no analysis. Below this level, the purpose is to illustrate the affairs of each division or department as though it were a separate business within a business.

Where the principles of *management by objectives* are applied, and targets are set in terms of revenue, expenditure etc., the departmental accounts should be so designed as to illustrate each manager's performance. The technique of management by objectives is discussed in relation to the office on pages 317–8 but may be applied in appropriate terms to any department of a business.

In order to avoid duplication of work, it is best to arrive at divisional or departmental totals and balances in the first place and then summarize these to give grand totals for incorporation in the financial accounts for the business as a whole.

COST ACCOUNTS

The cost accounts should enable costs to be studied in relation to the purposes for which they are incurred. The financial accounts of a business provide useful, but limited, information in this respect. They show what is the state of the business, but little of why that state exists. Management must know which of its products and which of its selling channels are the more profitable; it must know which components of the overall cost of operation are rising or falling. Whereas divisional or departmental accounts are concerned with areas of responsibility, cost accounts provide an analysis of revenue and expenditure according to products, processes, jobs or other classifications, and where appropriate they show these results of actual performance in comparison with predetermined standards.

This information is usually provided at frequent intervals. Whereas financial accounts may be prepared annually or quarterly, the results of the business as shown by the cost accounts may be produced monthly, weekly or, in part, daily.

For the purpose of costing, expenditure is usually classified firstly under three broad headings: labour, material and oncost. Although they will be further subdivided according to the particular needs of the business, it is convenient to consider the work of the office under these headings.

Labour   If the cost headings under which labour needs to be dissected are few, as is the case in some process or departmental costing systems, it may be possible to make the dissection on the wages sheets (see page 210). If the entire wages of any one employee can always be charged to a single cost heading, the names can be arranged on the wages sheets in groups to correspond with the cost headings, and sub-totals of the gross wages can be taken and posted to the cost accounts. Where, however, each employee's time in any week or day may be charged to several different cost headings, it will be necessary to post the cost accounts from the time sheets, clock cards or other detailed records of working time. Generally, this is done in one of two ways: either by calculating on, say, a time sheet, the actual cost of each employee's wages and posting the cash values to the cost accounts or, alternatively, by posting the hours worked to the cost accounts, and valuing the hours accumulated under each job or other cost heading at standard rates. Where the different jobs being handled at any one time are numerous, it is usual to allot job numbers to facilitate identification. Indirect labour, which cannot be dissected to any particular job, product or department, is usually accumulated separately and apportioned as a percentage on direct labour or on some other arbitrary basis.

Materials   The charging of materials presents a slightly different problem and normally some form of stores delivery note is the basis of the charge (see page 213). When raw materials are purchased the normal accounting entry is to credit the supplier's personal account and debit the nominal account. For cost accounting purposes, as well as for the control of the store, the goods may also be charged to a stores control account (see page 216). When materials are issued from a store for a particular job, they are accompanied by the stores delivery note indicating the process or job for which they are to be used. When valued, the note is used as a medium for crediting the stores control account and charging under the appropriate cost heading. Reference has already been made to the method of calculating the cost of raw materials (see page 219).

Oncosts   Oncosts are treated in the cost accounts in a variety of ways according to the nature of the business. Some may be apportioned to jobs, products or processes as a percentage of material or labour cost or on some other basis; others may be apportioned departmentally. Whatever the method of treatment, it is usually necessary to maintain an analysis by nominal accounts. This analysis may be made when invoices are passed for payment or when oncost materials are drawn from store, according to when it is first possible to identify the appropriate cost heading. Two main principles should be applied: costs should be charged in the cost accounts as early as possible in the clerical processes, and duplication of records for the financial accounts and cost accounts should be avoided.

OTHER MANAGEMENT INFORMATION

Purchase statistics   The requirements of the buying department have been mentioned in Chapter 15 (Stock control). In addition to information for the control of ordering and for following up deliveries, the management may also require to know the commitments according to the date when payment is due, so that they may ensure that cash will be available to meet liabilities.

Production statistics   The statistical requirements of the factory management and supervision are discussed in Chapter 16 (Production records).

Sales statistics   Much useful information can be provided to the management with little additional clerical work, and reference has already been made to this in Chapter 11 (Sales accounting).

Financial statistics   These may include statements of cash-in-hand, debtors, creditors, bad and doubtful debts, and current value of investments.

Personnel statistics   Reference has been made in Chapter 14 (Wages) to the maintenance of central staff records from which information can be provided as to employees engaged and leaving, rates of pay etc.

FIGURES FOR PLANNING

Planning is the responsibility of management, but plans involve paper work, and paper work is the responsibility of the office. As always, the office is the servant, and whilst interpretation of the information gathered may be suggested by those more familiar with figures, it is management which in fact determines policy on the basis of these interpretations.

Whatever plans are in course of preparation, the records of the office will be found of value in providing details of past experience. On the production side, the office may be called upon to cost new products or new plant, or to show the probable effect on the business of a rise in price of a raw material, or an increase in wage rates. The sales department may require to know the cost of distributing goods over a wider area, or to have some market survey carried out.

In larger businesses particularly, the office may be called upon to estimate the profitability of new ventures of considerable magnitude. Whether the project be large or small, the primary task of the office is to take the initial plans of the management and, in consultation with the appropriate managers and technicians, to translate them into terms of probable revenue and expenditure. If existing production methods are to be continued, the costs will already be available in the office. If, on the other hand, new processes are involved, the office must co-operate with the technical experts in estimating their cost. The engineer can state the anticipated output of the machine, the time-study man can estimate the hours of labour, and the production manager can state the raw materials to be used. From its own records, the office is able to put a value on each of these items, and so build up a costing.

The office manager should not regard this task as merely one of valuing a list of items provided for him. From his experience of the business as illustrated in the accounts and other records, he must be prepared to offer criticism, comment and advice. It will be observed that this process requires, in addition to a knowledge of costs, a familiarity with the technical operations, and it is essential that clerks engaged on this work should be highly trained for their duties. To take but one example, in dealing with the costs of the raw materials, the clerk will need to take into consideration, not merely the basic costs, but carriage, packaging, storage rent, storage handling, and all the manifold additional costs which are involved before the raw material is delivered at the bench or machine.

In principle, the evaluation of management plans is always the evaluation of alternative courses of action. In the simplest state, management may have to decide whether to make a change or continue existing policy. Sometimes, however, management must choose from among a number of possible plans. For example, the office may be required to calculate the optimum level of production or rate of expansion, rather than evaluate a clear-cut proposition. In the more complex situations it may be necessary to use mathematical and operational research techniques. These can include:

(a) *Discounted cash flow*   This technique is used in decision making. It takes into account the fact that payments in the current year cost more than equivalent payments in future years.

(b) *Industrial models*   These also are concerned with decision making. The process involves the use of mathematical models to determine the probable effect of experimental ideas in complex business situations.

(c) *Value analysis*   The value concept seeks to improve quality at the same cost, or maintain quality at a reduced cost. It is concerned with the careful measurement of the effects of using alternative processes and materials to achieve the required result.

(d) *Critical path analysis* This technique is designed to enable projects to be completed on time whilst also fulfilling specifications and keeping within budgeted costs. It is a charting process which has regard to such matters as time-cost relationships.

Whilst the office may provide from its records some of the data, the application of mathematical techniques is usually a matter for specialists.

When the plan is put into operation, steps need to be taken to compare performance against the plan. To permit of this subsequent control, the plan must be stated in terms which will allow a comparison to be made with the financial and cost accounts, and other records. If such a comparison is not possible, a review will be necessary; both plans and office records need to be couched in terms which truly reflect the operation of the business.

ACCOUNTING COMPARISONS

A figure in isolation has no meaning; it must be compared with some other figure. For example, sales of £1000 may be an improvement when compared with £900, but a disaster when compared with £10 000. Comparisons may be of several kinds:

(a) *Historical comparison,* as where one year's accounts are set beside those for a previous year, so that changes may be evaluated item by item and in total.

(b) *Management ratios,* as where one figure is related to another within the same account, e.g. gross profit in relation to sales turnover, or net profit in relation to investment.

(c) *Interfirm comparison,* as where one business compares its results with those of others in the same industry or trade.

(d) *Budgetary control comparison,* as where revenue, expenditure, assets and liabilities are estimated in advance according to management plans, and the actual figures as revealed by the accounts are compared with them to produce budget variances.

(e) *Standard or marginal cost comparison,* as where standard costings are prepared for factory jobs, operations, processes etc. (see page 230). The goods produced are evaluated at the standard costs of material, labour etc. and the results compared with the corresponding actual costs as shown in the cost accounts to produce cost variances.

(f) *Project comparisons,* as where a major project is planned and evaluated in terms of estimated investment, revenue and expenditure, and the actual results as revealed by the accounts are compared with these estimates.

Some of these methods require no more than the presentation of accounts in a suitable form and a few calculations which the accountant may make personally. Others require that the accounts or other office records be kept in a manner to facilitate comparisons and to produce detailed explanations of any variances which are significant. The ability to explain variances without unreasonable effort is important. Investigations by senior clerks are costly and the time spent in obtaining detailed information can be greatly reduced if the vouchers supporting accounts etc. are systematically filed with this task in mind.

The work which the office may be called upon to do in the setting of standards for comparison is discussed above under Figures for Planning.

INTEGRATED ACCOUNTING

Office management has long been aware of the high cost of operating separate systems for producing financial accounts, cost accounts and other management information. For example, the routine act of selling can generate entries on:

delivery note
invoice
sales journal
sales account (debit)
warehouse stock record
customer statement
sales account (credit)
cash book
bank statement
commission statement
customer sales record
sales analyses.

Not all of the information about sale or payment will appear on every record, but there is considerable duplication.

The possibility of integrating accounting processes requires the application of the O & M techniques described in Chapter 24. This process is made the more practicable with the development of the computer.

The data concerning a sale can be assembled partly from files containing 'fixed information' such as names and addresses, product descriptions, prices and terms etc., and partly from the customer's order. Once all the data are available, invoicing, accounting, stock control, sales analysis and other processes can be carried out automatically by extraction and summarization.

In most business concerns the development and integration of management information systems evolves over time through a predictable series of stages:

(1) In the beginning the main emphasis is upon the financial accounts.

(2) Subsequently, various management information techniques are adopted independently, but with increasing sophistication.

(3) When the need is recognized, a third stage occurs in which attempts are made to integrate the information systems with each other and with the financial accounts.

(4) In the final stage the availability of computers offer the opportunity for the complete integration of all the systems.

Each stage may take several years and there is often some overlapping of stages. In consequence, decades may elapse before the pattern of management information is developed as one integrated whole. The future trend is, however, clear: a movement towards the capture of basic data to be processed to produce all the required results. In furthering this trend, every opportunity should be taken to eliminate duplication of work by integrating separate but related systems.

Accounts and statistics prepared by the office for the information of the management must be pertinent, accurate and prompt. They must give the key information which will lead management to take action or to make further inquiry. They must not be misleading through inaccuracy or vagueness. They must be available as soon after the events to which they refer as is economically possible; any delay in management being able to correct undesirable tendencies represents a loss to the business.

It has already been pointed out that the nature of control statistics must depend upon the nature and peculiarities of the business; it must also depend upon the level of management by which the figures are to be used. The foreman may require detailed daily returns of production, to enable him to review the position within his field of responsibility. The managing director requires less detailed information, but covering a much wider field. The mode of presentation of control statistics will also vary with the requirements of individual managers. The facility with which different persons comprehend different statistical statements must be taken into account. Some people are able readily to comprehend the significance of facts presented in the form of involved tabulations; others need to have them simplified or are better able to understand charts.

The responsibility of the office is to produce the information at the time and place and in the form required by the management. The publication of extracts from the office records is, however, not enough. The manager of an office producing management information should examine the figures produced from the point of view of the general management. He should ask himself the questions: 'If I were the manager receiving these statistics, could I act upon them? If I could not, what other information would I require?' He should look for abnormal trends, and differences between actual results and standards and, having located them, seek the practical reasons in order to be able to present the full facts. It is important that the administrative manager should not live in a world of figures without appreciating their significance.

The more the office can know of the practical problems of the business, the better will it serve the management; the more the office can speak to management in its own language, the better will it be understood.

18   Insurance

The safeguarding of security is one of the prime functions of management. It is concerned with protecting a business at minimum cost from fortuitous losses which might put its finances in jeopardy. Much of the risk can be covered by insurance but the handling of risk is more properly dealt with by a comprehensive strategy based on all the resources available. This approach is called risk management.

RISK MANAGEMENT

Risk management can involve three stages:

(*1*) *Identification*   This concerns the identification of all the risks to which the enterprise is liable. Some risks are obvious, such as the loss of property through fire, theft and loss in transit, and liability for injury to employees or to third parties. Some risks are less obvious, for example the liability for negligent or tortious acts of employees, and their identification, requires knowledge combined with imagination. A first step is to identify areas that are liable to risk and the associated events that can give rise to loss. A second step is to identify possible causes of loss resulting from natural phenomena, breach of natural laws and man's activities. The third step is to identify the resulting damage to property, personal injury, legal liability and loss of earnings.

(*2*) *Evaluation*   This requires that risks shall be measured according to likelihood and value.

(*3*) *Management*   This requires the exercise of judgment. Among the possibilities are:

(*a*) Avoidance. A risk may be avoided by:

(i) a change in location, procedure, materials, process or equipment;
(ii) giving up the activity that gives rise to the risk.

(*b*) Reduction. Risks can be reduced in a variety of ways:

(i) by physical security devices such as locks, alarms, pressure gauges, safety guards on machines, sprinklers and safety doors;

247

(ii) by procedural devices such as inspections, security patrols, checks on employees, frequent clearing of flammable waste and by the institution of controls;

(iii) by education and training in safe methods of working and in procedures for dealing with emergencies;

(iv) by providing for risk reduction when designing production processes.

(c) Transfer. This is the legal assignment of potential losses to another party:

(i) by insurance which is the most common form of transfer;

(ii) by a contractural device such as a change in the terms of buying, selling or leasing.

(d) Retention. A business may assume the risk itself and make appropriate financial reserves for this purpose. This may be a prudent decision, for example, for an enterprise with a large fleet of vehicles; whilst there would be a legal requirement to insure against third-party risks, the enterprise could itself carry the costs of repairs to vehicles arising from accidents.

In summary, risk management involves exploring the costs of alternative methods of protecting an enterprise from fortuitous losses.

INSURANCE ADMINISTRATION

Many large concerns appoint a manager to be responsible for making recommendations about risk management and insurance. In smaller organizations, this responsibility may be given to the company secretary or the office manager.

The responsibilities of an insurance manager include:

(a) identifying risks and recommending how these risks are to be covered;

(b) placing and maintaining the insurances;

(c) making recommendations relating to risk reduction; and

(d) dealing with claims.

These responsibilities require the manager to maintain contact with all parts of the business so that he may be aware of the changes in risk situations, of security measures or the lack of them, of the alternative ways of managing the risks and of the associated costs of these alternatives.

Ideally, the insurance manager should visit all the principal premises at intervals, partly because of the value of personal contact, partly because the written word is often inadequate to convey all the relevant information, and partly because he has expertise to offer. He may also require that some inspections are made by specialists.

Contracts may be a source of risk and the insurance manager should ensure that someone is responsible for identifying legal liabilities that need to be considered in relation to insurance and risk management. Contracts to be so examined include leases, contracts of sale, supply or service, construction contracts and hire of premises.

It is important that the insurance manager is informed at once of all incidents causing damage to property and injury to persons, or other matters for which the organization may be held liable; sometimes a standard form is used for this purpose. The legal department, if there is one, may also be involved in some cases.

LEGAL ASPECTS OF INSURANCE

An insurance 'policy' is a contract between the insurer and the insured and, as such, subject to the law which governs contracts generally. Because of the special nature of insurance, however, there are special principles which are also applied.

Utmost good faith Contracts of insurance are contracts *uberrimae fidei* or of the utmost good faith. In practice, this means that a person or company making a proposal to an insurer must disclose all the material facts. These facts are those which would influence the insurer in accepting the risk at all, or in accepting it at a particular premium rate. If material facts are not disclosed, the insurer has the option of declaring the contract void and refusing to pay any claims made by the insured.

Insurable interest Insurance is not gambling. For a policy to be enforceable, the insured must have a legally recognized interest in the property or other subject matter of the contract. For example, a company is not entitled to insure a building against fire unless it will suffer financial loss as the result of a fire in that building. It is not necessary for the insured to own the building; the company might sustain loss of a mortgage, or as a tenant with a legal liability to make good fire damage under the terms of its lease.

Indemnity The intention of insurance is that the insured, on suffering financial loss, shall have this loss made good, no more and no less. This principle cannot, of course, apply in life or personal-accident insurance.

Contribution If the insured has more than one policy covering the same loss, the principle of indemnity prohibits his having that loss made good more than once. If there are two or more insurances, the loss will be shared by the insurers.

Subrogation Again, in applying the principle of indemnity, an insured person cannot obtain damages from a third party and also claim for the same loss from an insurer. If he chooses to claim from the insurer, then his right to recover damages from a third party passes to the insurer.

THE INSURANCE MARKET

There are many insurance companies, some specializing in certain types of risk and some covering a wide range of business. In addition to the companies, Lloyd's underwriters handle a variety of risks as well as the marine insurance for which they are famous.

The first consideration is to insure with a company which is financially sound and likely to be able to meet claims made on it. The buyer then has the choice of placing insurance business with:

(*a*) one company, which may be convenient in practice and beneficial if a discount is offered because of the value of total premiums;

(*b*) several companies, each giving a more specialized service.

The buyer may also consider the benefits of using a broker as an intermediary because of his professional competence, experience, special expertise and access to Lloyd's and other specialized markets. This knowledge will include the advantages or otherwise of using particular companies or the possibility of advantageous policy wordings to the benefit of the buyer.

When a loss occurs, the insurer may appoint a 'loss adjuster' whose duty it then is to ascertain whether the loss is covered by the policy and, if so, the amount of the settlement. His professional integrity requires that he acts equitably in the interests of both parties. The insured party can also appoint a 'loss assessor' to negotiate the claim.

FIRE

Insurance against fire and its effects is perhaps the most common form of insurance protection. A standard policy covers fire, lightning and, to some extent, explosion. There are many exclusions: fire and explosion is excluded if caused by:

(*a*) its own spontaneous fermentation;

(*b*) a process involving heating;

(*c*) earthquake or subterranean fire;

(*d*) nuclear explosion;

(*e*) riot, civil commotion, civil war, rebellion, revolution or insurrection;

(*f*) war, invasion, hostilities or act of foreign enemy.

Some of these risks, but not those relating to war, can be recovered by an additional premium.

Fire must be accidental so far as the insured party is concerned. Arson is covered provided it does not occur with the consent of the insured.

Explosion of domestic boilers and domestic gas lighting or heating is covered, but explosions caused by non-domestic boilers, pressure vessels, dust and chemicals have to be covered separately. Damage by concussion may need separate cover.

An additional premium may be required to cover non-fire damage by aircraft and anything dropped from them but sonic booms are not covered, the latter being the responsibility of the Government.

A fire policy may be extended by an extra premium to cover damage by storm, tempest, flood and bursting or overflowing of water tanks, pipes and apparatus.

When taking out fire insurance the buyer has to understand what property is covered. A standard specification may include the building together with landlord's fixtures and fittings, machinery, plant, stock and materials in trade and all other contents, the property of the insured or held in trust or on commission for which he is responsible. There may be exclusions and possible extensions.

There may be a limit on the value of money, stamps, documents, business books, patterns, models, plans, designs and employees' personal belongings. Computer records may also be limited in value and require an additional premium.

Professional fees for reinstatement of the premises may be covered by an extra premium. These would include fees for architects, surveyors, solicitors and engineers but not fees caused by making a claim for the damage.

Reinstatement may involve the application of by-laws or building regulations that were not previously in force; such costs can be heavy and their cover would require an extra premium.

Rent may be insured by an owner-occupier to pay for alternative accommodation, or by a tenant obliged to pay even though the premises are unusable.

THEFT

When considering theft and insurance against it, the owner must have regard to a variety of factors. Of prime importance is the extent to which goods are vulnerable because of their worth and the ease with which they can be removed and exchanged for cash.

The next consideration is the cost of security. For most concerns, the vulnerable stocks can be concentrated in particular stores and given special protection. This can be done by a shop, hotel or restaurant for cigarettes, wines and spirits; a manufacturing plant can have a special store for precious metals; a jeweller will require protection for almost the entire stock. Vulnerable areas can be protected but only at a cost for strong-rooms, safes, warning systems and personnel occupied on controls or surveillance. Security is so complex a subject that it may be wise to pay for expert advice.

Deciding how to insure against theft involves:

(*a*) determining the relationship between the cost of insurance and the cost of security—the better the security, the lower the premium; the poorer the security, the higher the premium.

(*b*) determining how far to insure, since the premium can be reduced in various ways, for example, by insuring only for an estimated first loss or by accepting a part of each loss, say the first £500.

A proposal form for insurance against theft calls for extensive information about the security of the area involved, about locks and other devices on doors, windows and skylights, times of occupancy and guards on duty at other times. If values are appreciable, the insurer may survey the premises from time to time. The policy may include such requirements as:

(*a*) care in the selection of employees;

(*b*) a limit on the total to be paid during the period of the policy;

(*c*) the keeping of detailed records of goods in and out.

Exclusions may include:

(*a*) riot, war etc., as in the case of fire;

(*b*) fire and explosion;

(*c*) losses caused by an employee, a member of the insured's family or anyone lawfully on the premises;

(*d*) items above a certain value unless listed in the policy.

LIABILITIES

This protects the insured against legal liabilities at common law and under statute for injury to persons, damage to property and other financial loss. There are three kinds of risk: third-party liability, products liability and employer's liability. The relevant policies are available separately or in any combination.

Third-party liability   This covers the liability to members of the public for injury or damage to property caused by defective premises and plant or negligent employees. Claims by members of the public can be substantial, as can legal defence costs which are also covered by the insurance.

Excluded, but covered by other policies, are:

(*a*) injuries to employees;

(*b*) damage to property owned by or in the custody of the insured;

(*c*) vehicles on the public highway, ships and aircraft;

(*d*) products liability.

There are other exclusions which can specifically be covered, e.g. employees' effects, leased property and property being worked upon.

War and riot risks cannot be insured. Nuclear and radioactive risks require special arrangements. Contractural risks are not covered unless the insured party would have been liable by law in any case.

There may be a limit on the total liability but this amount is substantial. The premium is usually based on payroll or turnover.

Products liability This covers liability for negligence at common law, liability under statute where proof of negligence may be unnecessary, and breach of conditions of sale. The potential liability of some manufacturers is huge, of which pharmaceuticals and aircraft are examples.

The basic insurance is in the area of 'claims for injury or damage caused by any defects in the products', but wordings vary; the insurance buyer needs to give careful attention to the wording.

The cover applies only when the products have left the insured's control so that injury to employees and damage to the insured's property are excluded.

Exclusions may include liability assumed by contract and liability for repairing or replacing faulty parts.

It is usual for there to be a limit on the liability for any one incident and on the total of claims during the period covered. The premium is usually based on turnover.

Employer's liability It is compulsory by law for employers to insure against liability for injury or disease sustained by employees arising out of their employment in Great Britain. Exempted employers are local government, police and nationalized industries. Certificates of insurance must be on display at the place of business and an uninsured employer is liable to a fine. The legislation prescribes the form of policy and the limit of indemnity.

Premiums are based on payroll and may be altered in the light of claims over a period of years. Many insurance companies offer inspection and advisory services.

PERSONNEL

There are three main aspects to financial compensation for death, injury, sickness and prolonged disability of employees:

(a) that required by law which has been dealt with above;

(b) that considered appropriate on humanitarian grounds or to avoid employee dissatisfaction.

(c) that which it is considered prudent to insure.

The range of policies available is comparatively limited.

Personal accident There is commonly available a policy which provides:

(a) a capital sum for death by accident, or loss of one or more limbs or eyes, or for permanent total disablement;

(b) weekly payments for up to two years for temporary total disablement or partial disablement.

It is possible to insure separately for one or more of these hazards but temporary partial disablement can only be covered if temporary total disablement is also covered.

There are some variations, for example:

(a) as to what constitutes permanent disablement; or
(b) as to whether the loss of two limbs or eyes provides a larger sum than the loss of one.

The premium is based on different rates per £1000 of capital sum for each risk.

Common grounds for exclusion are drug taking, suicide, wilful exposure to needless risks, private flying and a variety of so-called hazardous sports.

Some concerns insure for a larger capital sum for executives than for others; some cover only executives and other favoured occupations.

Many companies, particularly the larger ones, do not insure in this way because they:

(a) have pension schemes which provide for payments on death before retirement, or pensions for early retirement through ill-health;
(b) regard the cost of sick pay over long periods for employees with service qualification as a normal business expense:
(c) find inadequate a policy that compensates for loss of limb or eye but excludes other serious and permanent injuries.

These considerations are less likely to apply in the case of small firms where paying for long absence by one or two employees would impose a serious burden and where compensation for a personal catastrophe would be beyond its resources.

Travel insurance   Some employers insure members of the staff when travelling overseas on business; some include travel by public transport in the UK. Even though a company may have a pension scheme which pays a substantial sum in the event of death before retirement, it is argued that death by misadventure whilst on business requires additional compensation. Travel insurance can usually be extended to cover medical expenses and loss of baggage.

Medical and surgical expenses   Insurance companies will cover payment for private medical care for the insured person and his family. This form of insurance is also provided by the British United Provident Association or by the Private Patients Plan.

MONEY

A normal policy covers loss of money from the insured's business premises, from contract sites, from the homes of specified senior employees, from a bank night-safe, in transit and in the hands of representatives and collectors. Money means cash, currency notes, cheques, postal orders, saving certificates and luncheon vouchers.

It is usually required that when the premises are closed:

(a) money above, say, £50 must be kept in a locked safe;

(b) money above some higher limit must be kept in a strong-room.

A strong-room may be expensive because it will have to meet standards set by the insurer. The insured may prefer not to retain large sums of money out of hours but employ a security service to take the money away and return it when the premises are re-opened; alternatively, a bank night-safe can be used. Either arrangement may not be needed every night but only when an extra amount is held, say just prior to pay day.

A policy usually covers losses caused by dishonest employees, but only provided the loss is discovered within a time limit which might be 48 hours.

Common exclusions include war and related acts, but not riot and civil commotion except in special circumstances as in Northern Ireland. Compensation to employees injured whilst in charge of money may be covered by an additional premium.

Fidelity guarantee   Under this, the insurer makes good the loss of cash or goods caused by the dishonesty of employees of the insured. The insurer examines the employees' occupational history, obtaining references and making such enquiries as are thought fit.

Because some losses may remain hidden for long periods, a policy specifies two periods beyond that of annual renewal:

(a) the period between misappropriation and discovery;

(b) the period between the date of leaving employment or cancelling the policy and the date of discovering the misappropriation.

There is a limit on the insurer's liability in any year.

There are individual policies or collective policies, for example:

(a) for several named employees each with a separate guaranteed limit;

(b) a blanket policy for certain categories of employee, without individual names and guarantee limits and where the employer is responsible for obtaining references.

Credit insurance   This protects a trader from loss caused by insolvency or failure to pay within 90 days of due date an admitted debt for goods delivered. Non-payment from political causes is excluded. Normally, the insurer takes about 80 per cent of the risk and the insured retains the rest.

A policy can be on whole turnover, for the whole world or for specified markets, or for a particular transaction. It may provide for the insurer to be able to abandon future cover for specified customers and countries. Normally, policies exclude government departments, public authorities and associated companies of the insured.

ALL-RISKS

An all-risks policy is wider than both fire and theft together but nonetheless does not cover every risk. It is appropriate for jewellery, works of art and other items of high individual value. Security requirements are stringent and there are many exclusions, for example money, breakage, damage by wear, tear or climate, and riot, war etc.

MOTOR

Private vehicles   There are three basic forms of cover:

(a) Road Traffic Act. This covers the legal liability to third parties for death or injury caused by the insured vehicle.

(b) Third party. In addition to covering the legal liability for death and injury, this covers damage to the property of third parties. Fire and theft cover can be added.

(c) Comprehensive. In addition to that provided by a third-party policy, this covers loss or damage to the insured car. The limit is the declared value of the car when the insurance is raised, but the market value is usual in the case of total loss. In case of damage, the policy covers removal to the nearest repairer, cost of repairs and redelivery. There is a lump-sum death benefit for the owner, and perhaps his wife, as well as sums for medical benefits, loss of sight or limbs and loss of personal effects.

The premium depends upon a number of factors:

(a) the way in which the vehicle is used; the premium is higher if the vehicle is used for business than if it is used for the social, domestic and pleasure purposes of the owner;

(b) cars garaged in the centre of large towns attract higher premiums than those garaged in rural areas;

(c) cars are grouped into six classes according to performance; the higher the performance, the higher the premium;

(d) the premium is increased if there is to be more than one driver, if the driver has a poor accident record and if the insurer is to pay the full cost of damage;

(e) the premium may be reduced by a no-claims bonus which may range from $33\frac{1}{3}$ per cent for one year to 60 per cent for four claim-free years.

Commercial vehicles   Again, there are three basic forms of policy:

(*a*) Road Traffic Act. This is the same as for private vehicles.

(*b*) Third party. This, also, is the same as for a private vehicle except that there is a limit on the insurer's liability for damage to property, but loading and unloading is covered provided this is done by the driver or other attendant.

(*c*) Comprehensive. Also as for a private vehicle except that personal accident, medical expenses and personal effects are not covered, nor are goods carried in the vehicle.

In determining premium, factors additional to those mentioned under private vehicles are weight and trade; a commercial vehicle can only be used for the trade stated in the policy.

Other vehicles   Motorcycles, motor scooters, mopeds and invalid carriages are covered by the three basic forms of policy provided for private cars. Otherwise:

(*a*) hire cars, coaches, buses and mobile tools have special policies;

(*b*) the motor trade has special policies for vehicles not owned by the insured; these cover road risks and internal risks separately;

(*c*) trailers towed by private vehicles are usually covered for third-party risks but not those towed by commercial vehicles; both need an additional premium for comprehensive cover.

General   All policies require the insured to protect the vehicle from loss or damage and to maintain it in good condition. If the vehicle is kept in the street the insurer should be informed. A vehicle with faulty brakes could cause an objection to a claim. Most policies exclude war, riot etc.

Temporary use outside the United Kingdom can be covered at extra cost. A 'green card' exempts the user in some foreign countries from taking a separate insurance.

BUSINESS INTERRUPTION

Whilst material damage insurances cover the loss of assets, business-interruption insurance covers the corresponding loss of earnings. The policy contains the formula by which the amount is calculated and is specific as to matters such as calculating loss in turnover, additional cost of working and loss of profit.

Compensation is payable only if there is material damage insurance in operation for the specific property, against the peril that caused the interruption and the material damage insurers have admitted liability. The sum assured has to be based on future earnings taking into account variations and trends so as to provide the amount that would have been available had there been no interruption.

CONTRACTORS ALL RISKS

This policy protects a party who requires work to be done and also the contractor against damage before the handover. It excludes, among other causes, risks that are not fortuitous, those directly associated with the manner of construction, war, riot etc.

GOODS IN TRANSIT

By land The parties to a contract of carriage are the haulier and the trader. A haulier is engaged in carrying goods for third parties and as such is liable at common law for loss or damage with some exceptions. Most hauliers operate with written conditions, under which, typically, the haulier is responsible, whether or not he is negligent, except in case of act of God, war, riot, fault of the trader, inherent vice of the goods or inadequate packing.

Goods in transit may be the subject of two insurances. The trader will require the widest possible cover and the haulier will require to cover the liability under his written conditions and those at common law. Some hauliers cover both sets of interests in one policy.

The insurer's liability has a money limitation based on package, load, location, accident or some combination of such factors. The premium may be calculated on yearly haulage charges or value of goods carried. The premium is determined by factors such as kinds of goods, types of vehicles, areas involved, overnight conditions, distance and conditions of carriage. Insurers may dictate terms concerning security, maintenance, drivers' references, variation of routes and other loss-prevention measures. There may be extra premiums for vulnerable goods such as spirits, tobacco and radios.

By sea and air Marine insurance is a specialized subject involving technical matters and variations in premium rates. In addition to the hazards of sea and air there are, for example, those of stevedores, porters and mechanical handling. Insurance brokers are widely used.

The responsibility for insurance is determined by the conditions of sale, for example:

(a) *Cost, insurance and freight (CIF)* Seller insures for the benefit of buyer until goods are unloaded at port of destination;

(b) *Cost and freight (C & F) or free on board (FOB)* Buyer has responsibility for the goods from time the goods are put on board the vessel;

(c) *Delivered warehouse* Seller responsible for delivery in sound condition to a named warehouse.

There is a standard marine policy to cover such perils as stranding, sinking, fire, collision, heavy weather and piracy, but not pilferage, bad stowage, sweat, rust and breakage. Coverage of additional perils is arranged by clauses commonly in use. A common clause 'warehouse to warehouse' avoids dispute as to the point at which damage occurred.

Policies can be for individual shipments or they can be floating or open. A floating policy covers all shipments of a particular type up to a total sum of money. An open policy covers all ships over a period with a monetary limit for any one ship. The premium is based on kind of goods and method of packing, type of vessel and whether on deck, regular air line or charter, extent of voyage, perils covered and claims experience.

General average　This occurs when a ship is in peril and part of the ship or cargo is sacrificed or expenditure is incurred to prevent further loss. This loss or cost is shared by every party with an interest in the ship on a basis declared by a specially-appointed general-average adjuster.

Particular average　This occurs when there is partial loss or damage and is paid to those with an interest in the goods concerned.

Actual or constructive loss　The insurer pays the total sum if the insured goods are totally destroyed or if there is constructive loss because the cost of recovery would exceed the value of the goods recovered.

Shipowner's liability　The Hague Rules make shipowners responsible for their servants' negligence including the handling and stowage of cargo, but not for errors in navigation or management of the ship, accidental fire, inadequate packing, acts of God, war, strike etc. Where these rules apply, shipowners cannot contract out and premiums are based on an assumption that some part of the losses can be recovered from the shipowners.

ENGINEERING

Boilers (other than domestic equipment), pressure vessels, lifts, hoists, cranes and other lifting and mechanical handling plant, and certain electrical installations have, by law, to be inspected under prescribed conditions. Only in the case of boilers and pressure vessels on motor vehicles is insurance compulsory, but because the hazards which give rise to the need for inspection also cause the exclusion of this same plant from general insurance policies there are special forms of engineering insurance. Inspection and insurance go hand-in-hand: insurance companies require to inspect plant that they insure and a substantial part of the insurance cost is used for inspection.

There are standard policies for the main types of equipment which, by law, are subject to inspection:

Boilers and pressure vessels   One policy covers the property of the insured and liability to third parties for injury to persons and property.

Lifts and hoists   Cover for damage to the equipment is separated from third-party cover for persons and their property being carried, and third-party property not being carried.

Cranes   The insurance is in three parts: breakdown, extraneous damage and third party. These can be insured separately or in combiation; some public-liability policies cover damage and injury caused by crane failure.

In each type of policy, what constitutes explosion or breakdown, the circumstances covered or excluded and the parts of the equipment covered, are carefully defined. Usually excluded are wear and gradually developing faults, as well as lightning, flood and earthquake, but each type of policy has its own exclusions and special extensions according to the hazards peculiar to the equipment.

There are other special forms of engineering insurance, including:

(*a*) Electrical plant used in generation, conversion and application of electrical power.

(*b*) Steam engines, fans and blowers, hydro-extractors, air compressors, pumps, steam and water turbines.

(*c*) Computers including readers, tape decks, disk drives, drums, stores and printers but excluding, for example, tapes and cards.

Not all of these require inspection by law.

Part 4
Environment

Too many offices are housed in premises ill-suited to their purpose: old houses and the partitioned-off corners of factories and warehouses. Office managers who have properly-designed modern office buildings can count themselves fortunate; the remainder have the task of making the best use possible of the accommodation at their disposal. But even the most modern office building is as much a 'tool' as a typewriter or any other piece of the equipment housed within it; if it is to contribute to overall efficiency it must be properly used. It is not the purpose here to deal with the design of office buildings, but rather with how to make the best use of the accommodation which is available.

The law lays down certain minimum standards in relation to accommodation. It should be noted that these are *minimum* standards for the *health* and *safety* of staff. The office manager is concerned also with efficiency, which may demand standards higher than those set by law.

All people work better if they are given the surroundings and equipment appropriate to their work, and the clerk is no exception to this rule. The office accommodation should be laid out and equipped so that the clerks are able to work throughout the day without wasteful movement, without distraction, and without being affected unduly by the mental fatigue which can accompany sedentary work.

19 Furniture and layout

The furniture of an office is made up of the desks, chairs and other equipment allotted to the individual clerks, or for general use.

Most clerks work at desks, while others work at machines with side-tables or other provisions for their papers and records. The design of desks and machine tables is of great importance: a properly laid out working area can contribute considerably to the clerk's efficiency. Within the working area, space is required for three major purposes:

(*a*) work in progress; that is, the forms and documents on which the clerk is writing or from which he is reading;

(*b*) machines and devices necessary to the job;

(*c*) storage; that is, the space in which incoming work, finished work, stationery, forms, reference books etc. can be kept during the day and put away at night.

It is not usually satisfactory to leave the clerks, and particularly junior clerks, to lay out their own working areas without assistance. It should be the supervisor's responsibility to study each clerk's requirements and to give guidance as to the places in which equipment and forms should be kept.

The elementary principles of motion study should be applied to the problem. Fig. 107 indicates those parts of the working area which are usually employed for various purposes. It should be examined as an example only; the correct use of space for any particular job can only be determined by the study of that job in relation to its environment. The layout of the working area may be affected by whether it is to the right or left of a gangway along which messengers will pass bringing work to the clerk or taking finished work away. Any peculiarities of the individual clerk must be given due consideration: those who are abnormally tall or short may need some rearrangement made for them, and those who are left-handed may require to have the entire layout reversed.

In selecting the furniture and other equipment to be used for a specific job, the following six questions should be considered:

(*a*) *Is the working area adequate?* Consideration should be given to the area needed not only for doing the job, but also for storing new work, finished work, and supplies of stationery, blank forms etc.

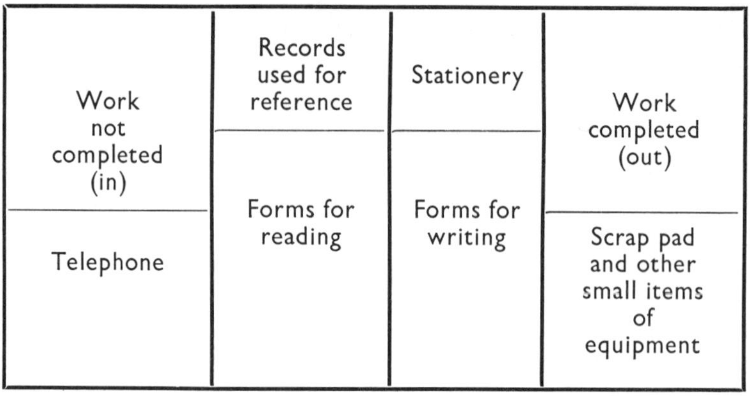

Work not completed (in)	Records used for reference	Stationery	Work completed (out)
	Forms for reading	Forms for writing	
Telephone			Scrap pad and other small items of equipment

Fig. 107   Diagram of desk working area

(b) *Can the clerk work comfortably?*   All the equipment and forms needed for the job should be within easy reach. Associated forms should be kept together, and those most frequently used should be nearest to hand.

(c) *Is the clerk enabled to use both hands?*   The jobs should be laid out so that the clerk is encouraged to use both hands simultaneously.

(d) *Can the job be supervised?*   The supervisor should be able to see the state of each clerk's work. Positions should be allocated for unfinished and finished work. It is preferable that all such work should be readily visible during the day so that nothing is overlooked.

(e) *Is the work adequately protected?*   Equipment, stationery and forms should be properly protected during the day and at night against dust, loss, damage or unauthorized access. In some cases this may entail removing the work in some container to be stored at night in a fire-proof safe.

(f) *Is there suitable provision for the clerk's personal effects?*   It is not reasonable to insist that clerks should leave handbags and other personal possessions of value in cloakrooms, where they may be pilfered. The provision of a personal drawer or locker in the desk is appreciated by the staff and helps to ensure tidiness in the office.

(g) *Can the working area be cleaned?*   A desk which is left at the end of the day covered with loose papers cannot be cleaned. Ideally, when the office cleaners arrive, they should be able to clean floors and all furniture without difficulty because all work has been put away.

DESKS

A desk is a work-bench which should be suited to the needs of the job. For most purposes, each clerk should have his own desk with a top measuring 4–5 ft (say, 1·2–1·5 metres) wide by 2 ft 6 in. (say, 0·75 metres) deep. The normal desk-top height is 2 ft 4½ in. (0·724 metres) from the floor to provide a comfortable working position. Those who use machines may need the surface a few inches lower to bring the keyboard to a convenient level.

To this working surface must be added such storage space as may be necessary, usually in the form of pedestals fitted with drawers or shelves. For many jobs, the general-purpose desk with one or two pedestals (Fig. 108) is suitable. Other types are described below.

Fig. 108   General-purpose desk *(Courtesy of Abbott Bros (Southall) Ltd.)*

Work stations   Clerks can sometimes work more efficiently if provided with an L-shaped desk or work station such as is illustrated in Fig. 109. The two working surfaces can be used in a variety of ways: a typist can do hand work on one and turn to the other when typing; a clerk can write at one and keep records for reference, or an adding or calculating machine, instantly available on the other. A swivel chair should be provided.

Work stations can also be assembled from standard units so as to provide exactly for a clerk's needs. Units may include a chassis, top, drawer and shelf pedestals, side tables and other fitments. Figure 110 illustrates an assembly in which a screen is incorporated on which a working surface and

Fig. 109   General-purpose work station (*Courtesy of Abbott Bros (Southall) Ltd.*)

storage units can hang within convenient reach. This is particularly appropriate for use in landscaped offices (page 273) because visual or acoustic screens, instead of standing separately, can be made part of the working position.

Typists' desks   If the maximum speed of operation and the minimum of fatigue are to be achieved, the typewriter keyboard should be at about normal desk height. Figure 109 shows how this is achieved by using the lower level of a work station. There are also specially designed desks having a well in which to place the typewriter or a shelf to one side.

Spine table (or 'Z') assembly   The spine table, which may have storage accommodation built into it, has single pedestal desks attached at each side (see Fig. 111). A number of these 'Z' formations may be placed together to form a working group and are particularly convenient where work is regularly passed from desk to desk.

Special-purpose desks   If a clerk is doing highly repetitive work and handling a large volume of forms, it is sometimes worthwhile having a special desk constructed according to the particular requirements of the job. It is, however, often cheaper and as effective to modify a general-purpose desk by the addition of a special fitment, such as a stationery rack or a sorting device, or to construct a work station from standard units.

Fig. 110   Screened work stations (*Courtesy of Hille International Ltd.*)

CHAIRS

The Offices, Shops and Railway Premises Act, 1963, requires that suitable seating shall be provided, with a footrest where this is necessary.

Specially designed chairs can play a large part in reducing fatigue and the consequent loss of output, particularly when used by machine operators and

Fig. 111   Spine table assembly (*Courtesy of the Tan-Sad Chair Co. (1931) Ltd.*)

typists. Most office chairs are adjustable both as to height and as to the position of the back-rest, so that they can be readily suited to the needs of individuals. Where adjustable chairs are used (see Fig. 112), the office manager should take steps to see that the adjustments are properly carried out for each clerk. Once a chair is correctly set, it should be labelled with the clerk's name. These precautions are of importance since, if a chair is transferred from one clerk to another without being readjusted, it may well do more harm than good.

The legs of chairs should be such as not to damage plastic floor tiles or carpet. The base of a swivel chair should have five splayed legs rather than four in order to ensure stability.

LAYOUT

The layout of an office is the arrangement of furniture, machines etc. within the space available. Having regard to the limitations imposed by the building, the objectives are as follows:

(*a*) *legal requirements* to be fulfilled (see page 281);
(*b*) *space* to be used to the greatest advantage;
(*c*) *services* to be available where needed: power, telephones etc.;
(*d*) *good working conditions* to be provided for everyone;
(*e*) *supervision* to be able to see the staff at work;
(*f*) *sense of belonging and loyalty* to the working group fostered;
(*g*) *communication and work flow* facilitated;
(*h*) *movement* of clerks between desks and filing etc. made easy;
(*j*) *noisy and distracting* operations segregated;
(*k*) *mutual interference* between clerks avoided;
(*l*) *privacy and security* provided where necessary.

Fig. 112   Office chairs (*Courtesy of the Tan-Sad Chair Co. (1931) Ltd.*)

Aids to planning   The office layout should be planned on paper before putting furniture, machines etc. into position. An outline of the room is drawn to scale on squared paper, showing the positions of doors and windows and of any obstructions such as pillars, buttresses and radiators. Blocks or small pieces of coloured paper cut to scale to represent the desks, filing cabinets, machines, cupboards etc. can then be arranged and rearranged on the plan until a suitable layout is obtained. When planning a landscaped office which will not be laid out in a rectangular pattern, paper with an hexagonal grid should be used instead of squared paper.

The plan should be thoroughly tested by marking on it the normal flow of work from one clerk to another, and the movements which clerks may have to make between their desks and filing cabinets or other pieces of equipment.

When planning a new layout, the views of staff should be heard. They may have useful ideas to contribute and will the more readily accept the eventual plan if they, or their representatives, have participated in its development. It is sometimes possible, particularly in the case of landscaped offices, to allocate space for sections and groups, permitting the staff to determine the detailed use of that space.

Space   In planning the office, adequate space must be allowed not only to house the furniture and other equipment but also to permit easy movement from one part of the room to another. Main gangways should be not less than 4 ft wide with subsidiary gangways not less than 3 ft. People passing along too narrow a gangway are liable to brush papers from desks or otherwise interfere with the work of others. The area to be allotted to one individual desk may need to be varied according to the nature of the job and to make allowance for any additional equipment which it is necessary to have in the immediate working area. It is sufficient to leave a space of 2–3 ft between desks for the clerk's chair.

The Offices, Shops and Railway Premises Act, 1963, requires that rooms in which people work shall allow 40 sq ft of floor space per person, or 400 cu ft where the ceiling height is less than 10 ft from the floor. This space is the total room space including that occupied by gangways, equipment etc. It is generally enough for efficient working but may have to be exceeded where there is an abnormal amount of machinery, filing or other equipment in general use.

Care must be taken in apportioning space to see that fire exits and fire-fighting appliances are readily accessible.

Services   The layout must have regard to the provision of services, principally power cables, telephone cables and cables linking terminals of any kind with a computer. A high degree of flexibility can be obtained by carrying cables in under-floor channels or above a false ceiling. The latter is less desirable as connections dropped from above are unsightly and may be liable to accidental damage. A less flexible arrangement is to run cables along the walls behind a skirting. In this case, there is a natural tendency to position those who need services near the walls, not always an ideal arrangement from other points of view.

Other services, such as drinking water and refreshment vending machines, are often sited in an area set aside and furnished as a staff lounge available for use in rest and refreshment breaks.

Private offices

Private offices are normally provided for those whose work is of a highly confidential or exacting nature, or entails frequent meetings. Whilst the occupant may be allowed to exercise some personal preference as to how the office is laid out, it should nonetheless be planned as a workplace. The general rules as to the allocation of the desk surface and the use of side tables should be observed.

Where visitors are to be received or meetings held, the layout should provide for these situations. A visitor should not be expected to face a window, or be expected to make notes without a surface on which to write.

It is increasingly the practice for a private office to be divided into two main areas: the first is a compact working area for the occupant; the second is an area for receiving visitors and holding small meetings at a conference table. One advantage of this arrangement is that confidential papers on the desk need not be removed when visitors arrive.

Status In addition to being a workplace, the private office was for long regarded as a symbol of status; a goal to be reached by the ambitious. This attitude is changing as part of the general change in social attitudes (see also Landscaped offices). The decision to provide a private room is now more likely to be taken on grounds of practical need.

Cellular offices

The cellular office may be of varying size, the intention being to provide a department, section or group of clerks with a separate room. In older buildings, this may be necessary because the structure imposes such an arrangement. Where, however, there are or can be large open areas, the trend is away from the cellular principle as being wasteful of space and expensive in many ways (see below under Comparison of alternatives).

There are some situations in which separate departmental offices are necessary. One example is a computer room which must be closely controlled as to temperature and humidity, and protected because of the value and vulnerability of the equipment in it. Another example is the cashier's office, where the walls and door form part of the security barriers against robbery.

One of the principal arguments in favour of cellular offices is that they are psychologically desirable, reinforcing a sense of belonging to a group of people clearly distinguished from others. This can strengthen group loyalty, but in so doing may weaken the wider loyalty to the organization as a whole.

When cellular offices are replaced by open or landscaped offices, it is still found desirable to provide some lines of demarcation, usually by the arrangement of desks, filing equipment and screens.

Open-plan offices

The open-plan office is one in which clerks, supervisors and sometimes managers too are accommodated in one large area. In order to obtain the maximum use of space, desks are usually arranged in straight lines by groups and sections. As compared with a combination of private and cellular offices, there are significant advantages and some disadvantages:

Advantages of the open-plan office are as follows:

(a) *Lower capital cost* for partitions, doors, heating, lighting, power and other services.

(b) *Better space utilization*, less space being taken up by partitions, doors, corridors etc.

(c) *Lower maintenance costs* in decoration, cleaning and for services generally.

(d) *Easier supervision* and possibly fewer supervisors.

(e) *Communication and work flow* facilitated.

(f) *Sharing of machines and equipment* becomes possible.

(g) *Flexibility of layout* when organizational changes are necessary.

(h) *Better working conditions* often possible.

(i) *Fewer indications of status* may encourage co-operation and participation.

Disadvantages of the open-plan office are as follows:

(a) *Reduced security* for confidential work and cash handling.

(b) *Distraction* through visitors and general movement.

(c) *Communal noise* may become excessive.

(d) *Infectious diseases* may spread.

(e) *Lowering of morale* through apparent regimentation and loss of individuality and reduced sense of belonging to a well-defined working group.

(f) *Apparent loss of status among senior staff.*

It will be noted that the advantages are savings in cost and ease of operation. The disadvantages can to some extent be avoided by segregating work which is confidential, noisy or distracting. There remain particularly the psychological disadvantages which may be summed up as 'many people do not like working in open offices'.

Various methods have been adopted for breaking up open floors without losing too many of the advantages which they afford. The boundaries between sections can be marked by arrangements of filing cabinets or counter-height storage units. Head-height partitions which are readily

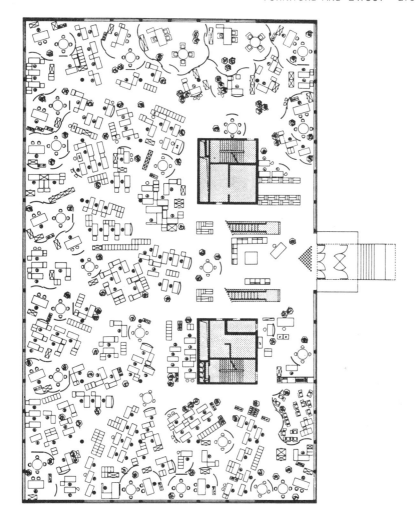

Fig. 113   Plan of a landscaped office (*Courtesy of Anbar Publications Ltd.*)
The ground floor of the Orenstein-Koppel building, Dortmund. It has 171 work stations (including 61 typists), one rest room (with 17 seats), 90 planters and 110 screens. The floor area is 2100 m²; 12·2 m² per work station

movable can be erected to give some sense of separation. Among the more important developments is the landscaped office which is discussed below.

Landscaped offices

The landscaped office is an open-floor arrangement which avoids the regimentation of the straight lines of desks found in the open-plan office (see Fig. 113). Desks are set out individually or in groups at different angles one from another; gangways change direction, skirting round areas of varying sizes. The layout reflects the ways in which people work and are organized.

The advantages of the open-plan office listed above are all obtained in the landscaped office, with one exception. Whilst there is still likely to be a better utilization of space as compared with the cellular office, less people will be accommodated than by the open-plan. Studies in Germany, where the landscaped office originated, suggest that whereas the cellular office makes direct use of 58–67 per cent of available space, the landscaped office makes direct use of 72–83 per cent.

Some of the disadvantages of the open-plan office can be eliminated or reduced in the landscaped office. There is less distraction, noise can be better controlled and the psychological effects of apparent regimentation and loss of group identity are reduced if not entirely removed.

It is usual to accentuate the boundaries between departments and, where necessary, individuals by positioning equipment or visual or acoustic screens. The general atmosphere is enhanced by the provision of growing plants, which also contribute to the demarcation of areas and gangways.

In the extreme, the whole of the administrative and clerical staff from the most junior clerk to the chief executive are in the same room. Those whose work is confidential may be protected by movable screens, often of no more than 50 in. high. Screens that are too high impede daylight and produce the impression of a maze of twisting corridors; the reverse of what is intended.

There is often resistance by managers and senior clerks to the proposal that they should join the general staff in one large office. The private office has been a status symbol and symbols are important in that they fulfil a human need. The symbol of status does not, however, have to take the form of a walled-in room: the manager in a landscaped office may be distinguished by a greater floor area, giving some degree of privacy, or by furnishings.

The prospect of moving from a private office to a landscaped office can be expected to cause anxiety. There is, however, evidence to support the view that once the change has been made, a manager may be happier in an open environment and have no wish to return to a lonely isolation. A similar change in attitude has been observed in some organizations when a separate management dining room has been replaced by a common restaurant used by all grades of staff.

In observing changes in customs, it must be accepted that they usually take place slowly. The changes in social attitudes implicit in the concept of the landscaped office have begun, but it may take a generation before they are complete.

Comparison of alternatives

Four types of office have been described: private, cellular, open-plan and landscaped. Not everyone is able to choose which style to adopt. It is often necessary to make the best possible arrangment within an existing building in which some interior walls cannot be demolished because they support the main structure. Newer buildings are usually more flexible, having been constructed with open floors.

The decision as to how to make the best use of the available space must take account of the cost of alterations and the benefits which may accrue immediately and in the long term. As a general guide, the list set out below shows where the advantages tend to lie. In each case the greatest advantage is marked A, and the lesser advantages B and C.

	Private or cellular	Open-plan	Landscaped
Space utilization	C	A	B
Flexibility	C	B	A
Communication/work flow	C	B	A
Mutual interference/distraction	A	C	B
Movement	C	B	A
Equipment sharing	C	B	A
Supervision	C	B	A
Security	A	C	B
Working conditions	C	B	A
Group loyalty	A	C	B
Status indication	A	C	B
Capital cost	C	A	B
Maintenance cost	C	A	B

This evaluation suggests that, where conditions permit and there are no overriding special factors, the landscaped office has more to offer than the other types.

20   Physical conditions

The clerk's work requires more mental than physical effort, and his working conditions must be planned with full recognition of this fact. He is required to concentrate for long periods, very often performing the same process over and over again. He is particularly liable to mental fatigue with its consequent lowering of output. This fatigue is largely the result of lack of physical movement, and is entirely different from that which affects those engaged in heavy manual labour. The cure for it, generally, is not rest, but exercise.

Concentrated work demands broadly two things: a clear brain and no distraction. Some people are born with the ability to reason and make mental calculations readily, but these people are exceptional. Exceptional also are those who are able to concentrate over long periods, ignoring the distractions which surround them. But whether a person has a natural ability for concentrated mental work or not, his efficiency is affected by his physical surroundings. It is the duty of the office manager to provide for his clerks conditions conducive to sustained good work, bearing in mind that he is providing for average people whose jobs are only of average interest.

The law requires that conditions shall not endanger the health and safety of workers generally. The Offices, Shops and Railway Premises Act, 1963 (see pages 282–4) and Regulations made under this Act set minimum standards which are enforceable. It must, however, be borne in mind that these standards are minima; the least that is necessary for health and safety. This chapter is concerned principally with the provision of conditions conducive to good work and good personnel relations. To meet these needs, conditions may often have to be better than those demanded by law.

DECORATION

The decoration of an office can have a noticeable effect upon the morale of the staff; drab surroundings are depressing, pleasant surroundings are conducive to good work.

A 'company standard' scheme should be avoided because it it is unlikely to suit every situation and, by repetition, soon becomes boring. Decoration schemes should be suited to each particular room; the scheme which can be attractively applied to a modern building may be altogether inappropriate in an old or converted building; that which suits a large room may appear ridiculous in a small room. The architectural style and the materials used in construction must be taken into account: concrete, brick, plaster, wood, metal, glass and plastic surfaces influence the overall decorative effect. The aspect of a room is also important: rooms which are not reached by direct sunlight and tend to be cool may need 'warm', cheerful colours containing red and yellow; others, facing the sun, may need 'cool' colours containing blue.

Entrance halls and public waiting areas   These should be appropriate to the business. Some might properly be strikingly modern, others homely or with a quiet dignity. None need be cold, uninviting or uncomfortable.

General offices   These should be decorated attractively but with particular regard to natural and artificial lighting. Some rooms, because of their shapes and aspects, may need the walls and other surfaces to reflect light. White and pale shades of yellow have particularly high reflective values but any pale tint may prove satisfactory. Stronger colours may then be used for doors and other wood or metalwork to provide contrast and interest. Colours should not be selected because they 'do not show the dirt'; it is better that they ensure adequate light without glare and are kept clean.

It is generally recognized that colours have some effect on human emotions: some are cheering, others depressing, some are restful, others stimulating. There is, however, no universal reaction to colours and preferences differ between individuals and between the sexes. New and imaginative schemes may be more readily accepted if the clerks are consulted and their views on alternative proposals obtained. It is the clerks who will spend many hours in the general office and they should find it pleasing to enter for the first time and to work in day after day.

The effect of a well-planned decoration scheme will be destroyed if the walls or screens are hung with calendars, notices, price lists etc. Proper provision should be made for whatever is necessary and this may include not only official noticeboards but a sheet of softboard for the display of unofficial material such as holiday postcards. Reproductions of good pictures may be displayed on the office walls with pleasing effect.

Perhaps as a reaction against the concrete and glass of office buildings, growing plants often form part of the decoration. These can be in pots, tubs or troughs and in the open or landscaped office may form part of the divisions between sections of the office.

Cloakrooms and lavatories   These should look, as well as be, clean. This does not necessitate the exclusive use of white finishes; pastel shades and contrasting colours can be introduced.

First-aid and rest rooms   These should be decorated in restful but attractive colours so as not to appear cold and impersonal.

CLEANLINESS

A clean and tidy office contributes not only to the health and general well-being of the clerks but also to the neatness and accuracy of work. People react to their surroundings: clerks working in a dirty, untidy office will tend to become untidy and careless in their work; clerks trained and working in clean, tidy surroundings will take a pride in the accuracy and appearance of their work.

Office cleaners should be adequately supervised and provided with the proper equipment and material for their work, including such devices as power-driven floor polishers and vacuum cleaners. However well the office is cleaned from day to day, in the course of time dirt will accumulate in filing cabinets, shelves and cupboards, and behind equipment and furniture which is placed against walls. A definite programme of special cleaning should be laid down and followed. When a section of the office is due for thorough cleaning, shelves, cupboards, cabinets and desks should be cleared of papers so that all accumulated dust and dirt can be removed.

VENTILATION

It is important that there should be a constant flow of clean fresh air through the office in order to combat fatigue. Many offices are air-conditioned, with air flow, temperature and humidity automatically controlled. In these cases, the required conditions will have been provided so long as the system is well designed and maintained.

In the absence of air-conditioning, there may be problems in maintaining a healthy atmosphere without draughts which are a source of irritation to clerks and one about which they feel strongly. To anyone moving about, the occasional draught of cold air means little; to a clerk seated at a desk it can be a grave distraction.

A number of devices can be used to reduce draughts, for example:

(*a*) Lobbies with inner and outer doors and sufficient space between them so that, when a person is passing through, both doors are not open at the same time. It is an added advantage if, in cold weather, the space between the doors can be raised to a high temperature so as to provide a 'cushion' of warm air to prevent cold draughts.

(*b*) Transparent plastic screens inside sash window frames so that, when the window is opened at the bottom, the stream of air does not come straight in, but is forced upwards and diffused.

(*c*) Fine-mesh screens which, when placed over the open portion of a window, break up the draught of air coming through without completely blocking the light.

(*d*) Wood or metal and glass screens placed round doorways.

Whilst draughts can be reduced, no general cure has yet been found. It remains for each office manager to use his ingenuity in dealing with the problem as it arises.

TEMPERATURE

The Office, Shops and Railway Premises Act, 1963, lays down minimum temperature requirements but these should normally be exceeded, the temperature of an office being kept at 19–21°C (67–70°F). A clerk's efficiency is impaired by an atmosphere which is either too cold or too hot. One of the requirements for proper concentration is that a clerk should not be conscious of himself; anyone who is uncomfortably hot or cold cannot concentrate fully on the job in hand. The ideal heating system for offices is one which gives an even heat throughout the room, without excessively hot or cold areas.

Whatever heating system is used, it is generally better to have a large number of small radiators or other heat sources well spread, than a small number of more powerful sources.

Office buildings with large areas of glass in the walls, whether as windows or as cladding, can become over-heated in sunny weather. This effect is best combated by the provision of exterior sunblinds. Interior venetian blinds are of some help, but are not so effective because they do not prevent the sun's rays from striking the glass surfaces.

LIGHTING

The importance of correct lighting in the office cannot be over-emphasized. A clerk who is engaged in close work throughout the day is, under the best of conditions, liable to eye strain with its attendant mental fatigue, irritability and other physical disorders. Bad lighting accentuates the possibility of low output and inaccurate work resulting from these causes.

A well-lit office is one in which the following three requirements are met:

(*a*) the light is well diffused with no sharp shadows cast;

(*b*) the intensity of light in any place is adequate for the work done there; too strong a light may be as bad as insufficient light;

(*c*) there is no glare, either direct, or reflected from surfaces such as the tops of desks or filing equipment.

In considering lighting we are concerned with the two kinds, natural and artificial.

Natural lighting Ideally, the office building should not be shaded by other buildings, should face away from the sun and have large windows.

Such a building is, however, seldom to be found and it is the office manager's responsibility to arrange the office so that the best possible use is made of the natural light available. Those clerks who do close work should be given positions near to the windows. Desks should not be placed so that clerks face the light, since the glare, both direct and reflected from the desk top, is a source of distraction. The ideal desk position is one in which the light falls from behind and slightly to the left of the clerk. Where the office windows face towards the sun, sunblinds should be provided so that the intensity of light and the glare can be reduced in sunny weather.

Artificial lighting   Office lighting systems can be broadly classified under four headings:

(a) *Fluorescent lighting* is generally used and fulfils the need for a direct but diffused light. The glare from unshaded tubes can be a source of distraction but this can be overcome by a variety of fittings.

(b) *Indirect lighting* by electric lamps provides a diffused light without glare. Suspended fittings reflect light upwards to the ceiling, which in turn reflects it downwards. Lamps, reflectors and ceilings must be kept clean if the light intensity is to be maintained.

(c) *Direct lighting* by shaded electric lamps suspended from the ceiling is generally regarded as unsatisfactory because it gives an ill-diffused light and casts shadows.

(d) *Individual desk or machine lighting* is not common but may be used where particular jobs require an abnormally high intensity of light.

Schemes should be designed to provide an adequate intensity of light wherever work is done. Light may be measured with a light meter, the intensity being expressed in terms of lumens (or foot-candles). For general office work, 20–30 lumens is generally regarded as satisfactory, although 10 lumens may prove adequate in some circumstances. Where sustained close work is done, an intensity of more than 30 lumens may be desirable.

ACOUSTICS

Loud noises and sharp and unexpected sounds are a frequent cause of distraction to clerical workers. Too often they are endured although some simple remedy could be found if time and thought were given to the matter.

In any enclosed space, sound waves reverberate; in an office they are successively reflected from hard surfaces such as walls, ceiling, floor and desk tops. The echoes and re-echoes give rise to a confused clatter. This can be avoided by 'absorbing' the sound waves on soft surfaces before they are able to travel far. There are broadly two methods of doing this.

General absorption Ceilings and sometimes parts of walls are treated with sound-absorbent acoustic tiles or other material. Because a high proportion of sound waves strike the ceiling before being reflected downwards to be heard, this method is often sufficient. By using carpet or other sound-absorbent floor covering, the reflection of sound waves upwards from the floor can also be prevented. General absorption should not be overdone; too little sound can be psychologically oppressive.

Local absorption Where a particular sources of noise can be identified, it is economical to absorb the sound waves at that point. Common examples are the placing of a felt pad under a typewriter or other machine, and the provision of an acoustic booth around a telephone in general use.

The following notes are examples of ways in which office managers can deal with some of the more common sources of distracting noise:

(a) *External sources* Ideally, offices should be sited away from busy streets or noisy industrial processes. The effect of external noises can be reduced by double-glazed windows.

(b) *Machines* Extremely noisy machines should be segregated in a room apart from the main office.

(c) *Doors* Banging doors should be fitted with rubber or felt stops or with hydraulic controls.

(d) *Telephones* Switchboards and telephone order clerks' desks should be segregated from the general office or screened with sound-absorbent material.

(e) *Interviewing* Lengthy interviews or conversations between clerks in the general office can cause distraction to others. The provision of a conference or interviewing room for general use as necessary should be considered.

(f) *Movement* Noise caused by the movement of clerks and messengers in the main office can be reduced by covering the floor (or at least the main gangways) with carpet, rubber flooring or linoleum with under-felt.

In landscaped offices, free-standing acoustic screens are commonly used to absorb excessive noise at critical points.

HEALTH AND SAFETY

There are several Acts of Parliament concerned with protecting the health and safety of office staff at work. In some cases, these Acts provide broad guidelines within which a Secretary of State may make more detailed regulations from time to time.

The extent and complexity of the laws now enacted (see also pages 304–5) make it impossible for an office manager to be expert in them, and he should when necessary take professional legal advice. In order to be able to seek such help he must, of course, be aware of the areas in which there may be restrictions on his freedom of action. The following defines the general scope of the principal Acts involved.

Health and Safety at Work Act, 1974   This Act is concerned with employees generally, including office staff. Among other things, it requires an employer to provide employees with a written statement of policy, organization and arrangements relating to health and safety at work, to give information as to risks which employees may face and as to training in safe practices. The office manager normally conforms with the arrangements for the whole of the organization of which his office forms part.

Offices, Shops and Railway Premises Act, 1963   Known briefly as the Offices Act, this legislation is of particular interest to the office manager. It requires employers to maintain minimum standards of working conditions and provides for the official inspection of offices to ensure that this is done.

Whilst the Act sets some of the minimum standards, the Secretary of State for Employment is given power to make, and later amend, Regulations under the Act. It is therefore necessary for management to ensure that the latest requirements are known. The following is a brief summary of the scope of the Offices Act, indicating the matters to which attention must be given.

(a) *Cleanliness*   Premises, furniture, fittings etc. must be kept clean.

(b) *Overcrowding*   Rooms where people work must allow 40 sq ft of floor space per person or, if the ceiling is lower than 10 ft from the floor, 400 cu ft. The space specified is the total space, including that occupied by equipment, gangways etc.

(c) *Temperature*   A reasonable temperature must be maintained where people work (except for short periods), i.e. a minimum of 16°C (60·8°F) after the first hour. A thermometer must be provided on each floor to enable employees to check the temperature.

(d) *Ventilation*   There must be provision of adequate fresh or purified air.

(e) *Lighting*   Natural or artificial lighting must be suitable and sufficient, windows being kept clean inside and outside and lighting equipment properly maintained.

(f) *Sanitary conveniences*   Sufficient and suitable sanitary conveniences must be provided, kept clean and properly maintained. Standards according to numbers of employees are prescribed by regulation.

(g) *Washing facilities*   Washing facilities must be provided under suitable conditions and include clean, running hot and cold water, soap and towels or other means of cleaning or drying.

(h) *Drinking water*   Adequate drinking water must be provided, piped or in a container where the water is renewed daily. Except where people drink from a jet, drinking vessels must be provided.

(i) *Clothing*   Accommodation must be provided for clothing not worn in working hours and facilities for drying clothing.

(j) *Seating*   Seats must be provided, and those for people who normally work sitting down must be suitable in design, construction and dimensions, with a foot-rest if necessary.

(k) *Floors, passages and stairs*   These must be soundly constructed and maintained, kept free from obstruction and slip-free. Stairs must have handrails etc., and floor openings must be fenced.

(l) *Machinery*   Dangerous parts of machines must be fenced. No person under the age of 18 may clean machinery if this exposes him to risk; no person may work a machine specified as dangerous unless fully instructed as to the dangers.

(m) *Heavy work*   No one may be required to lift, carry or move a load likely to cause injury.

(n) *First aid*   A first-aid box or cupboard in the charge of a responsible person must be provided for each 150 employees or fraction of that number. Where there are more than 150 employees, one of the responsible persons must be trained in first aid and must be available during working hours. A notice indicating the person's name must be displayed.

(o) *Fire precautions*   Adequate means of escape must be provided, and appropriate fire-fighting equipment. Premises are required to be inspected and certified as having adequate safeguards, but some smaller offices are exempt from this requirement. Fire exits must be clearly marked and escape routes kept free from obstruction. Fire alarms must be provided and tested periodically, and occupiers of premises must ensure that all employees are familiar with the escape routine.

(*p*) *Notification of accidents*   Accidents causing death, or disabling a person from doing his usual work for more than three days, must be notified to the local authority (or other enforcing authority).

(*q*) *Abstracts*   Either the prescribed abstracts of the Act or the prescribed booklet has to be displayed in a prominent position, or employees must be given a copy of the special explanatory booklet prescribed for that purpose.

Employer's Liability (Defective Equipment) Act, 1969   Under this Act, an employer is made responsible for personal injury suffered by an employee as the result of defects in equipment provided by the employer. The employee is entitled to claim compensation even though the defect arose from faulty manufacture or other cause not directly under the employer's control.

Employer's Liability (Compulsory Insurance) Act, 1969   Employers (other than certain employers in the public sector) are required to maintain approved insurance against liability for bodily injury or disease sustained by employees in the course of their employment (see also page 253).

Penalties   Offences under these Acts are punishable by fines. It is important to note that where the employer is a limited company, it may be possible to take legal proceedings also against responsible directors and managers.

Part 5
Personnel

The following chapters deal with three aspects of personnel policy:

Staffing Describing some of the aids used by management in providing staff for the office.

Rewards Dealing with wages, conditions of employment and with other less tangible rewards such as satisfaction and interest in the work.

Training Dealing with education and training for clerical workers, for office supervisors and for office managers, with particular reference to the requirements of Industrial Training Boards.

The principles relating to office personnel policy do not differ essentially from those adopted in other departments of a business. The practices adopted in applying these principles, however, sometimes differ in important respects. In these three chapters, particular attention is paid to those matters in which the practices differ, whilst only passing reference, if any, is made to those in which practices are common.

21 Staffing

The provision of an adequate staff to do the work that must be done, now and in the future, is a vital function of management. The process of staffing begins with consideration of the *work* to be done. This must be apportioned as jobs, each suitable for a person of defined skill and capability. The jobs so created must be organized by groups and sections to permit supervision and control. Finally, people must be selected to do the jobs. In this chapter, the subject is dealt with under six main headings: Work Analysis, Work Measurement, Job Evaluation and Grading, Job Construction, Organization, and Recruitment and Selection. These processes can be carried out in a variety of ways: in a large office they may be formalized; in a smaller office they may be informal, but the chain of events should nevertheless be the same.

WORK ANALYSIS

The staffing stems from the work to be done and the first step must therefore be to establish the tasks. Work may be analysed in varying degrees of detail and the following terms are generally used:

Job   The work assigned to a person.

Task   Part of a job having a readily recognizable beginning and end and making a substantial contribution to that job or the system of which it forms part. Examples might be the typing of letters from recorded dictation as part of a typist's job, or the preparation of clock cards as part of a wages clerk's job.

Operation   Part of a task which requires a distinguishable group of movements, for example, setting up and feeding paper into a typewriter as distinct from the operation of typing.

Element   Part of an operation which is the smallest usefully distinguishable action, for example, picking up a piece of paper and positioning it on a desk-top.

Elements and operations are of importance in method study. In staffing, it is not necessary to go into such detail; it is sufficient to determine and record:

(*a*) the main tasks;

(*b*) the volume of work expressed in appropriate units, e.g. forms handled, letters typed etc.

(*c*) a rough estimate of the total time taken on each task each week or other appropriate period.

In analysing clerical work, the main tasks are often found to be surrounded by minor tasks such as answering the telephone and raising queries with a supervisor. The job may also include dealing with inquiries from customers, suppliers or management. It is difficult, if not impossible, to define precisely these incidental tasks which may vary from day to day. They are therefore best grouped under general headings and the volume estimated in terms of time spent.

As a rough guide, office jobs have been found to contain on average seven or eight main tasks. Ready-made definitions of nearly 1000 common office tasks are published by the Institute of Administrative Management in *Office Job Evaluation* (see Bibliography).

WORK MEASUREMENT

Work analysis provides a list of tasks and the volume of work in each task expressed in suitable units. The next step is to measure this work in terms of time, which may be the actual time taken on a particular occasion, the average time taken over a number of occasions or an assessment of the time which should be taken when reasonable skill and effort are applied. It is this latter, the *standard time*, which is important because from it can be calculated the number of staff required as distinct from the number currently employed.

In measuring work in terms of time, it must be accepted that some clerks can work faster than others; it is also true that everyone adjusts the rate of working to the pressure of work. This was summed up in 'Parkinson's Law': *work expands to fill the time available.* Within wide limits, whether it is a busy day or a slack day, the work lasts from the time of opening the office until the time of closing. When work is measured this variation must be taken into account and time standards must assume that a clerk is exercising reasonable skill and reasonable effort such as might be sustained on average throughout the working day.

There are various methods by which work can be measured, some relatively exact and some less accurate. If it is the intention to pay an output bonus, accuracy is important. In most cases, however, office work is measured for the purposes of planning and control in circumstances in which:

(a) the workload may fluctuate from day to day and from hour to hour;
(b) no two units of work may be exactly alike, e.g. letters, invoices, payroll lines;
(c) there are unpredictable minor tasks to be done as they arise;
(d) there is mental work which cannot be observed as can manual work;
(e) there are decisions to be taken.

Whilst in theory it is possible to make allowance for all of these factors, in practice the cost of measuring the work precisely may exceed any savings to be gained by so doing. It may therefore be preferable to set standards which are loose since loose standards are better than no standards and are likely to be adequate as a basis for assessing the number of staff necessary.

Averaging actual performance   Much can be gained from the mere recording and analysing of actual performance. Clerks can be given time sheets and asked to record the tasks done, the time taken and the number of units of output. If these records are kept over an extended period including busy times and slack times, it will be seen how the output in units an hour varies and which clerks are able to give a consistently good performance.

Care must be taken in drawing conclusions from such records and in setting standards based upon them. The actual performance, even at busy times, may be low. Studies made by some well-known businesses showed that the overall average actual performance in their offices was 51 per cent of what might reasonably be expected, with a maximum of 80 per cent and a minimum of 30 per cent. It is unwise to assume that what is being done is satisfactory. The best of clerks can do no more than the work provided and will set a working pace to spread it over the day.

Simple timing   This is a method whereby almost anyone can establish a reasonable standard time for work which he understands. It is therefore suitable for use by supervisors or O & M officers in measuring routine tasks. In all systems of work measurement, the objective is to discover what is an acceptable normal performance. In simple timing, everything possible is normalized; the work, the clerk doing the work and the working conditions. The procedure may be summarized as follows:

(1) select a unit of output which can be readily counted and recorded, e.g. an invoice rather than a line of an invoice;
(2) prepare batches of work which can be expected to take 20–30 minutes each. Each batch should contain the same number of units and be a normal mixture of the easy and the difficult;
(3) select a normal clerk (neither the best nor the worst) and explain what is to happen. It is important that the clerk selected shall be willing to co-operate and try to work normally;

(4) give the clerk successive batches of work and record the time taken to complete each one;

(5) from the accumulated results, assess what is a reasonable standard time after adding a relaxation allowance (see Relaxation allowance, below).

It may be necessary to discard the record of the first one or two batches. When a clerk knows that he is being timed, he may become nervous and work at an unnatural pace, probably abnormally quickly. This effect passes, however, and the subsequent times can be accepted as normal. Provided that the batches of work are normal, the times taken should not vary greatly. If they do, the work should be examined and the clerk questioned in order to discover the reasons. Abnormalities which arise regularly must be the subject of a time allowance and it is necessary to understand their nature and frequency.

Activity sampling   This is a statistical method by which the use of a person's time can be determined, even though he does a variety of tasks at no fixed intervals during the day. An observer merely records what is being done at random points of time. A very large number of observations are necessary, perhaps as many as 1000, if adequately accurate results are to be obtained, but these may be spread over an extended period. From the records, it is established how many times each operation was observed. To take a simplified example, a telephone operator's work observed over some weeks might give the following result:

Observed dealing with external calls	200 times (20%)
Observed dealing with internal calls	300 times (30%)
Observed idle (no calls to be handled)	500 times (50%)

The percentage of times that each operation was observed may be taken to be the percentage of the average day spent in that activity. In the example, the operator is idle half of the day and it may be assumed could deal with increased telephone traffic without assistance. It must be noted that the effort expended is not rated and the result illustrates actual and not potential performance.

Activity sampling is useful in determining such things as idle time when work is not available, time spent in telephoning, dealing with queries etc. It may also help in analysing a job in which there is a mixture of work of several types or grades (see Job Evaluation and Grading, below).

Time study   The work is broken down into elements which are then timed repeatedly with a stop-watch. As the time taken is recorded, the worker's application and industry are *rated* to the base of 100. If the performance in terms of skill and effort is normal, the rating is 100; if less than normal, a rating below 100 is recorded; if above normal, a rating above 100 is recorded. The ratings are used to adjust the actual times taken so as to arrive at the normal standard times to be adopted. Relaxation allowances are added (see Relaxation allowance, below).

Time study can only be carried out by trained specialists able to rate the skill and effort applied. It is the method used in factories where there is a regular sequence of operations. Whilst the technique has been used in offices, conditions are rarely such that its application is economic.

Predetermined motion-time systems (PMTS)   There are several systems which come under this general description, including Methods Time Measurement (MTM) and Master Clerical Data (MCD). All are based on the fact that, within reasonable and definable limits, all skilled people require the same amount of time to perform a particular movement, for example, reaching for a given distance, grasping a sheet of paper, positioning it. By using advanced techniques such as slow-motion picture analysis, standard times are established for all fundamental human motions.

In applying a system, the work to be studied is analysed into a sequence of fundamental motions. These are then evaluated according to the predetermined standard times, the total of these providing a standard for the whole operation. By using these synthetic times, it is possible to build up accurate standards for most routine operations. PMTS must, however, be introduced by specialists and it is usual to employ consultants for the purpose.

Relaxation allowance   Whenever standard times are being established through observation it is necessary to add an allowance for relaxation. It cannot be assumed that clerks will be able to sustain continuous output throughout the working day. The normal basic allowance for personal needs, etc. is 8 per cent and to this should be added a variable percentage to allow for physical effort, adverse working conditions, continuous concentration and monotony. For most office work, the total relaxation allowance will be between 10 per cent and 15 per cent of the basic standard time.

JOB EVALUATION AND GRADING

Different tasks require different skills and different *degrees of skill*. Job evaluation and grading are techniques which seek to provide a means of measuring the relative values of tasks and jobs according to the levels of skill, knowledge and experience necessary to their proper performance. Job evaluation is the assessment of the relative value of a task or job; job grading is the placing of a task or job into a particular category according to that assessment.

Although the ultimate objective may be to grade a job, it is usual to evaluate work at the task level first. It can then be seen whether a job contains work of one grade only or is a mixture of tasks of two or more grades calling for reconstruction.

Job evaluation   There are various methods of job evaluation, but all seek to define the extent to which different attributes are present. A typical system might examine the job according to the following factors:

	Possible points
Knowledge or skill required to do the job	45
Responsibility—supervising, training or instructing others	15
Trust—handling of money, valuables or confidential information	10
Contacts—departmental or outside the business	10
Physical effort—exertion and precision	10
Mental effort—concentration, accuracy, judgement	10
	100

Each factor is weighted according to its importance by allotting a total possible number of points as shown.

In evaluating a particular job, points are awarded out of the total possible for each factor. For example, a simple routine job requiring little training might score only 5 points for knowledge, whilst a job involving advanced accounting techniques might score the maximum of 45 points. When each factor has been assessed, the total points for the job indicate its value in relation to other jobs similarly evaluated. It must be borne in mind that the awarding of points is only a way of expressing an opinion. The use of numbers instead of words does not make the result any more accurate. Indeed, those who use points systems often find it necessary to define in words the job characteristics which are to be associated with different scores.

The Institute of Administrative Management system of Job Evaluation and Grading enables the separate process of job evaluation to be avoided because it provides definitions of common office tasks already graded (see Job grading, below).

Job grading   Job-grading systems of one sort and another are to be found in most large office organizations. They usually provide for a small number of grades (usually less than ten) which correspond with the generally accepted levels of skill and responsibility. Many businesses adopt or modify the Institute of Administrative Management (IAM) Job Grading scheme which provides eight basic grades lettered A–H as defined in Fig. 114. Until 1976, the IAM scheme included only grades A–F and the larger organizations at their discretion sub-divided Grade F into F1, F2 etc. as was considered necessary. The original Grade F is now split into Grades F, G and H and tasks are identified accordingly.

The IAM scheme is of particular value because those who use it can avoid much of the work of job evaluation. The book describing the scheme in detail provides nearly 1000 common task definitions with their grades.

With the aid of this, it is only necessary to match a task with its standard definition in order to ascertain its grade.

In some schemes, there is a separate grading scale for each of the principal types of skill, e.g. Typing and Secretarial, Computer Operation, General Clerical. This is found helpful in establishing related salary scales.

Job grading serves a variety of purposes. By enabling management to classify work realistically, it simplifies staffing, aids in the fixing of fair wage scales, in selecting and placing clerks in suitable jobs, and in planning training and promotion.

Where the size of the organization makes it appropriate, the grading scheme is sometimes extended beyond Grade H to include various levels of management. The nature of management work is such, however, that it cannot be described as tasks to be performed. Jobs are more properly defined in terms of responsibilities borne, and evaluated by a points system which takes into account factors such as the need for technical knowledge and managerial experience, the number of staff controlled, the influence of decisions taken on revenue, cost, profitability etc.

JOB CONSTRUCTION

It is open to the office manager to arrange the work in any reasonable way and apportion tasks so as to create jobs suitable for the unskilled, the semi-skilled, the skilled and the highly skilled. In doing this, regard must be had to the long-term as well as the short-term benefits. For example, to construct very simple jobs may reduce training time and produce a high output in the short term. In the long term, it may lead to a high rate of staff turnover through boredom and lack of opportunity, an increase in the total amount of training necessary for replacements and a lack of clerks suitable for promotion when the need arises. In order to achieve the maximum benefit for both employer and employee, the following principles should be applied:

Volume   The workload in terms of volume should be reasonable, allowance being made for routine tasks, unpredictable tasks and relaxation (see Work Measurement, above).

Type of skill   The assortment of tasks included in a job should call for a limited range of skills, e.g. be predominantly concerned with typing and the use of language, or accounting and the use of figures.

Degree of skill   All tasks within a job should call as far as possible for the same degree of skill, i.e. be of the same job grade (see Job Evaluation and Grading, above).

Satisfaction   A job should not be a burden; it should be absorbing and satisfying. The individual tasks and the job as a whole should be such that

Grade A. Tasks which require no previous clerical experience; each individual task is allotted and is either very simple or is closely directed.

Grade B. Tasks which, because of their simplicity, are carried out in accordance with a limited number of well defined rules after a comparatively short period of training. These tasks are closely directed and checked, and are carried out in standard routine with short period control.

Grade C. Tasks which are of a routine character and follow well defined rules, but which require either some experience or a special aptitude for the task, and which are carried out according to a standard routine and are subject to short period control.

Grade D. Tasks which require considerable experience, but a limited degree of initiative, and which are are carried out according to a predetermined procedure. The tasks are carried out according to a standard routine which may vary, but will not vary enough to necessitate any considerable direction.

Grade E. Tasks which may require one or more of the following—
    (a) a basic level of professional or specialised knowledge, for example Part I or II of the A.C.M.A. (Associate of the Institute of Cost and Management Accountants) examinations;
    (b) performance or control of clerical or administrative work requiring mostly routine decisions, but occasional use of discretion and initiative;
    (c) work supervision of a range normally of two to six clerical staff. The number supervised may vary according to the complexity or level of the work.

Grade F. Tasks which may require one or more of the following—
    (a) professional or specialised knowledge equivalent to an intermediate level examination of an appropriate professional association, for example the Institute of Administrative Management's Certificate in Administration Management, Part II or III of A.C.M.A. examinations;

Fig. 114 IAM grading scheme (1976)—grade definitions

(b) performance or control of complex clerical or routine administrative work requiring occasional decisions of a non-routine type, and some use of judgement or initiative or routine matters;

(c) supervision of a range normally of five to twelve clerical staff, in a section compact enough to enable full personal control to be directly maintained. The numbers supervised may vary according to the complexity or level of the work, and may include E grade assistants.

Grade G. Tasks which may require one or more of the following—

(a) professional or specialised knowledge equivalent to a university first degree or to an advanced but not necessarily final qualification of an appropriate professional association, for example final years of A.C.A., the Institute of Administrative Management's Diploma in Administrative Management, or Part III or IV of A.C.M.A.;

(b) performance or control of work of wide complexity or importance requiring regular non-routine decisions and a regular use of judgement and initiative in the execution of predetermined policies;

(c) supervision of a range normally of nine to twenty clerical staff. Control of clerical work may be exercised through two or more grade E or F supervisors; or supervision of a smaller number of grade E or F professional or specialist staff. The numbers supervised may vary according to the complexity or level of the work.

Grade H. Tasks which may require one or more of the following—

(a) professional or specialised knowledge equivalent to a university first degree with some experience or a final qualification of an appropriate professional association such as A.C.A., the Institute of Administrative Management's Diploma in Administrative Management, or A.C.M.A.;

(b) performance or control or work of significant complexity or importance requiring an extensive measure of judgement or initiative and responsibility for some contribution towards the development of departmental policies as well as for their execution;

(c) supervision of a range of normally twenty or more clerical staff. The numbers supervised may vary according to the complexity or level of the work, but control will normally require a deputy and two or more grade E or F supervisors; or supervision of a smaller number of grade E, F or G specialist staff.

the clerk, having regard to his level of experience, can become genuinely interested in the work. It is false to assume that the best results are obtained by creating jobs in which the work is so simple as to be boring. By adding responsibilities to routine work, the job is said to be 'enriched'.

Personal development A job should be so constructed that the experience gained in doing it makes a significant contribution to the personal development of the clerk and to his preparation for promotion to work of a higher grade.

The jobs in an office must be considered as a whole as well as individually. In maintaining a contented staff, reasonable prospects of promotion must be provided. There must be jobs of all grades available in such proportions as to satisfy normal ambition.

ORGANIZATION

As an office increases in size, it becomes more and more necessary to organize it according to some logical plan, rather than allow the form to be the result of successive expedients. In re-planning an existing organization, or in setting up an entirely new one, there are certain practical steps which can be taken as follows (it is presumed that jobs have already been constructed and graded according to the principles enunciated above):

(a) Sort the jobs according to their nature The object is to bring together those jobs which are related because:

(i) they contribute to the same system, e.g. sales invoicing, wages etc., or
(ii) they require the same type of skill, e.g. typing.

(b) Group related jobs into primary working units (Groups) If clerks are to give of their best, they require informal leadership as members of groups of 'family' size with which they can feel a close association. The ideal size of group depends upon the complexity of the work because this determines the amount of supervisory attention necessary. As a guide, the span of control of a Group Leader might be:

(i) about six clerks, where the duties vary from one clerk to another;
(ii) up to twelve clerks, where the duties of clerks are simple and identical;
(iii) fewer than six clerks, where the work is complicated or gives rise to exceptional cases requiring individual attention.

The Group Leader is normally a working supervisor, spending on average about 25 per cent of his time in supervisory duties and the remainder in work of appropriate grade. The work of a group should form a related whole, being concerned with a system (e.g. wages group, sales-invoicing group) or with a skill or service (e.g. typing group).

(c) Assemble groups into secondary working units (Sections) The working units or groups should in turn be grouped to form sections, the second level of supervisory responsibility. Each section should, as far as possible, be composed of groups engaged in similar or related work (see Fig. 115). The number of groups in a section is again dependent upon the complexity of the work, being usually between four and eight. The head of a section is normally a full-time supervisor, spending on average about 75 per cent of his time in supervisory duties and having a wider scope of responsibility than the group leader.

(d) Security provisions It is a principle long recognized that office work should be so arranged as to minimize the possibility of fraud and other dishonest acts. In designing the organizational structure, care should be taken to separate tasks in such a way that the collusion of a number of persons is necessary to defraud or commit acts of industrial espionage.

Organization charts

The pattern of an organization can be represented in the form of a chart which can serve a number of purposes. In planning, the chart is a means of expressing the plans concisely. In reorganization, it provides a basis for consideration and discussion. At any time, it is a compact record of how the office operates. An organization chart can show:

(*a*) the way in which jobs are grouped;
(*b*) the titles of the jobs, groups and sections so formed;
(*c*) the chain of command, showing to whom each person is directly responsible.

The form of the chart should be suited to its purpose. Fig. 115 shows a chart which is particularly suited to illustrating an organization composed of groups and sections. The title of each section is entered in a 'box' together with the numbers and grades of the clerks employed. The composition of each group within the section is similarly defined. The alphabetical grading of the clerks used in this example follows the IAM system described under Job Grading above.

Charts may be supported by other sheets giving, for example, detailed job descriptions, definitions of responsibility and the names of those doing the various jobs. It is better that this be done rather than to over-burden the chart with detail which may obscure the general picture.

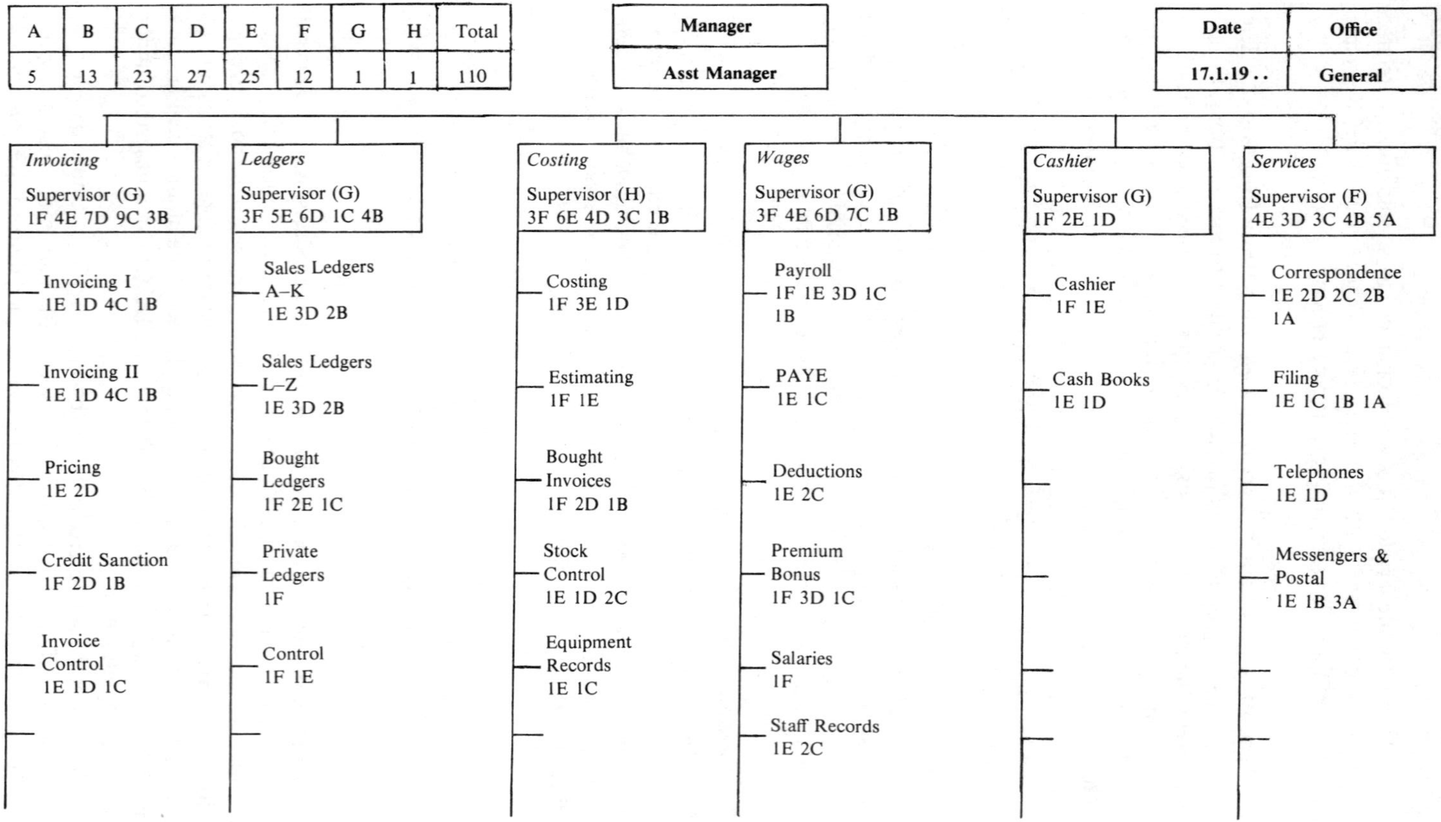

Date	Office
17.1.19..	General

Manager	
Asst Manager	

A	B	C	D	E	F	G	H	Total
5	13	23	27	25	12	1	1	110

Invoicing
Supervisor (G)
1F 4E 7D 9C 3B

- Invoicing I
  1E 1D 4C 1B
- Invoicing II
  1E 1D 4C 1B
- Pricing
  1E 2D
- Credit Sanction
  1F 2D 1B
- Invoice Control
  1E 1D 1C

Ledgers
Supervisor (G)
3F 5E 6D 1C 4B

- Sales Ledgers A–K
  1E 3D 2B
- Sales Ledgers L–Z
  1E 3D 2B
- Bought Ledgers
  1F 2E 1C
- Private Ledgers
  1F
- Control
  1F 1E

Costing
Supervisor (H)
3F 6E 4D 3C 1B

- Costing
  1F 3E 1D
- Estimating
  1F 1E
- Bought Invoices
  1F 2D 1B
- Stock Control
  1E 1D 2C
- Equipment Records
  1E 1C

Wages
Supervisor (G)
3F 4E 6D 7C 1B

- Payroll
  1F 1E 3D 1C 1B
- PAYE
  1E 1C
- Deductions
  1E 2C
- Premium Bonus
  1F 3D 1C
- Salaries
  1F
- Staff Records
  1E 2C

Cashier
Supervisor (G)
1F 2E 1D

- Cashier
  1F 1E
- Cash Books
  1E 1D

Services
Supervisor (F)
4E 3D 3C 4B 5A

- Correspondence
  1E 2D 2C 2B 1A
- Filing
  1E 1C 1B 1A
- Telephones
  1E 1D
- Messengers & Postal
  1E 1B 3A

Fig. 115 Office organization chart

RECRUITMENT AND SELECTION

The techniques already described in this chapter enable an office manager to determine his staffing needs and express them concisely. It remains to select and appoint people to do the various jobs as vacancies occur. The problem lies in recognizing when a person's characteristics and abilities match those required. Sometimes jobs will be filled by engaging clerks from outside; sometimes by transfer or promotion from within the organization. In either case, the procedure is fundamentally the same, although it is obviously easier to form sound judgements when the candidate for a job is already well known.

It is likely that the final decision to appoint a candidate will be taken after interviewing by one or more persons representative of management, supervision and the personnel department. Whilst there is no substitute for the personal interview, it can be made more effective by the use of quality rating and testing which are considered below.

Quality rating   By work analysis, jobs are defined in terms of what has to be done. Quality rating is a means of defining these same jobs in terms of the human characteristics or qualities necessary. The principal qualities of significance in office work are listed and defined in Fig. 116. They fall into five groups: Technical, Physical, Intellectual, Emotional and Volitional. It will be seen that qualities listed are simple and basic. Complex qualities such as 'leadership' or 'ability to settle queries' are avoided. If, for example, a person is unable to settle queries, it is important to know why this is so. The reason could be lack of knowledge of some aspect of the business which could easily be corrected by training, or it might be something less easily corrected such as an inborn lack of imagination.

The first step in quality rating is to consider the particular job and select from the list of qualities those which are significant in its performance. These should then be sorted according to degree of importance and it is usually adequate to place them into five categories according to requirements as follows:

Much above average
Above average
Average
Below average
Much below average

In practice, qualities which are required at degrees below average are of so little importance as to be discarded. The remainder are set out on a rating form as illustrated in Fig. 117. Except in highly responsible jobs, the number of qualities required to the highest degree is small and in routine jobs there may be none.

In applying the rating, the primary task is to decide to what extent, if at all, the candidate falls short of the standards required for the job. For this

Technical qualities

Experience of Job	.	Experienced in this particular job.
Office Practice	.	Familiar with different kinds of clerical work.
Education	. .	Well educated, including self-education.
The Business	.	Familiar with the organization and activities of the particular business.
Office Management	.	Experienced in supervising clerks and clerical jobs.
Accounting	.	Familiar with the principles and practice of Accounting.
Cost Accounting	.	Familiar with the principles and practice of Management Accounting.
Statistics	. .	Able to examine figures by statistical methods.
Time Study	. .	Familiar with the principles and practice of time study.
Computer Programming	. .	Experienced in writing and testing computer programs.
Arithmetic	. .	Practised in Arithmetic.
English	. .	Versed in good English style.
Commercial Practice	.	Familiar with Commercial Law and procedure.
Shorthand	. .	Able to write and read Shorthand.
Typewriting	. .	Able to type satisfactorily.
Audio-typing	. .	Able to type from recorded dictation.

Personal qualities

Physical

Physique	. .	Physically strong, healthy, able to get about.
Good Appearance .	.	Pleasing to others in appearance.
Hearing	. .	Able to hear clearly what is said.
Sight	. .	Able to read easily documents, machine dials and the like.
Clear Speech	. .	Able to speak so as to be easily understood.
Legibility	. .	Able to write so that others can read it easily.
Neatness	. .	Neat and tidy in work.
Manual Dexterity .	.	Capable and quick with the hands.

Intellectual

Concentration	. .	Able to concentrate on the matter in hand, to take care.
Memory	. .	Able to remember accurately.
Reliability	. .	Accurate in work and reliable in statement.
Ability to learn	.	Able to apprehend new ideas.
Wide Interests	.	Interested in other things, desirous of knowledge.
Reasoning	. .	Able to argue, clear in thought, analytical.
Practical Mind	.	Inclined and able to test theories by practical experiment.
Judgement	. .	Able to weigh up and choose rightly, has a sense of proportion.
Imagination	.	Able to create new ideas or a new arrangement of ideas.
Lucidity	. .	Able to express his thoughts clearly.

Emotional

Dash	. .	Quick to respond, energetic, lively.
Confidence	.	Self-reliant, convinced of the value of his efforts.
Sensitivity	. .	Receptive to outside impressions; sympathetic.
Acceptability	.	Able to get on with people and disposed to mix with others.

Volitional

Obedience	. .	Prepared to work under authority and to observe rules.
Willingness	. .	Willing to assist others.
Persistence	. .	Determined to continue in a course, even against opposition.
Self-control	. .	Prepared to resist the effect of strain and excitement.
Trustworthiness	. .	Morally reliable, conscientious.

Fig. 116 Quality rating list

QUALITY RATING	JOB TYPE: CREDIT CONTROL CLERK	MUCH ABOVE AVERAGE	ABOVE AVERAGE	ABOUT AVERAGE	BELOW AVERAGE	MUCH BELOW AVERAGE
GRADE E	PARTICULAR JOB (IF ANY) *Wholesale Group*					
DATE *2.6.19..*	NAME *R. Jones*					

CONSIDER THE INDIVIDUAL AND THE EXTENT TO WHICH HE OR SHE IS--	MUCH ABOVE AVERAGE	.	-1	-2	-3	-4
Able to weigh up and choose rightly, has a sense of proportion	Judgment	✓				

	ABOVE AVERAGE	.	-1	-2	-3
Familiar with the Company's organization and activities	The Company		✓		
Versed in good English style	English		✓		
Able to speak so as to be easily understood	Clear Speech	✓			
Able to remember accurately	Memory	✓			
Accurate in work and reliable in statement	Reliability	✓			
Able to express his thoughts clearly ...	Lucidity	✓			
Morally reliable, conscientious	Trustworthiness	✓			

	AVERAGE	.	-1	-2
Familiar with different kinds of clerical work	Office Practice	✓		
Familiar with the principles and practice of Accounting	Accounting	✓		
Practised in Arithmetic	Arithmetic	✓		
Able to hear clearly what is said	Hearing	✓		
Able to read easily documents, machine dials and the like	Sight	✓		
Able to write so that others can read easily	Legibility		✓	
Neat and tidy in work	Neatness	✓		
Able to argue, clear in thought, analytical	Reasoning	✓		
Self-reliant, convinced of the value of his efforts	Confidence	✓		
Prepared to work under authority and to observe rules	Obedience	✓		
Willing to assist others	Willingness	✓		

Fig. 117   Quality rating form

reason the form provides for the recording of deficiencies to different degrees in the columns on the right. If a quality is required to a degree above average, but is only possessed by the person to an average degree, a tick will be placed against it in the average column, indicating that there is a deficiency of one degree. Whether a deficiency constitutes a serious objection or not depends upon the prospects of improving the quality by training or special care.

When the form has been completed, the overall significance of the deficiencies recorded should be considered and summarized in a short report supporting the judgement reached.

Undue importance should not be attached to the rating form itself; valuable as it is in assisting the formulation of sound judgements, it is no substitute for the judgement itself. The use of this system serves five main purposes:

(*a*) it ensures that the requirements of the job are systematically considered and assessed;

(*b*) it ensures that consideration is given to the degree to which a clerk possesses all the significant qualities;

(*c*) it provides a means of conveying opinions to others and a basis for the discussion of the suitability of a candidate for a job;

(*d*) it assists in determining what training and experience is necessary to develop a clerk's full potentialities;

(*e*) it provides a means of recording the clerk's deficiencies at a particular time and a basis for the subsequent evaluation of progress.

Testing   Some of the qualities necessary to the performance of a job can be evaluated by testing. Tests may be seen as falling into four main types, being concerned with:

(*a*) *ability* to perform specific tasks, as when the applicant for a typing job is asked to demonstrate speed and accuracy;

(*b*) *aptitude* for doing specific types of work, as when a school-leaver is given simple tests in language, arithmetic or facility in sorting names into alphabetical order;

(*c*) *intelligence*, as when a potential O & M officer is given tests which demonstrate the ability to reason from data to a conclusion;

(*d*) *medical*, as when physical qualities (e.g. sight and hearing) are of particular importance.

The simpler ability and aptitude tests can be designed and applied with little difficulty, although it will probably be found convenient to adopt those published by the National Institute of Industrial Psychology and others. The testing of intelligence, however, requires special skills and unless trained personnel are available, outside agencies should be employed to make the assessment. Where all applicants for employment are seen by a doctor, the latter should be asked to test any physical characteristics which are significant in the performance of the job.

Interviewing Although important positive information is obtainable by testing, many of the qualities required to do a job can only be assessed by human judgement. The interview remains the most important means of selection. The National Institute of Industrial Psychology has devised a seven-point plan which suggests that the interviewer must consider the following aspects of the candidate: physical qualities; attainments and experience; intelligence; special aptitudes; interests; disposition; circumstances. The time available to form a considered judgement of a person's suitability under these headings is limited and may be as little as half an hour. The interview should therefore be planned in advance and conducted with clear objectives in view. A 'chat' to see if the candidate 'seems all right' is not good enough.

(*a*) *Preparation* Before commencing, the interviewer should have a clear appreciation of the job. If formal methods are used, this will be available as a definition obtained by work analysis, supported by a quality rating (see Fig. 117). In addition, facts of significance to the candidate must be known, e.g. working hours, working conditions, conditions of employment, promotional prospects, social facilities etc.

(*b*) *Preliminary information* It is usual to ask an applicant for employment to complete a form, giving personal information and details of education, training and experience. The interviewer should study this in advance and decide which aspects are to be discussed with the candidate in greater depth. If the candidate is already employed and is being considered for transfer or promotion, the personnel record should be examined.

If tests have been completed, the results should be evaluated. If there is reason to believe that the candidate has not given a fair impression of ability or aptitude, perhaps because of nervousness, this should be noted.

(*c*) *Conducting the interview* Interviews should be in private and in pleasant surroundings and the candidate should be seated comfortably and without any distractions.

Although planned, the interview should proceed as an informal conversation. Whilst the interviewer may glance at the quality rating or other notes to ensure that nothing is overlooked, and make brief notes, the impression of recording answers to a predetermined list of questions must be avoided. Attention must be paid to the manner in which the candidate responds; hesitation or the evasion of questions may be significant.

The length of the interview and the number of interviews accorded to an applicant will vary with the nature of the job. A single half-hour interview may be enough to decide whether or not a young person is suitable for a relatively junior position. In selecting someone to fill a senior position, it may be necessary to devote much more time and to have applicants interviewed by several people.

Whilst the interviewer requires to learn about the candidate, it must be remembered that the candidate also wishes to learn about the job and the employer. There is little to be gained by engaging a suitable applicant who will leave after a short time because of some dissatisfaction. Basic information about the job, conditions and prospects should be volunteered and the candidate invited to ask questions which should be answered frankly.

(*d*) *Evaluating the results*   Immediately after the interview has ended, the interviewer should supplement the brief notes made whilst the proceedings are still freshly remembered. If a quality rating form has been prepared, this should be completed so that any deficiencies can be seen and judged.

It is not to be expected that any candidate will be perfect, having every required quality to the required degree. Some deficiencies may be capable of correction and therefore acceptable; others may be more fundamental and make the candidate totally unsuitable. Systematic preparation, testing and interviewing will help to determine not only whether a person is suitable or unsuitable, but why.

Whilst objective evaluation of the person in relation to the job is important, the overall personality must also be considered. The candidate selected will become one of a group and influence the relationships within that group. In addition to determining ability to do a job, the interviewer must be satisfied that the individual will fit happily into the team.

LAWS RELATING TO EMPLOYMENT*

There are many Acts of Parliament which define the relationships between employer and employee and influence staffing policy and practice. In some cases, these Acts provide broad guidelines within which a Secretary of State may make more detailed regulations from time to time.

The scope of the law now makes it a separate study (see also pages 281–4). The office manager should not seek to be his own expert, but rather rely on professional legal advice. In order to be able to seek such help he must, of course, be aware of the areas in which there may be restriction on his freedom of action. To offend against the law may lead to the employer being prosecuted in the Courts, or having to defend cases before tribunals. It must be noted that under some Acts the legal responsibility falls not only on the employer (which may be a limited company) but on the director or manager concerned personally.

---

* Much of this section is reproduced by permission of the Institute of Administrative Management from *Office Administration*, ed. Mills and Standingford (Pitman), 3rd edition.

The following defines the general scope of the principal Acts involved:

Contracts of Employment Act, 1963 as amended Requires a minimum period of notice to terminate employment after a qualifying period of employment; requires employers to give written particulars of terms and conditions of employment including rates of pay, intervals between payments, hours of work, sick pay, pension, holidays, trade union membership, grievance procedure, length of notice to be given and date of expiry of contract (if for a fixed period).

Race Relations Act, 1968 Makes it unlawful to discriminate against a person on grounds of colour, race, ethnic or national origins in advertisements, employment, training, promotion or dismissal; employers may discriminate to secure a balance of different racial groups.

Sex Discrimination Act, 1975 Makes it unlawful to discriminate directly or indirectly on grounds of sex or marital status in matters of employment, e.g. staff advertising, recruitment, promotion, transfer, training, benefits or facilities, except where the sex of a person is a genuine qualification for a job.

Equal Pay Act, 1970 Requires that employers shall accord equal treatment to men and women as regards terms and conditions of employment (including pay), except in matters which are (a) subject to laws regulating the employment of women, (b) concerned with childbirth, and (c) concerned with pensions, retirement, marriage or death.

Redundancy Payments Acts, 1965, 1969 as amended Require employers to compensate employees made redundant by a scale of redundancy pay related to the rate of pay and the length of service.

Trade Unions and Labour Relations Act, 1974 Concerned principally with trade union practices and the rights of trade union members, including the right to strike; lays down procedures for the settlement of disputes as to fair and unfair dismissal.

Employment Protection Act, 1975 Concerned with (a) industrial relations and the settlement of disputes by conciliation or force of law, (b) the provision by employers of information to trade unions, (c) the rights of employees in relation to payment, medical suspension, maternity pay and reinstatement, trade union membership, time off for union or public duties and dismissal, and (d) redundancy procedure.

22 Rewards

The principal reward for work done is an adequate salary coupled with just conditions of employment. But this alone is not sufficient. Human beings also look for other, less tangible, rewards, among them satisfaction and interest in their work. This chapter is therefore divided into two sections, the first dealing with wage practices and conditions of employment, and the second with work satisfaction.

WAGE PRACTICES AND CONDITIONS OF EMPLOYMENT

Whereas many tradesmen in other fields reach their maximum earning capacity in their early twenties, the clerk has seldom mastered his craft so soon. He can continue to increase his knowledge and ability, and thus progress to more highly skilled and responsible jobs, throughout almost the whole of his working life. For this reason, clerical wage scales traditionally have numerous steps by which remuneration is to be increased in proportion to increasing skill and responsibility. Most wage scales have this in common: there is a basic rate for the job with a margin to allow for differences in age or for the skill with which the job is performed.

Grade scales Where work is graded by some such system as that described in the previous chapter, wage rates are related to the grading system. Generally, a minimum and a maximum is set for each grade, for example:

Grade A £26·00–£29·00
Grade B £30·00–£33·00
Grade C £34·00–£38·00

Thus, in the example, a clerk doing Grade B work will earn not less than £30·00 and not more than £33·00, the actual point being determined by the efficiency of the individual. This range provides scope for some advancement in salary whilst the clerk remains in the one grade, and it is to be expected that when the time for promotion to the next grade approaches, the rate will approximate to the minimum for that grade.

Sometimes a more elastic scale is provided by overlapping the rates for the different grades, thus:

Grade A £26·00–£32·00
Grade B £30·00–£36·00
Grade C £34·00–£42·00

There may be separate grade scales for different skills, e.g. the scale for typewriting and private secretarial jobs may differ from that for general clerks.

Merit scales   Where a grade or other type of scale provides for upper and lower limits, the actual amount paid may be purely discretionary but the assessment is more likely to be just—and accepted as just—if some formula is used. It is not easy to judge the relative merits of clerks without some common yardstick. Whilst intangible qualities such as loyalty or a pleasant personality have some importance, merit at work should be assessed as far as possible by consideration of such factors as:

Output in terms of quantity;
Quality having regard to accuracy, judgement, neatness;
Ability to deal with difficult situations, queries, correction of errors etc.;
Willingness and ability to help and advise others when necessary;
Mobility or ability to do a variety of tasks;
Punctuality and reliability in attendance.

Merit must be assessed at infrequent intervals, possibly half-yearly or even yearly. If judgements are to be just, they must be based on performance over the entire period since the previous assessment and not unduly influenced by recent events. To this end, it is necessary to maintain simple records of attendance, output, errors, experience gained etc.

It is common practice to assess the merit of a person, whether in relation to a single factor or as a whole, according to a five-point scale, e.g.

Much below average	Below average	Average	Above average	Much above average

or

Indifferent	Fair	Good	Very good	Excellent

The Institute of Administrative Management publishes a merit rating plan with its job-grading scheme described in the previous chapter.

Clerks are rated according to the definitions given in Fig. 118. The rates of pay may then be fixed according to a scale in which the overspill ratings Superior (+1) and Outstanding (+2) are equal to the Starter and Qualified ratings of the grade next above (see Fig. 119).

Starter. This rating is assigned when the job holder has started in a grade either as a newcomer or as a result of promotion and has the ability to tackle the new job. It represents the degree of efficiency which can reasonably be expected during the period that the job holder is learning the work.

Qualified. This rating is assigned when the job holder has completed the learning period and is qualified to perform satisfactorily all the normal aspects of a job in the grade without further instruction.

Experienced. This rating is assigned when the job holder has been in the grade for some time and has not only mastered all the normal aspects of a job in the grade but also acquired a sufficient knowledge and understanding of its implications to be able to deal reliably with all the circumstances likely to arise.

Superior (or +1). This rating is only assigned when a job holder, in addition to the acquisition of knowledge and experience, continually demonstrates an ability to perform work in the grade in a noticeably superior manner.

Outstanding (or +2). This rating is confined to those of outstanding ability in the job grade. Generally speaking it is used only for those who are fully capable of doing higher grade work or for those who have performed their jobs in a consistently superior manner with accumulating experience for a number of years, or are very versatile in other work of the same grade, or recognised as leaders among other staff of the same grade.

Fig. 118   IAM Merit-rating definitions

Age scales   In fixing wage scales, it is customary to provide special age rates for the more junior clerks. A minimum is set for each age from, say, 16 to 21, so that, for example:

at 16 the minimum is £26·00
at 17 it is   £28·50
at 18 it is   £31·50, and so on.

This method can be combined with a grade scale so that each clerk will be

Job Grade	MERIT RATING				
	Normal			Overspill	
	Starter	*Qualified*	*Experienced*	*Superior* (+1)	*Outstanding* (+2)
A	£26·00	27·25	28·50	30·00	31·50
B	£30·00	31·50	33·00	34·50	36·00
C	£34·50	36·00	38·00	40·00	42·00

Fig. 119   Example from job/merit wage scale

paid at least the minimum for his age, or the minimum for his grade, whichever is the greater.

Job and age scales   An alternative method is to fix an 'adult rate' (not necessarily related to the legal age of adulthood) for each class of job with an ascending scale for juniors. For example, the adult rate for a typist might be set at £49·00. Younger typists are then paid as follows:

at age 17 £28·00   at age 21 £40·00
at age 18 £31·00   at age 22 £43.00
at age 19 £34·00   at age 23 £46·00
at age 20 £37·00   at age 24 £49·00

Office salaries analyses   Businesses need to compare their own rates with those of similarly placed organizations. To assist in these comparisons, the Institute of Administrative Management regularly conducts nationwide surveys and analyses the rates paid for different grades and types of job. The results are available to anyone interested.

Long-service premiums   It is sometimes the practice to pay a premium for long service so that, in addition to the job rate, a clerk will receive extra amounts after, say, five, ten and fifteen years' service.

Adult workers doing low-grade work   At one time it could be assumed that unskilled or semi-skilled office work would ordinarily be done by young people. The rates of pay offered for jobs of, say, IAM Grades A, B and C were such as to attract clerks up to the age of about 20. In many areas, insufficient young clerks are available to fill the junior positions and their places are taken by adults, mostly men nearing or over normal retirement age and married women aged 30 and over who may have children at school. Clerks in these categories are sometimes paid rates in excess of those normally associated with the grades of work done.

Bonus   Incentive bonuses directly based on output are seldom offered in offices because of the inherent difficulties in measuring and recording the work with a sufficient degree of accuracy (see page 288). Bonuses have been paid in circumstances in which:

(*a*) the work is highly repetitive routine, e.g. copy-typing forms or card/tape punching, or

(*b*) the work of a group can reasonably be related to some simple unit, e.g. all the work of a sales office related to the number of sales invoices completed.

The outcome, however, is not always satisfactory because discontent may arise. Those who are eligible for bonus may feel 'cheated' when given work which is difficult because of abnormalities or queries. They may also resent variations in earning potential when there are fluctuations in the amount of work available. Once clerks become used to receiving higher levels of pay, they expect these to continue as of right and resent any reduction which is not 'their fault'.

Unless a bonus scheme is uniform throughout all sections of an office, there is likely to be discontent among those who are unable to qualify for bonus however hard they work. This discontent will be felt particularly when a clerk is transferred or even 'promoted' from a job in which bonus can be earned to a job for which there is a fixed basic rate only.

Some factories are already turning away from premium bonus and it seems unlikely that offices generally will adopt it. The present tendency is towards establishing by measurement what is a reasonable workload and expecting management and supervision:

(*a*) to ensure that each clerk is provided with an adequate flow of work;

(*b*) to train and stimulate clerks to maintain a proper level of output;

(*c*) to reward consistently good performance by merit increases and by promotion to better paid jobs.

Payment of salaries   It is becoming common practice to pay clerks, particularly those in senior grades, by transfer to their bank accounts and to pay them monthly rather than weekly.

Overtime   Clerks, other than the more senior, are usually paid for overtime, either at basic rate or with increment varying from one-fifth to double time. Where there are peak loads of work followed by slack periods, compensation for overtime often takes the form of equivalent time off when the work permits.

Sick pay   Generous provision for sick pay has long been common practice in offices, the amount and duration usually depending upon service.

Other Conditions

Pensions   Most large businesses have superannuation schemes for their employees. The conditions vary, but most schemes in industrial and commercial offices are contributory and with 60–65 as the age of retirement.

Hours of work   The office must open to meet the needs of the business served. The working week varies accordingly between thirty-five and forty hours exclusive of meal breaks. The generally accepted normal is about thirty-seven-and-a-half hours.

The five-day week, Monday to Friday inclusive, predominates. For the staff it provides a longer weekend break and saves travelling time and fares. For the employer it saves the cost of opening the office which may exceed the value of work done. In some businesses, Saturday morning working is necessary for some, if not all, of the office staff. In such cases, employees may take turns in attending and may be compensated for the Saturday morning by overtime payment or time off on another day.

Part-time working   A large proportion of office staff consists of married women with domestic and family responsibilities. Some of these find it inconvenient or impossible to work the normal office hours, and prefer:

(a) to work mornings or afternoons only; or
(b) to work shorter hours, starting late and finishing early; or
(c) to work only on certain days of the week.

Such arrangements are often convenient because of variations in the office workload. Tasks which cannot be started until the morning mail has been opened and sorted can perhaps begin at 10 a.m. A wages office may need a full staff only during the middle of the week.

Hourly rates of pay for part-time clerks are sometimes marginally higher than those for full-time staff to allow for travelling and meal expenses which are likely to be the same however short or long the working day.

Flexible working hours   Flexible working hours or flexitime is a system by which clerks are allowed to start and finish work as they choose, provided that:

(a) they work within the earliest and latest times laid down;
(b) they are present during the 'core' time when everyone is expected to be at work, say 10 a.m. until 3.30 p.m.;
(c) they work an agreed total of hours within a specified period, e.g. a week or a month.

In the larger offices, it is usual to install time-recording equipment (Fig. 120) operated by the clerk using a key or identity card. This arrangement ensures that there is no misunderstanding as to the hours worked by each person.

With flexitime, the employee has greater freedom and with it often demonstrates a corresponding sense of responsibility. So long as the work is done satisfactorily, there is no feeling of guilt about being late for work or having time off for personal reasons. The married woman in particular is able to co-ordinate her work with domestic and family responsibilities without having to watch the clock too closely; those with travel difficulties can perhaps avoid the rush hours. An off-setting disadvantage for some may be that there is likely to be less overtime, with its opportunity for additional earnings.

The employer may find that he is able to select recruits from a wider range of applicants because he can offer working hours to suit more people. Morale is generally found to improve with flexible hours, providing a happier working environment for everyone. In some circumstances, flexible hours may be better suited to the workload and result in a reduction of overtime outside normal office hours. On the other hand, it is necessary to ensure that the office is supervised from the earliest starting time to the latest finishing time, and to provide for the recording of irregular hours of attendance. In some cases, there may be difficulty in ensuring that jobs which entail contact with suppliers or customers are always staffed during the traditional business hours.

Where flexitime is worked, it appears to be popular, particularly in large city centres where there are travel problems.

Meals and meal breaks   If mental alertness is to be maintained throughout the day, meal breaks should be carefully arranged so that long periods of uninterrupted work are avoided. No main spell of work should exceed three and a half hours. It is common practice to provide short tea or coffee breaks of about ten minutes during the morning and afternoon. In some offices, refreshments are brought to the clerks' desks; in others, clerks are encouraged to go to a canteen, tea bar or vending machine. The argument for the latter arrangement is that some benefit is gained from the change of surroundings and slight exercise. With the introduction of vending machines, some managements permit clerks to leave their desks at will to obtain refreshments.

Holidays   A minimum of three weeks' holiday with pay is usual. Often there are additional holidays for senior staff or those with long service.

Staff handbooks   A carefully compiled staff handbook can be an important factor in establishing good relations with the staff. It should set out the conditions of employment and office rules, and describe the welfare services,

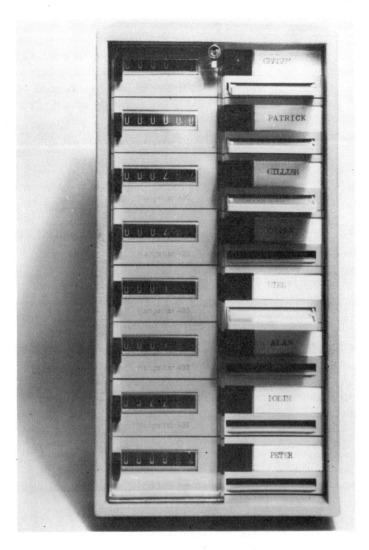

Fig. 120   Time-recording equipment (*Courtesy of Hengstler Flextime Ltd.*)

conditions of work, sports-club facilities and training programmes. Often in a larger business a separate handbook is issued to the office staff. To be fully effective, it should not be a mere book of rules or a legal document but give a lively and intelligible account of the whole working environment. It should seek to make the newcomer feel welcome in his new surroundings and glad to become a member of the organization.

Care should be taken not to overpaint the picture: the effect of disappointment in the light of experience is worse than that of initial misgivings which are later dispelled.

Trade unions   Historically, office workers have not had a tradition of unionization. The clerk who was discontented tended to leave his employer and seek another job rather than band together with his associates to take joint action. It may be assumed that their attitudes reflected their conditions of work. This does not mean that they were eternally contented, but rather that if they had real grievances they were able to obtain redress as individuals.

Among the advantages which clerks enjoyed, as compared with other workers, were:

(*a*) *Favourable Labour Market.* The number of clerical workers employed increased year by year for more than half a century and severe unemployment was not felt.

(*b*) *Prospects.* By tradition, the clerical worker who responded to training and developed his capabilities could expect, and usually obtained, increased rewards through promotion or merit assessment.

(*c*) *Mobility.* If unhappy in his job, the skilled clerical worker could move to another employer irrespective of industry. When one industry was suffering hard times, he could move to one which was expanding.

(*d*) *Contact with Management.* Through the nature of his work, the clerk was in direct contact with supervision and management, sometimes at high level. He was, therefore, able to mention any grievance informally before it became oppressive. Again, through the nature of his training and work, he was better able than many workers to make his feelings known directly without requiring a 'shop steward' to speak on his behalf.

However, union activities, already commonplace in national and municipal government services and in nationalized industries, are increasing in industrial and commercial offices, particularly under the influence of industrial legislation.

The office manager may or may not be directly involved in negotiation with union representatives on major issues. Either way, it is his duty to be aware of, and to conform with, agreements entered into by his employer and a union. He is also wise to maintain personal contact with his staff and their union representatives so that he may understand their views. He may then be able to prevent grievances or at least act promptly when they come to his notice. If he does not have the power to act, he should report matters to his superior and make such recommendations as seem to him necessary. Delay in settling minor grievances can in time build up an atmosphere of discontent.

Publicity is always given to industrial disputes; rarely to the many thousands of organizations in which there is co-operation and mutual understanding. If management at all levels plays its proper part in ensuring just rewards and reasonable working conditions, industrial peace can prevail.

WORK SATISFACTION

Adequate payment and good conditions of work are not by themselves sufficient to provide the satisfaction in work that people require if they are to give of their best. Some of the difficulties attaching to monetary incentives have been mentioned earlier in this chapter, and the office manager needs to concern himself with the problem of stimulating the interest of his clerks in their work in order to obtain increased output and higher standards of quality.

Every effort should be made to develop a community of interest between the individual and the others with whom he works; in short, to stimulate a good team spirit. Most people can only find pleasure in work through the satisfaction of playing a part in an effective team doing a job which is regarded as worth while. And the team, or primary group should be of such a size (numbering between, say, six and twelve) that the individual is in personal contact with each member of it in the course of his work. The practical test is that the individual should feel that the success of the group is as his own success, and the failure of the group is as his own failure.

Good team spirit is not fortuitous but requires certain favourable conditions. These conditions require that there shall be a stated and commonly accepted objective known to every member of the group. Those who do the work must know that it has a purpose, and must clearly understand what that purpose is. Moreover, the group must realize its potentialities as a whole, and each individual must recognize the part which he can play within the group. Much will depend upon the personal influence of the manager, but there are certain specific means which can be adopted to stimulate satisfaction in work, and these are discussed below.

Joint consultation   The development of ideas about the effective management of human resources, reinforced by legislation, is inevitably leading towards more employee participation in management. Although employees have not had the power of decision, consultation between management and employees is not new. In the smaller and medium-sized businesses, representatives of the office staff are usually included in a works or production committee representing the entire organization. Where a large office staff is employed, there may be a separate office committee, since the particular problems and interests of the office are not necessarily the same as those of the factory.

The function of joint committees composed of representatives of the workers, supervisors and management is not merely to deal with working conditions affecting the individual, but also to take an interest in the effective running of the business. These committees are not, however, executive, but are intended:

(*a*) to provide a two-way stream of information; employees informing management of their ideas and of any causes of dissatisfaction, and management informing employees of current problems and intended action;

(*b*) to provide for joint consultation between employees and management on policy whilst it is still in the formative stage, so that before managerial decisions are made the employees' ideas and reactions may be considered.

When such committees are first formed, matters discussed usually centre around working conditions, employee services, education, discipline, absenteeism and lateness, social and recreational activities, canteen facilities, and grievances. Questions relating to wages are usually excluded, but the discussion of wage rates from a general, but not individual, point of view may be permitted.

In the more advanced stage of development, staff committees are able to deal with suggestions regarding the work, and problems of efficiency, production and general operating policy. When major changes in method are proposed, committees may be one of the means of consultation and communication between management and staff. In this way the representatives of the employees can have a part in the management of the enterprise even though only in an advisory capacity.

Suggestion schemes Suggestion schemes (sometimes called improvement schemes) enable staff to make their ideas known to management, confident that these will receive serious consideration. There is, of course, nothing to prevent clerks from making proposals orally or in writing but many are diffident, fearing that they may be ridiculed or regarded as criticizing a superior. A formal scheme which openly encourages suggestions helps to overcome this diffidence. The benefits which may accrue include:

(*a*) the tangible improvements which result directly or indirectly from suggestions made;

(*b*) the stimulation of staff to take a greater interest in their work and environment.

Usually, forms are provided and suggestion boxes set up so that clerks may make suggestions without directly approaching a supervisor or manager and without drawing attention to themselves. The boxes are emptied periodically and the forms passed to a committee composed of representatives of management and staff. This committee is responsible for making sure that each suggestion receives proper consideration in the right quarter.

Most schemes provide cash awards for suggestions which are implemented with or without amendment. In some cases, small awards are given to encourage further effort, even though the suggestion may have proved impracticable.

Few suggestion schemes flourish unless members of the staff are repeatedly encouraged to put forward their ideas for consideration. Whenever problems arise which the clerks themselves might help to solve, management and supervision should draw attention to them. Personal encouragement generally achieves the greatest interest, but this can usefully be supplemented by poster and other publicity and by the publication of awards.

Explanation of purpose   It happens that in the office the reason why work is done is often less obvious than in other spheres of activity. Yet unless the reason for a job is clearly understood, it is unlikely that the person doing it will give of his best.

Generally, during training is the most convenient time to give an explanation of purpose, and no clerk should be instructed in a job until the purpose has first been explained. But once is not sufficient; full appreciation of purpose will not always be attained during training, when so much is new. Once the clerk has settled down to the new job, the supervisor should discuss the purpose with him again, if necessary at some length. If the full explanation requires a visit to one of the operative departments, it may be better to defer this visit until the clerk has become familiar with the work relating to it.

For the more junior levels, it may be necessary to take pains to simplify the explanation, but it will be found that the trouble taken is well justified by the results obtained.

Management by objectives   In this section on Work Satisfaction, ideas have been discussed which concern developing 'a community of interest between the individual and the others with whom he works'. This, among other things, concerns team spirit, joint consultation and stimulating people to think about ways of improving the work in the light of its purposes.

One more approach may be mentioned: creating a climate of management by objectives. This starts with establishing an appropriate relationship between the office manager and the supervisors who report directly to him. This relationship will need to take into account a number of ideas which have already been touched upon.

The manager and his supervisors are working together in the office to achieve a series of objectives. These objectives form the purpose or the mission of the department for which the manager is responsible. It is the office manager's duty to establish these objectives by discussions with the managers of those departments of the business which the office serves.

The office manager also has the duty to interpret the objectives to his immediate subordinates. These objectives are unlikely to be clearly understood if the manager merely states them to his subordinates, either orally or in writing. There needs to be full and open discussion so that the information obtained by the office manager may be shared with his supervisors working together as a team. The supervisors will need this opportunity to discuss and explore the purpose of the department if they are to collaborate to the full. This may include contributing ideas which will involve the office manager in going back to the departments to make further suggestions.

When the total purpose of the department is understood it is then appropriate, against the background of the team discussions, for the manager to discuss with each supervisor in turn the purpose of his particular section. Once there is mutual agreement on the purpose of a section, the manager and the supervisor should agree upon the targets which the supervisor is to try to achieve in the immediate future, perhaps the following six months. These are likely to concern changes and improvements: the supervisor may be responsible for helping to install a change in method; there may be a requirement to improve the training of his subordinates; it may be desirable to raise the output or improve certain aspects of quality.

Ideally, the supervisor, having taken part in the general discussion on the overall purpose of the office, should take the lead in stating the purpose of his section and in detailing the appropriate targets which he hopes to achieve in the immediate months ahead. He should be invited to go away and think about his ideas and to come back with proposals. In thinking about his targets he should be given an opportunity to include those aspects which will give him personal satisfaction. If a supervisor is able, in reality, to contribute to the setting of objectives or targets he will thereby increase his commitment; people support what they have helped to build.

After the objectives or targets have been agreed the supervisor should be invited to recommend the basis on which performance will be measured. Unless targets are capable of measurement the supervisor will not be able to get satisfaction out of achievement when the time comes to review performance. The crucial aspect of this process is that manager and supervisor agree in advance what performance is required and how that performance is to be measured. In short, 'the rules of the game' are worked out and agreed beforehand.

Something like an ideal state of affairs will have been reached if at the end of the agreed period the supervisor, without prompting from his manager and having reviewed his own performance on his own behalf, suggests to his manager that they should review together his performance and set up new targets for a further period.

If a climate of management by objectives is to be fully effective it has to operate on all levels. The office manager will need to work in this relationship with the senior manager to whom he reports. The supervisors will need to establish a similar relationship with their group leaders and the group leaders with their clerks.

Status   Throughout history and in all walks of life, it has been normal for the leader to enjoy greater rewards than are accorded to those who are led. It is also normal human behaviour to grant to leaders outward signs or symbols of their position in society. These symbols are sought, displayed, esteemed and envied even though they have little or no money value. In the armed services, the symbol may be a badge on a uniform; in business, it is likely to be a combination of privilege and working conditions.

The office traditionally has its status symbols. These may include additional holiday entitlement, even though it may not be wholly taken, and the 'right' not to be paid for overtime worked. The more readily-visible symbols may be a private office, a larger desk, a better chair, a loud-speaking telephone, a carpet or a private secretary. To some extent these symbols may be necessary to the job, but they are also valued as outward signs of status.

With the trend towards a greater equality of financial reward (the narrowing of 'differentials') and the increased use of open and landscaped offices, the status symbol has a new and perhaps greater significance. Provided that it is generally recognized, the symbol can be quite simple. In one European organization, for example, management and staff work together in one landscaped office and have the same furniture with one exceptional item. For management and supervision, a visitor's chair is provided and according to level within the organization this chair is upholstered in a distinctive colour. A person's position is thus displayed, not in anything which is enjoyed by him personally, but by the mere colour of the chair offered to his visitor.

There are those who decry the status symbol as unnecessary and perhaps even degrading. Humans are, however, imperfect and appear to need to display their successes in some way. The fulfilling of this need is one of the rewards for work.

23 Training

Work, whether done by a clerk or by the office manager, is the result of a combination of time spent, effort expended and skill employed. The ultimate productivity of a day's work depends to a large extent on the third factor of skill. The typist able to work quickly and accurately may achieve twice as much in the hour as one who is faltering and uncertain what to do. The clerk who knows enough to be able to settle queries without reference to a supervisor will produce far more than one who can deal only with straightforward cases.

The purpose of training is to develop skill and, through skill, to raise the productivity of the individual. There are several ways in which a job may be learnt, some efficient and some inefficient. In the past, the untrained clerk was often told to sit beside a more experienced person and learn by watching and copying. This method was slow and costly in that the trainee was paid a full wage over an extended training period. It is now recognized that the most economical method is planned, intensive instruction aimed at producing maximum output in the shortest possible time.

The speed with which people learn is influenced to a considerable extent by the attitudes of their superiors and colleagues. The learner must feel protected during the period in which skill is being developed. There must be no ridicule of early attempts and there must be encouragement rather than criticism. Trainees need to know when they are doing well, and how they might do better. They must be given adequate opportunity to try again and again; patience is an essential of good teaching.

Training is encouraged in Britain through the operation of the Industrial Training Act with its system of levy and grant which is described below. It is important that this system, where it applies, should not overshadow the main purpose of instruction. The earning of grants is a secondary consideration; they are no more than a contribution towards costs already incurred. The true benefit comes from more and better work for the salary paid.

It should also be noted that the skill derived from training is valueless unless it is fully employed. Time and money spent in developing a clerk's ability is wasted if thereafter the clerk is given no more work to do than before. Training should be part of a scheme which includes job grading and work measurement to ensure that each clerk's potential is fully utilized.

THE INDUSTRIAL TRAINING ACT, 1964

The purpose of this Act is to ensure the provision of adequate training for employment in industry and commerce for everyone over the compulsory school age. It established an Industrial Training Board for each industry or group of industries, to be responsible for securing the provision of training courses and facilities, and the Central Training Council as an advisory body.

Each Board has the power to raise a compulsory levy on all the firms in its industry in order to provide funds for its purposes. This levy is usually a fixed sum per employee or a percentage of a firm's payroll. The money so raised is available to make grants to firms to cover wholly or in part the cost of training activities carried out with the Board's approval. Funds can also be used for research and the direct provision of training facilities.

The conditions to be fulfilled before firms receive training grants are laid down by the individual Boards, varying from one industry to another. It is normally a condition that training within a firm shall be supplemented, particularly for young people, by release for related further education in a technical college. Firms applying for grants must be prepared to keep prescribed records and submit their training schemes to inspection.

It is an offence under the Act, punishable by fine, to fail to provide information lawfully demanded by a Board. The wilful furnishing of false information may lead to a fine, imprisonment or both. In the case of a limited company, any director, secretary or manager may be found guilty of an offence and be liable to fine or imprisonment.

Central Training Council recommendations

The training of office workers—from the most junior of clerks to the office manager—presents problems common to all industries. Because of this, the Central Training Council set up a Commercial and Clerical Training Committee to advise the various Industrial Training Boards as to the action they should take. The recommendations of this committee (*Training for Commerce and the Office*, HMSO) have been accepted by the Boards in principle, although each board is free to make such variations as it wishes in framing its rules.

That which follows is in accordance with the Commercial and Clerical Training Committee's recommendations which are representative of general basic practice.

THE ELEMENTS OF OFFICE TRAINING SCHEMES

Approved training schemes must generally contain four elements, which are:

Induction training	Job training
Skill training	Further education

Whilst these can each be considered in isolation, they all contribute to one total effect: the development of a skilled office worker, able to undertake a variety of jobs with understanding.

It should be noted in this connection that approved training schemes go beyond the training of a person to do what is immediately necessary. In the case of young people in particular, it is the intention that they should be prepared for a career in office work. Early training should enable a clerk to be transferred or promoted in due course to other jobs with the minimum of further training. In some businesses, it has been the practice to give no instruction beyond that which is necessary to do a single job. This has been shown to be a short-sighted policy. The young are able to learn much more quickly than older people and advantage should be taken of this fact. The time and effort spent will be amply repaid in increased efficiency and in the ability to undertake greater responsibility at an earlier age.

Induction training

The purpose of induction training is to introduce the newly-engaged employee to his environment. An induction course should therefore be given to every newcomer, no matter what his previous experience.

On coming into the business for the first time, everything will be strange: the premises, the people, the traditions, the rules etc. The newcomer must become familiar with these before he can do his work with understanding, and the sooner he settles in, the better. If he is left to gather informaion by chance, it may be many months before the necessary background knowledge has been assimilated.

The induction training programme should start on the new employee's first day and be spread over, say, three weeks. An intensive course is likely to confuse the trainee by requiring that too much information should be absorbed at one time. An hour of instruction each day is more effective than two whole days of instruction. The course might include the following:

(*a*) *On the first day.* Receive and welcome. Conduct round the premises with particular attention to position of cloakroom, lavatories, canteen, main departments and fire exits. Take to the office in which the trainee will work and introduce to:

(i) supervisor;
(ii) a few colleagues (too many introductions confuse and embarrass);
(iii) a 'friend', one colleague who will be asked to help and advise when necessary.

Explain terms of employment, office rules, etc.

(*b*) *Spread over the ensuing weeks.* Sessions conducted by the office manager, personnel officer, training officer and others as may be appropriate, which may be informal talks or tours of departments. The trainee may be given duplicated notes so that points of detail can be studied at leisure. A typical plan might include such subjects as:

(i) history of the business;
(ii) products, materials and processes (with visits to stores and factory);
(iii) markets and new developments;
(iv) company organization and principal officials;
(v) organization of the trainee's own department and the duties of individuals;
(vi) training and further education programme;
(vii) promotional prospects.

In most businesses, newcomers undergo induction training individually and instruction can be personal and informal. In the larger organizations, it may be possible to form small groups to go through the induction course together. Where the cost is warranted, use can be made of films and other visual aids; even a simple photograph may save time and make an explanation more effective.

Induction training is of special importance to the office worker who deals with words and figures. It affords an opportunity to show the business as a reality and give the words and figures meaning.

Skill training

Office work entails the use of a number of basic skills which can be more effectively taught away from the job in the first instance. No one, for example, would attempt to teach typewriting as part of the job training: it is accepted that a minimum degree of speed and accuracy must be attained before practical work is attempted. The same principle can be applied to a number of other basic skills.

How and where basic skill training is given depends mainly on the number of hours of instruction necessary and the facilities available. If the teaching time is short, arrangements can probably be made in the office; if not, it may be better to make use of external facilities. The following are examples of basic skills, showing where instruction might be given:

At a technical or commercial college

Typewriting	Commercial calculations
Book-keeping	Duplicating

In the office

Handling incoming mail	Reception of visitors
Handling outgoing mail	Photocopying
Sorting	Adding–listing
Filing	machine operation
Use of the telephone	Petty-cash accounting

It is the intention of the Industrial Training Act that office workers should be trained beyond the requirements of the immediate job. The training programmes for young people in particular should include instruction in the operation of a representative range of office machines and devices.

Where, as will often be the case, the training programme includes day-release for further education, the course attended is likely to provide some skill training. Inquiries should be made as to the nature and extent of this so as to avoid duplication.

Job training

The ultimate purpose of all training is that the trainee shall be able to do a job with skill and understanding, and so reach a high level of productivity. The elements of induction, skill training and further education all contribute to this but only yield their benefits through the job.

The responsibility for job training falls directly upon the office manager and his supervisors. It was at one time general practice to let one clerk be trained by another. This method is now obsolete because it is slow and usually leads to the teaching of incorrect procedures and the passing on of bad working habits. It is now generally accepted that job training is best done by the trainee's immediate superior. The office manager trains the supervisor; the supervisor trains the group leader; the group leader trains the clerk.

Training—or teaching—is a form of communication; the passing of information from one person to another. The principles that should be applied in communication generally must therefore be applied in teaching, and the following are of particular importance.

Responsibility   The responsibility for effective teaching lies entirely with the teacher. If the trainee fails to learn, it is because the trainer has failed to find the right way of conveying his ideas.

Purpose   If the purpose is known, knowledge becomes understanding. Before the trainer explains what is to be done, he must explain the purpose to be achieved.

Association of ideas   New ideas can only be assimilated if they are related to something already understood. The trainer must find out what the trainee already knows and then build on that knowledge.

From the general to the particular   Details have little meaning except as the parts of a whole. The trainer must first explain things in general terms so that the whole job and the system of which it forms part are understood. The trainee will then be able to appreciate the significance of the various tasks to be performed.

From the normal to the exceptional   The normal procedure should be taught first. Only when this has become familiar should the trainee be introduced to the exceptional cases and variations from the basic routine. If the normal and the exceptional are taught together, the trainee is likely to become confused and the teaching process will take longer.

Teach by stages   People cannot assimilate more than a limited amount of new knowledge at one time. Instruction should be given by stages in a logical order and time allowed between stages for the new ideas to be digested.

Repetition   No one learns by being told what to do once only. For knowledge to be retained by the memory, it must be repeated several times. Patient repetition pays because it results ultimately in the establishing of correct working habits.

Job training methods

There are three main stages to be accomplished in carrying out a job training programme:

Preparation
Instruction
Follow-up

One example of this approach is the Training Within Industry (TWI) Job Instruction programme sponsored by the Department of Employment.

Preparation   The trainer must be fully prepared before starting to teach. He must know exactly what is to be taught and the order in which it should be taught. Time spent in preparation is seldom wasted.

Few jobs, if any, are so simple that they can be taught in one lesson. The first step is, therefore, to break the job down into its component tasks and arrange these in a logical order so that the first provides a basis of understanding for the second, and so on. The best order may not always be from the first operation to the last; it is sometimes more effective to teach the closing stages first. Each task should then be broken down if necessary into stages which are reasonably self-contained and which can be taught in 20–30 minutes.

Each such stage of training should be made the subject of a 'break-down', which is no more than a brief series of notes to guide the trainer. It will be seen from the example in Fig. 121 that the break-down shows the simple steps to be taken in doing the work, the order in which they must be taken, and the 'special points'. The special points are the matters which require particular attention if the work is to be done in every way correctly.

JOB TRAINING BREAK-DOWN

Section __Cashiers__   Job __Writing a Cheque__

Equipment Required __Should be written in ink but good in__

_____ __law if written in pencil or by__ _____

_____ __typewriter__ _____

Divisions of the Job	Normal Procedure	Variations and Special Points
Date	Day, Month, Year	If a cheque is presented before the date it bears, it will be returned.
Payee's name	All initials or full Company title. Start close to the word "Pay". Rule line after name.	Initials of Companies with long names can only be used if the payee has arranged this with the bank.
Amount in words	Over £1·00: pounds in full, pence in figures. Under £1·00: Number of pence and the word "pence" written in full. Start at extreme left of line and leave no gaps.	Show two figures for pence. ½ not acceptable.
Amount in figures	Start against £ sign. Separate pounds and pence with a hyphen, e.g. £1–45. Check words and figures agree.	If less than £1 write zero and two figures of pence. "p" or "pence" not to be written.
Signature	As specimen held at bank.	
Error correction	Strike out – write in – initial.	
Counterfoil	Date, payee, amount.	

Fig. 121 Job training break-down

Instruction   Instruction should take place at the desk or machine where the work will normally be done. Everything necessary should be there and correctly positioned. The trainer should take the clerk's chair and the trainee should sit comfortably in a position to watch what is done.

The trainer's first task is to talk informally with the trainee to put him at his ease and also to find out what is already known. This conversation should lead naturally into the actual instruction and, as soon as the trainer has established a point of contact, he should relate the job to it and proceed:

(*a*) to explain the purpose of the job;

(*b*) to describe the system and the job in general terms with particular reference to what happens *before* and *after* the tasks which the trainee is to undertake.

Having assured himself that the trainee has an adequate appreciation of the system and can understand the part which the job plays in it, the trainer should turn to the first breakdown. Step by step, he should do the work and at the same time explain what he is doing and why. This simultaneous demonstration and explanation is important because it appeals to two senses at once: sight and hearing. The process should be repeated several times.

As soon as it is thought that the trainee has grasped the sequence of steps and the associated special points, he should be allowed to change places with the trainer. The trainee should be asked to do the work and, as the trainer has been doing, explain what is happening and give the reasons for it. When necessary he should be corrected and additional explanation and demonstration given.

When the trainer is satisfied that the operations have been mastered, he should leave the trainee to work alone for perhaps an hour until the pattern of working has become established by repetition. Whilst it is important that the trainee should not feel the embarrassment of being constantly observed, the trainer should remain available to answer questions. Where the trainer is the immediate supervisor, this presents no difficulty as he will be going about his other duties in the vicinity.

When the steps in the first breakdown have been mastered and practised, the next stage of the job can be taught in the same way, and so on until the whole of the job has been covered.

Follow-up   A person who has just been taught a new job, however thoroughly, is still a beginner. He may have mastered the normal routine, but will for some time be faced with queries and exceptional cases which he does not understand. The trainer must examine the completed work and watch the job being done from time to time over the ensuing weeks, or even months. Any tendency to depart from the correct method of working should be corrected as soon as it is noticed. Good working habits are invaluable: they ensure that the job is done always in the right way and in the shortest time. Habits usually take some weeks to form but once established they are hard to break. Follow-up to ensure that good habits are formed is an essential part of training and the time spent is amply rewarded.

FURTHER EDUCATION

The Industrial Training Act, 1964, requires that Industrial Training Boards shall recommend 'the nature and length of training . . . and the further education to be associated with the training'. It may therefore be assumed that any approved training scheme will contain an element of further education whenever this is appropriate.

There is a comprehensive pattern of courses available at colleges of further edcation. These lead to examinations and, for those who are successful, the award of various certificates, diplomas and degrees. The intention is that anyone may progress from level to level as far as is appropriate to his needs or as far as his natural ability will allow. There are no dead ends and a person who was unsuccessful at school may still aspire to a degree or to a professional or management qualification. A ladder of progress is provided which may be climbed by the ambitious, starting at a point appropriate to the educational standard previously attained and finishing at whatever point is dictated by personal capacity.

This pattern of courses and qualifications is broadly illustrated in Fig. 122. The standards of general education adopted in the scheme are:

General Certificate of Education (GCE) with 4 passes at Ordinary (O) level;
General Certificate of Education (GCE) with 2 passes at Advanced (A) level;
University Degree or Diploma.

According to the standard attained, a person may commence business studies at an appropriate level, subsequently proceeding to higher qualifications. The principal awards for England and Wales are described below; there are separate but approximately similar awards for Scotland.

Syllabuses for many of the courses are not fixed nationally although they must be approved by the Business Education Council. Details should therefore be obtained from the principal of the local college of further education.

Employees attending courses as part of an approved training scheme are normally released from work on full pay by:

(*a*) *Day-release*, when they attend a technical college regularly, usually for one day a week or a half-day and evening;

(*b*) *Block release*, when they attend a technical college full-time usually for several weeks in the year;

(*c*) *Sandwich course*, when they alternate periods of full-time study at a university or college with periods of practical experience in the business.

Certificate in office studies   The course of study is suitable for those who have no educational qualification and consists of two compulsory subjects, (*a*) English (including General Studies) and (*b*) Clerical Duties, and two further subjects selected from a range which may differ from college to college and include, for example:

Social Studies
Law and the Individual
Typewriting and Office Machinery
Store-keeping

Study is normally by day-release over a period of two years commencing at age 16 or over. Admission at age 15 is at the discretion of the college.

Ordinary national certificate (ONC) in business studies   Students are required to be aged 16 or over and to have four or more GCE 'O' level passes in suitable subjects. Instruction is on a part-time basis, spread over

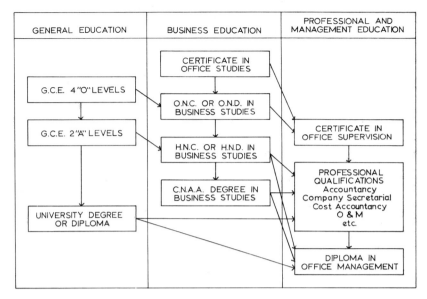

Fig. 122 The pattern of further education

two years, with four subjects taken in each year. The following is typical and indicates the range of subjects which may be taken:

First Year
Economics I

Second Year
Economics II
English

and three subjects selected from
Accounting I
Modern Language I
Economic History
Economic Geography

and two subjects selected from
Accounting II
Mercantile Law
Transport
Functions and Organization of the Office

Ordinary national diploma (OND) in business studies   This diploma is awarded following a full-time course of study extending over two years. Conditions for entry and subjects are similar to those for the ONC, but levels of attainment are higher. More subjects are studied and there is time for liberal and private study.

Higher national certificate (HNC) in business studies   Students are normally required to possess the ONC in Business Studies or have two or more GCE 'A' level passes in appropriate subjects. There is provision for entry by those who do not possess either of these qualifications and inquiries should be made at colleges in exceptional cases. Instruction is on a part-time basis, spread over two years and normally three subjects are studied in each year. The following is typical of the range of subjects which may be taken:

Economics
Accounting
Cost Accountancy
Marketing
Secretarial and Administrative Practice
Business Organization
Modern Language
Purchasing
Work Study
Organization and Methods

In selecting subjects, consideration should be given to possible further study, as for professional or management qualifications or for a degree. There are arrangements whereby some professional bodies grant exemption from examination to holders of this certificate.

Higher national diploma (HND) in business studies   This Diploma is awarded following a course extending over two years full-time or three years on a sandwich basis. Students should normally be aged 18 or over, and the level of attainment on entry is similar to that for the HNC. Courses are designed to provide a combination of general and specialized business education. Economics is a compulsory subject throughout the course and, in addition, the student must take four other subjects in each year. The range available is similar to that for the HNC.

As in the case of the HNC, optional subjects should be selected with regard to possible further study and exemption from professional examinations.

Degree in business studies   Ordinary and honours degrees in business studies are awarded by the Council for National Academic Awards (CNAA).

Diploma in management studies (DMS)   A postgraduate diploma in management studies is awarded by the CNAA. Minimum entry qualifications are a degree, HND or HNC; in the case of those over 27, four or more years of suitable employment may suffice. A typical one-year full-time course might include the following subjects:

Human Sciences
Management and Organization
Basic Mathematics and Statistics
Management Economics
Personnel Management and Industrial Relations

Quantitative Business Analysis
Management Accounting
Marketing
Business Policy
Production and Purchasing

Other certificate courses   For many purposes, the system of courses leading to National Certificates, Diplomas and Degrees provides the most appropriate plan for further education. There are, however, other courses available which lead to examinations in single subjects or groups of subjects. The examining bodies include The Royal Society of Arts, The London Chamber of Commerce, and various regional institutions.

Single subject certificates are granted in a comprehensive range of general and commercial subjects. Certificates and diplomas are awarded for groups of subjects at senior and junior levels and may be designed for particular office skills, e.g. private secretaries, cost clerks.

Certificates in office supervision   Certificates at a level suitable for office supervisors and junior managers are awarded by the Institute of Administrative Management and by the National Examinations Board for Supervisory Studies.

Courses at colleges may be on day-release or block-release, or held in the evenings. Students will usually be expected to have some preliminary qualifications such as the Certificate in Office Studies or the ONC in Business Studies. Older students who have not passed a qualifying examination may be admitted to courses if their practical experience is approved as adequate preparation for study.

Students may be expected to attend a short residential course in addition to college lectures, and to undertake a project and prepare a report on it.

Professional and management qualifications   Trainees for more responsible positions may be required to specialize in one of the several technical aspects of office work, which include:

Accountancy
Company Secretarial Practice
Cost Accountancy
Organization and Methods
Personnel Management

Courses leading to the examinations of the professional institutions in these fields are available at colleges and from correspondence schools.

The potential office manager requires more than a technical education and may proceed to a course of study leading to the Diploma awarded by the Institute of Administrative Management. To be admitted to this course, students should normally hold the HNC in Business Studies, a professional qualification or university degree.

The regulations governing the examinations of professional bodies usually include the granting of exemption under certain circumstances. The office manager who is required to advise on professional or management courses for trainees is advised always to consult the latest syllabus and regulations.

PLANNING AND CONTROLLING TRAINING SCHEMES

The need for training arises when new employees are engaged and when existing employees are transferred from one job to another. The extent of the training necessary will vary from one person to another. All new employees require an induction course, but this is not necessary on transfer within the business. All young people require basic skill training and further education; the older and more experienced may not. All who undertake new jobs require job training.

In every case, the training should be planned and it will be found convenient for this purpose to use separate forms for the four elements: induction, basic skill training, job training and further education. Copies of the plan should be provided for the manager or supervisor, for the training officer (where one exists) and for the trainee. Having set a plan, the progress and effectiveness of training should be controlled and recorded on the same form.

Where schemes are to be approved by an Industrial Training Board, it may be necessary to keep records in a prescribed manner. The specimen form in Fig. 123 should, therefore, be taken only as a guide in principle. The essential information to be recorded is as follows:

Name of trainee and other general information;
Subjects or tasks to be taught;
Stages by which instructon is to be given;
Planned date by which each stage is to be completed;
Actual date of completion of each stage;
Trainer's initials or other identification;
Trainer's comments on the trainee's performance;
Training officer's comments.

The conditions for receipt of training grants from Industrial Training Boards vary, but it may be necessary to extend the record as shown to give details of time spent and cost incurred.

Trainee's work book   Trainees may be required to keep a work book as a more detailed record of training activities. This usually takes the form of a loose-leaf binder in which are kept:

(a) trainee's copy of the training plan;
(b) notes taken during training, and essays written;

(*c*) specimen forms and written instructions received;

(*d*) copies of reports arising from projects undertaken (by the more senior trainees).

The purposes are to stimulate interest and to enable the office manager, supervisor and training officer to assess progress. These purposes can only

BASIC SKILL TRAINING RECORD					
Section: Name:					
Supervisor in Charge:					
Subject	Planned Date	Actual Date	Trained By	Trainer's Comments	Cost Information

INCOMING MAIL
  Pre-sort
  Opening
  Cash and cheques
  Sorting
  Delivery					

FILING
  Explanation
  Marking-up
  Sorting
  Putting away
  Finding
  Recording out					

DUPLICATING
  Explanation
  Preparing masters
  Setting up machine
  Running machine
  Cleaning down
  Storing masters					

TELEPHONE
  Visit to switchboard
  Making calls
  Receiving calls					

RECEPTION
  Receiving visitors
  Tracing people
  Turning visitors
    away					

Training Officer's Comments:					

Fig. 123   Training record form

be achieved if work books are examined regularly and the contents discussed with the trainees.

TRAINING FOR SUPERVISION AND MANAGEMENT

Succession planning   Training for supervision and ultimately for management should commence as early as possible in the individual's career. It may take many years to develop a good supervisor or manager and it is unwise to wait until a vacancy is imminent before training someone to fill the position. Management has the duty to plan ahead and to ensure that a sufficient number of people are being developed in anticipation of eventual need.

Selection of trainees   In some businesses, it is the policy to engage men and women specifically as supervisory and management trainees. Whilst this method has much to recommend it, it should not be the only way in which senior members of the staff are recruited. The ability to take charge of others may be found among those who started as junior clerks as well as among university graduates. There should never be any artificial barrier to promotion and every opportunity should be given to those who may develop later in life.

The ultimate selection of a candidate for a particular post will depend upon the specific qualities which the work demands. When a potential supervisor or manager is selected, perhaps some years in advance of actual promotion, a more general assessment must be made of intelligence and aptitude. Use may be made of the technique of Quality Rating described in Chapter 21. This is not only an aid in judging the suitability of a person, but provides an indication of special training requirements.

Supervisory training programmes

Following an exhaustive enquiry by a Joint Training Board Committee, the Department of Employment issued a report on *Training for Office Management* (HMSO, 1975). From this and *Training for Office Supervision* (HMSO, 1968) the following list has been extracted to illustrate the scope of office supervisory and management training.

(1) the firm's objectives, products, policies and methods;
(2) the firm's organization and functions of departments;
(3) the firm's personnel policy;
(4) the work for which the manager/supervisor is responsible;
(5) inter-departmental contacts;
(6) decision making;
(7) delegation;
(8) oral and written communication;

(9) office methods and systems;
(10) use of machines and equipment, including EDP;
(11) output planning and control;
(12) inspection and quality control;
(13) work simplification;
(14) clerical work measurement;
(15) security;
(16) job evaluation and grading; salary structures;
(17) recruitment and selection of staff;
(18) interviewing;
(19) staff training and instructional methods;
(20) leadership and motivation of staff;
(21) industrial relations;
(22) staff appraisal and merit rating;
(23) safety, fire precautions and health hazards;
(24) legal aspects of the job.

The first five of the items listed must of necessity be taught within the particular business. The remainder are concerned with clerical work and the techniques of supervision and can be studied in general terms at colleges of further education.

Training courses must be planned individually according to the trainee's level of knowledge and experience and according to the requirements of the job. In the stages immediately preceding appointment to a supervisory position, the job should be analysed and the trainee's abilities compared with the results. This will reveal any deficiencies in the trainee so that steps may be taken to make these good. When, however, a trainee is being developed over a period of years, a more general pattern of preparation can be adopted:

Working experience
Technical education
Supervisory education
Job analysis
Job training
Evaluation of training
Continued development

Working experience   The potential supervisor needs to gain as wide a personal experience of clerical work as possible. The young trainee can be moved from job to job and from department to department. The older candidate may already have done a sufficient variety of jobs. Trainees who enter business after a university or technical education are often able, because of their facility in learning, to gain practical experience quickly. They should not be held back but allowed to move on as soon as a job has been mastered. It may, however, be an important part of experience to discover what it is like to undertake repetitive routine to the point of boredom.

Technical education   Some trainees, particularly those who are likely to progress to management, may require technical education to a professional level. Courses are available at colleges (see page 330) or through correspondence schools.

Supervisory education   The burden of supervisory training which falls on management can be greatly reduced by arranging that trainees undergo courses leading to certificates in office supervision (see page 331).

Job analysis   Each supervisory position is to some extent unique. The general experience, technical and supervisory education has therefore to be supplemented by specific job training. Because a supervisor's job entails the bearing of responsibility rather than the doing of work, training methods differ from those used in the case of a clerk. The job must be analysed so as to produce a supervisory *job specification*. This should show such things as:

(*a*) the purposes which the section of the office fulfils;

(*b*) the services which it provides to the business;

(*c*) the manager to whom the supervisor will be responsible;

(*d*) the staff to be controlled;

(*e*) the work which the supervisor must do personally and that which should be delegated to subordinates;

(*f*) the nature and limits of the supervisor's authority to act without reference to a superior;

(*g*) the supervisor's relationships with other departments;

(*h*) the reports on work, staff etc., which the supervisor must render to the office manager.

Job training   The duration of job training will vary according to the size of the section and the complexity of the work which it does. A few weeks may suffice for a trainee about to take charge of a small group doing routine work; in some cases, months may be necessary. The training plan should be laid by reference to the job specification, the objective being to make good the individual's deficiencies in knowledge, experience and understanding.

If the trainee has had a thorough preparatory training, including further educational courses, the need for special tuition will be reduced. Given, for example, a general knowledge of supervisory techniques, it remains only to demonstrate the applications in use in the particular office.

It is the office manager's task to direct the training and to take part in each stage personally. There should be regular meetings between manager and trainee, at which the various aspects of the job are discussed. These meetings are essential because they serve to establish mutual understanding which will enable manager and supervisor to work as a team.

The instructional methods used may be varied and wherever possible should be such that the trainee learns by doing something, as well as by listening to explanations. Some examples of methods follow:

(a) *Visits*   The trainee is sent to those departments of the business with which the section normally deals, to see how they operate. If, for example, the section is concerned with stock control, there should be a visit to the stores department lasting some days. The objectives are to learn the practical and clerical procedures and to meet the people who work there.

(b) *Projects and exercises*   The office manager gives the trainee a series of assignments which call for investigation and the preparation of a report or other written evidence of what has been learnt. Each assignment should have a definite objective. For example, the trainee might be required to prepare job instruction breakdowns (or check those already in existence) for all the jobs on the section. In doing so, the trainee will learn the work of the section and at the same time ensure that the means of training clerks are available. Other suitable assignments might include work simplification, personnel audit, errors analysis, work measurement.

(c) *Participation in meetings*   Trainees are invited to attend meetings between the office manager and existing supervisors in order to hear and, as understanding develops, participate in the discussion of problems.

(d) *Work books*   Trainees are required to keep work books in which to accumulate written evidence of training activities and the related specimens. As a final summary of what has been learnt, the trainee may prepare in collaboration with the office manager a *statement of responsibilities*. This should set out briefly the essential elements of the supervisor's job. In particular, it should define responsibilities and the limits of authority; the work which the supervisor must do personally and that which should be delegated to subordinates. The statement of responsibilities will, by its very nature, cover the matters contained in the job specification. It need not, however, be in the same form and should be the means of clarifying anything which the trainee and his office manager feel is necessary.

Evaluation of training   The utlimate test of effective training is that the supervisor is able to carry out the job to the office manager's satisfaction. It is not to be expected that the initial preparation and job training will be entirely successful. Many of the problems of supervision can only be fully appreciated when they have been experienced; mistakes of judgement will be made. The office manager should, from time to time, reconsider the supervisor's performance in the light of the job specification and supplement the original training where necessary.

Continued development   Once appointed, the supervisor may have a long career ahead. Sound though the initial training may have been, it must be supplemented to ensure familiarity with new ideas, methods, machines etc, as they emerge. Supervisors, if qualified, should be encouraged to join the Institute of Administrative Management and to attend meetings, discussion groups, exhibitions and courses outside the business from time to time. Much will be gained from the supervisor getting away from the narrow confines of the office to meet others with similar interests and problems.

Management training programmes

The office manager has often to fulfil another function as well, being the company secretary, accountant, cost accountant or holding an equivalent position in local government etc. Where this is the case, technical education should have been continued to embrace courses leading to the appropriate professional qualification. This by itself is not, however, an adequate preparation for management. The trainee needs a firm grounding in office practice and management techniques.

The potential office manager should have been trained as a supervisor and have had some supervisory experience. It may therefore be assumed that a management training programme will build upon that foundation. The techniques of management and supervision have much in common but the manager needs to have studied these in greater depth. Further education should therefore be extended and trainees released to attend courses leading to the Institute of Administrative Management's Diploma (see page 331).

Job training for management follows a pattern similar to that described above for supervision: the job is analysed and a job specification prepared. Training is directed by a manager personally through regular meetings with the trainee and the various methods described for supervisory training are employed.

The manager's responsibility is, however, wider than that of the supervisor and demands a deeper appreciation of policy and purpose. Management is concerned with the effectiveness of the service which the office gives as well as with efficiency. Much of the training must, therefore, be devoted to developing an understanding of objectives so that wide decisions may be taken which serve the long-term interests of the business as well as the immediate needs. However thorough the training before appointment, perhaps as an assistant manager in the first instance, it must be continued thereafter by the discussion of problems and situations as they arise. Whenever questions are asked, the answers should be given and the implications discussed as fully as may be necessary to develop a full understanding.

Effective management can only be ensured as a continuing process if managers are kept up-to-date in their knowledge and ideas. To this end, they should be encouraged to take an active part in suitable activities outside the business, such as those organized by the Institute of Administrative Management. Attendance at meetings, exhibitions, refresher courses etc. should be planned as part of the manager's normal working life. The time 'lost' in absence from the office is usually more than paid for by the stimulation of new ideas through contact with the outside world.

Part 6
Planning and control

The task of office management includes planning every aspect of the work of the office and the provision of controls as a means of ensuring that these plans are carried out. Throughout the preceding parts of this book continual reference has been made to the principles to be followed in planning the methods to fulfil specific clerical functions. In addition, there are certain general principles and certain techniques which experience has shown to be worthy of adoption.

The planning of methods and the designing of forms are important among the office manager's duties and a systematic approach to these tasks is desirable. But plans, however well drawn, are not enough; it cannot be assumed that they will be followed exactly when once they have been put into effect. The passing of time brings change, however gradual; human fallibility gives rise to slackness and inaccuracy. The office manager must at all times be checking the effectiveness of his department's work. The performance of this duty will be simplified by the institution of systematic controls from day to day and audits at longer intervals.

The art of writing reports and the procedure for conducting meetings are also dealt with in this part. Whilst these subjects are pertinent to planning and control, the student is recommended to pay attention to them from a wider point of view. They are matters of general importance to managers and supervisors in no matter what department they serve.

24   Methods

Anyone making a careful analysis of office work may well be struck by the simplicity of the operations involved. Whatever the purpose of the information handled and whatever the type of record involved, all clerical work consists of the carrying out of a number of simple elementary operations. These are:

Writing, or making original records.
Copying, including posting and duplicating.
Computing, or adding, subtracting and calculating.
Comparing, or checking one item against another.
Sorting, including classifying.
Filing and indexing.
Communicating, or conveying verbal and written information.

These operations are in themselves simple but it is rarely that any one of them is carried out in isolation. It has been shown, for example, in Chapters 10 and 11, how the method of dealing with customers' orders from their receipt to the dispatch of the goods (including the various accounting and cost-accounting operations incidental to the transaction) requires a chain of operations, possibly carried out by a number of clerks, each having a share in the overall process. Therefore, if a clerical procedure is to be carried out smoothly and correctly, the method must be carefully planned so that the work of all concerned is properly co-ordinated.

The complexity of office systems is accentuated by two main causes:

(a) *Specialization*   In order to obtain the advantages of specialization, one item of information may pass through many operations each performed by a different clerk.

(b) *Information for several purposes*   One item of information may be used to serve a number of different purposes; if so, the several operations required to fulfil each purpose may need to be carefully 'dovetailed'.

Specialization

As businesses have increased in size, so also have the offices which serve them, and this growth has been accompanied by a higher degree of specialization in clerical work. Whilst at one time it was normal for the preparation of an invoice to be the work of one clerk, it is now often the result of a series of processes, each undertaken by a separate clerk. And the same tendency is to be observed in keeping ledgers, paying accounts and almost every office function.

Sometimes there is a tendency to introduce specialization merely for its own sake: it is assumed that the higher the degree of specialization, the more efficient the method. This is wrong because there is a point beyond which further specialization results in a drop in efficiency arising from two causes:

(*a*) every additional clerk introduced into the chain of operations results in additional time being spent in the physical handling of forms;

(*b*) every clerk working on a form must spend time in reading all or part of what is written on it before he can undertake the next operation. It is, therefore, economical of effort if a clerk, having read from a form, can carry out as many operations as feasible based upon the same information.

If specialization is to be effective, it must yield advantages which more than offset the losses resulting from these two causes. Furthermore, over-specialization has often led to the introduction of extremely dull jobs. If a job is so simple that the clerk is unable to make full use of his intellectual powers, and is unable to feel any sense of pride and achievement in doing it, he will lose interest in his work and be more liable to make errors.

Specialization should be introduced only in order to achieve one of the following objects:

(*a*) *To separate different skills*   Mechanization is a principal cause of specialization. An invoice may have the address written by an addressing machine, the values worked out on a calculating machine, and the details written by a typewriter.

(*b*) *To separate simple from complex tasks*   The junior clerk should not be given tasks beyond his comprehension, and the senior clerk should not waste his ability on junior work. Moreover, a senior clerk is unlikely to find interest in a very simple job and in consequence may become careless or frustrated.

(*c*) *To use specialized knowledge*   A clerk with a wide range of duties cannot be expected to have more than a superficial understanding of each; he may be able to follow the various routines, but will not accumulate the detailed knowledge which enables him to recognize errors and take steps to correct them.

(*d*) *To permit independent checking*   If a clerk checks his own work by going over it a second time, he may make the same error on both occasions. It is, therefore, usual to employ clerks whose duty it is to check the work of others.

(e) *To prevent fraud* Many clerical functions are concerned directly or indirectly with the receipt and payment of cash, and precautions are necessary to ensure that opportunities for fraud are, as far as possible, removed. One such precaution is to divide the work between different clerks so that fraud is not possible except by a number of persons in collusion.

Information for several purposes

Many different departments or officials of a business may be interested in precisely the same information. When, for example, an entry is made in respect of raw materials which have been purchased and delivered, the departments concerned with this information may include:

(a) *Buying*, which requires to know that the order has been executed;

(b) *Stores*, where the receipt of the goods has to be recorded so that a control may be exercised over them;

(c) *Production*, which may need to be informed of the materials available;

(d) *Accounting*, which will authorize payment and enter details in the appropriate financial accounts;

(e) *Cost accounting*, which must be informed so that when the raw materials are eventually withdrawn from store and used, they may be charged under a cost heading at the appropriate price.

In practice, the use of information for a variety of purposes is a frequent occurrence in office work and many other examples will have been found in Part 3. In every case it tends to make the method complex and its planning a matter for careful thought.

THE NEED FOR REVISION

The organizational structure of an office and the methods which it employs require frequent revision. Systems which were once efficient become inefficient and must be investigated and re-planned. The principal reasons for this deterioration are:

(a) changes in the business which the office serves;

(b) technical advances in office methods and equipment;

(c) changes in the office services required by management.

Changes in the business An office provides a service for a particular business. The systems which it employs must be suited to that business, its organization an its activities. If the business remains unaltered, the system may well continue to operate satisfactorily. Most businesses, however, are constantly changing: new products, materials, processes and machines are introduced, new markets and marketing methods are developed, new departments are created. Every such change tends to make some office system less effective.

When a major alteration is made, the need for re-planning the related office systems is obvious and action will be taken. It is often the minor changes which cause the most difficulty. Individually, they may not warrant more than small revisions of procedure; cumulatively, they are likely to create problems which can be solved only be complete overhaul.

Technical advances   New computers, machines and devices, and modifications of those already existing, are frequently introduced. That which was best for its purpose ten years earlier may become obsolete. Advances continue to be made also in the ideas underlying office methods as, for example, the use of statistical and mathematical techniques to replace more detailed methods and to make possible controls that would otherwise not be economical.

Changes in the office services   Office systems are designed to provide the services which the management of the business requires. As a business develops and as new management techniques are introduced, the nature of the services demanded changes and systems must be revised accordingly. The most frequent changes are often in the information required for use in planning and control. Sometimes whole new systems may be introduced. It is more likely, however, that management will ask for additional information piecemeal and the office will make minor alterations to procedure in order to provide it. The cumulative effect of many such minor changes is to render a system inefficient so that re-design becomes necessary.

THE O & M SERVICE

The planning of methods is one of the fundamental duties of office management. The office manager must ensure that an adequate proportion of his time is devoted to this task, however difficult it may be to put aside urgent day-to-day matters. The planning of a system requires time for investigation and thought, for the most effective and economical method can only be found by full inquiry into the sources of information and the detailed analysis of the steps necessary to achieve the desired purpose. In a large office, the manager, unable himself to give sufficient time to this work, will need to appoint an organization and methods (O & M) specialist to investigate and plan under his direction. An O & M specialist, freed from all other duties, is able to give concentrated thought to the devising of systems, leaving the manager, to whom he reports, the task of criticizing and amending or approving the proposals made.

The term 'organization and methods' (abbreviated as O & M) came into use because office methods are inseparably linked with the organizational structure of the business as a whole, and of the office. To take a simple example, the method of sales invoicing and the design of the invoice form are influenced by the organization of the sales department and by the way in which orders are received and executed. If the sales organization is changed, it is likely that the invoicing system will have to be revised. Within the office, the organization by sections and groups will be influenced in turn by the system, and by the human skills and equipment which it employs.

When planning methods, it is necessary to study the associated parts of the organization; when planning the organization, it is necessary to study the associated office methods. The business organization and the place of the office within it have been discussed in Chapter 1; the office organization has been discussed in Chapter 21. In that which follows, the principal concern is with methods.

In designing systems, the aim should be to evolve methods which:

(*a*) achieve a useful purpose;
(*b*) are appropriate to the purpose;
(*c*) are based on the use of accurate information;
(*d*) are economical.

PLANNING METHODS

O & M, like any other specialization, has its own techniques and important among them is the methodical approach to the revision of office methods. This seeks to discover the facts and to produce an efficient system based upon them. On the face of it, the methodical approach may seem unnecessarily detailed and pedantic. Experience has shown, however, that it is likely to yield far better results than either the adoption of apparently inspired 'good ideas', or the copying of what others have done. No two businesses are the same and, if the office methods are to serve a business well, they must be specially designed.

The methodical approach can be regarded as having a number of main stages, as follows:

(*a*) preliminary survey;
(*b*) investigation;
(*c*) design of a simple method;
(*d*) use of machines and equipment;
(*e*) costing and comparison of methods;
(*f*) design of forms;
(*g*) installation.

It is important that each of these stages (which are more particularly described below) should be undertaken and completed in the order shown. Computerization, for example, cannot be considered before it has been determined what processes must be carried out; forms cannot be designed until it is known whether the work on them will be done by hand or machine.

In the course of investigation, it may be determined that the work should be done by computer. Whilst the general principles set out below will still apply, there are special considerations which are dealt with on pages 359–62.

Preliminary survey

Before a full investigation is made, it is necessary to carry out a brief preliminary survey so as to be able to define the scope and objectives of the inquiry.

Office work is arranged in systems which fulfil one or a number of purposes. A system is usually easily identifiable, e.g. sales invoicing, wages, cash control, purchase ledger, production control. Although these terms are familiar, it must not be assumed that every office has its work arranged in the same way. In a small business, the 'accounts' system may embrace both sales and purchases ledgers. In a very large business, there may be separate systems for keeping the raw-material purchases ledger and for keeping the expense purchases ledger. It is part of the preliminary survey to determine what constitutes a separate system in the particular case.

A system, although separate for the purposes of O & M investigation, is usually linked with one or more other systems. The wages system, for example, may have links with cash control, cost accounting and personnel records. If the broadest view is taken, all the systems in an office may be regarded as parts of one whole. The revision of all the work of an office at once would, however, be a task too complex to undertake. It is therefore normal in the first instance to accept the boundaries between systems as they exist and examine each separately.

As the result of the survey, a judgement will be formed as to the effectiveness of the services provided and the efficiency of the methods employed. As a basis on which to form this judgement, the answers to the following questions should be obtained.

Purpose What are the end-products of the system? What purpose or purposes do they serve? Have any of the end-products been added since the system was originally designed? Is the purpose relevant to current requirements? Should the service rendered by the office in respect of this particular function be reviewed afresh in collaboration with the managers concerned?

Age For how long has the system been in operation? Could its age be taken as *prima facie* evidence of its obsolescence?

Machines and equipment Are the machines and other items of equipment obsolete or nearing the end of their useful lives? To what extent is use made of machines and devices? When was the possibility of greater mechanization last considered? Is there computer or other machine-time available but unused?

Office space   How much space does the operation of the system occupy? Could the space be put to better use if ways were found of reducing the need?

Staff   How many clerks of various grades and skills are employed? Has the increase in salary cost in relation to machinery cost shifted the balance in favour of greater mechanization? Does the present system require highly-skilled clerks, the need for whom might be avoided by other means?

Cost   What is the total cost of operating the system? What is the average cost of providing a 'unit of service', e.g. raising one invoice, paying one employee? How does this compare with the value of the service to the business? How does it compare with the cost of equivalent service in other businesses?

Problems   What difficulties are experienced in operating the system, e.g. errors, queries, peak loads of work, regular overtime or shift working?

Investigation

When there is evidence that a system is in need of revision, a full investigation should be made, embracing both purpose and method.

Purpose   If the preliminary investigation has established the need for a full investigation, the reasons must be stated and accepted by all concerned. It may be that the original purpose of the system is no longer valid. It cannot be assumed that because office work is done, it must serve a useful purpose. The needs of the business may have changed since the system was installed and some of its end-products may be of little significance under current conditions. Conversely, new needs may have arisen and are not being satisfied. Alternatively, it may be that whilst the purpose is still valid, the means by which it is fulfilled need to be improved in order to reduce cost and/or to improve accuracy, appearance and timeliness.

With the reason for the investigation identified, it is necessary to make a final check to identify with equal clarity the purposes to be served by the system in the future. The O & M investigator should discuss these with management and the outcome should be a mutually agreed re-statement of what is required.

Methods of investigation   The purposes having been defined, the investigation can proceed in one of two alternative but equally important ways which are described in more detail below.

If there is an existing system which fulfils all or most of the purposes, the next step may be to examine and record this system with a view to criticizing and improving it. If the purposes are new and there is no existing system, the approach must obviously be different. The investigation must be focused on the required end-products, and on the nature and sources of the data necessary to produce them. This approach is known as the *A–Z* method. It concentrates firstly on defining the end products (*Z*), secondly on the collection of data (*A*) and, finally, at the system-design stage, on the processes necessary to convert *A* into *Z*.

The *A–Z* method may also be preferred where there is an existing procedure because:

(*a*) the procedure is obviously so unsatisfactory or obsolete that little can be learned from studying it; or

(*b*) the purposes are being so radically altered or extended that the procedure is no longer pertinent.

Study of existing system   The existing procedure should be examined and recorded as concisely as possible. Long and detailed written statements may confuse rather than assist. It is necessary to establish *what* is done, *how* it is done, *where*, by *whom* and *why*. Much of this information can be expressed by specimen forms and flow charts; the remainder can be appended as brief notes.

One commonly adopted means of investigation is that known as 'method analysis', Copies of all forms used are assembled, each one being filled in

METHOD ANALYSIS	System:		Form:		
	Date:		Average usage per week		
Associated Forms					
Reference	Operation Description	Operations per Form	Est. Time per Form	Problems and Suggestions	

Fig. 124   Method-analysis form

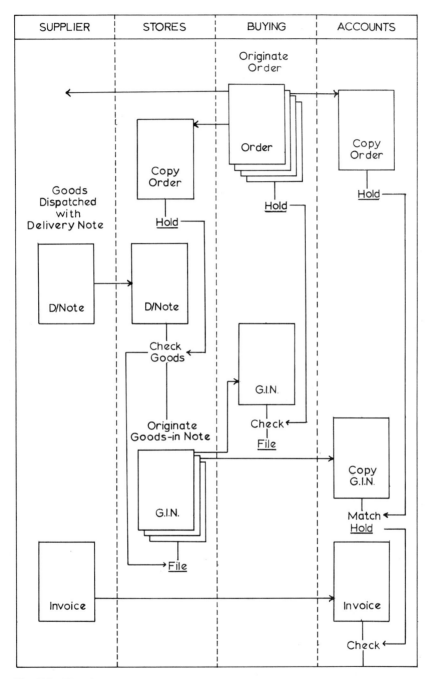

Fig. 125 Flow chart

with typical entries. These are then sorted according to the purposes which they serve; in general, a form may be:

(*a*) an end-product of the system;
(*b*) means of collecting and recording data;
(*c*) a means of processing data to arrive at the end-product (a working-paper).

Some forms will be principal forms and others subsidiary, e.g. those used in exceptional situations or in settling queries.

Starting with the principal forms, the processes carried out on each are identified. Notes may be made on method-analysis forms, an example of which is given in Fig. 124. If there are more than a few forms,.it may be necessary to clarify the way in which each moves from department to department and from clerk to clerk. Simple flow charts such as that shown in Fig. 125 provide a useful means of illustrating movement and the relationship of one form to another.

In investigating a procedure, care must be taken to obtain the true facts. It is not enough to be told what is done; the investigator must see what is done and be satisfied that nothing is overlooked. The following rules should be observed:

(*a*) interview clerks at their desks under normal working conditions;
(*b*) observe what is done first, and then ask questions about it;
(*c*) note any unofficial records which may be in use;
(*d*) note what is normal and also any exceptions to the general rule;
(*e*) note apparent difficulties and encourage clerks to discuss their problems and grievances in relation to their jobs.

A–Z method   By this method, the investigation is concentrated in two main areas.

End-products (Z)   The intended users of the information to be produced are interviewed to discover *what* is wanted, *why, where, when* and *by whom.* It is not usually sufficient to accept without question what managers and others say in answer to questions. The investigator, approaching with an open mind and probably having a greater knowledge of what information is already available in the office and elsewhere, should be able to make valuable suggestions.

Data (A)   Having established what is to be produced, the investigator can infer from this the data necessary. The next questions to be answered are *where* can those data be obtained reliably, from *whom, when* and *how.* The *how* is of special importance since the form of the initial record should be such that the end-product can be produced with minimal effort. This stage in the investigation may involve interviewing salesmen, storemen, drivers, factory supervisors and other non-clerical staff. It is they who know the facts at first hand because they are present when the incidents to be recorded take place. In the course of such interviews, enquiries should be made as to any unofficial paper-work which is done and which might become part of the official system.

Where there is an existing system, this should not be completely ignored. Although it is not examined in detail and recorded, there may be by-products which were overlooked when the purposes were defined.

Design of a simple method

When the facts as to the existing method have been established and recorded or the original data and the end-products have been established, the next step is to design a simple, logical method of processing the original data so as to arrive at end-products which serve the desired purposes with the fewest possible operations.

Office methods start with the gathering of primary information or data; simple facts about the business and its dealings. These data are then processed within the office to produce the end-products. In designing or redesigning a system, however, it is necessary to start with the end-product. When this has been firmly established, consideration can be given to the data required and the processes which it must undergo.

End-products   Those forms which represent the end-products of the system are criticized in the light of the newly defined objectives. It may be possible to eliminate some altogether. In others, there may be superfluous matter to be deleted or additions to be made where the investigation has disclosed useful purposes which had been overlooked.

Primary information (data)   Having established the end-products, it is possible to determine the data necessary to produce them. The forms used in data collection are criticized to ascertain:

(a) that everything necessary can be accurately recorded;
(b) that there is no superfluous information on them;
(c) that information is being obtained from the best source.

Accurate information can be obtained only from someone who knows the facts at first-hand. This person is often a foreman, storeman, driver, factory operative or other non-clerical worker and due regard must be paid to difficulties in entering forms.

Method   It remains to consider the processes by which the primary information is converted into the end-products. Firstly, the operations noted on the method-analysis forms should be re-examined. If whole forms have already been eliminated, the work done on them can also be eliminated. Any variations in the detail of end-products or data will also demand a change in processing.

When the operations have been amended in the light of these fundamental changes, they are examined from the point of view of efficient working.

Combination   Are there any operations at present done by different people which might usefully be combined? Every time a form is passed unnecessarily from one person to another, time and effort are wasted. Work which is broken down into very simple, repetitive tasks may be boring. Combination may not only save time, but increase job interest and thereby the quality of the work.

Separation   Conversely, it may be found that operations are so grouped that a clerk has an unnecessarily complicated job, or one which combines tasks of different grades (see Chapter 21). By a rearrangement of duties, output may be increased, training time reduced, and better use made of the abilities of senior clerks. Where operations are computerized, it may emerge that the integration of systems has brought disadvantages. A complicated computer program serving several purposes may save machine-time, but cause delay in producing results which a separate program might have produced earlier.

Sequence   Are the operations performed in a logical sequence? For the end-products to be produced quickly and efficiently, there should be a smooth flow of work. 'Back-tracking' and 'double-handling' must be eliminated.

Quality   Does the method produce work of adequate quality in terms of accuracy, appearance and the exercise of judgement? It may be that insufficient checks are imposed in the early stages of the system and that this leads to major difficulties which can only be overcome by employing senior staff to investigate and correct mistakes in the final stages.

General review   When the methods have been examined from the various aspects mentioned above, the system must be considered as a whole. Does it serve the required purposes? Does it proceed logically from data to end-product?

Use of machines and equipment

One of the classical errors in designing systems is to assume that machines and equipment will inevitably improve productivity. Another is to assume that the largest, fastest, newest or most automatic must be the best. Even the fact that the application of machines and equipment will reduce the cost of an existing manual system is not proof that the best solution has been found. If the manual methods are inefficient, they might be improved and still be the most economical.

The case for machines and equipment must be proved in terms of money, which is the measure of all economic activity. The overall costs of alternative methods must be compared and the cheapest fulfilling the requirements must be selected.

The first step is design a simple system using mainly handwork. The purpose is to establish what has to be done and the logical sequence of doing it, and to provide a basis for comparison with alternative methods.

Simple machines and devices   The next step is to see whether the application of simple machines and devices would result in any improvement. Simple machines are those which carry out one of the basic clerical operations listed at the beginning of this chapter; they are 'tools' to improve the productivity of skilled clerks. One example is the typewriter, which only writes but enables a person to write more legibly, more compactly and faster than is possible by hand. Other examples, taken at random, are adding–listing machines, desk calculators, wheel indexes and addressing machines.

Complex machines and equipment   Finally, it should be considered whether more complex, automatic machines and equipment might offer still greater advantages by carrying out a number of basic operations, simultaneously or in sequence, with some measure of automatic control. Complex machines and equipment embrace not only the whole range of computers, but word-processing machines, collating and mailing machines, telecommunications equipment etc.

Where the simple machines and devices are tools to aid skilled clerks who might otherwise do the work by hand, complex machines and equipment are usually set to follow a predetermined routine under the control of an operator or automatically in varying degrees. In general, the complex and automatic can only be justified where there is a substantial volume of repetitive work to be done.

Where a computer is to be used, it may be necessary to make a fresh appraisal of the existing boundaries between systems. If two or more systems have data in common or processes in common, combination may be beneficial.

Costing and comparison of methods

When the possibilities of mechanization and the use of equipment have been explored, a decision must be made as to which of two or more possible methods should be adopted. Cost of operation is always important, though not the only consideration. It may be decided to spend money on office work in order to obtain the end-products more quickly, because this will enable the business to operate more profitably. The search is not for the cheapest method of doing paper-work, but for the cheapest method by which all the requirements of management may be fulfilled.

Each possibility from a simple hand system to one using a main-frame computer should be costed. The necessary office space, staff, machines, stationery etc. is estimated, and a *total annual cost* calculated. It is, of course, essential that the basis of costing should be the same in each case so that comparison can be made. The principal elements of cost are as follows.

Staff   The number of each of the various grades of staff required to operate a system should be estimated. The cost of salaries and other incidental expenses can then be calculated in accordance with the scales in use within the business. This may be the largest cost component and also the most difficult to assess; it is often under-estimated. Care must therefore be taken and full provision made covering absences due to holidays and sickness, low output during training etc.

Machines and equipment   The capital cost should be ascertained and then converted into an annual cost. In some cases it will suffice merely to divide the capital cost by the number of years service which can be expected. Where substantial sums of money are involved, more complex formulae may be used, taking into account the interest on investment, taxation, and possibly other allowances.

Maintenance   This is the cost of maintaining machines and equipment in good working order, including repairs, overhauls and spare parts. Routine maintenance is often the subject of a long-term contract at a fixed annual fee.

Stationery and sundries   Major items of stationery and sundries such as machine ribbons, inks and chemicals for duplicators etc., should be costed. Minor items can, of course, be ignored as they are unlikely to influence any decision.

Premises   Office premises are costly, especially in city centres. Rents, rates and other expenses should be estimated where significant.

Installation costs   In addition to the running costs of a system, there may be substantial costs associated with preparation and installation. The importance of these costs will vary according to circumstance. In the case of a simple hand system, they may not be worthy of consideration. The installation of a mechanized system, on the other hand, may require a substantial expenditure. If, for example, a sizeable computer is to be installed, the premises may require alteration and specialist staff may have to be engaged or trained months in advance of operation.

Design of forms

The design or re-design of forms is, of necessity, left until the logic of the system and the extent of mechanization have been established. For example, an invoice form to be filled in by machine will differ from one to be filled in by hand. To design it before the method is known is to waste time.

A form is a tool of office work and should be treated as such. It is a means of communicating and recording information and an aid in carrying out clerical work. Of all the means used in the office, it is probably the most important. The right number of well-designed forms will achieve maximum efficiency; too many forms make for complexity, unnecessary work and high operating cost; badly-designed forms lead to errors and omissions.

There should be as few different types of forms as possible and departments should be discouraged from designing their own instead of adopting those in common use. Each form should serve as many purposes as possible, provided that they are all related. If all the information required at one time can be concentrated on one sheet of paper, handling, copying and checking will all be greatly reduced. Care should be taken, however, not to carry the concentration of information beyond the point of convenience. If there is too much detail on a single form, it becomes complicated and can increase the liability to error. Also, the smooth flow of work may be impeded if two clerks need to refer to the same form at the same time.

Form-design process   Form design should be carried out systematically in a series of stages, as follows:

(a) list the items to appear on the form and check that each serves a purpose;

(b) determine the order in which the items should appear to suit the convenience of the person *entering* the form;

(c) determine the order in which the items should appear to suit the convenience of the person *reading and using* the form;

(d) compromise as may be necessary between (b) and (c);

(e) determine the space necessary for each item;

(f) prepare rough layouts leading to a final draft.

The following are among the more important items in designing forms.

Title   Every form should bear a brief title which should, wherever possible, be self-explanatory. If the form is to be filled in by a member of the public or by another business, an amplifying note may need to be added.

Order of information   The spaces for the entry of information should be arranged in some logical order which will facilitate both the making of the entries and the subsequent use of the information. For example, if two forms are used in conjunction, the information which is common to each should be arranged in the same order.

Spacing   Adequate space, but no more, should be allotted for the entry of each item. Where entries are to be made by hand, feint ruled lines should be provided. Where entries are to be made by machine, the space should be left unruled, so as to avoid having to adjust the machine to obtain exact alignment. Printed descriptions should be arranged to coincide with the spacing of the machine; for example, three or six lines to the inch should be adopted if the form is to be entered on a typewriter.

Columns   Where possible, columns should be headed with brief and self-explanatory titles; the use of code titles should be avoided. The width of columns should be determined by the information to be entered rather than by the size of the heading. Forms are often wrongly designed with columns of varying widths merely because the titles use words of different lengths.

Sizes   The use of standard sizes of paper for forms simplifies handling and filing, and avoids waste in printing or duplication. In each case, the smallest suitable size should be selected, bearing in mind the volume of information to be entered and the use to which the form is to be put. The traditional British standard sizes are brief (13 × 16 in.), foolscap folio (8 × 13 in.) and quarto (8 × 10 in.). From these can be cut a number of useful sizes.

As an alternative to quarto and foolscap, use can be made of *International Papers Sizes*. These have dimensions which always bear the relationship $1:\sqrt{2}$, and when a sheet is folded or cut in half this relationship remains unchanged. The international sizes which are of most general use in offices are:

Code	millimetres	inches (approx.)
A3	297 × 420	$11\frac{3}{4} \times 16\frac{1}{2}$
A4	210 × 297	$8\frac{1}{4} \times 11\frac{3}{4}$
A5	148 × 210	$5\frac{7}{8} \times 8\frac{1}{4}$
A6	105 × 148	$4\frac{1}{8} \times 5\frac{7}{8}$
A7	74 × 105	$2\frac{7}{8} \times 4\frac{1}{8}$

Paper   The type and quality of paper used should be appropriate to the purpose, having regard to the extent to which it will be handled and the method of making entries. The following are some examples of the principal considerations:

(a) *Physical handling*   If a form will be handled many times, or is to be retained for reference over a long period, a good quality of paper is necessary. If, on the other hand, it is to be handled once or twice only, a less expensive paper will suffice. Extreme examples are the paper used for hand-posted ledgers and the flimsy paper used for taking carbon copies of correspondence.

(b) *Appearance*   The quality of paper used has a considerable effect upon the appearance of forms. For example, invoices are sometimes on high-quality paper in order to create a good impression on the customer. Generally, a form on good paper commands greater respect than one on poor paper.

(c) *Methods*   Paper must be suited to the clerical processes through which it will pass. If entries are to be made in ink, a non-absorbent paper is necessary; if in pencil, almost any type is adequate. If several carbon copies of a form are to be taken, a thin paper is necessary. Some classes of duplicating and copying machines can only be used effectively with particular types of paper. For example, the stencil duplicator often requires an absorbent paper, and the spirit duplicator requires a non-absorbent paper.

Make up   Many forms are prepared so that a number of copies can be made at the same time. They may be in pad form, perforated so as to be easily detachable, or in the form of continuous stationery for use in a manifold register or machine. Sometimes it is necessary that forms which are similar in general appearance shall be more readily distinguished. This can be achieved by the use of different coloured papers and inks, or by adding bold symbols which can be recognized at a glance. When carbon copies are to be made, forms can be coated with carbon on the back in the appropriate places so as to avoid the handling of carbon paper.

General appearance   The completed design should present a neat and straightforward appearance. Entry spaces should, as far as possible, be aligned vertically and horizontally. The work of entering is reduced if the clerk can follow a horizontal or vertical pattern rather than having to dodge from one part of the form to another. The use of a variety of unmatched printing types should be avoided, and heavy type for emphasis used sparingly.

Simplicity   Forms should, above all, be simple. Over-elaboration, often carried out from a desire to make the form more easily understood, generally leads only to confusion.

Installation

When a new system has been planned, it is necesssary to obtain the approval of all concerned and then proceed to the installation.

Procedure statements   Some written statement of what is proposed must be prepared. Those who have to approve the plan have to study it; those who will operate the system require a guide to which they can refer. Procedure statements (or manuals) should be as brief as possible. Full use should be made of specimen forms and flow charts which are readily intelligible. The text can then be limited to an introductory summary and such further explanations as may be necessary to make the intention clear beyond doubt.

The statement should concentrate firstly on the normal procedure. There will, almost certainly, be exceptions to the normal but these will only confuse the reader if interspersed with the general rules to be followed. Any special instructions as to detail are best dealt with separately in an appendix. The general principles of report writing apply (see Chapter 27).

Responsibility for installation   The responsibility for installing and operating the new system from the beginning rests with the office manager and supervisors. O & M is an advisory and not an executive function, and should not therefore be involved beyond the preparatory stages. In practice, it is to be expected that the investigator will be present when operation commences to help and advise, but not to take charge.

Changeover   There are three principal methods of replacing an existing system. Firstly, the new system may be installed by stages. In a wages system, for instance, the attendance records might be installed first without disturbing the payroll procedure. Then, when this part of the routine has become firmly established, the method of preparing the payroll might be changed. Secondly, the new methods might be installed completely for successive blocks of work. Using wages again as an example, the entire system might be applied first to the employees in one or two departments only. As soon as the procedure has been satisfactorily established in this limited application, it could be extended by stages until it covered all departments of the business. Thirdly, the new method could be introduced in parallel with the existing method. The work would be done by both systems until it was seen that the new one was working satisfactorily; the old would then be discontinued. This procedure is usually necessary when installing systems using a computer.

Rarely is it safe to install new methods in one move. However carefully the planning may have been done, unforeseen difficulties may arise: staff have to acquire new working habits and are unlikely to work at what will ultimately be normal speed; there will be questions to be asked and answered.

Forms control

If every department of a business is free to create new forms the number in use and the cost of processing them will almost certainly become excessive. Because a narrow, departmental view is taken, records will be duplicated wholly or in part and clerical 'empires' will grow. To combat this tendency, a central control of forms, perhaps by the O & M department, can be instituted.

All forms are registered and specimens of them held centrally. A new form is only authorized when it has been ascertained that its purpose cannot be served by an existing form, by an additional copy of an existing form or by drawing on information already available elsewhere.

DESIGNING COMPUTER METHODS

The principles enunciated above apply as much to the design of computer methods as they do to the design of hand methods. It is still necessary to investigate, to establish the purposes to be fulfilled, to define the processes to convert data into end-products, to design forms and to install the new system.

In practice, there may be a computer already available, and what can be done limited by its capacity. There is then little point in designing an 'ideal' system only to find that it cannot be carried out by that machine. The O & M staff must understand the computer, what it can do and what it cannot do.

In some organizations, there is a separate computer O & M department. Whilst it enables specialists to be employed, this arrangement has its dangers. If a computer O & M department carries out an investigation, it may assume that the work must be done by the computer; it will be prejudiced. O & M work requires an open mind, seeking the best way of doing work, by whatever means. Sometimes the required results can be produced quicker by hand, and with little more work than is necessary to collect and record data for computer input. There have been cases in which the initial cost of systems analysis and programming has been greater than the amount of any possible economy in running cost.

Division of responsibilities   Although there must be collaboration between the O & M department and the computer department, there should be a clear division of responsiblity. This is usually as follows:

O & M department   responsible for discovering and defining management requirements, designing systems, producing feasible job specifications and approving the output from test runs.

Computer department   Responsible for writing and testing programs to fulfil the requirements of the job specifications and for the operation of the computer when the system has been installed.

Initial investigation   The first stages in the design of computer methods are no different from those in any O & M investigation. It is necessary to establish the purposes, the desired end-products, the nature and sources of data, and the logic leading from data to results. If it is then concluded that computerization may be a valid method, a feasibility study (or justification survey) is carried out to discover whether or not there would be acceptable cost or other advantages.

Feasibility study (justification survey) The purpose of the feasibility study is to establish facts which are significant in relation to computer operation, for example:

(*a*) *Storage* What long-term and immediate-access storage will be required, and is this within the capacity available?

(*b*) *Input* What will the volume of input be? How and from what sources will data be collected, and will this be item by item or in batches? How frequently must data be fed into the computer? What will be the cost of data capture?

(*c*) *Output* What printed output will be required and how frequently? Is visual-display unit enquiry required and how frequently must files be updated so that reliable information can be available?

(*d*) *Timetable* How often must programs be run? Must programs always be on line? Will the work interfere with other jobs, existing or planned?

(*e*) *Volumes and cost* What is the estimated initial cost of systems analysis and programming? How many items of data will be processed? What is the estimated computer running time in normal hours, in overtime or in shift working?

From such information, it will be possible to determine whether the available computer can do the work and, if so, what will be the estimated cost. Computer running time is usually costed at a rate per minute, but if there is idle machine and staff time to be taken up, a realistic view of the true additional cost must be taken. Equally, the possible effect on future plans of absorbing time now must be evaluated. Eventually, a computer may become fully used and the taking up of what appears to be 'free' time may lead to the purchase of another larger computer—a cost element which cannot be ignored.

The initial costs of systems analysis and programming are often of greater importance than the running costs. These initial costs can be likened to investments which must be recovered over the lifetime of the program and are best expressed as a cost per unit of work to be done. As a simplified example, let it be assumed that the design, programming and testing of an invoicing system will cost about £5000. It is anticipated that the system will operate without major change for five years, so that the cost can be written off at the rate of £1000 a year. Whether this is justifiable or not will depend on the number of invoices to be produced. For 1000 invoices a year, the average cost of £1 each might compare unfavourably with the cost of hand work. For 10 000 invoices a year, the average cost of 10p each might be attractive.

The fact that a computer can do a job—and it can do most things—does not mean that it should be used. A computer only becomes economical when its capacity for fast, repetitive work is sufficiently employed.

Computer job specification The job specification must provide all the information necessary to enable the computer systems analyst to prepare flow charts and the programmer to write programs. It should start with a general introduction, stating purposes and providing such background knowledge as may be necessary to understanding the intentions. This should be followed by sections dealing with the following:

(a) *Summary of output* listing what has to be produced and supported by realistic specimens and such notes as are necessary to explain abbreviations and short headings.

(b) *Summary of data* defining each item and the maximum number of digits or alphabetical characters for which provision must be made, and supported by specimens of any data collection forms.

(c) *Coding systems* to be adopted.

(d) *Volumes* of data and output.

(e) *Processing instructions* showing how results are to be obtained from the data.

As the computer systems analyst and programmer do their work, they should maintain contact with the O & M system designer to ensure that there are no misunderstandings.

Installation In installing computer systems, it must be remembered that the computer's operations are part only of the procedure as a whole. The O & M department has to plan and advise on what has to be done by clerical and non-clerical staff in collecting and recording data. It has also to make proposals as to the action to be taken when the computer's results have been produced.

Computer services

Package systems For systems commonly employed in business, it may be possible to purchase or hire programs from a computer supplier or a 'software house'. Standard 'package' programs are available for payroll, invoicing, accounting, budgetary control, stock control etc., and also for more sophisticated systems associated with business planning and forecasting. Provided that such packages fulfil the required purposes, they are likely to cost less than the designing of special systems and the writing of the associated programs. It must, however, be accepted that they may not match the peculiarities of a particular organization in all respects. Management must then decide whether the additional cost of the special system is jutified by what it will produce.

Computer bureaux   Computer bureaux provide a variety of services from system design, through programming, to operation. Some have small computers and may specialize in one or a few services, e.g. payroll preparation. Others have very large capacity computers and are able to undertake almost any kind of work. The smaller business may find it more economical to buy service than to install, staff and operate its own computer. It is not to be assumed that small computers suit small businesses. They may well be better served by a few hours a month of the time of a very large computer than by many days of a smaller one.

Any business may benefit from the occasional use of a large computer. A visible-record computer may be adequate for daily operations but unable to carry out processing required monthly or quarterly. If equipped with a punched paper tape or magnetic-recording output, the visible-record computer could accumulate data throughout the month ready to be fed into a larger computer at the month end. An example of such an arrangement would be data accumulated in the course of invoicing and stock control being sent monthly to a bureau to be further processed on a larger computer to produce customers' accounts and statements, and sales analyses.

25   Day-to-day controls

Day-to-day controls of output and of the quality of work produced are as essential in the office as they are in other departments. This chapter describes briefly some of the methods more commonly used in setting standards and in controlling the work by reference to them.

Whatever procedure is adopted, control has the dual purpose of ensuring that the work is completed on time and that the clerks are kept fully occupied. Parkinson's Law 'work expands to fill the time available' is somewhat negative and its complement is equally true and generally more productive; 'an individual's capacity for work expands to complete the work available'. The best results are often obtained by providing a satisfactory working environment and ensuring that reasonable quantities of work are made available in a steady flow.

QUALITY CONTROL

The standards of quality of office work may be expressed in terms of accuracy, appearance and judgement. Failure to achieve the desired standards is not always readily obvious and constant control must be exercised. All work must be checked and scrutinized to ensure that it has been adequately carried out, and part at least of this checking and scrutiny should be undertaken personally by supervisors or managers.

Accuracy

The importance of accuracy needs no emphasis. Every system should be devised with a view to minimizing the possibility of error, and should include provision for routine checks to trap and correct errors as soon as they occur. The control over accuracy is exercised largely by seeing that the routine checks are properly applied, by scrutiny of finished work and by recording and analysing the nature and causes of errors made.

Checking   Wherever possible, each operation should be checked before any subsequent operation is carried out, so that if an error has been made it will not lead to further incorrect work. For example, in a manual system the entries on a wages sheet showing the number of hours worked by each employee should be checked before the hours are multiplied by the rates to produce the gross wages.

There are four common methods of checking:

(*a*) *The independent check*   Here the work of one clerk is checked by another who repeats the operations involved.

(*b*) *The 'blind' check*   This is usually applied only to calculating operations. It is similar to the independent check except that the checker produces an independent answer before having access to the original answer.

(*c*) *'Self-balancing' processes*   The simplest example of this method is the 'square balancing' of the casts of several columns of figures. In this case a grand total of all the cross-cast totals should agree with a grand total of all the vertical totals. If they agree, it can be assumed that the additions are correct, subject to the chance of compensating errors. Another example is when the total of amounts posted on an accounting machine is compared with a pre-list.

(*d*) *Automatic check*   Where a computer is used, it is possible to program for data to be checked automatically for completeness, to some extent for accuracy (see check digits, page 152) and for plausibility, e.g. as to whether a figure lies between an expected minimum and maximum or has an acceptable relationship with some other figure. It is normal, whenever automatic checks cause data to be rejected by a computer, for a report to be printed out or displayed on a screen.

Scrutinizing   Wherever possible, all finished work should be examined for possible errors by a supervisor or an experienced senior clerk. With application and practice it is possible to develop an ability to detect errors merely by looking for any item which appears to be out of the ordinary. This faculty is not quickly acquired and clerks should be taught to examine figures critically early in their career.

Computer control   Computer users often have a small computer control section of experienced senior clerks with responsibility for ensuring:

(*a*) that data are complete, apparently correct and properly authorized;

(*b*) that batch and other control totals are recorded;

(*c*) that data are input at the correct time;

(*d*) that error reports from the computer are investigated and any necessary corrections made;

(*e*) that error records are maintained for analysis (see page 365);

(*f*) that print-outs from the computer are apparently correct so far as control totals show this;

(*g*) that print-outs are controlled and distributed promptly to management and the office.

The actual control checks imposed should be designed to suit the needs of the system. A computer rarely makes an error. The purpose of computer control is to ensure that the human processes, before data reach the computer, before data are processed, and after results are printed, are carried out accurately, promptly and honestly.

Appearance

The neatness and general appearance of clerical work is of importance, especially in the case of correspondence and forms which are to go outside the business. The impression created by letters, invoices and the like may have a considerable effect upon reputation and goodwill. There is only one means of control, and that is scrutiny. The work of junior clerks should be scrutinized by a senior clerk as a matter of routine. Supervisors and the office manager himself should regularly examine sample batches of work to see that proper standards are maintained.

Judgement

The element of decision enters into most clerical work, and a proper sense of judgement is necessary in all but the junior tasks. For example, a clerk answering a routine letter will make his decision as to what he writes and as to the tone in which he writes, and damage may be done to the business if he judges wrongly. The control exercised in such a case may take the form of a complete check, all outgoing letters being scrutinized and signed personally by an executive. Similarly, for most other tasks involving judgement, an adequate control can only be maintained if the finished work is scrutinized by a manager, a supervisor or by an experienced clerk. Controls by means of records are not possible for this aspect of quality.

Analysing errors

Clerical errors come to light in three ways:

(*a*) by the routine checks imposed as part of the office systems;

(*b*) by scrutiny and audit; and

(*c*) by complaints received from customers, suppliers and others outside the business.

Whenever the frequency of errors is such as to give cause for concern, a record of errors discovered should be kept with a view to analysing them to ascertain their nature, the causes and the persons responsible. It is not uncommon for a special form (sometimes called an errors docket) to be used. Errors dockets should be examined by the responsible supervisor, who should discuss the causes of the errors with the clerks concerned. These interviews should not take the form of a reprimand unless the clerk is obviously careless. What may appear at first to be carelessness may in fact be ignorance. The best results are often obtained by an objective discussion on the assumption that both supervisor and clerk are equally anxious to locate the true cause and prevent a recurrence of the error.

The errors recorded should be analysed under types, causes and persons responsible. Whilst some errors will be the result of carelessness, others may be found to arise from ill-designed systems or other causes which lie within the control of management rather than the clerks.

Some examples of common causes of errors are given below:

(a) *Poor selection of staff*   Certain jobs make special demands on intellectual qualities such as concentration, memory, reliability and judgement, or physical qualities such as hearing and sight.

(b) *Insufficient training*   Supplementary training should be given when errors arise from lack of understanding.

(c) *Vague instructions*   Instructions should be complete and unambiguous; they should never be given in haste. Clerks should be encouraged to ask questions when in doubt.

(d) *Conditions of strain*   Clerks should not be expected to work under unreasonable pressure or be subject to frequent interruption.

(e) *Poor working conditions*   Environment should be such that clerks can concentrate without distraction.

(f) *Unsatisfactory forms and equipment*   Forms should be designed to make it easy for the clerk to take the right action and to make omissions readily apparent. Machines and equipment should be maintained in proper condition.

OUTPUT CONTROL

It is of the essence of control that there shall be a standard or plan and that subsequent actual performance shall be compared with it. The mere recording of what is actually achieved is of little value in the absence of a 'yardstick' against which to measure the good and the bad. Standards must be reasonably capable of achievement. It is not enough to set vague targets such as 'being up-to-date at the end of the month', unless account has been taken of the volume of work to be done and the staff and machines available to do it.

For control purposes, clerical work can be regarded as falling into four broad categories:

(*a*) work which must be completed by a given time, e.g. payroll, which must be completed so that wages can be paid at the appointed time, or sales accounts which must be ready for the dispatch of statements to customers on a particular day of the month;

(*b*) continuing processes, in which the flow of work varies, e.g. purchase-invoice passing, where the number of invoices received through the post each day is unpredictable—passing on the day of receipt is not essential, but the number in hand must be kept within reasonable limits;

(*c*) work which must be fitted in at regular but longer than daily intervals, e.g. weekly, monthly, quarterly, annually;

(*d*) work which is of a special nature and cannot be foreseen, e.g. inquiries by management.

The cycle of daily routine is usually only one factor of several. In the extreme case, it is necessary to co-ordinate:

daily cycle of routine with possible peak loads within the day;
weekly cycle of routine arising possibly on some days only;
monthly cycle of routine creating peak loads at various times;
varying demands for unpredictable special tasks to be done.

Given unlimited resources, there would be no problem: idle staff and machines could be called on as work became available. If, however, a satisfactory level of productivity is to be maintained throughout each day, careful planning and control are essential. The methods by which these can be achieved are described below.

Work measurement

In order to plan realistically, it is necessary to express both the work and the available resources according to a common unit of measurement. The resources, whether human or mechanical, are most conveniently measured in terms of time: available minutes, hours and days. If time is to be the unit, then the work must also be expressed in this way as man-hours or machine-hours of work. Whereas the resources are actual time available, the work must be expressed as *standard time:* the amount of time that is necessary to do the work under normal conditions. To establish a reliable standard time for completing a particular unit of work, there must be work measurement by one of a number of methods available (see pages 288–91).

In selecting units of work to be measured, regard must be had to convenience in recording actual work at the control stage. The work of typing sales invoices might be very accurately measured according to the number of typewriter key depressions made, but to count these could well take longer than the work itself. Some less detailed unit such as an 'average invoice' is more practical because the units can be counted easily or calculated by reference to the invoice serial numbers. For control purposes, an average unit of work allowing for a normal incidence of queries and other difficulties is usually adequate and preferable. In general, the unit of work should relate to the *task* rather than the operation (see definitions on page 287).

Work scheduling

Work scheduling is the name commonly used to describe the preparation of standard programmes showing when each task should be done. The purpose of a work schedule is to provide a means whereby the work can be planned to ensure:

(*a*) an even distribution of the workload over the week or month, with as few peak loads and idle periods as possible;

(*b*) the provision of the number of clerks necessary to complete each task by the appointed time;

(*c*) a reasonable output from each clerk—neither too much nor too little;

(*d*) sufficient elasticity to allow time for special tasks as they may arise.

The work schedule should list all the tasks which must be done, grouped according to whether the cycle of routine is daily, weekly, monthly or on some other basis. Against each task should be shown:

(*a*) the work unit adopted;

(*b*) the estimated volume of work in terms of units per day, week etc.

(*c*) the standard time per unit;

(*d*) the total standard time per day, week etc. ((*b*) × (*c*));

(*e*) the grade/job classification showing the type of clerk necessary to do the work;

(*f*) the earliest possible starting time when work becomes available;

(*g*) the latest permissible finishing time;

(*h*) the number of clerks necessary to provide the standard time (*d*) within the limits imposed by (*f*) and (*g*).

With this information, a programme of work can be established. In practice, it is useful to have skeleton programmes for the daily, weekly and monthly cycles of routine work. The programme for any particular day or week is then constructed by bringing together the appropriate parts of these skeletons.

The object is to assign to each clerk a reasonable amount of work of appropriate grade in such a way that the whole of the work is accomplished in due time. In some sections of an office, this may be a relatively simple task, as for example where the whole of the work is routine data encoding. Where, however, a variety of tasks of differing grades must be co-ordinated as parts of a system, the plan will rarely be satisfactory at first draft. Alternative patterns will have to be considered before the one which gives the best overall result is found. If, for example, the work schedule showed the following, a number of alternative programmes would be possible:

Volume: 100 forms a week
Standard Time: 10 minutes a form (16 hours 40 minutes a week)
Earliest Start: 9 am Monday
Latest Finish: 3 pm Tuesday

Office hours are 9 am to 5 pm with one hour of breaks, giving a net seven working hours. The available time is 1 day 5 hours = 12 hours; the standard time required is 16 hours 40 minutes. One clerk is, therefore, not enough, but having regard to other work to be fitted into the programme, the following are among several possible arrangements:

(*a*) one clerk for 12 hours, supported by another for 4 hours 40 minutes at any time within the permitted limits;

(*b*) two clerks each working for 8 hours 20 minutes, starting at any time between 9 am and 1.40 pm on Monday.

Whatever formula is adopted, it is prudent to plan to finish before the due time so as to allow for contingencies.

It may sometimes be found to be impossible to allocate work so that all the requirements as to finishing times are fulfilled without peak loads and idle time resulting. Such situations should be discussed with management so that it may be decided whether the cost of carrying surplus staff at certain times is justified.

When expressing a work programme, whether as a list, chart or other form, provision should be made for recording and comparing the actual performance (see below).

Group output control

The responsibility for recording output and reporting significant deviations from the work programme is usually delegated to section supervisors and group leaders. The method of recording will depend upon the nature of the work, which is likely to fall into one of the four principal categories already defined on page 367. The illustrations given below should be regarded as examples only. The form adopted should be suited to the tasks and the needs of the person using it.

Work to be completed by a given time   A bar chart (or Gantt chart) as illustrated in Fig. 126 is a convenient means of planning and controlling output when starting and finishing times are important. Payroll preparation is a typical example of this situation: a sequence of tasks must be carried out and the ultimate completion depends as much on the first task as the last. The plan is represented by a dotted line. For 'Entry', this line indicates that the process is continuous from 9 am on Monday, but is divided according to the payrolls for various departments of the business. For checking, which is

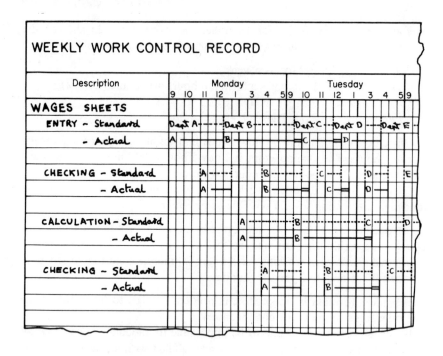

Fig. 126 Work-control chart

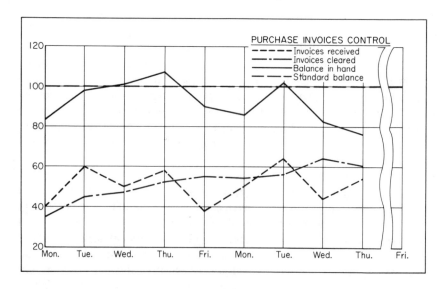

Fig. 127 Work-control graph

a shorter process, there are breaks in the flow of work when other tasks can be fitted into the programme.

The value of a control chart is largely lost unless it is consulted hour by hour and the actual performance recorded against the standard. In Fig. 126, the actual time taken is entered as a heavy line, doubled to show where the work was behind schedule. Colours are often used to denote standard, actual and excess times. A chart of this kind provides supervision and management with a means of checking progress quickly so that action may be taken before a crisis arises.

Continuing processes   The graph illustrated in Fig. 127 shows a standard balance, being the number of purchase invoices in hand regarded as a 'safe level'. A line representing the actual balance day by day shows how this moves in relation to the standard and indicates when action is necessary to avoid an accumulation of work. The number of invoices received and cleared are similarly recorded, enabling abnormal movements to be seen. All the relevant information is thus concentrated on one sheet.

Another method is to keep a 'work in progress account' in which the balance in hand is analysed to differentiate between work not yet started and queries awaiting solution, e.g.:

	Monday	*Tuesday*	*Wednesday*
Standard Balance	100	100	100
Opening Balance	84	98	102
add Received	60	51	57
	144	149	159
deduct Cleared	46	47	52
Closing Balance	98	102	107
Awaiting attention	62	67	66
Queries up to 7 days old	10	12	15
Queries 7–14 days old	16	14	17
Queries over 14 days old	10	9	9

Other work   Work which arises at weekly, monthly or longer intervals, such as the preparation of reports and accounts, should ideally be fitted into the routine programme and shown on the same control record. In practice, a separate check list may be all that is necessary.

Special tasks which cannot be foreseen must also be recorded by addition to the normal control sheet or separately, so that output in relation to resources can be judged as a whole. Because these tasks cause fluctuations in the workload, it is important to record and review the time spent on them at, say, monthly intervals.

Individual output control

Where the volume of work varies but little, the manner in which the work schedule is followed may itself provide a sufficient control over individual performance. Where, however, the volume of work fluctuates from day to day, the work done by the clerks, individually or in groups, may be recorded and the actual times compared with the standards. Daily time sheets should be made out by whoever is responsible for giving out the work. Time sheets should show:

(a) *The Work Accomplished*—the job description and the number of units completed (e.g. invoices, ledger postings).

(b) *The Standard Time*—the standard time allowed per unit multiplied by the number of units completed.

(c) *The Actual Time:*

(i) the starting and stopping times for the working day;
(ii) the time spent in meal breaks and any time lost through such as machine breakdowns or indisposition;
(iii) the time spent on unmeasured work.

The design of the time sheet will depend upon the types of job to be recorded. Increased output can often be stimulated by marking the standard time on each batch of work so that the clerk can check his performance as each job is completed.

At the end of the day, the total time at work, less any lost time and time on unmeasured work, should be compared with the standard time for the work accomplished and the reason for any significant differences ascertained. The principal purpose is to enable management and supervision to keep a control on the work of individuals. Results should be made known to the clerks and praise or encouragement given.

Consultant services

Some consultants will install control systems under distinctive names, e.g. Group Capacity Assessment (GCA), Clerical Work Improvement Programme (CWIP) and Variable Factor Programming (VeFac). These systems apply the principles set out in this chapter and, whilst they have differences in application, may be summarized as follows.

Because full O & M investigations take time, the *existing procedures* are accepted initially. *Work measurement* is carried out by one of the methods described in Chapter 21 and standard times established. If immediate *method improvement* is possible, changes are made. The balance between work to be done and staff available is improved by *work scheduling. Group output standards* per day or week are set in broad terms. Where a central office processes returns from branches, the standard times for tasks might be summarized to a total time allowance for one branch/day. Ordinarily, the group will be shown to have staff in excess of what is necessary if the supervisor obtains a reasonable output from each clerk.

Group output control is then installed. The output in terms of the broad units adopted is evaluated in terms of standard time. This is then compared with the actual time available within the group and an index of efficiency calculated which indicates the *supervisor's performance.* Control is over the group and its supervisor and not over the individual clerk. *Over-staffing is to be corrected* by the supervisor over a reasonable period. He may absorb additional work or ensure that clerks who leave the group are not replaced. If the supervisor does not effect improvement at a satisfactory rate, his manager must help by diagnosing causes and giving suitable *guidance and training.*

26   Audit 22/2/81

The purpose of the official audit, as carried out by professional accountants is well established. In the case of a limited company, the powers and duties of the auditor are defined by statute, and the auditor, as an agent of the shareholders, is appointed by them at the annual general meeting. Also, most private businesses make use of the services of professional accountants, although in this case the extent of the duties is settled by agreement between the auditors and the owners of the business.

It is also a common practice, particularly among larger businesses, for a continuous internal audit to be conducted by a special staff in the employ of the business. This enables a more detailed check to be imposed at reasonable cost and errors to be more quickly rectified than would otherwise be the case. Internal audits need not be considered as necessarily confined to the verification of records; they may be extended also to office methods and to personnel practices. It is with these three types of internal audit that this chapter is concerned.

THE RECORDS AUDIT

The purpose of the records audit is the detection of errors or fraud with a view to their subsequent correction and prevention. It should be remembered that:

(a) *errors* include not only straightforward clerical mistakes but also omissions and errors of principle in record keeping, and

(b) *fraud* includes not only falsification of accounts but also fraud by other persons outside the office made possible by loopholes in the office systems.

Planning the audit

An audit is the better for having been planned beforehand. Nonetheless, it is of the essence of auditing that the auditor must be ready to depart from the plan in order to investigate any matter which arouses his suspicion.

An overall plan should be prepared within which each job should be planned in the light of its relative importance. The length of time to be spent on each job should be determined, and a job programme drawn up dividing it into stages and showing how each stage is to be tackled. Regard must also be had to the convenience of those who are concerned with producing or using the records. The process of auditing should interfere as little as possible with the work of the office.

Conducting the audit

The purpose of the audit in relation to errors is to detect significant tendencies, intentional or otherwise, to depart from recognized and authorized principles. An audit is rarely concerned with achieving absolute accuracy; that is the province of routine checking. The purpose of the audit is to ensure that proper checks have in fact been made and to test the standard of accuracy achieved. Generally, this is done by a 'snap' or 'roving' check on a proportion of the work.

The more straightforward part of an audit consists of comparing records with the original information, verifying additions and other calculations, and checking all controls and reconciliation statements. Particular attention should be paid to transactions involving cash or anything which is of such a nature as to be easily subject to fraud.

To secure *prima facie* accuracy of entries is not enough. An audit should also be concerned with ensuring that nothing has been omitted. In selected cases, the auditor may make a complete check of a transaction. For example, in the case of a purchase, the auditor may need to satisfy himself on such questions as the following:

(a) *The order*   Was the order to the supplier placed by an authorized buyer?

(b) *The goods*   Was a record made of the goods received? To what purpose were the goods put; are they still in existence as the property of the business, or is there evidence of their having been sold or used in a production process?

(c) *The payment*   Does the invoice conform with an authorized order and with the record of goods received? Have the goods been already paid for? Have the correct entries been made in the books of account?

As a result of examining individual transactions, the auditor must give consideration to more general questions:

(*a*) Is there any failure to make out orders regularly and properly?
(*b*) Is a proper record made of goods as soon as they are received?
(*c*) Do the methods provide adequate safeguards against error and fraud?
(*d*) Are there any unnecessary records being produced?
(*e*) Are the clerks carrying out the method satisfactorily?

Other types of transaction receive similar treatment. In dealing with sales, the auditor may take selected items and trace every operation from the receipt of the customer's order, including the dispatch of the goods, the acknowledgement of their receipt and the establishment of an entry in the bank statement for the customer's payment. The complete chain of events is not necessarily carried out at one time; the sales may be investigated on one occasion and cash receipts on another.

Apart from dealing with individual transactions in the manner described, the audit may cover a variety of other matters of which the following are but examples:

(a) *Cash*   Is the cash in hand the same as the amount recorded in the cash book? Has the balance at the bank according to the cash book been reconciled with the bank statement?

(b) *Stock in trade*   Are there adequate records of the stocks? Are stocks properly controlled? Has a proper valuation of the stocks been made?

(c) *Work in progress*   Has a proper value been put on uncompleted work?

(d) *Equipment*   Is a proper record of equipment maintained? Is the valuation correct? Has due allowance been made for obsolescence and depreciation?

(e) *Buildings and land*   Has the business proper title to its property? Is it correctly valued?

 The fact that a thorough internal audit may be made does not remove the right or need for the official auditor to investigate the same matters. The advantage of the internal audit is that it may be carried out sooner than the official audit and in time to prevent serious consequences from the repetition of mistakes or fraud.

The audit report

The need for an internal audit exists because, in a large business, members of the management cannot personally inspect all that is going on. The purpose of the report, therefore, is to bring to their attention any matter of which they should be aware and on which they should take action. At the same time, the auditor is in a position to make recommendations and to advise all those who are concerned with the matters covered by his audit. The nature of the report and the person to whom it is addressed will depend upon the importance of the subject. In the case of a minor error it may be sufficient if its is reported to the clerk concerned or to a supervisor. More serious errors may need to be reported to the local management. Matters of policy or errors of principle may need to be reported to the higher management. The auditor's task is not complete until the appropriate level of authority has been put in a position to give due consideration to the result of his investigation.

THE METHODS AUDIT

As the name implies, the purpose of the methods audit is to examine the efficiency of the methods in operation and to report on the need for any reorganization. Its purpose may also include the making of recommendations as to the nature of such reorganization, although not in detail unless confined to minor adjustments to the existing method. It is this difference that distinguishes methods auditing from methods planning, even though both may be the work of the O & M department. The methods audit may take the form of:

(*a*) a 'follow-up' to check the effectiveness of a particular system which has been in operation for some time;

(*b*) a check on one particular aspect of all the methods of the office, e.g. the condition and utilization of equipment.

The methods audit as a follow-up

In a previous chapter, reference was made to the work of the O & M specialist in the planning of office methods. Once a plan has been accepted by the management and the method has been installed, the planner's duties are at an end. The very nature of the planner's work is such as to make it unwise for him to have anything to do with the day-to-day operation of the method once it has been installed. If he is to be free to give full thought and attention to each new problem as it is presented to him, he cannot at the same time be concerned with the operation and final adjustment of other systems unless matters of major significance arise. It is, however, an advantage for a planner to re-examine or audit systems after they have been in operation for a few months.

It is also valuable for a further inspection to be made after a system has been in operation for a number of years. Here the purpose is to examine the effects of the passage of time. Often the most important consideration is the possibility of a change in conditions. If the nature of the business changes (and it may do so imperceptibly) the method originally installed may have become unsuited to the new conditions. For example, an invoicing system, originally designed to deal with a small range of items, may become unsatisfactory if, over a period, there is a steady increase in the size of the range. Almost equally important are the changes which may have taken place in the system itself. Often, numerous small and comparatively insignificant changes in systems may be instituted which, whilst they appear to be expedient at the time, are from a long-term point of view unsatisfactory; extemporary changes may be made to deal with unforeseen eventualities, additional checks may be instituted to avoid errors, or local changes may be made without due regard to what takes place in other departments of the business.

The purpose of the methods audit is to take the long-term view of these changes and to decide whether conditions have so altered as to merit a complete reorganization of the system or whether only minor adjustments are required. It is convenient if the methods auditor can compare the existing methods with those described in the report of the system as originally installed, so as to ascertain what changes have taken place and to consider the reasons for them. If only minor adjustments are necessary, they may be made in conjunction with the local management, with little formality. If, on the other hand, a completely new method is required, it is a matter not for audit but for planning.

Other types of methods audit

Considerable benefits result from occasional audits of particular aspects of office methods and equipment. The follow-up audit is concerned with one particular system as a section of the work of the office. The audit of one aspect of all systems covers a cross-section and enables useful comparisons to be made. The two approaches should not be regarded as alternative, but rather as complementary; in surveying the office from two angles, much may come to light that would otherwise remain unnoticed. The following are examples of subjects for audit, together with some typical questions to which answers should be sought.

(a) *Equipment*   Is equipment being maintained in good repair? Are any items obsolete and due for replacement? Is full use being made of equipment or does it lie idle for part of the working day? Is it being used or operated correctly?

(b) *Stationery*   Are the stocks of stationery properly stored? Are there stocks of obsolete stationery? Are proper ordering levels maintained? Are the forms and general stationery suited to current requirements?

(c) *Filing*   Are the files in good order? Can records be located within a reasonable time? Are obsolete records cleared at suitable intervals or are records retained for longer than is necessary?

(d) *Furniture*   Are the desks and chairs and other items of furniture being maintained in good condition? Are they suited to their purpose? Is proper use being made of drawers and other fitments? Is proper use being made of adjustable chairs?

(e) *Space and layout*   Is the best use being made of the space available? Has the layout deteriorated? Have new conditions arisen which require a revision of the layout? Is the office kept tidy? Are the provisions of the Offices, Shops and Railway Premises Act, 1963, being fulfilled?

(f) *Cleanliness* Is the office regularly and satisfactorily cleaned? Have the cleaners adequate equipment? Does paintwork require washing down? Is any redecoration necessary? Should desks and cupboards be turned out?

(g) *Lighting* Are proper standards of lighting maintained? Are the fitments cleaned regularly? Are windows clean?

(h) *Communications* Are the communication services adequate? Is proper use made of the facilities available?

THE PERSONNEL AUDIT

No aspect of office management is more important than the personnel policy, and its concomitant, the reaction of the clerks to that policy. Whatever else may be deferred, problems relating to the clerks as people must be handled promptly as they arise from day to day. At the same time, it is necessary to take a long-term view of the personnel policy and its cumulative effect upon the way in which the clerks carry out the work of the office.

A personnel audit is a deliberate attempt to assess the soundness of the existing personnel policy and the success with which it is being put into practice. The audit can cover a wide field embracing, as it may, not merely the clerk at work, but the clerk's remuneration, his progress, his physical and mental health, and the discipline and morale of the office. It may also be necessary to include the making of comparisons with the policies and practices adopted in other businesses. Clearly an audit of this nature calls for considerable tact and discrimination. It need hardly be said that human beings cannot be subjected to scrutiny in the same way as can records and methods. What has to be done must be done unobtrusively. The necessary inquiries are usually matters for the personal attention of the office manager, but where a personnel officer is available, he or she may, with advantage, give assistance.

Like all other audits, the personnel audit should be a continuous process, with different aspects being dealt with in turn. The following is a representative selection of the subjects which may be surveyed:

(a) *Selection* Do the current methods of selection and recruitment produce the type of clerk required? If engagement tests are used, is there reasonable correlation between the results of the tests and the actual performance of the clerks at their jobs?

(b) *Training* Are the methods of training effective? Are the clerks able to tackle their jobs effectively as a result of the training given, or do they have to learn many of their duties by experience? Does the training engender a feeling of confidence among both the management and the clerks? Are the training schemes approved for Industrial Training Board grant?

(c) *Grading*   Are the jobs properly graded? Are there anomalies in the grading? Is the grading system understood by the clerks?

(d) *Workload*   Is the work satisfactorily allocated to the various clerks? Has the work been measured? Is individual output suitably recorded?

(e) *Salary scales*   Are the salary scales fair and just? Have the clerks confidence in the salary structure? Are the rates commensurate with those paid for similar work elsewhere? Do the rates meet legal requirements or those of a trade union agreement?

(f) *Progress*   Does the normal clerk make steady progress? Are there clerks who have been kept too long on one job? Are the clerks aware of the opportunities which exist for progress, and do they feel that they are given a fair chance to take advantage of these opportunities? Are clerks who are capable of doing a better job held in inferior jobs because of the lack of suitable posts or for other reasons?

(g) *Discipline*   Are reasonable standards of discipline maintained? Is discipline impartially enforced? Is attendance and time-keeping satisfactory? Do clerks conform to the office rules? Are the rules reasonable having regard to local conditions and general practice?

(h) *Meals*   Are meal breaks satisfactory as to time and duration? Are canteen meals and drinks of reasonable quality?

(j) *Morale*   Are the clerks interested in their work? Do the clerks consider that the management are interested in them as individuals? Is there a good team spirit? Do the clerks feel that the management are interested in the work they do and regard it as important? Do the clerks identify themselves with the interests of the business, and do the clerks count the successes of the business as their successes, and the failures of the business as their failures? What is the rate of staff turnover, and how does it compare with similar businesses in the same area?

(k) *Welfare*   Are there adequate facilities to enable staff to receive advice and assistance on personal problems? Do they make use of these services?

(l) *Physical conditions*   Are the physical conditions adequate and reasonable? Are the clerks satisfied with the heating, lighting, seating, ventilation, lavatories and cloakrooms? Is drinking water satisfactory? Are the standards being maintained or are they deteriorating?

(*m*) *Safety*   Are the stipulated fire and other safety precautions being observed?

(*n*) *Legal requirements*   Are current legal requirements being satisfied (see pages 281, 304 and 321)?

To obtain the answers to many of these questions, it is necessary for the person carrying out the audit to try to look at these matters through the clerks' eyes; to try to ascertain their true reactions. Where unfavourable results are obtained, it is necessary to seek the reasons and to find methods of overcoming the difficulties. Because these matters concern human beings, and because human motives are often difficult to understand, the solution to any problem which the audit brings forth may require penetrating and sympathetic thought.

THE AUDIT RESPONSIBILITY

A critical examination of the work produced and of the methods and the personnel policy is the duty of every supervisor. The internal audit covers the same ground but with this important difference; it is an inspection made by an independent party on behalf of the management.

In a very large business the records audit, the methods audit and the personnel audit may each be undertaken by different authorities. A special staff may find full time employment on auditing the records, the methods audit may be carried out by an O & M specialist, and the personnel audit may be carried out by a personnel officer. In a small business the three audits may to some extent be carried out by the office manager himself. Obviously, in these latter circumstances, the audits will not be as detailed or of the same character as the audits in a large business. But they may well be worthy of the name, if the office manager is able to free himself from time to time in order to take a detached view of his responsibilities.

To some extent, the three types of audit may overlap, but this is neither a disadvantage nor is it necessarily wasteful. In each case the angle of approach is different. Errors and bad work, for example, would certainly be covered by the records audit. The methods audit might very well go over the same ground if it were thought that the errrors were caused by a fault in the system adopted. The personnel audit might deal with the same subject if it were considered that the errors were caused by poor supervision, inadequate training, or dissatisfaction in work. This is not to suggest that the same ground would be covered in turn by successive audits. In practice it is rarely possible to take into consideration at any one time all the different aspects of accounting, methods, and personnel; no single audit is ever likely to be complete in itself.

27   Reports

In business, reports are prepared for a variety of purposes. Some reports are of a routine nature, such as the statistics which are regularly produced by the office for the information of the management in controlling the affairs of the business; others are of a special nature, as when decisions have to be taken outside the ordinary day-to-day affairs of the business and a special investigation is made. Reports can, therefore, be considered generally under two heads—routine reports and special reports.

Although information may be gathered by clerks in the office, the task of preparing the report or at least of editing the final draft, usually falls upon the manager. The office is the repository of the records of the business and the office manager must, therefore, be responsible for producing that information in suitable form. The extent to which his time is occupied with this activity will depend, of course, upon the requirements of directors and other managers, but it will also depend very largely on how far he has been successful in training his subordinates to deal with such matters on his behalf.

In preparing reports, there is an art which can be studied and cultivated. Information and recommendations placed before the management of the business are of little value unless they assist the formation of judgements and lead to decisions being taken. A report which does not stimulate thought and lead eventually to action may be of passing interest, but it serves no useful purpose. It will almost certainly not justify the cost of its preparation.

A good report should contain all the relevant facts, it should marshal these facts in logical order, discuss them in simple language and arrive at some conclusion.

SPECIAL REPORTS

It is convenient in the first instance to deal fully with the principles to be applied in preparing special reports, and then to refer to routine reports in the light of those principles. Reports may be prepared by individuals or by committees, but in either case the work of drafting must be that of an individual, or of a number of individuals each dealing with separate sections of the report. Where a report is published by a committee, the committee's duties, as a body, consist of considering and editing drafts, and giving approval to the final product. In the paragraphs which follow, consideration is given to each stage of investigation, drafting, editing and final publishing.

Briefing

Whoever is charged with the task of carrying out an investigation and of reporting, must have his terms of reference clearly defined. When he is given his brief it should be seen clearly that he knows the answers to three questions:

(a) *Why?*   It is possible for anyone familiar with, and having access to the records of the business, to produce information blindly on request. If, however, the management problem to be solved is such that a special report is called for, whoever is to be responsible for reporting must understand fully what the problem is.

(b) *Who?*   Any speaker or writer has perforce to assume the level of the existing knowledge of those to whom he is imparting information. Communication is always between persons; the conveying of ideas from one mind to another. In preparing a report, it is therefore essential to know what must be stated and what can be taken as already understood, and the writer must therefore know at the outset who will read and act upon it.

(c) *When?*   Given unlimited time, it might be possible to produce a well-constructed report based upon a very thorough investigation. It is often the case, however, that speed is essential; any delay in arriving at a conclusion may be costly. Those who commission reports must therefore consider the relative importance of speed as against accuracy and other qualities. It may be that information expressed in broad terms and obtainable quickly is preferable to detailed information laboriously gathered over weeks or even months. An understanding as to the time available should be reached before the task is commenced.

Framework

Before gathering any information, the subject should be considered in broad terms, and the framework of the report drawn up. This framework need consist only of headings and sub-headings, and will, in fact, be the first draft 'table of contents' of the report. It will represent the master plan of the investigation and the report which will come from it. Sometimes it is wise to obtain agreement as to the framework in consultation with all those concerned before the investigation begins, thus ensuring that there is no doubt as to its nature and scope.

Investigation

With the aid of the framework, it is possible for the investigator to arrange for much, if not all, of the information required to be gathered simultaneously. Requests for information should be couched in exact terms. It is generally convenient, in the first place, to draft the form in which figures are to be presented in the report and from this form to design any working sheets which are necessary to enable the figures to be marshalled from the records. If no records exist and it is necessary that information shall be gathered specially for the purpose of the report, special forms should be prepared. The forms should be issued with such written or verbal instructions as are necessary to make their use absolutely clear, and every opportunity should be given for questions to be asked. If it is necessary for the investigator to gather opinions as well as facts, it is best that he should do so personally, so that he can assess the reactions of individuals. If the number of opinions to be gathered is large (as in the case of a market research consumer survey) then the work of a team of investigators should be closely supervised and co-ordinated by one person.

Form of the report

Reports should be set out in such a way that they can be easily read, and that reference can be made without difficulty to any part. In particular, it should be borne in mind that not all who read and consider the report will wish to study the whole of it in detail. It may happen that a well prepared report need not be read right through before decisions can be taken upon it. There is no one way in which a report should be set out; the layout must differ according to the purpose of the report and the person for whom it is intended. There is, however, a widely accepted form of report which is used in business and in the reports of Government Committees, and it is this form which is commented upon below.

Heading   The report should be given a main heading which indicates as concisely as possible its contents. If a short heading is not capable of describing adequately the contents of the report, it should be followed by an amplifying sentence or paragraph.

Table of contents   This should consist of headings and sub-headings describing the various sections and sub-sections of the report, and indicating the numbers of the pages on which they are to be found. This table serves two purposes: it facilitates reference to sections and sub-sections, and it enables the reader to become familiar with the general pattern of the report before he starts to read it.

Introduction   This first section of the report should serve to prepare the reader's mind for the recommendations and information which are to follow. It should state the terms of reference which the writer was given and it should define the problem to be solved, the attendant circumstances and any general or specific assumptions which have been made.

Summary of recommendations   This section should state as concisely as possible the recommendations which the writer makes. Bearing in mind that the reader may come to his decision without making a close study of the detail of the report, care should be taken to see that any deficiencies in the facts on which the argument leading to the recommendations is based are referred to briefly in this section. In making recommendations, the terms of reference should be covered in full, and this may mean that conclusions based on facts and figures are not enough. It may be necessary to include opinions (taking care to define them as such) and also to comment on the possible human reactions which may result from putting the recommendations into practice.

The argument   This section should show how the conclusions were reached; it will be the longest part of the report proper but it should be as concise as possible having regard to all the relevant facts and figures being included. If, however, the volume of information collected (even in its summarized form) is too great to include in the body of the argument, the writer should consider segregating the more voluminous portions as appendixes. There is a danger that the reader may lose his grip of the main argument if he is asked to study too much detail in the course of his reading. Reference should be made in the text to the appropriate appendix.

Appendixes   These may consist of statistical tables, specimens of forms, minority reports where the members of a committee are not unanimous in their recommendations, and any other matter which is essential to the report but likely to confuse the reader if presented mixed in with the main arguments.

Drafting

The technique of preparing a framework enables the writer to draft his report section by section as the investigation proceeds. The final drafting of the argument and of the conclusions must, of course, be left until the whole of the facts have been marshalled and given due consideration.

Few find the preparation of a report an easy task. A high standard of report writing connotes a high standard of written English. Mastery of English is not easily attained but it is something worth striving after. Continual criticism is necessary to this end. Anyone, by practice, can achieve a fluency in writing or speaking; it is the achievement of both fluency and quality that is so rarely attained. It is not the purpose of this chapter to deal with matters which more properly belong to textbooks on English, but the few brief hints which follow may be of assistance to those entering on a career in management:

(*a*) Keep to the subject. In the course of investigation, interesting facts may come to light which have no bearing on the terms of reference of the report. They should be rigidly excluded. If it is considered necessary to make these extraneous facts known, they should be reported separately.

(*b*) Strive for simplicity. The good report is one which is easy to read. Use simple words and straightforward sentences, and ensure that each part of the report leads easily into the next argument step by step.

(*c*) Be positive, use positive statements. The use of negatives is liable to be confusing. Provided that the report includes statements of the facts and of what is recommended, it should not be necessary to state what is not true or not recommended.

(*d*) Be certain that you know the meaning of every word that you use. Refer to a dictionary whenever in doubt. Avoid slang.

(*e*) If in doubt as to how to punctuate sentences, refer to a textbook and make sure of the basic rules.

(*f*) If you find any difficulty in expressing an idea, do not keep on turning it over in your mind, but put it down on paper as best you can. However imperfect this first attempt may be, it will provide something that you can examine and revise word by word until you are satisfied.

(*g*) Always read over everything that you have written; do not regard it as finished until you are satisfied that it expresses your meaning.

Editing

The draft report should always be edited in the first place by the writer, as has been suggested in the last of the hints given in the preceding paragraph. It frequently happens that the report is further edited by one or more people in addition. The process of editing should be complete; that is to say, it should not be concerned merely with the expression but also with the adequacy and apparent accuracy of the facts and the logic of the argument leading to the conclusions.

Presenting the report

Reports should be presented in a form appropriate to the purpose to be served. They are normally typewritten, duplicated, or printed, according to the number of copies required, and only rarely is a single copy prepared and presented in manuscrupt. As with all written documents, the reports should be laid out in a manner pleasing to the eye and facilitating reference to isolated sections and sub-sections. Where necessary, a wide margin should be left to enable the reader to make notes. If the report is to be handled and referred to frequently over a long period, it should be bound in a cover for protection. Some reports are produced in quite elaborate style, particularly

than dictatorship, and history contains some evidence in support of this.

The committee in business is used as a means of ensuring understanding and co-operation not only among members of the management, but also between management and subordinates.

Meetings may be considered as falling into two broad types. Firstly, there are those meetings which are held regularly by standing committees whose business is continuous. Under this heading come committees of management for the purpose of co-ordinating the activities of different departments or functions of the business, staff committees of various sorts at which representatives of management and staff meet together, and sports and social committees concerned with organizing leisure time activities. Secondly, there are special meetings which may be convened to discuss particular problems. Meetings of this type are more commonly confined to members of the management, when representatives of different departments get together in order to discuss and resolve problems which affect them all.

The office manager may well spend a greater proportion of his time attending committee meetings than do other members of the management. The work of the office is affected by all activities of the business; any decisions which are reached in connection with manufacturing, selling or other policy are likely to affect the systems for which the office manager is responsible. It is therefore desirable that he should be present, and take part in discussions to which he can usually make a useful contribution.

PROCEDURE

The following is an outline of the basic committee procedures. Many committees, however, are conducted with appreciably less formality than is indicated below; quite frequently there are no resolutions, no voting, and sometimes no formal minutes. The minimum requirement, perhaps, if affairs are to be conducted in a business-like way, is that there should be a chairman, an agenda, and notes on the action which is agreed upon. Nonetheless, it is advisable that office managers should be aware of the procedures from which informal methods are derived.

Constitution   The members of a committee may be appointed by some authority or may be the elected representatives of others. For example, the members of a committee of managers may be appointed by the general manager, whilst the members of a staff committee may be delegates elected by various groups of employees to represent their points of view. In the case of elected committees, it is usually necessary to have the procedure for election, and such matters as the terms of office of its members, and the appointment and duties of officers, fully recorded in writing and agreed by all concerned. In other cases, a mere list of the members of the committee may be sufficient for all purposes.

Terms of reference   The terms of reference of any committee should be clearly stated and made known to all its members.

Officers   The officers of a committee should consist of at least a chairman and a secretary. If these officers are not appointed when the committee is constituted, the chairman should be elected by the committee from among its members at the first meeting. The secretary may be appointed from among the members of the committee, or may be someone, not a member of the committee, appointed to be in attendance but having no right to take part in the discussion or to vote on any motion.

Convening meetings   All members of a committee should be given proper notice of each meeting. Notices giving details of the time and place of the meeting should be sent out by the secretary in good time, so that members have an opportunity of arranging their other appointments.

The agenda   The agenda, outlining the business which the meeting is to transact, should be provided to members in advance, and is usually sent out with the notice convening the meeting. The secretary normally drafts the agenda and obtains the chairman's agreement before it is circulated. Copies of any important reports or correspondence referred to in the agenda should be sent with it, so that members may have a full opportunity to study them before coming to the meeting. An example of a combined notice of meeting and agenda is given in Fig. 128. Some chairmen adopt the practice of noting on the agenda the approximate time to be allotted to each item. Whilst such a time table obviously cannot be strictly followed to the extent of stifling discussion, it can have the effect of ensuring that an undue proportion of the time of the meeting is not given to the first item on the agenda, leaving the remainder to be dealt with in haste.

Quorum   No committee can fulfil its purpose unless its meetings are attended by a reasonable proportion of its members. It is the usual practice, therefore, to establish a quorum, that is, a minimum number of members who must be present before the committee can function.

The chairman's duties   It is desirable that the chairman of a committee shall be a person who is experienced in committee work and who has the necessary ability to control the meeting.

The chairman's responsibilities are briefly as follows:

(*a*) to ensure that the business of the committee is conducted in an orderly manner and in accordance with the agenda;

(*b*) to ensure that the matters discussed are within the terms of reference of the committee, and that they are put before the meeting in such a form as to be clearly understood by the members;

STAFF COMMITTEE

A Meeting of the Staff Committee will be held in the Board Room on Thursday 21st October, at 3.0 p.m.

AGENDA

1. Apologies for absence (if any).
2. Minutes of the previous meeting to be read and confirmed.
3. Matters arising from the minutes.
4. Reports of Standing Sub-committees (copies enclosed)
   (a) Canteen
   (b) Staff Suggestions.
5. Working conditions in the office.
6. Arrangements for the election of Staff Delegates in December.
7. Any other business.

Fig. 128 Committee agenda

(*c*) to conduct the meeting in such a way that each member has a reasonable opportunity to speak;

(*d*) to see that any resolution passed by the committee is couched in terms which leave no doubt as to its meaning;

(*e*) to keep the meeting to the point under discussion and to ensure that time is not wasted.

The duties of a chairman call for tact, sympathy and, sometimes, a sense of humour. If members hold strong and conflicting opinions on the business in hand, he must endeavour to steer the meeting towards a removal of the differences, or towards some compromise which will satisfy all. The chairman must also be a person capable of upholding the 'dignity of the chair'; he must be able to give decisions justly, so that no member of the committee may feel that he is not being permitted to play his full part in the proceedings.

Putting a motion   The greater part of the business of a committee is dealt with by some member moving a resolution, which is subsequently debated by the members, and either rejected, or passed in its original, or an amended form. It is the duty of the chairman to see that motions put before the committee are in concise terms, clearly understood, and leave no reasonable doubt as to their meaning. It is usual for the resolution to be moved by a proposer, and seconded by another member of the committee before the chairman puts it before the meeting for discussion.

Putting amendments   Any member who does not agree with the motion as it is put is at liberty to propose an amendment to it. An amendment has the effect of altering by addition, deletion or substitution the wording of the motion as put by the proposer and seconder. It may not be a direct negative of the motion, but may seek to defer discussion until some later date.

The discussion   In the course of discussion, the chairman should see that each member of the committee has a reasonable opportunity to give his opinion. It is accepted custom that all remarks shall be addressed to the chairman, and not to individual members or to the committee as a whole. This procedure helps to remove the personal element from discussion, with its possibilities of bad feeling or frayed tempers.

Voting   After adequate time had been allowed for discussion, it is the chairman's duty to put the motion to the vote. If any amendments have been proposed and seconded in the course of discussion, the amendments are put to the meeting first. The chairman should read the motion or amendment carefully to make certain that there is no doubt in members' minds as to the point at issue, and then ask for the votes of those in favour, followed by those against. He is responsible for the counting of the votes and the announcing of the result. Where the number of votes cast for and against are equal, the chairman may have a casting vote.

Sub-committees   Some committees are large, and do not lend themselves to the discussion of detail. In these cases, it is usual for the committee to appoint from among its members smaller sub-committees for particular purposes. A sub-committee may be set up in order to discuss one particular point and to report back its recommendations to the main committee, or there may be standing sub-committees, which meet regularly to deal, in detail, with particular aspects of the main committee's work.

Minutes The secretary is responsible for preparing minutes of the proceedings of the meeting. These should be a concise record of the names of those present and of the business transacted. Details of the discussion should not normally be included; the final resolutions are sufficient. At each meeting, the secretary is called upon to read the minutes of the previous meeting. The meeting having agreed them as a true record, the chairman then signs them to signify that they have been adopted. In order to save the time of the meeting, copies of the minutes are often circulated to members in advance so that they may read them at their convenience and be ready to approve or object.

Bibliography

The following is a short list of books recommended for further reading and reference:

Forms and methods design

Simplifying Office Work, Oliver Standingford (Pitman, London).

How to Design a Procedure, G. J. Mills and Others (Institute of Administrative Management, Beckenham).

The Design of Forms in Government Departments, Management Services Division of the Civil Service Department (Her Majesty's Stationery Office, London).

Setting up an Organisation and Methods Section, L. G. S. Mason (Institute of Administrative Management, Beckenham).

Procedure Charts for Administrative Work (Institute of Administrative Management, Beckenham).

Office equipment

Business Equipment Guide (B.E.D. Business Books Limited, Wallington).

Office services and procedures

Filing (Second Edition), Oliver Standingford (Institute of Administrative Management, Beckenham).

Clerical Quality Control, D. C. Arnall and T. S. Hall (Institute of Administrative Management, Beckenham).

Better Offices (The Institute of Directors, London).

The Open Plan Office, E. John Browne (Institute of Administrative Management, Beckenham).

The Effective Use of Secretarial Services, D. L. Wallace (Institute of Administrative Management, Beckenham).

Office management

Office, Oliver Standingford (BBC Publications, London).

Office Administration (Third Edition), edited by Mills and Standingford (Pitman, London).

A Guide to effective Office Supervision (Institute of Administrative Management, Beckenham).

Staffing

Office Salaries Analysis (Institute of Administrative Management, Beckenham).

Office Job Evaluation, Keith Scott (Institute of Administrative Management, Beckenham).

Offices Hours and Payment Practices (Institute of Administrative Management, Beckenham).

Office Staff Holidays, Turnover and Other Procedures (Institute of Administrative Management, Beckenham).

Index

Accident prevention, 282
Accommodation, 268–84
  aids to planing, 270
  acoustics, 280–1
  cellular offices, 271
  cleanliness, 278
  decoration, 276–78
  landscaped offices, 273–5
  legal requirements, 281–4
  lighting, 279–80
  open-plan offices, 272
  private offices, 271
  services, 270
  space, 270
  status, 271
  temperature, 279
  ventilation, 278–80
Accounting—
  comparisons, 243–4
  cost, 239–41
  departmental, 239
  financial, 238
  integrated, 244–6
Accounting equipment—
  mechanical, 163–5
  electronic, 105–58
Accounting services, 169–246
  cash control, 191–8
  management information, 237–46
  production records, 223–36
  purchases, 184–90
  sales, 169–83
  stock control, 212–22
  wages, 199–211
Accuracy, 363–66
Acoustics, 280–1
Activity sampling, 290
Adding machines—
  listing, 159–60
  non-listing, 162–3
Addressing equipment, 88–91
Agenda, 394
Alphabetical classification, 59–60
Application forms, 200, 210–11
Attendance records, 200, 204–8
Audit, 374–81
  methods audit, 377–80
  personnel audit, 379–81
  records audit, 374–77
  responsibility, 381
Automatic equipment—
  accounting machines, 163–5
  calculators, 160–2
  card indexes, 75
  computers, 105–58
  filing, 70
  postal, 32–5
  telephone answering, 48
  typewriters, 20–4

Bank paying-in slip, 192, 193
Banking cash, 194
Basic clerical operations, 341
Batch production by computer, 153
Binary arithmetic, 108–9
Binders, loose-leaf, 64–5
Bonus, 310
Box files, 64
Branch cash control, 196
Business organization, 3–4
Byte computer store, 126

Calculating machines, 159–63
  adding-listing, 159–60
  electronic, 160–2
  key-driven, 162–3

Calculating machines—*contd.*
  printing, 162
  programmable, 161–2
  rotary, 163
Card indexes, 74–81
Cards—
  magnetic, 121–2
  punched, 124
  slotted, 80–1
Cash control, 191–8
  banking, 194
  branches, 196
  cash book, 191, 193–4
  cash payments, 193
  cash received, 192–3, 194
  cheque-writing machines, 194–5
  computer systems, 196
  forms, 191–2, 196
  petty cash, 195
  security, 196–8
  stamps, tickets, etc., 195
  wages, 195
Cellular offices, 273
Central staff records, 211
Central Training Council, 321
Centralization of office control, 6
Centralized filing, 73
Centralized typing services, 29–31
Check digits, 152–3
Chairman of meeting, 390–2
Chairs, 267–8
  legal requirements, 281
Charts—
  control, 227–8, 369–1
  organization, 4, 7, 297
Checking clerical work—
  accuracy, 363–5
  analysing errors, 365–6
  appearance, 365
  judgement, 365
Checking computer data, 150, 152–3
Checking purchase invoices, 187–9
Checking stocks, 215
Cheque-writing machines, 194–5
Cheques, 192–5
Chronological filing classification, 62
Civil Evidence Act, 1968, 71
Classification for filing, 58–62
Cleaning offices, 278, 282–3

Clerical operations, basic, 341
Clerical salaries analyses, 309
Clock cards, 204–8
Colleges of further education, 327–32
Committee procedure, 388–93
  agenda, 390
  chairman, 390–2
  constitution, 389
  convening meetings, 390
  discussion, 392
  minutes, 393
  officers, 390
  putting a motion, 392
  putting amendments, 392
  quorum, 390
  sub-committees, 392
  terms of reference, 390
  voting, 393
Committees, staff, 315–6
Communication services (*see also*
     Telecommunication services)
  centralized typing services, 29–31
  computer assisted typing pools, 31
  conveyors, 37
  dictation, 25–8
  messenger services, 35–6
  oral, 13–16
  postal section, 33–5
  postal services, 31–2
  principles, 13–14
  secretarial duties, 28–9
  selecting the means, 14–15
  shorthand v. dictating machines, 27
  strenographic machines, 27
  typewriters, 17–20
  typing pools, 29–31
  word processing, 20–4
  written, 16–24
Computers and their use, 136–58
  batch production, 153
  check digits, 152–3
  computer filing, 72–4
  computer-originated micro-records,
    71, 130
  computer usage, 150–4
  data bank, 154
  data capture, 151
  Datapost, 150
  data storage, 153

designing computer methods, 359–62
examples of computers, 140–8
human aspects, 157–8
installing a computer, 154–7, 359–62
instructions to operators, 115, 152
inter-active mode, 153–4
intermediate computers, 138–40,
    144–7
mainframe computers, 137–8, 147–8
mode of use, 153–4
telecommunication, 148–50
visible record computers, 136–7,
    140–4
Computer components, 111–32,
    148–50
backing stores, 126
central processor, 132
communication controller, 150
direct data entry, 112–14, 131–2
diskettes, 116
disks, 115, 117, 127
documents readers, 119–20
edge-punched cards, 124
front-end processor, 150
immediate access store, 125–6
input, 111–25
key-to-disk, 115
laser beam printer, 130
line printer, 129–30
magnetic cards, 122
magnetic drums, 128
magnetic edge striped cards, 122
magnetic output, 132
magnetic stripe cards, 121–2
magentic tape, 114–15, 126–7
microfilm, 130
modem, 149
multiplexer, 149–50
off-line entry, 114–25
on-line entry, 112–4
output, 129–32
portable data-capture unit, 118
printed output, 129–30
punched cards, 124
punched output, 132
punched paper tape, 124
read only storage, 126
serial printer, 129
special purpose terminals, 116–7

storage, 125–9
visual display unit, 112–14, 131–2
visible record computer, 112
Concertina files, 35–6
Conditions of employment (see Employ-
    ment conditions)
Confravision, 48
Continuous stationery, 20
Contracts of Employment Act, 305
Control—
    charts, 227–8, 369–71
    of ledger posting, 178–80
    output, 363–73
Conveyors, 37
Costing, 227–31, 239–41
Costing of office methods, 358–4
Credit sanction, 170–1
Critical path analysis, 243

Data bank, 154
Data capture, 151
Datapost, 150
Data processing (see Computers and
    their use; Computer com-
    ponents; Data processing fun-
    damentals; Data processing
    miscellaneous equipment;
    programming)
Data processing fundamentals, 105–10
    benefits, 109–10
    binary system, 108–9
    components of a computer, 108
    functions, 105, 107
    systems, 106–7
Data processing miscellaneous, 159–66
    adding-listing machines, 159–60
    electronic calculators, 160–2
    electronic printing calculators, 162
    electronic programmable calculators,
        161–2
    key-driven calculators, 162–3
    mechanical book-keeping machines,
        163–5
    mechanical calculators, 162–3
    posting boards, 165–6
    ready reckoners, 163
    rotary calculators, 163
Data transmission, 148–50
Datel (see Data transmission)

Day-to-day controls, 363–73
  output control, 366–73
  quality control, 363–66
Decoration, 276–78
Delivery notes, 170, 213, 240
Departmental accounts, 239
Desk files, 69
Desks, 263–6
  special purpose desks, 266
  spine table assembly, 266
  typists's desks, 266
  work stations, 265
  working area layout, 263–5
Dictating, 25–8
  machines, 25–6
  shorthand v. dictating machines, 27
Diffusion transfer photocopying, 96
Direct positive photocopying, 96
Discounted cash flow, 242
Document readers for computer input, 119–20
Drawer filing, 70
Dual spectrum photocopying, 97
Duplicating (see Reprography)
Dyeline photocopying, 97

Earnings record card, 200
Edge-punched cards, 124
Education (see Training and Education)
Electronic calculators, 160–2
Electrostatic photocopying, 97
Employers Liability (Compulsory Insurance) Act, 1969, 253, 284
Employers Liability (Defective Equipment) Act, 1969, 284
Employment Protection Act, 1975, 305
Employment conditions—
  financial (see Wage practices)
  flexible working hours, 311–2
  holidays, 312
  hours of work, 311
  meals and meal breaks, 312
  part-time working, 311
  staff handbooks, 312–3
  trade unions, 314
Envelope sealing machines, 34
Equal Pay Act, 1970, 305
Error analysis, 365–6
Explanation of purpose, 317

Export invoicing, 173

Fasteners, paper and file, 67–9
Figures for planning, 241–3
Filing, 57–82
  alphabetical classification, 59–60
  automatic filing, 70, 75
  centralized filing, 73
  classification, 58–62
  chronological classification, 62
  computer filing, 73–4
  computer originated micro-records, 71
  desk filing, 69
  destruction of filing, 72
  drawer filing, 70
  equipment, 63–71
  fasteners, 67–9
  fire resisting equipment, 70–1
  folders, 66–7
  geographical classification, 60
  horizontal filing, 69
  indexing, 74–82
  lateral filing, 69, 70
  long-term storage, 72
  loose-leaf binders, 64–5
  micro-filing, 71
  numerical classification, 61–2
  operating a filing system, 71–2
  revolving filing, 70
  shelving, 69–70
  small containers, 63–9
  storage equipment, 69–71
  subject classification, 60–1
  systems, 57–62
  transfer files, 72
  vertical filing, 69
Financial accounts, 238
Fire precautions, 283
Fire resisting filing equipment, 70–1
First aid, 283
Flap sorters, 35
Folders and files, 63–71
Form design, 382–6
Forms—
  application, 200, 210–11
  bank paying-in slip, 192, 193
  bonus record, 229
  cash book 191, 193–4

cash receipts list, 192
cheque, 192–5
cost estimate, 227
cost summary, 229
delivery note, 170, 213, 240
earnings record card, 200
goods received record, 185, 188–9
invoice, 170–3
job record, 228
material requisition, 227
material schedule, 225
operation schedule, 225–7
operation ticket, 227
order, 170–1, 185
pay packet, 200, 209
pay slip, 200, 209
receipt, 192, 193, 194
sales journal, 174–7
sales ledger, 177–82
staff record, 200, 210–11
statement of account, 178, 182
stock account, 213, 240
stores requisition and delivery note,
  213
time and attendance record, 200,
  204–6
Forms control, 358
Franking machines, 35
Front-end computer processor, 150
Furniture and layout, 263–75
  cellular offices, 271
  chairs, 267–8
  desks, 264–6
  landscaped offices, 273–4
  layout, 268–75
  open-plan offices, 272
  special purpose desks, 266
  spine table assembly, 266
  typists' desks, 266
  work stations, 265
  working area, 263–4
Further education, 327–32

Gelatine transfer photocopying, 96
Geographical filing classification, 60
Goods received record, 185–6
Grading clerical work, 291–3
Grading salaries, 306–7
Group output control, 369–72

Guardbooks, 64

Health and safety, 281–4
Heat and transfer photocopying, 97
Heating, 279, 282
Holiday pay, 209, 312
Hours of work, 311

Incentives, 310
Income tax calculation, 208
Indexing, 74–82
  automatic card index, 75
  signals, 81–2
  slotted cards, 80–1
  staggered card index, 80
  strip index, 76
  vertical card index, 74–5
  visible books, 78
  visible card index, 77
  wheel index, 78–9
Individual output control, 372
Induction training, 322–3
Industrial Training Act, 1964, 321, 327
Industrial Training Boards, 320–1, 332
Installation of computers, 154–7,
  359–62
Installation of systems, 357–8, 361
Insurance, 247–60
  administration, 248–9
  all risks, 256
  business interruption, 257
  contractors' all risks, 258
  credit, 255–6
  employer's liability, 253
  engineering, 259–60
  fidelity guarantee, 255
  fire, 250–1
  goods in transit, 258–9
  legal aspects, 249–50
  liabilities, 252–3
  market for insurance, 250
  medical expenses, 254
  money, 255
  motor, 256–7
  personal accident, 253–4
  personnel 253–4
  products liability, 253
  risk management, 247–8
  theft, 251–2

Insurance—*contd.*
third party liability, 252–3
travel, 254
Integrated accounting, 244–6
Interest in work (*see* Work satisfaction)
Internal telephone systems—
Post Office, 38–49
private, 50–1
Interrogation of computer
storage, 112–14, 131–2
Interviewing, 299–304
Investigation, O & M, 344–59
Invoices, —
purchase, 187–9
sales, 170–3

Job construction, 293–6
Job evaluation and grading, 291–3
Job training, 324–7
Joint consultation, 315–19

Key-driven calculators, 162–3
Keymaster system, 42

Landscaped offices, 273–5
Lateral filing, 69–70
Layout of offices, 268–70
aids to planning, 270
general offices, 268–75
legal requirements, 282
private offices, 271
space, 270
Ledger—
bought ledger, 187, 189
cash postings, 193–4
cost accounts, 239–41
sales ledger, 177–82
stock accounts, 213, 217–21
Legal aspects of employment, 281–4,
304–5, 321
Letter opening machines, 33
Lever arch files, 63–4
Levy and grant, 320
Lighting, 279–80, 282
Long-service premiums, 308
Loose-leaf binders, 64–5
Lying time for wages, 209

Machines, application of, 352–4

Magnetic records (*see* Computer
components)
Mailing machines, 33–5
Mainframe computers, 137–8, 144–7
Management by objectives, 317–8
Management information, 237–46
accounting comparisons, 243–4
cost accounts, 239–41
divisional or departmental accounts,
239
figures for planning, 241–3
financial accounts, 238
integrated accounting, 244–6
other management information, 241
Management training, 330–32, 338
Manifold posting boards (*see* Posting
boards)
Manifold registers, 101–2
Meals and meal breaks, 314
Measurement of clerical work, 288–91,
372–3
Mechanical accounting machines,
163–5
Meetings (*see* Committee procedure)
Merit rating, 307
Messenger services, 35–6
Method analysis, 348–51
Methods, 341–62
costing and comparison, 353–4
computer methods design, 359–62
computer services, 361–2
design of simple methods, 351–2
form design, 354–7
forms control, 358
installation, 357–8
investigation, 347–51
machines and equipment, 352–4
need for revision, 343–4
O & M service, 344–5
planning methods, 345–58
preliminary survey, 346–50
specialization, 341–3
Methods audit, 377–9
Micro-photographic copying, 71,
97–101
Micro-records, computer, 130
Minutes of meetings, 393
Models for decision making, 242
Modem, 149

Multiplexer, 149–50

Nano-second, 109
Noise reduction, 280–1
Numerical filing classification, 61–2

O & M service, 344–62
Office accommodation (see Accommodation)
Office cleaning, 278, 282
Office management and administration—
  contribution to productivity, 3
  definition of, 7–8
  relationship with other managers, 4–7
  study of, 9
  technique of, 7–8
  terminology, 8
  training for, 326–38
Office salaries analysis, 309
Offices, Shops and Railway Premises Act, 1963, 282–4
Offset litho duplicators, 87–8
Open-plan offices, 272–3
Optical readers, 119–20
Order forms—
  buyer's orders, 185
  sales orders, 170
Organization, 3–8, 296–7
Organization charts, 4, 7, 297
Output control of clerical work—
  consultant services, 372–3
  group output control, 369–72
  individual output control, 372
  work measurement, 288–91, 367–8
  work scheduling, 368–9
Overcrowding, 270, 282
Overtime payment, 310

Paper, 356–7
  fasteners, 67–9
  folding machines, 35
P.A.Y.E., 200, 208
Payroll (see Wages)
Pensions, 311
Personal assistants, 29
Personnel audit, 379–81
Petty cash, 195

Photographic copying, 93–101
Physical conditions, 276–84
  accident prevention, 282
  acoustics, 280–1
  cleanliness, 278, 282
  clothing, provision for, 283
  decoration, 276–8
  drinking water, 283
  fire precautions, 283
  first aid, 283
  legal requirements, 281–4
  lighting, 279–80, 282
  overcrowding, 282
  safety precautions, 283
  sanitary conveniences, 283
  seating, 267–8, 283
  temperature, 279, 282
  ventilation, 278–9, 282
  washing facilities, 283
Planning information, 241–3
Post binders, 64
Post Office telephones (see Telephones)
Postal equipment—
  envelope sealing, 33
  franking, 33–5
  letter opening, 33
  mailing, 35
  paper folding, 35
  sorting, 35
Postal section, 32–5
Posting boards, 165–6, 179, 193, 202, 214, 235
Predetermined motion-time systems, 291
Preliminary methods survey, 346–7
Print room, 91–3
Private offices, 271
Production records, 223–236
  cost control, 233–4
  costing, 230–1
  forms, 225–9 231–3
  loading, 231
  mechanized methods, 234–6
  planning, 230
  progressing, 232–3
  quality control, 233
Programming for computers, 132–5
  assembler programs, 133
  compiler programs, 133
  executive programs, 133

Programming for computers—*contd.*
  languages—
    high level, 133
    low level, 133
    machine, 133
    source, 133
  operating systems, 133–4
  packaged programs, 133, 361–2
  software, 133–4
  users and programs, 134–5
Public address systems, 54
Punched cards, 124
Punched paper tape, 124
Purchases, 184–90
  accounting, 189–90
  checking invoices, 187–9
  forms, 185–7
  making payment, 190
  receiving goods, 187
  stock replenishment, 215–7
  using a computer, 190

Quality control, 233
Quality rating, 299–302

Race Relations Act, 1968, 305
Radiotelephony, 48
Ready reckoners, 163
Receipts, 192, 193, 194
Receiving goods, 187
Records audit, 374–7
  audit report, 376–7
  conducting the audit, 375–6
  planning the audit, 374–5
Recruitment and selection, 298–304
Redundancy Payments Act, 1965,
    1969, 305
Reflex photocopying, 96
Remuneration (*see* Rewards)
Reports, 382–7
  briefing, 383
  drafting, 385–6
  editing, 386
  form of report, 384
  framework, 383
  investigation, 384
  presentation, 384–7
  routine reports, 387
  special reports, 382–7

Reprography, 83–102
  addressing, 88–91
  diffusion transfer, 96
  direct positive, 96
  dual spectrum, 97
  duplicating, 83–93
  dyeline, 97
  electrostatic, 97
  gelatine transfer, 96
  heat transfer, 97
  manifold registers, 101–2
  microphotography, 97–101
  office print room, 91–3
  offset litho, 87–8
  photocopying, 93–102
  reflex, 96
  selecting equipment, 83–4
  spirit hectographic, 84–5
  stencil, 85–7
  typeset, 88
  xerography, 97
Revolving filing, 70
Rewards, 306–19
  conditions of employment, 306–14
  wage practices, 306–11
  work satisfaction, 315–19
Ring binders, 64
Rotary calculators, 163

Safety precautions, 279–82
Salaries analysis, 309
Salary scales, 306–11
Sales accounting, 174–83
  basic entries and operations, 178–9
  collecting payment, 182
  customer records, 183
  forms, 174–8
  integration of systems, 182
  ledger posting methods, 179–82
  quantity analysis, 183
Sales analysis, 183
Sales invoicing, 169–73
  accepting orders, 170–1
  addressing invoices, 173
  export invoicing, 173
  forms, 170, 173
  invoice preparation, 171–3
Sales journal, 174–7
Sales ledger (*see* Sales accounting)

Sales records, 183
Sales statistics, 183
Sanitary conveniences, 285
Scheduling work—
    factory, 225–7
    office, 368–9
Seating, 267–8, 283
Secretarial duties, 28–9
Security services, 196–8
Selection of staff, 297–304
Sex Discrimination Act, 1975, 305
Shelving for filing, 69–70
Shorthand writing, 27
Sick pay, 209, 311
Signals—
    audible, 54–5
    filing and indexing, 81–2
Skill training, 7–8
Slotted cards, 80–1
Sorting devices, 35, 37, 80–1
Specialization in office work, 341–3
Spirit hectographic duplicators, 84–5
Staff—
    committees, 315–6
    handbooks, 312–3
    records, 200, 210–11
Staffing, 287–305
    job construction, 293–6
    job evaluation and grading, 291–3
    law relating to employment, 304–5
    organization, 296–7
    recruitment and selection, 298–304
    work analysis, 287–8
    work measurement, 288–91
Staggered card index, 80
Statement of account, 178, 182
Stationery, continuous, 20
Statistics, 241
Status, 271, 319
Stencil duplicators, 85–7
Stenographic machines, 27
Stenography, 25–7
Stock control, 212–22
    availability of stocks, 217
    checking stocks, 215
    cost account dissection, 240
    degrees of stock control, 222
    forms, 213
    inactive stocks, 217

mechanized methods, 220–1
records in cash, 217–20
records in kind, 214–5
replenishing stocks, 215–6
valuation, 221–2
work in progress, 222
Strip index, 76
Subject filing classification, 60–1
Suggestion schemes, 316–17
Supervisory training, 331, 334–8
Suspension filing, 67

Tagged cords, 67
Telecommunications, 38–56
    closed-circuit television, 56
    computer data transmission, 148–50
    facsimile telegraph, 53
    Post Office telephones, 38–49
    private internal telephones, 50–1
    public address systems, 54
    staff location, 55
    telegraphs and cables, 51–2
    telenote, 54
    teleprinters, 52–3
Telegraphs, and cables, 51–2
Telephones, 38–51
    answering sets, 48
    confravision, 48
    extensions, 40–2
    keymaster system, 42
    Post Office, 38–49
    private branch exchange, 42–4, 49
    private circuits, 46
    private internal systems, 50–1
    radiotelephony, 48
    special circuits, 47
    sundry equipment, 45–6
Teleprinter, 52–3
Telex (see Teleprinter)
Testing applicants, 301
Thong binders, 64
Time sheets—
    factory, 200, 204–8, 227
    office, 372
Time study, 288–1, 310, 367–8, 372–3
Trade unions, 314
Trade Unions and Labour Relations
    Act, 1974, 305
Training and education, 320–38

Central Training Council, 321
certificate and diploma courses,
    327–32
further education, 327–32
induction training, 322–3
Industrial Training Act, 1964, 321,
    327
Industrial Training Boards, 320–1,
    332
job training, 324–27
levy and grant, 320
management training, 330–2, 338
office training schemes, 321–27
planning and controlling training,
    332–4
skill training, 323–4
supervisory training, 331, 334–38
Training Within Industry (TWI), 325–7
Typeset duplicators, 88
Typewriters, 17–20
    carriage sizes, 18
    continuous stationery, 20
    line spacing, 17–18
    manual v. electric, 19
    portable, 19
    ribbon, 19
    tabulating mechanism, 18–19
    type, 17
    variable type, 19–20
    word processing, 20–4
Typewriting, 17–31
Typing pools and services, 29–31
Typists' desks, 266

Value analysis, 242–3
Variable-type typewriters, 19–20
Ventilation, 278–9, 282
Vertical card indexes, 74–5
Vertical filing, 69
Visible books, 78
Visible card indexes, 77
Visible record computers, 112, 136–7,
    140–4
Voting (see Committee procedure)

Wages, 199–211
    accounting, 210
    cost account dissection, 233–6, 240
    forms, 200, 204–8, 210–11

holiday pay and sick pay, 209
    income tax calculation, 208
    lying time, 209
    pay packets, 209
    pay slips, 209
    payment, 195, 209
    payroll preparation, 201–4, 210
    protection from fraud, 195, 210
    recording time and work, 204–8,
        225–7, 232–3
Wage practices and conditions of
    employment, 306–11
    adults doing low grade work, 309–10
    bonus, 310
    long service premiums, 309
    non-financial conditions (see Employ-
        ment conditions)
    office salaries analysis, 309
    overtime, 310
    payment of salaries, 310
    pensions, 311
    salary scales, 306–9
    sick pay, 311
Wallet files, 64
Washing facilities, 281
Wheel index, 78–9
Word processing, 20–4
    computer-assisted typing, 31
    electronic, 20–4
        applications, 24
        initial recording, 20–1
        recall, 22
        results, 22–4
        punched hole, 24
Work analysis, 287–8
Work measurement, 288–91, 367,
    372–3
Work satisfaction, 315–19
    explanation of purpose, 317
    joint consultation, 315–16
    management by objectives, 317–18
    status, 271, 319
    suggestion schemes, 316–17
Work scheduling—
    factory, 225–7
    office, 368–9
Work stations, 265–6

Xerography, 97